MznLnx

Missing Links Exam Preps

Exam Prep for

Economics Today

Miller, 12th Edition

The MznLnx Exam Prep is your link from the texbook and lecture to your exams.
The MznLnx Exam Preps are unauthorized and comprehensive reviews of your textbooks.

All material provided by MznLnx and Rico Publications (c) 2010
Textbook publishers and textbook authors do not particpate in or contribute to these reviews.

MznLnx

Rico
Publications

Exam Prep for Economics Today
12th Edition
Miller

Publisher: Raymond Houge
Assistant Editor: Michael Rouger
Text and Cover Designer: Lisa Buckner
Marketing Manager: Sara Swagger
Project Manager, Editorial Production: Jerry Emerson
Art Director: Vernon Lowerui

Product Manager: Dave Mason
Editorial Asitant: Rachel Guzmanji
Pedagogy: Debra Long
Cover Image: Jim Reed/Getty Images
Text and Cover Printer: City Printing, Inc.
Compositor: Media Mix, Inc.

(c) 2010 Rico Publications

ALL RIGHTS RESERVED. No part of this work covered by the copyright may be reproduced or used in any form or by an means--graphic, electronic, or mechanical, including photocopying, recording, taping, Web distribution, information storage, and retrieval systems, or in any other manner--without the written permission of the publisher.

Printed in the United States
ISBN:

For more information about our products, contact us at:
Dave.Mason@RicoPublications.com

For permission to use material from this text or product, submit a request online to:
Dave.Mason@RicoPublications.com

Contents

CHAPTER 1
The Nature of Economics — 1

CHAPTER 2
Scarcity and the World of Trade-Offs — 8

CHAPTER 3
Demand and Supply — 18

CHAPTER 4
Extensions of Demand and Supply Analysis — 27

CHAPTER 5
The Public Sector and Public Choice — 33

CHAPTER 6
Taxes, Transfers, and Public Spending — 48

CHAPTER 7
The Macroeconomy: Unemployment, Inflation, and Deflation — 53

CHAPTER 8
Measuring the Economy's Performance — 63

CHAPTER 9
Global Economic Growth and Development — 77

CHAPTER 10
Real GDP and the Price Level in the Long Run — 89

CHAPTER 11
Classical and Keynesian Macro Analyses — 97

CHAPTER 12
Consumption, Income, and the Multiplier — 104

CHAPTER 13
Fiscal Policy — 113

CHAPTER 14
Money, Banking, and Central Banking — 121

CHAPTER 15
Money Creation and Deposit Insurance — 135

CHAPTER 16
Domestic and International Dimensions of Monetary Policy — 145

CHAPTER 17
Stabilization in an Integrated World Economy — 157

CHAPTER 18
Policies and Prospects for Global Economic Growth — 165

CHAPTER 19
Consumer Choice — 171

CHAPTER 20
Demand and Supply Elasticity — 179

Contents (Cont.)

CHAPTER 21
Rents, Profits, and the Financial Environment of Business — 183

CHAPTER 22
The Firm: Cost and Output Determination — 195

CHAPTER 23
Perfect Competition — 203

CHAPTER 24
Monopoly — 210

CHAPTER 25
Monopolistic Competition — 218

CHAPTER 26
Oligopoly and Strategic Behavior — 227

CHAPTER 27
Regulation and Antitrust Policy in a Globalized Economy — 237

CHAPTER 28
Labor Demand and Supply — 248

CHAPTER 29
Unions and Labor Market Monopoly Power — 256

CHAPTER 30
Income, Poverty, and Health Care — 265

CHAPTER 31
Environmental Economics — 274

CHAPTER 32
Comparative Advantage and the Open Economy — 280

CHAPTER 33
Exchange Rates and the Balance of Payments — 286

ANSWER KEY — 298

TO THE STUDENT

COMPREHENSIVE

The *MznLnx* Exam Prep series is designed to help you pass your exams. Editors at MznLnx review your textbooks and then prepare these practice exams to help you master the textbook material. Unlike study guides, workbooks, and practice tests provided by the texbook publisher and textbook authors, *MznLnx* gives you **all** of the material in each chapter in exam form, not just samples, so you can be sure to nail your exam.

MECHANICAL

The MznLnx Exam Prep series creates exams that will help you learn the subject matter as well as test you on your understanding. Each question is designed to help you master the concept. Just working through the exams, you gain an understanding of the subject--its a simple mechanical process that produces success.

INTEGRATED STUDY GUIDE AND REVIEW

MznLnx is not just a set of exams designed to test you, its also a comprehensive review of the subject content. Each exam question is also a review of the concept, making sure that you will get the answer correct without having to go to other sources of material. You learn as you go! Its the easiest way to pass an exam.

HUMOR

Studying can be tedious and dry. MznLnx's instructional design includes moderate humor within the exam questions on occassion, to break the tedium and revitalize the brain

Chapter 1. The Nature of Economics

1. _____ is exchange of capital, goods, and services across international borders or territories. In most countries, it represents a significant share of gross domestic product (GDP.) While _____ has been present throughout much of history, its economic, social, and political importance has been on the rise in recent centuries.
   - a. Import license
   - b. Incoterms
   - c. Intra-industry trade
   - d. International trade

2. _____s is the social science that studies the production, distribution, and consumption of goods and services. The term _____s comes from the Ancient Greek οἰκονομῖα from οἶκος (oikos, 'house') + νΟεμος (nomos, 'custom' or 'law'), hence 'rules of the house(hold)'. Current _____ models developed out of the broader field of political economy in the late 19th century, owing to a desire to use an empirical approach more akin to the physical sciences.
   - a. Economic
   - b. Inflation
   - c. Opportunity cost
   - d. Energy economics

3. A _____ is a place of residence or refuge and comfort. It is usually a place in which an individual or a family can rest and be able to store personal property. Most modern-day households contain sanitary facilities and a means of preparing food.
   - a. 100-year flood
   - b. 130-30 fund
   - c. Home
   - d. 1921 recession

4. _____ was a survey conducted by the U.S. Department of Justice to gauge the prevalence of alcohol and illegal drug use among prior arrestees. It was a reformulation of the prior Drug Use Forecasting (DUF) program, focused on five drugs in particular: cocaine, marijuana, methamphetamine, opiates, and PCP.

Participants were randomly selected from arrest records in major metropolitan areas; because no personally identifying information is taken from each record chosen, the resulting data can be correlated to arrest rates, but not to the total population of persons charged.

   - a. AD-IA Model
   - b. Arrestee Drug Abuse Monitoring
   - c. ACCRA Cost of Living Index
   - d. ACEA agreement

5. Necessary _____s:

If x is a necessary _____ of y, then the presence of y necessarily implies the presence of x. The presence of x, however, does not imply that y will occur.

Sufficient _____s:

If x is a sufficient _____ of y, then the presence of x necessarily implies the presence of y.

   - a. Cause
   - b. Global justice
   - c. Materialism
   - d. Deductive logic

6. An _____ is the magnum opus of the Scottish economist Adam Smith. It is a clearly written account of economics at the dawn of the Industrial Revolution, as well as a rhetorical piece written for the generally educated individual of the 18th century - advocating a free market economy as more productive and more beneficial to society.

Chapter 1. The Nature of Economics

The work is credited as a watershed in history and economics due to its comprehensive, largely accurate characterization of economic mechanisms that survive in modern economics; and also for its effective use of rhetorical technique, including structuring the work to contrast real world examples of free and fettered markets.

   a. AD-IA Model
   b. ACCRA Cost of Living Index
   c. ACEA agreement
   d. Inquiry into the Nature and Causes of the Wealth of Nations

7. _____ is a branch of economics that deals with the performance, structure, and behavior of a national or regional economy as a whole. Along with microeconomics, _____ is one of the two most general fields in economics. It is the study of the behavior and decision-making of entire economies.
   a. Macroeconomics
   b. New Trade Theory
   c. Human capital
   d. Market structure

8. _____ is a branch of economics that studies how individuals, households and firms and some states make decisions to allocate limited resources, typically in markets where goods or services are being bought and sold. _____ examines how these decisions and behaviours affect the supply and demand for goods and services, which determines prices; and how prices, in turn, determine the supply and demand of goods and services.

Whereas macroeconomics involves the 'sum total of economic activity, dealing with the issues of growth, inflation and unemployment, and with national economic policies relating to these issues' and the effects of government actions on them.

   a. Fixed exchange rate
   b. Human capital
   c. Microeconomics
   d. Market structure

9. _____ is used to assign the available resources in an economic way. It is part of resource management.

In strategic planning, is a plan for using available resources, for example human resources, especially in the near term, to achieve goals for the future.

   a. 100-year flood
   b. 1921 recession
   c. 130-30 fund
   d. Resource allocation

10. _____ was a Scottish moral philosopher and a pioneer of political economy. One of the key figures of the Scottish Enlightenment, Smith is the author of The Theory of Moral Sentiments and An Inquiry into the Nature and Causes of the Wealth of Nations. The latter, usually abbreviated as The Wealth of Nations, is considered his magnum opus and the first modern work of economics.
   a. Alan Greenspan
   b. Adolph Fischer
   c. Adam Smith
   d. Adolf Hitler

11. An Inquiry into the Nature and Causes of the _____ is the magnum opus of the Scottish economist Adam Smith. It is a clearly written account of economics at the dawn of the Industrial Revolution, as well as a rhetorical piece written for the generally educated individual of the 18th century - advocating a free market economy as more productive and more beneficial to society.

The work is credited as a watershed in history and economics due to its comprehensive, largely accurate characterization of economic mechanisms that survive in modern economics; and also for its effective use of rhetorical technique, including structuring the work to contrast real world examples of free and fettered markets.

a. The New Industrial State
b. Wealth of Nations
c. Capital and Interest
d. Banks and Politics in America

12. In economics supernormal profit _____ or pure profit or excess profits, is a profit exceeding the normal profit. Normal profit equals the opportunity cost of labour and capital, while supernormal profit is the amount exceeds the normal return from these input factors in production.

_____ is usually generated by an oligopoly or a monopoly; however, these firms often try to hide this from the market to reduce risk of competition or antitrust investigation.

a. ACCRA Cost of Living Index
b. Operating profit
c. Accounting profit
d. Abnormal profit

13. In ethical philosophy, _____ is the principle that an action is rational if and only if it maximizes one's self-interest. The view is a normative form of egoism. However, it is different from other forms of egoism, such as ethical egoism and psychological egoism.

a. 100-year flood
b. 130-30 fund
c. 1921 recession
d. Rational egoism

14. Economic _____ is defined as an excess distribution to any factor in a production process above that which is required to induce the factor into the process or any excess above that which is necessary to keep the factor in its current use..

Classical Factor _____ is primarily concerned with the fee paid for the use of fixed (e.g. natural) resources. The classical definition is expressed as any excess payment above that required to induce or provide for production.

a. 1921 recession
b. 130-30 fund
c. 100-year flood
d. Rent

15. An Inquiry into the Nature and Causes of _____ is the magnum opus of the Scottish economist Adam Smith. It is a clearly written account of economics at the dawn of the Industrial Revolution, as well as a rhetorical piece written for the generally educated individual of the 18th century - advocating a free market economy as more productive and more beneficial to society.

The work is credited as a watershed in history and economics due to its comprehensive, largely accurate characterization of economic mechanisms that survive in modern economics; and also for its effective use of rhetorical technique, including structuring the work to contrast real world examples of free and fettered markets.

a. The General Theory of Employment, Interest and Money
b. The Bell Curve
c. Wealth and poverty of nations
d. The Wealth of Nations

16. CÄ"terÄ«s paribus is a Latin phrase, literally translated as 'with other things the same.' It is commonly rendered in English as 'all other things being equal.' A prediction, or a statement about causal or logical connections between two states of affairs, is qualified by _____ in order to acknowledge, and to rule out, the possibility of other factors which could override the relationship between the antecedent and the consequent.

A _____ assumption is often fundamental to the predictive purpose of scientific inquiry. In order to formulate scientific laws, it is usually necessary to rule out factors which interfere with examining a specific causal relationship.

a. Deflator
b. Dead cat bounce
c. Regrettables
d. Ceteris paribus

17. In economics and sociology, an _____ is any factor (financial or non-financial) that enables or motivates a particular course of action, or counts as a reason for preferring one choice to the alternatives. It is an expectation that encourages people to behave in a certain way. Since human beings are purposeful creatures, the study of _____ structures is central to the study of all economic activity (both in terms of individual decision-making and in terms of co-operation and competition within a larger institutional structure.)

a. Economic reform
b. Isocost
c. Epstein-Zin preferences
d. Incentive

18. A _____ is one scenario provided for evaluation by respondents in a Choice Experiment. Responses are collected and used to create a Choice Model. Respondents are usually provided with a series of differing _____s for evaluation.

a. 1921 recession
b. 100-year flood
c. 130-30 fund
d. Choice Set

19. _____ is the a method of technical and economic research of the systems for purpose to optimize a parity between system's consumer functions or properties and expenses to achieve those functions or properties.

This methodology for continuous perfection of production, industrial technologies, organizational structures was developed by Juryj Sobolev in 1948 at the 'Perm telephone factory'

- 1948 Juryj Sobolev - the first success in application of a method analysis at the 'Perm telephone factory'.
- 1949 - the first application for the invention as result of use of the new method.

Today in economically developed countries practically each enterprise or the company use methodology of the kind of functional-cost analysis as a practice of the quality management, most full satisfying to principles of standards of series ISO 9000.

- Interest of consumer not in products itself, but the advantage which it will receive from its usage.
- The consumer aspires to reduce his expenses
- Functions needed by consumer can be executed in the various ways, and, hence, with various efficiency and expenses. Among possible alternatives of realization of functions exist such in which the parity of quality and the price is the optimal for the consumer.

The goal of _____ is achievement of the highest consumer satisfaction of production at simultaneous decrease in all kinds of industrial expenses Classical _____ has three English synonyms - Value Engineering, Value Management, Value Analysis.

a. Residual value
b. Real net output ratio
c. Monopoly wage
d. Function cost analysis

20. _____ is a specific term used in companies' financial reporting from the company-whole point of view. Because that use excludes the effects of changing ownership interest, an economic measure of _____ is necessary for financial analysis from the shareholders' point of view

_____ is defined by the Financial Accounting Standards Board, or FASB, as e;the change in equity [net assets] of a business enterprise during a period from transactions and other events and circumstances from nonowner sources. It includes all changes in equity during a period except those resulting from investments by owners and distributions to owners.e;

_____ is the sum of net income and other items that must bypass the income statement because they have not been realized, including items like an unrealized holding gain or loss from available for sale securities and foreign currency translation gains or losses.

a. Real income
b. Windfall gain
c. Per capita income
d. Comprehensive income

21. _____ is the process by which the government, central bank (ii) availability of money, and (iii) cost of money or rate of interest, in order to attain a set of objectives oriented towards the growth and stability of the economy. Monetary theory provides insight into how to craft optimal _____.

_____ is referred to as either being an expansionary policy where an expansionary policy increases the total supply of money in the economy, and a contractionary policy decreases the total money supply.

a. 100-year flood
b. 1021 recession
c. Monetary policy
d. 130-30 fund

Chapter 1. The Nature of Economics

22. _____ is the branch of economics that incorporates value judgments (that is, normative judgements) about what the economy ought to be like or what particular policy actions ought to be recommended to achieve a desirable goal. _____ looks at the desirability of certain aspects of the economy. It underlies expressions of support for particular economic policies.
   a. Broad money
   b. Buy-side analyst
   c. Normative economics
   d. Bord halfpenny

23. _____ is the branch of economics that concerns the description and explanation of economic phenomena (Wong, 1987, p. 920.) It focuses on facts and cause-and-effect relationships and includes the development and testing of economics theories.
   a. Positive economics
   b. 100-year flood
   c. Regulatory economics
   d. 130-30 fund

24. _____ is the application of experimental methods to study economic questions. Experiments are used to test the validity of economic theories and test-bed new market mechanisms. Using cash-motivated subjects, economic experiments create real-world incentives to help us better understand why markets and other exchange systems work the way they do.
   a. Economic
   b. Evolutionary economics
   c. Economic development
   d. Experimental economics

25. In economics, _____ is a measure of the relative satisfaction from consumption of various goods and services. Given this measure, one may speak meaningfully of increasing or decreasing _____, and thereby explain economic behavior in terms of attempts to increase one's _____. For illustrative purposes, changes in _____ are sometimes expressed in units called utils.
   a. Expected utility hypothesis
   b. Ordinal utility
   c. Utility function
   d. Utility

26. The _____ or gross domestic income (GDI), a basic measure of an economy's economic performance, is the market value of all final goods and services produced within the borders of a nation in a year. _____ can be defined in three ways, all of which are conceptually identical. First, it is equal to the total expenditures for all final goods and services produced within the country in a stipulated period of time (usually a 365-day year.)
   a. Market failure
   b. Co-operative economics
   c. Public economics
   d. Gross domestic product

27. An inverse or negative relationship is a mathematical relationship in which one variable, say y, decreases as another, say x, increases. For a linear (straight-line) relation, this can be expressed as y = a-bx, where -b is a constant value less than zero and a is a constant. For example, there is an _____ between education and unemployment -- that is, as education increases, the rate of unemployment decreases.
   a. ACEA agreement
   b. ACCRA Cost of Living Index
   c. AD-IA Model
   d. Inverse relationship

28. In economics and business, specifically cost accounting, the _____ point (BEP) is the point at which cost or expenses and revenue are equal: there is no net loss or gain, and one has 'broken even'. A profit or a loss has not been made, although opportunity costs have been paid, and capital has received the risk-adjusted, expected return.

For example, if the business sells less than 200 tables each month, it will make a loss, if it sells more, it will be a profit.

a. Trailing twelve months
b. Break-even
c. Stylized fact
d. Decoupling plus

29. The _____ is an important selective, mainly private, international organization designed by its founders to supervise and liberalize international trade. The organization officially commenced on 1 January 1995, under the Marrakesh Agreement, succeeding the 1947 General Agreement on Tariffs and Trade (GATT.)

The _____ deals with regulation of trade between participating countries; it provides a framework for negotiating and formalising trade agreements, and a dispute resolution process aimed at enforcing participants' adherence to _____ agreements which are signed by representatives of member governments and ratified by their parliaments.

a. World Trade Organization
b. Blotto game
c. Differential games
d. Differences in Differences

30. In mathematics, a _____ system is a system which is not linear, that is, a system which does not satisfy the superposition principle, or whose output is not proportional to its input. Less technically, a _____ system is any problem where the variable(s) to be solved for cannot be written as a linear combination of independent components. A nonhomogeneous system, which is linear apart from the presence of a function of the independent variables, is _____ according to a strict definition, but such systems are usually studied alongside linear systems, because they can be transformed to a linear system of multiple variables.

a. Nonlinear
b. Nonlinear system
c. 130-30 fund
d. 100-year flood

Chapter 2. Scarcity and the World of Trade-Offs

1. In economics, _____ are the resources employed to produce goods and services. They facilitate production but do not become part of the product (as with raw materials) or significantly transformed by the production process (as with fuel used to power machinery.) To 19th century economists, the _____ were land (natural resources, gifts from nature), labor (the ability to work), and capital goods (human-made tools and equipment.)
   a. Long-run
   b. Factors of production
   c. Productive capacity
   d. Production function

2. In microeconomics, _____ is quite simply the conversion of inputs into outputs. It is an economic process that uses resources to create a good or service that is suitable for exchange. This can include manufacturing, storing, shipping, and packaging.
   a. Variability
   b. Bucket shop
   c. Characteristic
   d. Production

3. In Marxian economics, _____ originally referred to the means of production. Individuals, organizations and governments use _____ in the production of other goods or commodities. _____ include factories, machinery, tools, equipment, and various buildings which are used to produce other products for consumption.
   a. Modigliani-Miller theorem
   b. Capital goods
   c. Capital formation
   d. Cost of capital

4. _____s is the social science that studies the production, distribution, and consumption of goods and services. The term _____s comes from the Ancient Greek oἰκονομῐα from oἶκος (oikos, 'house') + νῐόμος (nomos, 'custom' or 'law'), hence 'rules of the house(hold)'. Current _____ models developed out of the broader field of political economy in the late 19th century, owing to a desire to use an empirical approach more akin to the physical sciences.
   a. Opportunity cost
   b. Inflation
   c. Energy economics
   d. Economic

5. _____ is the increase in the amount of the goods and services produced by an economy over time. It is conventionally measured as the percent rate of increase in real gross domestic product, or real GDP. Growth is usually calculated in real terms, i.e. inflation-adjusted terms, in order to net out the effect of inflation on the price of the goods and services produced.
   a. AD-IA Model
   b. ACCRA Cost of Living Index
   c. ACEA agreement
   d. Economic growth

6. A _____ is an object whose consumption increases the utility of the consumer, for which the quantity demanded exceeds the quantity supplied at zero price. _____s are usually modeled as having diminishing marginal utility. The first individual purchase has high utility; the second has less.
   a. Luxury good
   b. Positional goods
   c. Good
   d. Search good

7. _____ according to Onuoha (2007) is the practice of starting new organizations or revitalizing mature organizations, particularly new businesses generally in response to identified opportunities. _____ is often a difficult undertaking, as a vast majority of new businesses fail. Entrepreneurial activities are substantially different depending on the type of organization that is being started.
   a. ACCRA Cost of Living Index
   b. ACEA agreement
   c. Entrepreneurship
   d. Intrapreneurship

Chapter 2. Scarcity and the World of Trade-Offs

8. _____ refers to the stock of skills and knowledge embodied in the ability to perform labor so as to produce economic value. It is the skills and knowledge gained by a worker through education and experience. Many early economic theories refer to it simply as labor, one of three factors of production, and consider it to be a fungible resource -- homogeneous and easily interchangeable. Other conceptions of labor dispense with these assumptions.
   a. Labour economics
   b. Human capital
   c. Monopolistic competition
   d. Monetary inflation

9. An _____ is a good that is intangible, meaning that it can not be touched, as opposed to a physical good. In an increasingly digitized world, _____s play a more and more important role in the economy. Virtually anything that is in a digital form and deliverable on the Internet can be considered an _____.
   a. Export-led growth
   b. Inelastic
   c. International free trade agreement
   d. Intangible good

10. _____s (economically referred to as land or raw materials) occur naturally within environments that exist relatively undisturbed by mankind, in a natural form. A _____'s is often characterized by amounts of biodiversity existent in various ecosystems.

Mining, petroleum extraction, fishing, hunting, and forestry are generally considered natural-resource industries.

   a. 130-30 fund
   b. 100-year flood
   c. 1921 recession
   d. Natural resource

11. _____ is a slogan popularized by Karl Marx in his 1875 Critique of the Gotha Program. The phrase summarizes the principles that, under a communist system, every person should contribute to society to the best of his ability and consume from society in proportion to his needs, regardless of how much he has contributed. In the Marxist view, such an arrangement will be made possible by the abundance of goods and services that a developed communist society will produce; the idea is that there will be enough to satisfy everyone's needs.
   a. State monopoly capitalism
   b. From each according to his ability, to each according to his need
   c. Proletarian internationalism
   d. Cultural Marxism

12. In general _____ refers to any non-human asset made by humans and then used in production. Often, it refers to economic capital in some ambiguous combination of infrastructural capital and natural capital. As these are combined in process-specific and firm-specific ways that neoclassical macroeconomics does not differentiate at its level of analysis, it is common to refer only to physical vs. human capital and seek so-called 'balanced growth' that develops both in tandem

Such analyses, however, fails to make distinctions considered critical by many modern economists.

   a. Consumer-to-business
   b. Physical capital
   c. Control premium
   d. Depository Institutions Deregulation and Monetary Control Act

13. _____ is used to assign the available resources in an economic way. It is part of resource management.

In strategic planning, is a plan for using available resources, for example human resources, especially in the near term, to achieve goals for the future.

Chapter 2. Scarcity and the World of Trade-Offs

a. 100-year flood
b. Resource allocation
c. 1921 recession
d. 130-30 fund

14. In economics supernormal profit _____ or pure profit or excess profits, is a profit exceeding the normal profit. Normal profit equals the opportunity cost of labour and capital, while supernormal profit is the amount exceeds the normal return from these input factors in production.

_____ is usually generated by an oligopoly or a monopoly; however, these firms often try to hide this from the market to reduce risk of competition or antitrust investigation.

a. ACCRA Cost of Living Index
b. Operating profit
c. Accounting profit
d. Abnormal profit

15. Economic _____ is defined as an excess distribution to any factor in a production process above that which is required to induce the factor into the process or any excess above that which is necessary to keep the factor in its current use..

Classical Factor _____ is primarily concerned with the fee paid for the use of fixed (e.g. natural) resources. The classical definition is expressed as any excess payment above that required to induce or provide for production.

a. 100-year flood
b. 130-30 fund
c. 1921 recession
d. Rent

16. _____ is a fee paid on borrowed assets. It is the price paid for the use of borrowed money , or, money earned by deposited funds . Assets that are sometimes lent with _____ include money, shares, consumer goods through hire purchase, major assets such as aircraft, and even entire factories in finance lease arrangements.

a. Asset protection
b. Internal debt
c. Insolvency
d. Interest

17. _____ or economic opportunity loss is the value of the next best alternative foregone as the result of making a decision. _____ analysis is an important part of a company's decision-making processes but is not treated as an actual cost in any financial statement. The next best thing that a person can engage in is referred to as the _____ of doing the best thing and ignoring the next best thing to be done.

a. Industrial organization
b. Economic ideology
c. Economic
d. Opportunity cost

18. _____ is a broad label that refers to any individuals or households that use goods and services generated within the economy. The concept of a _____ is used in different contexts, so that the usage and significance of the term may vary.

Typically when business people and economists talk of _____s they are talking about person as _____, an aggregated commodity item with little individuality other than that expressed in the buy/not-buy decision.

Chapter 2. Scarcity and the World of Trade-Offs

a. 130-30 fund
b. 100-year flood
c. 1921 recession
d. Consumer

19. A _____ is a situation that involves losing one quality or aspect of something in return for gaining another quality or aspect. It implies a decision to be made with full comprehension of both the upside and downside of a particular choice.

In economics the term is expressed as opportunity cost, referring the most preferred alternative given up.

a. Market microstructure
b. Trade-off
c. Capital outflow
d. Stylized fact

20. _____ is a common concept in economics, and gives rise to derived concepts such as consumer debt. Generally _____ is defined by opposition to production. But the precise definition can vary because different schools of economists define production quite differently.

a. British canal system
b. Basis of futures
c. Discrete choice
d. Consumption

21. _____ is an online peer-reviewed magazine published by the Agricultural ' Applied Economics Association (AAEA) for readers interested in the policy and management of agriculture, the food industry, natural resources, rural communities, and the environment. _____ is published quarterly and is available free online. It is currently one of three outreach products offered by AAEA, along with the more timely Policy Issues and the forthcoming Shared Materials section of the AAEA Web site.

a. 100-year flood
b. Choices
c. 1921 recession
d. 130-30 fund

22. Economics:

- _____, the desire to own something and the ability to pay for it
- _____ curve, a graphic representation of a _____ schedule
- _____ deposit, the money in checking accounts
- _____ pull theory, the theory that inflation occurs when _____ for goods and services exceeds existing supplies
- _____ schedule, a table that lists the quantity of a good a person will buy it each different price
- _____ side economics, the school of economics at believes government spending and tax cuts open economy by raising _____

a. Demand
b. Procter ' Gamble
c. Bon
d. G20

23. In economics, _____ is the ratio of the percent change in one variable to the percent change in another variable. It is a tool for measuring the responsiveness of a function to changes in parameters in a relative way. Commonly analyzed are _____ of substitution, price and wealth.

a. Elasticity
b. ACFA agreement
c. ACCRA Cost of Living Index
d. Elasticity of demand

24. Price _____ is defined as the measure of responsiveness in the quantity demanded for a commodity as a result of change in price of the same commodity. It is a measure of how consumers react to a change in price. In other words, it is percentage change in quantity demanded by the percentage change in price of the same commodity.
   a. Elasticity
   b. ACEA agreement
   c. ACCRA Cost of Living Index
   d. Elasticity of demand

25. _____ in economics and business is the result of an exchange and from that trade we assign a numerical monetary value to a good, service or asset. If Alice trades Bob 4 apples for an orange, the _____ of an orange is 4 apples. Inversely, the _____ of an apple is 1/4 oranges.
   a. Lerner Index
   b. Price ceiling
   c. Price
   d. Price dispersion

26. _____ is defined as the measure of responsiveness in the quantity demanded for a commodity as a result of change in price of the same commodity. It is a measure of how consumers react to a change in price. In other words, it is percentage change in quantity demanded as per the percentage change in price of the same commodity.
   a. 130-30 fund
   b. 1921 recession
   c. 100-year flood
   d. Price elasticity of demand

27. Cǣterǣs paribus is a Latin phrase, literally translated as 'with other things the same.' It is commonly rendered in English as 'all other things being equal.' A prediction, or a statement about causal or logical connections between two states of affairs, is qualified by _____ in order to acknowledge, and to rule out, the possibility of other factors which could override the relationship between the antecedent and the consequent.

A _____ assumption is often fundamental to the predictive purpose of scientific inquiry. In order to formulate scientific laws, it is usually necessary to rule out factors which interfere with examining a specific causal relationship.

   a. Regrettables
   b. Dead cat bounce
   c. Ceteris paribus
   d. Deflator

28. _____ occurs when the economy is operating at its production possibility frontier (PPF.) This takes place when production of one good is achieved at the lowest cost possible, given the production of the other good(s.) Equivalently, it is when the highest possible output of one good is produced, given the production level of the other good(s.)
   a. Productive efficiency
   b. Lean consumption
   c. Fixed exchange rate system
   d. Recursive economics

Chapter 2. Scarcity and the World of Trade-Offs

29. Competition law, known in the United States as _____ law, has three main elements:

- prohibiting agreements or practices that restrict free trading and competition between business entities. This includes in particular the repression of cartels.
- banning abusive behaviour by a firm dominating a market, or anti-competitive practices that tend to lead to such a dominant position. Practices controlled in this way may include predatory pricing, tying, price gouging, refusal to deal, and many others.
- supervising the mergers and acquisitions of large corporations, including some joint ventures. Transactions that are considered to threaten the competitive process can be prohibited altogether, or approved subject to 'remedies' such as an obligation to divest part of the merged business or to offer licences or access to facilities to enable other businesses to continue competing.

The substance and practice of competition law varies from jurisdiction to jurisdiction. Protecting the interests of consumers (consumer welfare) and ensuring that entrepreneurs have an opportunity to compete in the market economy are often treated as important objectives. Competition law is closely connected with law on deregulation of access to markets, state aids and subsidies, the privatisation of state owned assets and the establishment of independent sector regulators. In recent decades, competition law has been viewed as a way to provide better public services.

a. Intellectual property law
b. United Kingdom competition law
c. Anti-Inflation Act
d. Antitrust

30. In economics and business, specifically cost accounting, the _____ point (BEP) is the point at which cost or expenses and revenue are equal: there is no net loss or gain, and one has 'broken even'. A profit or a loss has not been made, although opportunity costs have been paid, and capital has received the risk-adjusted, expected return.

For example, if the business sells less than 200 tables each month, it will make a loss, if it sells more, it will be a profit.

a. Trailing twelve months
b. Break-even
c. Decoupling plus
d. Stylized fact

31. In calculus, a function f defined on a subset of the real numbers with real values is called _____, if for all x and y such that x >≤ y one has f(x) >≤ f(y), so f preserves the order. In layman's terms, the sign of the slope is always positive (the curve tending upwards) or zero (i.e., non-decreasing, or asymptotic, or depicted as a horizontal, flat line) Likewise, a function is called monotonically decreasing (non-increasing) if, whenever x >≤ y, then f(x) >≥ f(y), so it reverses the order.

a. 1921 recession
b. 130-30 fund
c. Monotonic
d. 100-year flood

32. _____ is a type of private equity investment, most often a minority investment, in relatively mature companies that are looking for capital to expand or restructure operations, enter new markets or finance a significant acquisition without a change of control of the business.

Companies that seek _____, will often do so in order to finance a transformational event in their lifecycle. These companies are likely to be more mature than venture capital funded companies, able to generate revenue and operating profits but unable to generate sufficient cash to fund major expansions, acquisitions or other investments.

   a. Mezzanine capital
   b. Growth capital
   c. Seed money
   d. Venture capital fund

33. _____ is a concept found in moral, political, and bioethical philosophy. Within these contexts, it refers to the capacity of a rational individual to make an informed, un-coerced decision. In moral and political philosophy, _____ is often used as the basis for determining moral responsibility for one's actions.

   a. AD-IA Model
   b. Autonomy
   c. ACEA agreement
   d. ACCRA Cost of Living Index

34. _____ is a term used to describe consumption expenditure that occurs when income levels are zero. Such consumption is considered autonomous of income only when expenditure on these consumables does not vary with changes in income. If income levels are actually zero, this consumption counts as dissaving, because it is financed by borrowing or using up savings.

   a. Indexed unit of account
   b. Austerity
   c. Economic interdependence
   d. Autonomous consumption

35. In economics, the _____ is a single mathematical function used to express consumer spending. It was developed by John Maynard Keynes and detailed most famously in his book The General Theory of Employment, Interest, and Money. The function is used to calculate the amount of total consumption in an economy.

   a. Real exchange rate puzzles
   b. Procyclical
   c. Consumption function
   d. Demand-Led Growth

36. In economics, _____ refers to the ability of a party to produce a good or service using fewer real resources than another entity producing the same good or service..A party has an _____ when using the same input as another party, it can produce a greater output. Since _____ is determined by a simple comparison of labor productivities, it is possible for a a party to have no _____ in anything. It can be contrasted with the concept of comparative advantage which refers to the ability to produce a particular good at a lower opportunity cost.

   a. Index number
   b. International economics
   c. Absolute advantage
   d. ACCRA Cost of Living Index

37. In economics, _____ refers to the ability of a person or a country to produce a particular good at a lower marginal cost and opportunity cost than another person or country. It is the ability to produce a product most efficiently given all the other products that could be produced. It can be contrasted with absolute advantage which refers to the ability of a person or a country to produce a particular good at a lower absolute cost than another.

   a. Financial export
   b. Comparative advantage
   c. Small open economy
   d. Dutch disease

38. _____ in economics refers to metrics and measures of output from production processes, per unit of input. Labor _____, for example, is typically measured as a ratio of output per labor-hour, an input. _____ may be conceived of as a metrics of the technical or engineering efficiency of production.

Chapter 2. Scarcity and the World of Trade-Offs

a. Piece work
b. Fordism
c. Production-possibility frontier
d. Productivity

39. In algebra, a _____ is a function depending on n that associates a scalar, det(A), to an n×n square matrix A. The fundamental geometric meaning of a _____ is a scale factor for measure when A is regarded as a linear transformation. _____s are important both in calculus, where they enter the substitution rule for several variables, and in multilinear algebra.

For a fixed nonnegative integer n, there is a unique _____ function for the n×n matrices over any commutative ring R. In particular, this function exists when R is the field of real or complex numbers.

a. 130-30 fund
b. Determinant
c. 1921 recession
d. 100-year flood

40. In finance, the _____s between two currencies specifies how much one currency is worth in terms of the other. It is the value of a foreign nation;s currency in terms of the home nation;s currency. For example an _____ of 102 Japanese yen to the United States dollar means that JPY 102 is worth the same as USD 1.

a. Interbank market
b. ACEA agreement
c. Exchange rate
d. ACCRA Cost of Living Index

41. _____ was a survey conducted by the U.S. Department of Justice to gauge the prevalence of alcohol and illegal drug use among prior arrestees. It was a reformulation of the prior Drug Use Forecasting (DUF) program, focused on five drugs in particular: cocaine, marijuana, methamphetamine, opiates, and PCP.

Participants were randomly selected from arrest records in major metropolitan areas; because no personally identifying information is taken from each record chosen, the resulting data can be correlated to arrest rates, but not to the total population of persons charged.

a. ACCRA Cost of Living Index
b. ACEA agreement
c. AD-IA Model
d. Arrestee Drug Abuse Monitoring

42. Necessary _____s:

If x is a necessary _____ of y, then the presence of y necessarily implies the presence of x. The presence of x, however, does not imply that y will occur.

Sufficient _____s:

If x is a sufficient _____ of y, then the presence of x necessarily implies the presence of y.

a. Global justice
b. Deductive logic
c. Materialism
d. Cause

43. An _____ is the magnum opus of the Scottish economist Adam Smith. It is a clearly written account of economics at the dawn of the Industrial Revolution, as well as a rhetorical piece written for the generally educated individual of the 18th century - advocating a free market economy as more productive and more beneficial to society.

The work is credited as a watershed in history and economics due to its comprehensive, largely accurate characterization of economic mechanisms that survive in modern economics; and also for its effective use of rhetorical technique, including structuring the work to contrast real world examples of free and fettered markets.

a. ACEA agreement
b. ACCRA Cost of Living Index
c. AD-IA Model
d. Inquiry into the Nature and Causes of the Wealth of Nations

44. _____ is exchange of capital, goods, and services across international borders or territories. In most countries, it represents a significant share of gross domestic product (GDP.) While _____ has been present throughout much of history , its economic, social, and political importance has been on the rise in recent centuries.

a. Intra-industry trade
b. Import license
c. Incoterms
d. International trade

45. _____ was a Scottish moral philosopher and a pioneer of political economy. One of the key figures of the Scottish Enlightenment, Smith is the author of The Theory of Moral Sentiments and An Inquiry into the Nature and Causes of the Wealth of Nations. The latter, usually abbreviated as The Wealth of Nations, is considered his magnum opus and the first modern work of economics.

a. Alan Greenspan
b. Adolph Fischer
c. Adolf Hitler
d. Adam Smith

46. An Inquiry into the Nature and Causes of the _____ is the magnum opus of the Scottish economist Adam Smith. It is a clearly written account of economics at the dawn of the Industrial Revolution, as well as a rhetorical piece written for the generally educated individual of the 18th century - advocating a free market economy as more productive and more beneficial to society.

The work is credited as a watershed in history and economics due to its comprehensive, largely accurate characterization of economic mechanisms that survive in modern economics; and also for its effective use of rhetorical technique, including structuring the work to contrast real world examples of free and fettered markets.

a. Capital and Interest
b. Wealth of Nations
c. The New Industrial State
d. Banks and Politics in America

47. An Inquiry into the Nature and Causes of _____ is the magnum opus of the Scottish economist Adam Smith. It is a clearly written account of economics at the dawn of the Industrial Revolution, as well as a rhetorical piece written for the generally educated individual of the 18th century - advocating a free market economy as more productive and more beneficial to society.

The work is credited as a watershed in history and economics due to its comprehensive, largely accurate characterization of economic mechanisms that survive in modern economics; and also for its effective use of rhetorical technique, including structuring the work to contrast real world examples of free and fettered markets.

a. The Bell Curve

b. The General Theory of Employment, Interest and Money

c. Wealth and poverty of nations

d. The Wealth of Nations

48. The _____ is the largest national economy in the world. Its gross domestic product (GDP) was estimated as $14.2 trillion in 2008. The U.S. economy maintains a high level of output per person (GDP per capita, $46,800 in 2008, ranked at around number ten in the world.)

a. ACEA agreement

b. AD-IA Model

c. ACCRA Cost of Living Index

d. Economy of the United States

49. _____ in business and accounting is a percentage of voting stock owned. This notion is different from economic interest that refers to a percentage of all the equity issued, including preferred stock, warrants, and so on. Ownership of more than 50% of voting shares gives the right of control and consolidation.

a. Participating preferred stock

b. Voting Interest

c. Bookrunner

d. Cashflow matching

Chapter 3. Demand and Supply

1. _____ is a fee paid on borrowed assets. It is the price paid for the use of borrowed money, or, money earned by deposited funds. Assets that are sometimes lent with _____ include money, shares, consumer goods through hire purchase, major assets such as aircraft, and even entire factories in finance lease arrangements.

   a. Insolvency
   b. Interest
   c. Asset protection
   d. Internal debt

2. Cēterīs paribus is a Latin phrase, literally translated as 'with other things the same.' It is commonly rendered in English as 'all other things being equal.' A prediction, or a statement about causal or logical connections between two states of affairs, is qualified by _____ in order to acknowledge, and to rule out, the possibility of other factors which could override the relationship between the antecedent and the consequent.

   A _____ assumption is often fundamental to the predictive purpose of scientific inquiry. In order to formulate scientific laws, it is usually necessary to rule out factors which interfere with examining a specific causal relationship.

   a. Regrettables
   b. Deflator
   c. Ceteris paribus
   d. Dead cat bounce

3. Economics:

   - _____, the desire to own something and the ability to pay for it
   - _____ curve, a graphic representation of a _____ schedule
   - _____ deposit, the money in checking accounts
   - _____ pull theory, the theory that inflation occurs when _____ for goods and services exceeds existing supplies
   - _____ schedule, a table that lists the quantity of a good a person will buy it each different price
   - _____ side economics, the school of economics at believes government spending and tax cuts open economy by raising _____

   a. G20
   b. Procter ' Gamble
   c. Bon
   d. Demand

4. Competition law, known in the United States as _____ law, has three main elements:

   - prohibiting agreements or practices that restrict free trading and competition between business entities. This includes in particular the repression of cartels.
   - banning abusive behaviour by a firm dominating a market, or anti-competitive practices that tend to lead to such a dominant position. Practices controlled in this way may include predatory pricing, tying, price gouging, refusal to deal, and many others.
   - supervising the mergers and acquisitions of large corporations, including some joint ventures. Transactions that are considered to threaten the competitive process can be prohibited altogether, or approved subject to 'remedies' such as an obligation to divest part of the merged business or to offer licences or access to facilities to enable other businesses to continue competing.

Chapter 3. Demand and Supply

The substance and practice of competition law varies from jurisdiction to jurisdiction. Protecting the interests of consumers (consumer welfare) and ensuring that entrepreneurs have an opportunity to compete in the market economy are often treated as important objectives. Competition law is closely connected with law on deregulation of access to markets, state aids and subsidies, the privatisation of state owned assets and the establishment of independent sector regulators. In recent decades, competition law has been viewed as a way to provide better public services.

 a. Intellectual property law
 b. Antitrust
 c. Anti-Inflation Act
 d. United Kingdom competition law

5. In economics, the _____ is an economic law that states that consumers buy more of a good when its price decreases and less when its price increases.

There are certain goods which do not follow this law. These include Veblen and Giffen goods

 a. Labour economics
 b. Business cycle
 c. General equilibrium theory
 d. Law of Demand

6. _____ is a term that encompasses the notion of individuals and firms striving for a greater share of a market to sell or buy goods and services. Merriam-Webster defines competition in business as 'the effort of two or more parties acting independently to secure the business of a third party by offering the most favorable terms.' It was described by Adam Smith in The Wealth of Nations (1776) and later economists as allocating productive resources to their most highly-valued uses. and encouraging efficiency.

 a. Competition in economics
 b. Path dependence
 c. Moral victory
 d. Cut-throat competition

7. _____ is the price of a commodity such as a good or service in terms of another; ie, the ratio of two prices. A _____ may be expressed in terms of a ratio between any two prices or the ratio between the price of one particular good and a weighted average of all other goods available in the market. A _____ is an opportunity cost.

 a. False economy
 b. Relative price
 c. False shortage
 d. Food cooperative

8. _____ in economics and business is the result of an exchange and from that trade we assign a numerical monetary value to a good, service or asset. If Alice trades Bob 4 apples for an orange, the _____ of an orange is 4 apples. Inversely, the _____ of an apple is 1/4 oranges.

 a. Price dispersion
 b. Price ceiling
 c. Price
 d. Lerner Index

9. In economics, a _____ is a table that lists the quantity of a good a person will buy it each different price See Demand curve.

 a. Demand schedule
 b. Dynamic efficiency
 c. Rational irrationality
 d. Discouraged worker

10. The Organization of the Petroleum Exporting Countries is a cartel of twelve countries made up of Algeria, Angola, Ecuador, Iran, Iraq, Kuwait, Libya, Nigeria, Qatar, Saudi Arabia, the United Arab Emirates, and Venezuela. The cartel has maintained its headquarters in Vienna since 1965, and hosts regular meetings among the oil ministers of its Member Countries. Indonesia withdrew its membership in _____ in 2008 after it became a net importer of oil, but stated it would likely return if it became a net exporter in the world.
    a. ACEA agreement
    b. AD-IA Model
    c. ACCRA Cost of Living Index
    d. OPEC

11. In international commerce and politics, an _____ is the prohibition of commerce (division of trade) and trade with a certain country, in order to isolate it and to put its government into a difficult internal situation, given that the effects of the _____ are often able to make its economy suffer from the initiative.

    The _____ is usually used as a political punishment for some previous disagreed policies or acts, but its economic nature frequently raises doubts about the real interests that the prohibition serves.

    One of the most comprehensive attempts at an _____ happened during the Napoleonic Wars.

    a. Optimum currency area
    b. International finance
    c. Embargo
    d. Overshooting model

12. In economics, the _____ can be defined as the graph depicting the relationship between the price of a certain commodity, and the amount of it that consumers are willing and able to purchase at that given price. It is a graphic representation of a demand schedule. The _____ for all consumers together follows from the _____ of every individual consumer: the individual demands at each price are added together.
    a. Lorenz curve
    b. Kuznets curve
    c. Wage curve
    d. Demand curve

13. The _____ curve theory is an economic theory regarding oligopoly and monopolistic competition. When it was created, the idea fundamentally challenged classical economic tenets such as efficient markets and rapidly-changing prices, ideas that underly basic supply and demand models. _____ was an initial attempt to explain sticky prices.
    a. Marshallian demand function
    b. Hicksian demand function
    c. Marginal demand
    d. Kinked Demand

14. The _____ theory is an economic theory regarding oligopoly and monopolistic competition. When it was created, the idea fundamentally challenged classical economic tenets such as efficient markets and rapidly-changing prices, ideas that underly basic supply and demand models. Kinked demand was an initial attempt to explain sticky prices.
    a. Kinked Demand curve
    b. Marginal demand
    c. Kinked demand
    d. Marshallian demand function

15. In algebra, a _____ is a function depending on n that associates a scalar, det(A), to an n×n square matrix A. The fundamental geometric meaning of a _____ is a scale factor for measure when A is regarded as a linear transformation. _____s are important both in calculus, where they enter the substitution rule for several variables, and in multilinear algebra.

    For a fixed nonnegative integer n, there is a unique _____ function for the n×n matrices over any commutative ring R. In particular, this function exists when R is the field of real or complex numbers.

Chapter 3. Demand and Supply 21

a. 100-year flood
b. 1921 recession
c. Determinant
d. 130-30 fund

16. In economics, _____s are any goods for which demand increases when income increases and falls when income decreases but price remains constant, i.e. with a positive income elasticity of demand. The term does not necessarily refer to the quality of the good.

Depending on the indifference curves, the amount of a good bought can either increase, decrease, or stay the same when income increases.

a. Monopoly price
b. Malinvestment
c. Financial result
d. Normal good

17. A _____ is an object whose consumption increases the utility of the consumer, for which the quantity demanded exceeds the quantity supplied at zero price. _____s are usually modeled as having diminishing marginal utility. The first individual purchase has high utility; the second has less.

a. Positional goods
b. Search good
c. Luxury good
d. Good

18. _____ was a Scottish-born American industrialist, businessman, and a major philanthropist. He was an immigrant as a child with his parents. He built Pittsburgh's Carnegie Steel Company, which was later merged with Elbert H. Gary's Federal Steel Company and several smaller companies to create U.S. Steel.

a. Andrew Carnegie
b. Alfred Marshall
c. Oskar Morgenstern
d. Eli Whitney

19. In consumer theory, an _____ is a good that decreases in demand when consumer income rises, unlike normal goods, for which the opposite is observed. It is a good that consumers demand increases when their income increases. Inferiority, in this sense, is an observable fact relating to affordability rather than a statement about the quality of the good.

a. Export-oriented
b. Independent goods
c. Information good
d. Inferior good

20. _____ is the controlled distribution of resources and scarce goods or services. _____ controls the size of the ration, one's allotted portion of the resources being distributed on a particular day or at a particular time.

In economics, it is often common to use the word '_____' to refer to one of the roles that prices play in markets, while _____ is called 'non-price _____.' Using prices to ration means that those with the most money (or other assets) and who want a product the most are first to receive it.

a. 1921 recession
b. 130-30 fund
c. 100-year flood
d. Rationing

21. _____ is a broad label that refers to any individuals or households that use goods and services generated within the economy. The concept of a _____ is used in different contexts, so that the usage and significance of the term may vary.

Chapter 3. Demand and Supply

Typically when business people and economists talk of _____s they are talking about person as _____, an aggregated commodity item with little individuality other than that expressed in the buy/not-buy decision.

a. 100-year flood
c. 1921 recession
b. 130-30 fund
d. Consumer

22. In economics, the _____ is a historical inverse relation between the rate of unemployment and the rate of inflation in an economy. Stated simply, the lower the unemployment in an economy, the higher the rate of increase in nominal wages in the economy. Rate of Change of Wages against Unemployment, United Kingdom 1913-1948 from Phillips (1958)

William Phillips, a New Zealand born economist, wrote a paper in 1958 titled The Relationship between Unemployment and the Rate of Change of Money Wages in the United Kingdom 1861-1957, which was published in the quarterly journal Economica.

a. Kuznets curve
c. Demand curve
b. Phillips curve
d. Wage curve

23. _____ is an online peer-reviewed magazine published by the Agricultural ' Applied Economics Association (AAEA) for readers interested in the policy and management of agriculture, the food industry, natural resources, rural communities, and the environment. _____ is published quarterly and is available free online. It is currently one of three outreach products offered by AAEA, along with the more timely Policy Issues and the forthcoming Shared Materials section of the AAEA Web site.

a. 100-year flood
c. 1921 recession
b. 130-30 fund
d. Choices

24. In competition law the _____ defines the market in which one or more goods compete. Therefore, the _____ defines whether two or more products can be considered substitute goods and whether they constitute a particular and separate market for competition analysis.

The _____ combines the product market and the geographic market, defined as follows:

1. A relevant product market comprises all those products and/or services which are regarded as interchangeable or substitutable by the consumer by reason of the products' characteristics, their prices and their intended use;
2. A relevant geographic market comprises the area in which the firms concerned are involved in the supply of products or services and in which the conditions of competition are sufficiently homogeneous.

The notion of _____ is used in order to identify the products and undertakings which are directly competing in a business. Therefore, the _____ is the market where the competition takes place.

a. Judgment summons
c. Leave of absence
b. Flextime
d. Relevant Market

Chapter 3. Demand and Supply

25. In economics, the _____ is the tendency of suppliers to offer more of a good at a higher price. The relationship between price and quantity supplied is usually a positive relationship. A rise in price is associated with a rise in quantity supplied.
    a. Mainstream economics
    b. Pegged exchange rate
    c. Consumer theory
    d. Law of Supply

26. In economics, _____ is the total amount of money available in an economy at a particular point in time. There are several ways to define 'money', but standard measures usually include currency in circulation and demand deposits.

    _____ data are recorded and published, usually by the government or the central bank of the country.

    a. Monetary economy
    b. Fiscal theory of the price level
    c. Monetary reform
    d. Money Supply

27. _____ is the term denoting either an entrance or changes which are inserted into a system and which activate/modify a process. It is an abstract concept, used in the modeling, system(s) design and system(s) exploitation. It is usually connected with other terms, e.g., _____ field, _____ variable, _____ parameter, _____ value, _____ signal, _____ device and _____ file.
    a. AD-IA Model
    b. Input
    c. ACCRA Cost of Living Index
    d. ACEA agreement

28. _____ in economics refers to metrics and measures of output from production processes, per unit of input. Labor _____, for example, is typically measured as a ratio of output per labor-hour, an input. _____ may be conceived of as a metrics of the technical or engineering efficiency of production.
    a. Fordism
    b. Piece work
    c. Production-possibility frontier
    d. Productivity

29. To _____ is to impose a financial charge or other levy upon a taxpayer by a state or the functional equivalent of a state.

    _____es are also imposed by many subnational entities. _____es consist of direct _____ or indirect _____, and may be paid in money or as its labour equivalent (often but not always unpaid.)

    a. 1921 recession
    b. 100-year flood
    c. Tax
    d. 130-30 fund

30. In economics, the _____ of an industry is used as an indicator of the relative size of firms in relation to the industry as a whole. It is calculated as the sum of the percent market share of the top n industries. This may also assist in determining the market structure of the industry.
    a. Rate-of-return regulation
    b. De facto monopoly
    c. Price takers
    d. Concentration ratio

31. In economics, _____ is the ratio of the percent change in one variable to the percent change in another variable. It is a tool for measuring the responsiveness of a function to changes in parameters in a relative way. Commonly analyzed are _____ of substitution, price and wealth.

Chapter 3. Demand and Supply

a. Elasticity of demand
b. ACEA agreement
c. ACCRA Cost of Living Index
d. Elasticity

32. In finance, the _____s between two currencies specifies how much one currency is worth in terms of the other. It is the value of a foreign natione;s currency in terms of the home natione;s currency. For example an _____ of 102 Japanese yen to the United States dollar means that JPY 102 is worth the same as USD 1.
a. ACCRA Cost of Living Index
b. Interbank market
c. ACEA agreement
d. Exchange rate

33. A _____ is an expression that compares quantities relative to each other. The most common examples involve two quantities, but any number of quantities can be compared. _____s are represented mathematically by separating each quantity with a colon, for example the _____ 2:3, which is read as the _____ 'two to three'.
a. 130-30 fund
b. Ratio
c. 100-year flood
d. Y-intercept

34. _____ is a common concept in economics, and gives rise to derived concepts such as consumer debt. Generally _____ is defined by opposition to production. But the precise definition can vary because different schools of economists define production quite differently.
a. Consumption
b. Discrete choice
c. Basis of futures
d. British canal system

35. _____ is a policy or ideology of violence intended to intimidate or cause terror for the purpose of 'exerting pressure on decision making by state bodies.' The term 'terror' is largely used to indicate clandestine, low-intensity violence that targets civilians and generates public fear. Thus 'terror' is distinct from asymmetric warfare, and violates the concept of a common law of war in which civilian life is regarded. The term '-ism' is used to indicate an ideology --typically one that claims its attacks are in the domain of a 'just war' concept, though most condemn such as crimes against humanity.
a. 130-30 fund
b. 100-year flood
c. Terrorism
d. 1921 recession

36. _____s is the social science that studies the production, distribution, and consumption of goods and services. The term _____s comes from the Ancient Greek oá¼°κονομῖα from oá¼¶κος (oikos, 'house') + vÏŒμος (nomos, 'custom' or 'law'), hence 'rules of the house(hold)'. Current _____ models developed out of the broader field of political economy in the late 19th century, owing to a desire to use an empirical approach more akin to the physical sciences.
a. Inflation
b. Economic
c. Energy economics
d. Opportunity cost

37. _____s are expenses that change in proportion to the activity of a business. In other words, _____ is the sum of marginal costs. It can also be considered normal costs.
a. Marginal cost
b. Cost-Volume-Profit Analysis
c. Variable Cost
d. Cost overrun

Chapter 3. Demand and Supply

38. In economics, _____ refers to either

   1. a simplifying assumption made by the new classical school that markets always go to where the quantity supplied equals the quantity demanded; or
   2. the process of getting there via price adjustment.

A _____ price is the price of a good or service at which quantity supplied is equal to quantity demanded. Also called the equilibrium price.

In simple terms, this means that markets tend to move towards prices which balance the quantity supplied and the quantity demanded, such that the market will eventually be cleared of all surpluses and shortages (excess supply and demand.) The first version assumes that this process occurs instantaneously.

   a. Market portfolio
   c. Market data
   b. Noise trader
   d. Market clearing

39. In economics, _____ is the total supply of goods and services produced by a national economy during a specific time period. It is the total amount of goods and services in the economy available at all possible price levels.
   a. Aggregate expenditure
   c. Aggregate supply
   b. Aggregation problem
   d. Aggregate demand

40. _____ is an economic model based on price, utility and quantity in a market. It predicts that in a competitive market, price will function to equalize the quantity demanded by consumers, and the quantity supplied by producers, resulting in an economic equilibrium of price and quantity. The model incorporates other factors changing equilibrium as a shift of demand and/or supply.
   a. Cross elasticity of demand
   c. Snob effect
   b. Supply and Demand
   d. Demand vacuum

41. _____ is a specific term used in companies' financial reporting from the company-whole point of view. Because that use excludes the effects of changing ownership interest, an economic measure of _____ is necessary for financial analysis from the shareholders' point of view

_____ is defined by the Financial Accounting Standards Board, or FASB, as e;the change in equity [net assets] of a business enterprise during a period from transactions and other events and circumstances from nonowner sources. It includes all changes in equity during a period except those resulting from investments by owners and distributions to owners.e;

_____ is the sum of net income and other items that must bypass the income statement because they have not been realized, including items like an unrealized holding gain or loss from available for sale securities and foreign currency translation gains or losses.

   a. Windfall gain
   c. Real income
   b. Comprehensive income
   d. Per capita income

42. A _____ is a public market for the trading of company stock and derivatives at an agreed price; these are securities listed on a stock exchange as well as those only traded privately.

The size of the world _____ was estimated at about $36.6 trillion US at the beginning of October 2008 . The total world derivatives market has been estimated at about $791 trillion face or nominal value, 11 times the size of the entire world economy.

a. Stock Market
c. 100-year flood

b. 1921 recession
d. 130-30 fund

Chapter 4. Extensions of Demand and Supply Analysis

1. _____ is the price of a commodity such as a good or service in terms of another; ie, the ratio of two prices. A _____ may be expressed in terms of a ratio between any two prices or the ratio between the price of one particular good and a weighted average of all other goods available in the market. A _____ is an opportunity cost.
   - a. Food cooperative
   - b. False economy
   - c. False shortage
   - d. Relative price

2. _____ in economics and business is the result of an exchange and from that trade we assign a numerical monetary value to a good, service or asset. If Alice trades Bob 4 apples for an orange, the _____ of an orange is 4 apples. Inversely, the _____ of an apple is 1/4 oranges.
   - a. Price ceiling
   - b. Price
   - c. Price dispersion
   - d. Lerner Index

3. A _____ is any systematic process enabling many market players to bid and ask: helping bidders and sellers interact and make deals. It is not just the price mechanism but the entire system of regulation, qualification, credentials, reputations and clearing that surrounds that mechanism and makes it operate in a social context.

   Because a _____ relies on the assumption that players are constantly involved and unequally enabled, a _____ is distinguished specifically from a voting system where candidates seek the support of voters on a less regular basis.

   - a. Two-sided markets
   - b. Price mechanism
   - c. Market system
   - d. Market equilibrium

4. In economics, a _____ may be either a subsidy or a price control, both with the intended effect of keeping the market price of a good higher than the competitive equilibrium level.

   In the case of a price control, a _____ is the minimum legal price a seller may charge, typically placed above equilibrium. It is the support of certain price levels at or above market values by the government.

   - a. Forward exchange market
   - b. Price support
   - c. Market neutral
   - d. January effect

5. In economics and related disciplines, a _____ is a cost incurred in making an economic exchange. For example, most people, when buying or selling a stock, must pay a commission to their broker; that commission is a _____ of doing the stock deal. Or consider buying a banana from a store; to purchase the banana, your costs will be not only the price of the banana itself, but also the energy and effort it requires to find out which of the various banana products you prefer, where to get them and at what price, the cost of traveling from your house to the store and back, the time waiting in line, and the effort of the paying itself; the costs above and beyond the cost of the banana are the _____s.
   - a. Total absorption costing
   - b. Psychic cost
   - c. Cost allocation
   - d. Transaction cost

6. In economics, and cost accounting, _____ describes the total economic cost of production and is made up of variable costs, which vary according to the quantity of a good produced and include inputs such as labor and raw materials, plus fixed costs, which are independent of the quantity of a good produced and include inputs (capital) that cannot be varied in the short term, such as buildings and machinery. _____ in economics includes the total opportunity cost of each factor of production in addition to fixed and variable costs.

Chapter 4. Extensions of Demand and Supply Analysis

The rate at which _____ changes as the amount produced changes is called marginal cost.

a. 1921 recession
c. 100-year flood
b. 130-30 fund
d. Total Cost

7. Economics:

- _____, the desire to own something and the ability to pay for it
- _____ curve, a graphic representation of a _____ schedule
- _____ deposit, the money in checking accounts
- _____ pull theory, the theory that inflation occurs when _____ for goods and services exceeds existing supplies
- _____ schedule, a table that lists the quantity of a good a person will buy it each different price
- _____ side economics, the school of economics at believes government spending and tax cuts open economy by raising _____

a. Demand
c. G20
b. Procter ' Gamble
d. Bon

8. _____, as defined by the _____ Association of America (Information technologyAA), is 'the study, design, development, implementation, support or management of computer-based information systems, particularly software applications and computer hardware.' _____ deals with the use of electronic computers and computer software to convert, store, protect, process, transmit, and securely retrieve information.

Today, the term _____ has ballooned to encompass many aspects of computing and technology, and the term has become very recognizable. The _____ umbrella can be quite large, covering many fields.

a. ACEA agreement
c. Information Technology
b. AD-IA Model
d. ACCRA Cost of Living Index

9. In economics, _____ is the total amount of money available in an economy at a particular point in time. There are several ways to define 'money', but standard measures usually include currency in circulation and demand deposits.

_____ data are recorded and published, usually by the government or the central bank of the country.

a. Monetary economy
c. Monetary reform
b. Fiscal theory of the price level
d. Money Supply

10. _____ is a common concept in economics, and gives rise to derived concepts such as consumer debt. Generally _____ is defined by opposition to production. But the precise definition can vary because different schools of economists define production quite differently.

a. Basis of futures
c. British canal system
b. Consumption
d. Discrete choice

Chapter 4. Extensions of Demand and Supply Analysis

11. _____ is a fee paid on borrowed assets. It is the price paid for the use of borrowed money, or, money earned by deposited funds. Assets that are sometimes lent with _____ include money, shares, consumer goods through hire purchase, major assets such as aircraft, and even entire factories in finance lease arrangements.

   a. Insolvency
   b. Internal debt
   c. Asset protection
   d. Interest

12. The Organization of the Petroleum Exporting Countries is a cartel of twelve countries made up of Algeria, Angola, Ecuador, Iran, Iraq, Kuwait, Libya, Nigeria, Qatar, Saudi Arabia, the United Arab Emirates, and Venezuela. The cartel has maintained its headquarters in Vienna since 1965, and hosts regular meetings among the oil ministers of its Member Countries. Indonesia withdrew its membership in _____ in 2008 after it became a net importer of oil, but stated it would likely return if it became a net exporter in the world.

   a. OPEC
   b. ACEA agreement
   c. ACCRA Cost of Living Index
   d. AD-IA Model

13. _____ is the controlled distribution of resources and scarce goods or services. _____ controls the size of the ration, one's allotted portion of the resources being distributed on a particular day or at a particular time.

   In economics, it is often common to use the word '_____' to refer to one of the roles that prices play in markets, while _____ is called 'non-price _____.' Using prices to ration means that those with the most money (or other assets) and who want a product the most are first to receive it.

   a. Rationing
   b. 100-year flood
   c. 1921 recession
   d. 130-30 fund

14. In international commerce and politics, an _____ is the prohibition of commerce (division of trade) and trade with a certain country, in order to isolate it and to put its government into a difficult internal situation, given that the effects of the _____ are often able to make its economy suffer from the initiative.

   The _____ is usually used as a political punishment for some previous disagreed policies or acts, but its economic nature frequently raises doubts about the real interests that the prohibition serves.

   One of the most comprehensive attempts at an _____ happened during the Napoleonic Wars.

   a. Overshooting model
   b. Optimum currency area
   c. Embargo
   d. International finance

15. The underground economy or _____ is a market where all commerce is conducted without regard to taxation, law or regulations of trade. The term is also often known as the underdog, shadow economy, black economy, parallel economy or phantom trades.

   In modern societies the underground economy covers a vast array of activities.

   a. Post-industrial economy
   b. Market economy
   c. Command economy
   d. Black market

Chapter 4. Extensions of Demand and Supply Analysis

16. A _____ is a government imposed limit on how high a price can be charged on a product. For a _____ to be effective, it must differ from the free market price. In the graph at right, the supply and demand curves intersect to determine the free-market quantity and price.

   a. Demand optimization
   b. Transactional Net Margin Method
   c. San Francisco congestion pricing
   d. Price ceiling

17. A _____ is a government- or group-imposed limit on how low a price can be charged for a product. In order for a _____ to be effective, it must be greater than the equilibrium price. An ineffective _____, below equilibrium price.

   A _____ can be set below the free-market equilibrium price.

   a. Flat rate
   b. Fire sale
   c. Factor price equalization
   d. Price floor

18. A _____ is a group of people who share or are motivated by at least one common issue or interest, or work together on a specific project(s) to achieve a common objective. _____s are also characterised by attempts to share and exercise political and social power and to make decisions on a consensus-driven and egalitarian basis. _____s differ from cooperatives in that they are not necessarily focused upon an economic benefit or saving (but can be that as well.)

   a. 1921 recession
   b. 100-year flood
   c. 130-30 fund
   d. Collective

19. Economic _____ is defined as an excess distribution to any factor in a production process above that which is required to induce the factor into the process or any excess above that which is necessary to keep the factor in its current use..

   Classical Factor _____ is primarily concerned with the fee paid for the use of fixed (e.g. natural) resources. The classical definition is expressed as any excess payment above that required to induce or provide for production.

   a. 100-year flood
   b. 1921 recession
   c. 130-30 fund
   d. Rent

20. _____ refers to laws or ordinances that set price controls on the renting of residential housing. It functions as a price ceiling.

   _____ exists in approximately 40 countries around the world.

   a. 100-year flood
   b. Rent control
   c. Tenant rights
   d. National Housing Conference

21. In economics, _____ is the ratio of the percent change in one variable to the percent change in another variable. It is a tool for measuring the responsiveness of a function to changes in parameters in a relative way. Commonly analyzed are _____ of substitution, price and wealth.

   a. ACCRA Cost of Living Index
   b. Elasticity of demand
   c. Elasticity
   d. ACEA agreement

Chapter 4. Extensions of Demand and Supply Analysis

22. In economics, the _____ is defined as a numerical measure of the responsiveness of the quantity supplied of product (A) to a change in price of product (A) alone. It is the measure of the way quantity supplied reacts to a change in price.

For example, if, in response to a 10% rise in the price of a good, the quantity supplied increases by 20%, the _____ would be 20%/10% = 2.

 a. Residual claimant
 b. Demand side economics
 c. Price elasticity of supply
 d. Frontier markets

23. The _____ was a worldwide economic downturn starting in most places in 1929 and ending at different times in the 1930s or early 1940s for different countries. It was the largest and most important economic depression in the 20th century, and is used in the 21st century as an example of how far the world's economy can fall. The _____ originated in the United States; historians most often use as a starting date the stock market crash on October 29, 1929, known as Black Tuesday.

 a. British Empire Economic Conference
 b. Causes of the Great Depression
 c. The Great Depression
 d. Great Depression

24. A _____ is the lowest hourly, daily or monthly wage that employers may legally pay to employees or workers. Equivalently, it is the lowest wage at which workers may sell their labor. Although _____ laws are in effect in a great many jurisdictions, there are differences of opinion about the benefits and drawbacks of a _____.

 a. Deregulation
 b. Minimum wage
 c. Permanent income hypothesis
 d. Permanent war economy

25. A _____, reserve bank, or monetary authority is the entity responsible for the monetary policy of a country or of a group of member states. It is a bank that can lend money to other banks in times of need. Its primary responsibility is to maintain the stability of the national currency and money supply, but more active duties include controlling subsidized-loan interest rates, and acting as a lender of last resort to the banking sector during times of financial crisis (private banks often being integral to the national financial system.)

 a. 100-year flood
 b. 130-30 fund
 c. 1921 recession
 d. Central bank

26. _____ is an economic concept with commonplace familiarity. It is the price that a good or service is offered at, or will fetch, in the marketplace. It is of interest mainly in the study of microeconomics.

 a. Noisy market hypothesis
 b. Paper trading
 c. Market Price
 d. Market anomaly

27. _____ is a term that encompasses the notion of individuals and firms striving for a greater share of a market to sell or buy goods and services. Merriam-Webster defines competition in business as 'the effort of two or more parties acting independently to secure the business of a third party by offering the most favorable terms.' It was described by Adam Smith in The Wealth of Nations (1776) and later economists as allocating productive resources to their most highly-valued uses. and encouraging efficiency.

Chapter 4. Extensions of Demand and Supply Analysis

a. Cut-throat competition
b. Moral victory
c. Path dependence
d. Competition in economics

28. In economics, an _____ is any good (e.g. a commodity) or service brought into one country from another country in a legitimate fashion, typically for use in trade. It is a good that is brought in from another country for sale. _____ goods or services are provided to domestic consumers by foreign producers. An _____ in the receiving country is an export to the sending country.
   a. Economic integration
   b. Import
   c. Incoterms
   d. Import quota

29. An _____ is a type of protectionist trade restriction that sets a physical limit on the quantity of a good that can be imported into a country in a given period of time. Quotas, like other trade restrictions, are used to benefit the producers of a good in a domestic economy at the expense of all consumers of the good in that economy.

Critics say quotas often lead to corruption (bribes to get a quota allocation), smuggling (circumventing a quota), and higher prices for consumers.

   a. Economic integration
   b. Import quota
   c. Agreement on Agriculture
   d. International Monetary Systems

30. _____ is that which is owed; usually referencing assets owed, but the term can also cover moral obligations and other interactions not requiring money. In the case of assets, _____ is a means of using future purchasing power in the present before a summation has been earned. Some companies and corporations use _____ as a part of their overall corporate finance strategy.
   a. Subordinated debt
   b. Participation loan
   c. Non-performing loan
   d. Debt

Chapter 5. The Public Sector and Public Choice

1. The _____ is the central United States governmental body, established by the United States Constitution. The federal government has three branches: the legislative, executive, and judicial. Through a system of separation of powers and the system of 'checks and balances,' each of these branches has some authority to act on its own, some authority to regulate the other two branches, and has some of its own authority, in turn, regulated by the other branches.
   a. Federal government of the United States
   b. 100-year flood
   c. 1921 recession
   d. 130-30 fund

2. In economics, an _____ or spillover of an economic transaction is an impact on a party that is not directly involved in the transaction. In such a case, prices do not reflect the full costs or benefits in production or consumption of a product or service. A positive impact is called an external benefit, while a negative impact is called an external cost.
   a. Environmental impact assessment
   b. Externality
   c. Existence value
   d. Environmental tariff

3. In economics, a _____ exists when the production or use of goods and services by the market is not efficient. That is, there exists another outcome where all involved can be made better off. _____s can be viewed as scenarios where individuals' pursuit of pure self-interest leads to results that are not efficient - that can be improved upon from the societal point-of-view.
   a. Market failure
   b. New Keynesian economics
   c. Consumer theory
   d. Perfect competition

4. _____ in economics and business is the result of an exchange and from that trade we assign a numerical monetary value to a good, service or asset. If Alice trades Bob 4 apples for an orange, the _____ of an orange is 4 apples. Inversely, the _____ of an apple is 1/4 oranges.
   a. Lerner Index
   b. Price ceiling
   c. Price
   d. Price dispersion

5. In economics, a _____ may be either a subsidy or a price control, both with the intended effect of keeping the market price of a good higher than the competitive equilibrium level.

   In the case of a price control, a _____ is the minimum legal price a seller may charge, typically placed above equilibrium. It is the support of certain price levels at or above market values by the government.

   a. Market neutral
   b. Forward exchange market
   c. January effect
   d. Price support

6. To _____ is to impose a financial charge or other levy upon a taxpayer by a state or the functional equivalent of a state.

   _____es are also imposed by many subnational entities. _____es consist of direct _____ or indirect _____, and may be paid in money or as its labour equivalent (often but not always unpaid.)

   a. 100-year flood
   b. 1921 recession
   c. 130-30 fund
   d. Tax

7. _____ is the process of changing the way taxes are collected or managed by the government.

   _____ers have different goals. Some seek to reduce the level of taxation of all people by the government.

a. Tax cap
b. Tax policy
c. Tax on cash withdrawal
d. Tax Reform

8. To tax is to impose a financial charge or other levy upon a taxpayer by a state or the functional equivalent of a state.

_____ are also imposed by many subnational entities. _____ consist of direct tax or indirect tax, and may be paid in money or as its labour equivalent (often but not always unpaid.)

a. Taxes
b. 100-year flood
c. 1921 recession
d. 130-30 fund

9. In economics, an externality or spillover of an economic transaction is an impact on a party that is not directly involved in the transaction. In such a case, prices do not reflect the full costs or benefits in production or consumption of a product or service. A positive impact is called an _____, while a negative impact is called an external cost.
   a. ACCRA Cost of Living Index
   b. AD-IA Model
   c. ACEA agreement
   d. External benefit

10. Many _____ are related to the environmental consequences of production and use

    - Systemic risk describes the risks to the overall economy arising from the risks which the banking system takes. That the private costs of banking failure may be smaller than the social costs justifies banking regulations, although regulations could create a moral hazard.

    - Anthropogenic climate change is attributed to greenhouse gas emissions from burning oil, gas, and coal. Global warming has been ranked as the #1 externality of all economic activity, in the magnitude of potential harms and yet remains unmitigated.

    a. Contingent valuation
    b. Total Economic Value
    c. Positive externalities
    d. Negative externalities

11. _____, short for Ecological taxation, can refer to:

A policy that introduces taxes intended to promote ecologically sustainable activities via economic incentives. Such a policy can complement or avert the need for regulatory approaches. Often, such a policy intends to maintain overall tax revenue by proportionately reducing other taxes, e.g. on human labor and renewable resources, in which case it is known as the green tax shift towards ecological taxation.

a. ACEA agreement
b. ACCRA Cost of Living Index
c. AD-IA Model
d. Ecotax

Chapter 5. The Public Sector and Public Choice

12. Examples of _____ include:

- A beekeeper keeps the bees for their honey. A side effect or externality associated with his activity is the pollination of surrounding crops by the bees. The value generated by the pollination may be more important than the value of the harvested honey.

- An individual planting an attractive garden in front of his house may provide benefits to others living in the area, and even financial benefits in the form of increased property values for all property owners.

- An individual buying a product that is interconnected in a network (e.g., a video cellphone) will increase the usefulness of such phones to other people who have a video cellphone. When each new user of a product increases the value of the same product owned by others, the phenomenon is called a network externality or a network effect. Network externalities often have 'tipping points' where, suddenly, the product reaches general acceptance and near-universal usage, a phenomenon which can be seen in the near universal take-up of cellphones in some Scandinavian countries.

- Knowledge spillover of inventions and information - once an invention (or most other forms of practical information) is discovered or made more easily accessible, others benefit by exploiting the invention or information. Copyright and intellectual property law are mechanisms to allow the inventor or creator to benefit from a temporary, state-protected monopoly in return for 'sharing' the information through publication or other means.

   a. Negative externalities
   b. Weighted average cost of carbon
   c. Travel cost analysis
   d. Positive externalities

13. A _____ is a group of people who share or are motivated by at least one common issue or interest, or work together on a specific project(s) to achieve a common objective. _____s are also characterised by attempts to share and exercise political and social power and to make decisions on a consensus-driven and egalitarian basis. _____s differ from cooperatives in that they are not necessarily focused upon an economic benefit or saving (but can be that as well.)
   a. 1921 recession
   b. 130-30 fund
   c. 100-year flood
   d. Collective

14. _____s is the social science that studies the production, distribution, and consumption of goods and services. The term _____s comes from the Ancient Greek οἰκονομία from οἶκος (oikos, 'house') + νόμος (nomos, 'custom' or 'law'), hence 'rules of the house(hold)'. Current _____ models developed out of the broader field of political economy in the late 19th century, owing to a desire to use an empirical approach more akin to the physical sciences.
   a. Inflation
   b. Economic
   c. Energy economics
   d. Opportunity cost

15. _____ is the increase in the amount of the goods and services produced by an economy over time. It is conventionally measured as the percent rate of increase in real gross domestic product, or real GDP. Growth is usually calculated in real terms, i.e. inflation-adjusted terms, in order to net out the effect of inflation on the price of the goods and services produced.
   a. Economic growth
   b. ACEA agreement
   c. AD-IA Model
   d. ACCRA Cost of Living Index

16. Under the system of feudalism, a _____, fief, feud, feoff often consisted of inheritable lands or revenue-producing property granted by a liege lord, generally to a vassal, in return for a form of allegiance, originally to give him the means to fulfill his military duties when called upon. However anything of value could be held in fief, such as an office, a right of exploitation (e.g., hunting, fishing) or any other type of revenue, rather than the land it comes from.

Originally, the feudal institution of vassalage did not imply the giving or receiving of landholdings (which were granted only as a reward for loyalty), but by the eighth century the giving of a landholding was becoming standard.

   a. Fiefdom
   b. 130-30 fund
   c. 1921 recession
   d. 100-year flood

17. In microeconomics, _____ is quite simply the conversion of inputs into outputs. It is an economic process that uses resources to create a good or service that is suitable for exchange. This can include manufacturing, storing, shipping, and packaging.
   a. Variability
   b. Bucket shop
   c. Characteristic
   d. Production

18. In Marxian economics, _____ originally referred to the means of production. Individuals, organizations and governments use _____ in the production of other goods or commodities. _____ include factories, machinery, tools, equipment, and various buildings which are used to produce other products for consumption.
   a. Modigliani-Miller theorem
   b. Cost of capital
   c. Capital formation
   d. Capital goods

19. A _____ is an object whose consumption increases the utility of the consumer, for which the quantity demanded exceeds the quantity supplied at zero price. _____s are usually modeled as having diminishing marginal utility. The first individual purchase has high utility; the second has less.
   a. Positional goods
   b. Luxury good
   c. Search good
   d. Good

20. Competition law, known in the United States as _____ law, has three main elements:

- prohibiting agreements or practices that restrict free trading and competition between business entities. This includes in particular the repression of cartels.
- banning abusive behaviour by a firm dominating a market, or anti-competitive practices that tend to lead to such a dominant position. Practices controlled in this way may include predatory pricing, tying, price gouging, refusal to deal, and many others.
- supervising the mergers and acquisitions of large corporations, including some joint ventures. Transactions that are considered to threaten the competitive process can be prohibited altogether, or approved subject to 'remedies' such as an obligation to divest part of the merged business or to offer licences or access to facilities to enable other businesses to continue competing.

Chapter 5. The Public Sector and Public Choice 37

The substance and practice of competition law varies from jurisdiction to jurisdiction. Protecting the interests of consumers (consumer welfare) and ensuring that entrepreneurs have an opportunity to compete in the market economy are often treated as important objectives. Competition law is closely connected with law on deregulation of access to markets, state aids and subsidies, the privatisation of state owned assets and the establishment of independent sector regulators. In recent decades, competition law has been viewed as a way to provide better public services.

a. Anti-Inflation Act
b. Antitrust
c. Intellectual property law
d. United Kingdom competition law

21. _____, known in the United States as antitrust law, has three main elements:

- prohibiting agreements or practices that restrict free trading and competition between business entities. This includes in particular the repression of cartels.
- banning abusive behaviour by a firm dominating a market, or anti-competitive practices that tend to lead to such a dominant position. Practices controlled in this way may include predatory pricing, tying, price gouging, refusal to deal, and many others.
- supervising the mergers and acquisitions of large corporations, including some joint ventures. Transactions that are considered to threaten the competitive process can be prohibited altogether, or approved subject to 'remedies' such as an obligation to divest part of the merged business or to offer licences or access to facilities to enable other businesses to continue competing.

The substance and practice of _____ varies from jurisdiction to jurisdiction. Protecting the interests of consumers (consumer welfare) and ensuring that entrepreneurs have an opportunity to compete in the market economy are often treated as important objectives. _____ is closely connected with law on deregulation of access to markets, state aids and subsidies, the privatisation of state owned assets and the establishment of independent sector regulators. In recent decades, _____ has been viewed as a way to provide better public services.

a. Patent
b. Personal Responsibility and Work Opportunity Reconciliation Act of 1996
c. Federal Reserve Police
d. Competition law

22. _____ is a concept found in moral, political, and bioethical philosophy. Within these contexts, it refers to the capacity of a rational individual to make an informed, un-coerced decision. In moral and political philosophy, _____ is often used as the basis for determining moral responsibility for one's actions.
a. AD-IA Model
b. ACCRA Cost of Living Index
c. ACEA agreement
d. Autonomy

23. _____ is a term used to describe consumption expenditure that occurs when income levels are zero. Such consumption is considered autonomous of income only when expenditure on these consumables does not vary with changes in income. If income levels are actually zero, this consumption counts as dissaving, because it is financed by borrowing or using up savings.

Chapter 5. The Public Sector and Public Choice

a. Economic interdependence
c. Autonomous consumption
b. Austerity
d. Indexed unit of account

24. In economics, the _____ is a single mathematical function used to express consumer spending. It was developed by John Maynard Keynes and detailed most famously in his book The General Theory of Employment, Interest, and Money. The function is used to calculate the amount of total consumption in an economy.

a. Demand-Led Growth
c. Procyclical
b. Real exchange rate puzzles
d. Consumption function

25. The _____ is an independent agency of the United States government, established in 1914 by the _____ Act. Its principal mission is the promotion of 'consumer protection' and the elimination and prevention of what regulators perceive to be harmfully 'anti-competitive' business practices, such as coercive monopoly.

The _____ Act was one of President Wilson's major acts against trusts.

a. Federal Trade Commission
c. 130-30 fund
b. 1921 recession
d. 100-year flood

26. A _____ is defined in economics as a good that exhibits these properties:

- Excludable - it is reasonably possible to prevent a class of consumers (e.g. those who have not paid for it) from consuming the good.
- Rivalrous - consumptions by one consumer prevents simultaneous consumption by other consumers. _____s satisfies an individual want while public good satisfies a collective want of the society.

A _____ is the opposite of a public good, as they are almost exclusively made for profit.

An example of the _____ is bread: bread eaten by a given person cannot be consumed by another (rivalry), and it is easy for a baker to refuse to trade a loaf (excludable

a. Private good
c. Veblen goods
b. Pie method
d. Merit good

27. In economics, a _____ is a good that is non-rivaled and non-excludable. This means, respectively, that consumption of the good by one individual does not reduce availability of the good for consumption by others; and that no one can be effectively excluded from using the good. In the real world, there may be no such thing as an absolutely non-rivaled and non-excludable good; but economists think that some goods approximate the concept closely enough for the analysis to be economically useful.

a. Happiness economics
c. Business sector
b. Neoclassical synthesis
d. Public good

28. In economics and especially in the theory of competition, _____ are obstacles in the path of a firm that make it difficult to enter a given market.

_____ are the source of a firm's pricing power - the ability of a firm to raise prices without losing all its customers.

Chapter 5. The Public Sector and Public Choice

The term refers to hindrances that an individual may face while trying to gain entrance into a profession or trade.

a. Barriers to entry
c. Net Book Agreement
b. Group boycott
d. Predatory pricing

29. _____ has several particular meanings:

- in mathematics
    - _____ function
    - Euler _____
    - _____
    - _____ subgroup
    - method of _____s (partial differential equations)
- in physics and engineering
    - any _____ curve that shows the relationship between certain input- and output parameters, e.g.
    - an I-V or current-voltage _____ is the current in a circuit as a function of the applied voltage
    - Receiver-Operator _____
- in fiction
    - in Dungeons ' Dragons, _____ is another name for ability score

a. Drawdown
c. Fiscal
b. Procter ' Gamble
d. Characteristic

30. _____ is a common concept in economics, and gives rise to derived concepts such as consumer debt. Generally _____ is defined by opposition to production. But the precise definition can vary because different schools of economists define production quite differently.

a. Consumption
c. Basis of futures
b. British canal system
d. Discrete choice

31. The _____ was a worldwide economic downturn starting in most places in 1929 and ending at different times in the 1930s or early 1940s for different countries. It was the largest and most important economic depression in the 20th century, and is used in the 21st century as an example of how far the world's economy can fall. The _____ originated in the United States; historians most often use as a starting date the stock market crash on October 29, 1929, known as Black Tuesday.

a. Causes of the Great Depression
c. The Great Depression
b. Great Depression
d. British Empire Economic Conference

32. The concept of a _____ introduced in economics introduced by Richard Musgrave (1957, 1959) is a commodity which is judged that an individual or society should have on the basis of some concept of need, rather than ability and willingness to pay. The term is, perhaps, less often used today than it was in the 1960s to 1980s but the concept still lies behind many economic actions by governments which are not performed specifically for financial reasons or by supporting incomes (eg via tax rebates.) Examples include the provision of food stamps to support nutrition, the delivery of health services to improve quality of life and reduce morbidity, subsidized housing and arguably education.

a. Credence good
b. Final good
c. Giffen good
d. Merit good

33. Unemployment occurs when a person is available to work and seeking work but currently without work. The prevalence of unemployment is usually measured using the _____, which is defined as the percentage of those in the labor force who are unemployed. The _____ is also used in economic studies and economic indexes such as the United States' Conference Board's Index of Leading Indicators as a measure of the state of the macroeconomics.
    a. AD-IA Model
    b. ACEA agreement
    c. ACCRA Cost of Living Index
    d. Unemployment rate

34. In economics, a _____ is a good or service whose consumption is considered unhealthy, degrading, or otherwise socially undesirable due to the perceived negative effects on the consumers themselves. It is over-consumed if left to market forces. Examples of _____s include tobacco, alcoholic beverages, recreational drugs, gambling, junk food and prostitution.
    a. Demerit good
    b. Private good
    c. Veblen goods
    d. Positional goods

35. In economics, _____ is the transfer of income, wealth or property from some individuals to others.

One premise of _____ is that money should be distributed to benefit the poorer members of society, and that the rich have an obligation to assist the poor, thus creating a more financially egalitarian society. Another argument is that the rich exploit the poor or otherwise gain unfair benefits.

    a. Redistribution
    b. 130-30 fund
    c. 100-year flood
    d. 1921 recession

36. A _____ is the transfer of wealth from one party (such as a person or company) to another. A _____ is usually made in exchange for the provision of goods, services or both, or to fulfill a legal obligation.

The simplest and oldest form of _____ is barter, the exchange of one good or service for another.

    a. RFM
    b. Payment
    c. Hard count
    d. Contingent payment sales

37. In economics, a _____ is a redistribution of income in the market system. These payments are considered to be nonexhaustive because they do not directly absorb resources or create output. Examples of certain _____s include welfare (financial aid), social security, and government subsidies for certain businesses (firms.)
    a. 130-30 fund
    b. 1921 recession
    c. 100-year flood
    d. Transfer payment

38. _____ is the removal or simplification of government rules and regulations that constrain the operation of market forces. _____ does not mean elimination of laws against fraud, but eliminating or reducing government control of how business is done, thereby moving toward a more free market.

The stated rationale for '_____' is often that fewer and simpler regulations will lead to a raised level of competitiveness, therefore higher productivity, more efficiency and lower prices overall.

a. SIMIC
b. Lucas-Islands model
c. Monetary policy reaction function
d. Deregulation

39. _____ are the divisions at which tax rates change in a progressive tax system (or an explicitly regressive tax system, although this is much rarer.) Essentially, they are the cutoff values for taxable income -- income past a certain point will be taxed at a higher rate.
   a. Privatized tax collection
   b. Gift tax
   c. Voluntary taxation
   d. Tax brackets

40. A _____ is a tax system with a constant tax rate. Usually the term _____ would refer to household income (and sometimes corporate profits) being taxed at one marginal rate, in contrast with progressive taxes that may vary according to such parameters as income or usage levels. _____es generally offer simplicity in the tax code, which has been reported to increase compliance and decrease administration costs.
   a. Flat tax
   b. 130-30 fund
   c. 1921 recession
   d. 100-year flood

41. An _____ is a tax levied on the financial income of people, corporations, or other legal entities. Various _____ systems exist, with varying degrees of tax incidence. Income taxation can be progressive, proportional, or regressive.
   a. ACCRA Cost of Living Index
   b. ACEA agreement
   c. AD-IA Model
   d. Income tax

42. _____ is the difference between a lower selling price and a higher purchase price, resulting in a financial loss for the seller. Pursuant to IRS TAX TIP 2009-35 'If your _____es exceed your capital gains, the excess can be deducted on your tax return, up to an annual limit of $3,000 ($1,500 if you are married filing separately.)'.
   a. 130-30 fund
   b. 1921 recession
   c. 100-year flood
   d. Capital loss

43. Total _____ is defined by the United States' Bureau of Economic Analysis as

income received by persons from all sources. It includes income received from participation in production as well as from government and business transfer payments. It is the sum of compensation of employees (received), supplements to wages and salaries, proprietors' income with inventory valuation adjustment (IVA) and capital consumption adjustment (CCAdj), rental income of persons with CCAdj, _____ receipts on assets, and personal current transfer receipts, less contributions for government social insurance.

   a. Broad money
   b. Direct Market Access
   c. Personal Income
   d. Malinvestment

44. In finance, a _____ is a debt security, in which the authorized issuer owes the holders a debt and, depending on the terms of the _____, is obliged to pay interest (the coupon) and/or to repay the principal at a later date, termed maturity. A _____ is a formal contract to repay borrowed money with interest at fixed intervals.

Thus a _____ is like a loan: the issuer is the borrower (debtor), the holder is the lender (creditor), and the coupon is the interest.

a. Carter bonds
b. Prize Bond
c. Callable
d. Bond

45. The _____ consists of a number of economic theories which describe the nature of the firm, company including its existence, its behaviour, and its relationship with the market.

In simplified terms, the _____ aims to answer these questions:

1. Existence - why do firms emerge, why are not all transactions in the economy mediated over the market?
2. Boundaries - why the boundary between firms and the market is located exactly there? Which transactions are performed internally and which are negotiated on the market?
3. Organization - why are firms structured in such specific way? What is the interplay of formal and informal relationships?

Despite looking simple, these questions are not answered by the established economic theory, which usually views firms as given, and treats them as black boxes without any internal structure.

The First World War period saw a change of emphasis in economic theory away from industry-level analysis which mainly included analysing markets to analysis at the level of the firm, as it became increasingly clear that perfect competition was no longer an adequate model of how firms behaved. Economic theory till then had focussed on trying to understand markets alone and there had been little study on understanding why firms or organisations exist.

a. Technology gap
b. Neo-Ricardian school
c. Theory of the firm
d. Marginal revenue product

46. _____ is a specific term used in companies' financial reporting from the company-whole point of view. Because that use excludes the effects of changing ownership interest, an economic measure of _____ is necessary for financial analysis from the shareholders' point of view

_____ is defined by the Financial Accounting Standards Board, or FASB, as e;the change in equity [net assets] of a business enterprise during a period from transactions and other events and circumstances from nonowner sources. It includes all changes in equity during a period except those resulting from investments by owners and distributions to owners.e;

_____ is the sum of net income and other items that must bypass the income statement because they have not been realized, including items like an unrealized holding gain or loss from available for sale securities and foreign currency translation gains or losses.

a. Real income
b. Per capita income
c. Windfall gain
d. Comprehensive income

Chapter 5. The Public Sector and Public Choice

47. In economics, _____ is the analysis of the effect of a particular tax on the distribution of economic welfare. _____ is said to 'fall' upon the group that, at the end of the day, bears the burden of the tax. The key concept is that the _____ or tax burden does not depend on where the revenue is collected, but on the price elasticity of demand and price elasticity of supply.
   a. 100-year flood
   b. Tax incidence
   c. 130-30 fund
   d. 1921 recession

48. _____s are payments made by a corporation to its shareholders. It is the portion of corporate profits paid out to stockholders. When a corporation earns a profit or surplus, that money can be put to two uses: it can either be re-invested in the business (called retained earnings), or it can be paid to the shareholders as a _____.
   a. Dividend cover
   b. Dividend
   c. Dividend payout ratio
   d. Dividend imputation

49. _____ is a broad label that refers to any individuals or households that use goods and services generated within the economy. The concept of a _____ is used in different contexts, so that the usage and significance of the term may vary.

Typically when business people and economists talk of _____s they are talking about person as _____, an aggregated commodity item with little individuality other than that expressed in the buy/not-buy decision.

   a. 130-30 fund
   b. 1921 recession
   c. 100-year flood
   d. Consumer

50. A _____ is a measure of the average price of consumer goods and services purchased by households. A _____ measures a price change for a constant market basket of goods and services from one period to the next within the same area (city, region, or nation.) It is a price index determined by measuring the price of a standard group of goods meant to represent the typical market basket of a typical urban consumer.
   a. Consumer Price Index
   b. Hedonic price index
   c. Lipstick index
   d. Cost-of-living index

51. _____ or government expenditure is classified by economists into three main types. Government purchases of goods and services for current use are classed as government consumption. Government purchases of goods and services intended to create future benefits, such as infrastructure investment or research spending, are classed as government investment.
   a. 100-year flood
   b. 130-30 fund
   c. 1921 recession
   d. Government spending

52. _____, in law and economics, is a form of risk management primarily used to hedge against the risk of a contingent loss. _____ is defined as the equitable transfer of the risk of a loss, from one entity to another, in exchange for a premium, and can be thought of as a guaranteed small loss to prevent a large, possibly devastating loss. An insurer is a company selling the _____; an insured or policyholder is the person or entity buying the _____.
   a. Insurance
   b. AD-IA Model
   c. ACCRA Cost of Living Index
   d. ACEA agreement

Chapter 5. The Public Sector and Public Choice

53. A _____ is a normalized average (typically a weighted average) of prices for a given class of goods or services in a given region, during a given interval of time. It is a statistic designed to help to compare how these prices, taken as a whole, differ between time periods or geographical locations.

Price indices have several potential uses.

a. Point of total assumption
c. Flat rate
b. Pecuniary externality
d. Price Index

54. In finance, the term _____ describes various legal measures taken to ensure that debtors, whether individuals, businesses honor their debts and make an honest effort to repay the money that they owe. Generally regarded as a subdivision of tax law, _____ is most often enforced through a combination of audits and legal restrictions. For example, a provision of the Federal Debt Collection Procedure Act states that a person or organization indebted to the United States, against whom a judgment lien has been filed, is ineligible to receive a government grant.

a. Capital note
c. Prosper Marketplace
b. Hard money loan
d. Debt compliance

55. _____ is a term that refers to any currency used as an alternative to the dominant national or multinational currency systems (usually referred to as national or fiat money.) Alternative currencies can be created by an individual, corporation they can be created by national, state or they can arise naturally as people begin to use a certain commodity as a currency. Mutual credit is a form of _____, and thus any form of lending that does not go through the banking system can be considered a form of _____.

a. ACCRA Cost of Living Index
c. AD-IA Model
b. ACEA agreement
d. Alternative currency

56. _____ in economic theory is the use of modern economic tools to study problems that are traditionally in the province of political science.

In particular, it studies the behavior of politicians and government officials as mostly self-interested agents and their interactions in the social system either as such or under alternative constitutional rules. These can be represented a number of ways, including standard constrained utility maximization, game theory, or decision theory.

a. Public interest theory
c. Separability problem
b. Public choice
d. Rational ignorance

57. In economics and sociology, an _____ is any factor (financial or non-financial) that enables or motivates a particular course of action, or counts as a reason for preferring one choice to the alternatives. It is an expectation that encourages people to behave in a certain way. Since human beings are purposeful creatures, the study of _____ structures is central to the study of all economic activity (both in terms of individual decision-making and in terms of co-operation and competition within a larger institutional structure.)

a. Economic reform
c. Isocost
b. Epstein-Zin preferences
d. Incentive

58. _____ refers to confiscation of private property with the stated purpose of establishing social equality.

Chapter 5. The Public Sector and Public Choice

Unlike eminent domain, _____ takes place beyond the common law legal systems and refers to socially-motivated confiscations of any property rather than to taking away the real estate. Just compensation to owners is given.

a. ACCRA Cost of Living Index
b. Expropriation
c. AD-IA Model
d. ACEA agreement

59. _____ is the controlled distribution of resources and scarce goods or services. _____ controls the size of the ration, one's allotted portion of the resources being distributed on a particular day or at a particular time.

In economics, it is often common to use the word '_____' to refer to one of the roles that prices play in markets, while _____ is called 'non-price _____.' Using prices to ration means that those with the most money (or other assets) and who want a product the most are first to receive it.

a. Rationing
b. 130-30 fund
c. 1921 recession
d. 100-year flood

60. Fractional-reserve banking is the banking practice in which banks keep only a fraction of their deposits in reserve (as cash and other highly liquid assets) and lend out the remainder, while maintaining the simultaneous obligation to redeem all these deposits upon demand. _____ necessarily occurs when banks lend out any fraction of the funds received from demand deposits. This practice is universal in modern banking.

a. Certificate of deposit
b. Bank secrecy
c. Fractional reserve banking
d. Repo Rate

46 Chapter 5. The Public Sector and Public Choice

61. A _____ is:

- Rewrite _____, in generative grammar and computer science
- Standardization, a formal and widely-accepted statement, fact, definition, or qualification
- Operation, a determinate _____ for performing a mathematical operation and obtaining a certain result (Mathematics, Logic)
    - Unary operation
    - Binary operation
- _____ of inference, a function from sets of formulae to formulae (Mathematics, Logic)
- _____ of thumb, principle with broad application that is not intended to be strictly accurate or reliable for every situation. Also often simply referred to as a _____
- Moral, an atomic element of a moral code for guiding choices in human behavior
- Heuristic, a quantized '_____' which shows a tendency or probability for successful function
- A regulation, as in sports
- A Production _____, as in computer science
- Procedural law, a _____ set governing the application of laws to cases
    - A law, which may informally be called a '_____'
    - A court ruling, a decision by a court
- In the U.S. Government, a regulation mandated by Congress, but written or expanded upon by the Executive Branch.
- Norm (sociology), an informal but widely accepted _____, concept, truth, definition, or qualification (social norms, legal norms, coding norms)
- Norm (philosophy), a kind of sentence or a reason to act, feel or believe
- 'Rulership' is the concept of governance by a government:
    - Military _____, governance by a military body
    - Monastic _____, a collection of precepts that guides the life of monks or nuns in a religious order where the superior holds the place of Christ
- Slide _____

- '_____,' a song by Ayumi Hamasaki
- '_____,' a song by rapper Nas
- '_____s,' an album by the band The Whitest Boy Alive
- _____s: Pyaar Ka Superhit Formula, a 2003 Bollywood film
- ruler, an instrument for measuring lengths
- _____, a component of an astrolabe, circumferator or similar instrument
- The _____s, a bestselling self-help book
- _____ Project (Run Up-to-date Linux Everywhere), a project that aims to use up-to-date Linux software on old PCs
- _____ engine, a software system that helps managing business _____s
- Ja _____, a hip hop artist
    - R.U.L.E., a 2005 greatest hits album by rapper Ja _____
- '_____s,' a KMFDM song

a. MET   b. Rule
c. Russian financial crisis   d. Bon

Chapter 5. The Public Sector and Public Choice

62. _____ is the electronic delivery and presentation of financial statements, bills, invoices, and related information sent by a company to its customers. _____ is also known as other payment models based on consumer-to-business and business-to-business:

- Electronic billingPP -- Electronic Bill Presentment ' Payment (typically focused on business-to-consumer billing and payment)
- EIPP -- Electronic Invoice Presentment and Payment (typically focused on business-to-business billing and payment)

a. ACEA agreement
b. ACCRA Cost of Living Index
c. EInvoice
d. Electronic billing

63. In economics, _____ is the ratio of the percent change in one variable to the percent change in another variable. It is a tool for measuring the responsiveness of a function to changes in parameters in a relative way. Commonly analyzed are _____ of substitution, price and wealth.

a. Elasticity of demand
b. ACEA agreement
c. ACCRA Cost of Living Index
d. Elasticity

64. In economics, the _____ is defined as a numerical measure of the responsiveness of the quantity supplied of product (A) to a change in price of product (A) alone. It is the measure of the way quantity supplied reacts to a change in price.

For example, if, in response to a 10% rise in the price of a good, the quantity supplied increases by 20%, the _____ would be 20%/10% = 2.

a. Frontier markets
b. Price elasticity of supply
c. Demand side economics
d. Residual claimant

Chapter 6. Taxes, Transfers, and Public Spending

1. A _____ is a bond which is worth a certain monetary value and which may only be spent for specific reasons or on specific goods. Examples include -- but are not limited to -- housing, travel and food _____s. The term _____ is also a synonym for receipt, and is often used to refer to receipts used as evidence of, for example, the declaration that a service has been performed or that an expenditure has been made.
    a. 130-30 fund
    b. 100-year flood
    c. 1921 recession
    d. Voucher

2. A _____ is a consumption tax charged at the point of purchase for certain goods and services. The tax is usually set as a percentage by the government charging the tax. There is usually a list of exemptions.
    a. 1921 recession
    b. Sales tax
    c. 100-year flood
    d. 130-30 fund

3. To _____ is to impose a financial charge or other levy upon a taxpayer by a state or the functional equivalent of a state.

   _____es are also imposed by many subnational entities. _____es consist of direct _____ or indirect _____, and may be paid in money or as its labour equivalent (often but not always unpaid.)
    a. 1921 recession
    b. 130-30 fund
    c. 100-year flood
    d. Tax

4. A _____ is a group of people who share or are motivated by at least one common issue or interest, or work together on a specific project(s) to achieve a common objective. _____s are also characterised by attempts to share and exercise political and social power and to make decisions on a consensus-driven and egalitarian basis. _____s differ from cooperatives in that they are not necessarily focused upon an economic benefit or saving (but can be that as well.)
    a. 130-30 fund
    b. Collective
    c. 100-year flood
    d. 1921 recession

5. _____ or government expenditure is classified by economists into three main types. Government purchases of goods and services for current use are classed as government consumption. Government purchases of goods and services intended to create future benefits, such as infrastructure investment or research spending, are classed as government investment.
    a. 1921 recession
    b. 100-year flood
    c. Government spending
    d. 130-30 fund

6. In finance, the term _____ describes various legal measures taken to ensure that debtors, whether individuals, businesses honor their debts and make an honest effort to repay the money that they owe. Generally regarded as a subdivision of tax law, _____ is most often enforced through a combination of audits and legal restrictions. For example, a provision of the Federal Debt Collection Procedure Act states that a person or organization indebted to the United States, against whom a judgment lien has been filed, is ineligible to receive a government grant.
    a. Capital note
    b. Prosper Marketplace
    c. Hard money loan
    d. Debt compliance

Chapter 6. Taxes, Transfers, and Public Spending

7. _____ is a term that refers to any currency used as an alternative to the dominant national or multinational currency systems (usually referred to as national or fiat money.) Alternative currencies can be created by an individual, corporation they can be created by national, state or they can arise naturally as people begin to use a certain commodity as a currency. Mutual credit is a form of _____, and thus any form of lending that does not go through the banking system can be considered a form of _____.
   a. ACCRA Cost of Living Index
   b. ACEA agreement
   c. AD-IA Model
   d. Alternative currency

8. _____ is a common concept in economics, and gives rise to derived concepts such as consumer debt. Generally _____ is defined by opposition to production. But the precise definition can vary because different schools of economists define production quite differently.
   a. Basis of futures
   b. Consumption
   c. British canal system
   d. Discrete choice

9. A _____ is a duty imposed on goods when they are moved across a political boundary. They are usually associated with protectionism, the economic policy of restraining trade between nations. For political reasons, _____s are usually imposed on imported goods, although they may also be imposed on exported goods.
   a. 130-30 fund
   b. 1921 recession
   c. 100-year flood
   d. Tariff

10. To tax is to impose a financial charge or other levy upon a taxpayer by a state or the functional equivalent of a state. _____ are also imposed by many subnational entities. _____ consist of direct tax or indirect tax, and may be paid in money or as its labour equivalent (often but not always unpaid.)

   a. 100-year flood
   b. 130-30 fund
   c. Taxes
   d. 1921 recession

11. _____ is a broad label that refers to any individuals or households that use goods and services generated within the economy. The concept of a _____ is used in different contexts, so that the usage and significance of the term may vary.

   Typically when business people and economists talk of _____s they are talking about person as _____, an aggregated commodity item with little individuality other than that expressed in the buy/not-buy decision.

   a. 130-30 fund
   b. 1921 recession
   c. 100-year flood
   d. Consumer

12. _____ in economics and business is the result of an exchange and from that trade we assign a numerical monetary value to a good, service or asset. If Alice trades Bob 4 apples for an orange, the _____ of an orange is 4 apples. Inversely, the _____ of an apple is 1/4 oranges.
   a. Price ceiling
   b. Lerner Index
   c. Price dispersion
   d. Price

Chapter 6. Taxes, Transfers, and Public Spending

13. _____ is an economic concept with commonplace familiarity. It is the price that a good or service is offered at, or will fetch, in the marketplace. It is of interest mainly in the study of microeconomics.
    a. Paper trading
    b. Market anomaly
    c. Noisy market hypothesis
    d. Market price

14. An _____ is a market form in which a market or industry is dominated by a small number of sellers (oligopolists.) Because there are few participants in this type of market, each oligopolist is aware of the actions of the others. The decisions of one firm influence, and are influenced by, the decisions of other firms.
    a. Oligopsony
    b. Oligopoly
    c. ACCRA Cost of Living Index
    d. ACEA agreement

15. _____ is an online peer-reviewed magazine published by the Agricultural ' Applied Economics Association (AAEA) for readers interested in the policy and management of agriculture, the food industry, natural resources, rural communities, and the environment. _____ is published quarterly and is available free online. It is currently one of three outreach products offered by AAEA, along with the more timely Policy Issues and the forthcoming Shared Materials section of the AAEA Web site.
    a. 100-year flood
    b. 1921 recession
    c. Choices
    d. 130-30 fund

16. _____ is exchange of capital, goods, and services across international borders or territories. In most countries, it represents a significant share of gross domestic product (GDP.) While _____ has been present throughout much of history , its economic, social, and political importance has been on the rise in recent centuries.
    a. Import license
    b. Intra-industry trade
    c. Incoterms
    d. International trade

17. _____s is the social science that studies the production, distribution, and consumption of goods and services. The term _____s comes from the Ancient Greek oá¼°κονομῐα from oá¼¶κος (oikos, 'house') + vῐŒμος (nomos, 'custom' or 'law'), hence 'rules of the house(hold)'. Current _____ models developed out of the broader field of political economy in the late 19th century, owing to a desire to use an empirical approach more akin to the physical sciences.
    a. Energy economics
    b. Economic
    c. Opportunity cost
    d. Inflation

18. In economics and sociology, an _____ is any factor (financial or non-financial) that enables or motivates a particular course of action, or counts as a reason for preferring one choice to the alternatives. It is an expectation that encourages people to behave in a certain way. Since human beings are purposeful creatures, the study of _____ structures is central to the study of all economic activity (both in terms of individual decision-making and in terms of co-operation and competition within a larger institutional structure.)
    a. Epstein-Zin preferences
    b. Incentive
    c. Isocost
    d. Economic reform

19. In statistics, the _____ problem occurs when one considers a set of statistical inferences simultaneously. Errors in inference, including confidence intervals that fail to include their corresponding population parameters are more likely to occur when one considers the family as a whole. Several statistical techniques have been developed to prevent this from happening, allowing significance levels for single and _____ to be directly compared.

Chapter 6. Taxes, Transfers, and Public Spending

a. Familywise error rate
c. Closed testing procedure
b. Multiple comparisons
d. Hypotheses suggested by the data

20. The Organization of the Petroleum Exporting Countries is a cartel of twelve countries made up of Algeria, Angola, Ecuador, Iran, Iraq, Kuwait, Libya, Nigeria, Qatar, Saudi Arabia, the United Arab Emirates, and Venezuela. The cartel has maintained its headquarters in Vienna since 1965, and hosts regular meetings among the oil ministers of its Member Countries. Indonesia withdrew its membership in _____ in 2008 after it became a net importer of oil, but stated it would likely return if it became a net exporter in the world.
   a. ACCRA Cost of Living Index
   c. OPEC
   b. ACEA agreement
   d. AD-IA Model

21. A _____ is the transfer of wealth from one party (such as a person or company) to another. A _____ is usually made in exchange for the provision of goods, services or both, or to fulfill a legal obligation.

The simplest and oldest form of _____ is barter, the exchange of one good or service for another.

   a. Contingent payment sales
   c. Hard count
   b. RFM
   d. Payment

22. In international commerce and politics, an _____ is the prohibition of commerce (division of trade) and trade with a certain country, in order to isolate it and to put its government into a difficult internal situation, given that the effects of the _____ are often able to make its economy suffer from the initiative.

The _____ is usually used as a political punishment for some previous disagreed policies or acts, but its economic nature frequently raises doubts about the real interests that the prohibition serves.

One of the most comprehensive attempts at an _____ happened during the Napoleonic Wars.

   a. Optimum currency area
   c. Embargo
   b. International finance
   d. Overshooting model

23. _____ is one of the four Ps of the marketing mix. The other three aspects are product, promotion, and place. It is also a key variable in microeconomic price allocation theory.
   a. Pricing
   c. Big ticket item
   b. Nonlinear pricing
   d. Two-part tariff

24. _____ is the act of compensating someone for an expense. Often, a person is reimbursed for out-of-pocket expenses when the person incurs those expenses through employment or in carrying out duties for another party.

Common examples are firms compensating individuals who buy supplies for their companies, or firms compensating employees on field or out-of-town assignments who pay for their stay and transportation.

   a. Customer not present
   c. Retail loss prevention
   b. Reimbursement
   d. Soft count

Chapter 6. Taxes, Transfers, and Public Spending

25. _____ is the development of economic wealth of countries or regions for the well-being of their inhabitants. It is the process by which a nation improves the economic, political, and social well being of its people. From a policy perspective, _____ can be defined as efforts that seek to improve the economic well-being and quality of life for a community by creating and/or retaining jobs and supporting or growing incomes and the tax base.
   a. Economic methodology
   b. Inflation
   c. Experimental economics
   d. Economic development

26. The _____ was a worldwide economic downturn starting in most places in 1929 and ending at different times in the 1930s or early 1940s for different countries. It was the largest and most important economic depression in the 20th century, and is used in the 21st century as an example of how far the world's economy can fall. The _____ originated in the United States; historians most often use as a starting date the stock market crash on October 29, 1929, known as Black Tuesday.
   a. Causes of the Great Depression
   b. The Great Depression
   c. British Empire Economic Conference
   d. Great Depression

27. In finance, _____ rate of profit or sometimes just return, is the ratio of money gained or lost on an investment relative to the amount of money invested. The amount of money gained or lost may be referred to as interest, profit/loss, gain/loss, or net income/loss. The money invested may be referred to as the asset, capital, principal, or the cost basis of the investment.
   a. Return on capital employed
   b. Return of capital
   c. Rate of return
   d. Capital recovery factor

28. _____ to the arrival of new individuals into a habitat or population. It is a biological concept and is important in population ecology, differentiated from emigration and migration.

   _____ is a modern phenomenon.

   a. ACEA agreement
   b. AD-IA Model
   c. ACCRA Cost of Living Index
   d. Immigration

29. In calculus, a function f defined on a subset of the real numbers with real values is called _____, if for all x and y such that $x \geq y$ one has $f(x) \geq f(y)$, so f preserves the order. In layman's terms, the sign of the slope is always positive (the curve tending upwards) or zero (i.e., non-decreasing, or asymptotic, or depicted as a horizontal, flat line) Likewise, a function is called monotonically decreasing (non-increasing) if, whenever $x \geq y$, then $f(x) \geq f(y)$, so it reverses the order.
   a. 130-30 fund
   b. 100-year flood
   c. 1921 recession
   d. Monotonic

Chapter 7. The Macroeconomy: Unemployment, Inflation, and Deflation

1. In economics, _____ are key economic variables that economists used to predict a new phase of the business cycle. A leading indicator is one that changes before the economy does; a lagging indicator is one that changes after the economy has changed. Examples of _____ include stock prices, which often improve or worsen before a similar change in the economy.
   a. Literacy rate
   b. Perfect competition
   c. Law and economics
   d. Leading indicators

2. A consumer price index (_____) is a measure of the average price of consumer goods and services purchased by households. A consumer price index measures a price change for a constant market basket of goods and services from one period to the next within the same area (city, region, or nation.) It is a price index determined by measuring the price of a standard group of goods meant to represent the typical market basket of a typical urban consumer.
   a. Lipstick index
   b. Hedonic price index
   c. Cost-of-living index
   d. CPI

3. _____s is the social science that studies the production, distribution, and consumption of goods and services. The term _____s comes from the Ancient Greek oá¼°κονομία from oá¼¶κος (oikos, 'house') + vĺŒμος (nomos, 'custom' or 'law'), hence 'rules of the house(hold)'. Current _____ models developed out of the broader field of political economy in the late 19th century, owing to a desire to use an empirical approach more akin to the physical sciences.
   a. Opportunity cost
   b. Economic
   c. Inflation
   d. Energy economics

4. In economics, the people in the _____ are the suppliers of labor. The _____ is all the nonmilitary people who are employed or unemployed. In 2005, the worldwide _____ was over 3 billion people.
   a. Refusal of work
   b. Time-and-a-half
   c. Labor force
   d. Swedish labour movement

5. The _____ is a US private, nonprofit research organization dedicated to studying the science and empirics of economics, especially the American economy. It is 'committed to undertaking and disseminating unbiased economic research among public policymakers, business professionals, and the academic community.' It publishes NBER Working Papers and books. The NBER is located in Cambridge, Massachusetts with branch offices in Palo Alto, California, and New York City.
   a. Luxembourg Income Study
   b. Citizens for an Alternative Tax System
   c. Paris Club
   d. National Bureau of Economic Research

6. The _____ was a serious economic depression in the United States that began in 1893. This panic is sometimes considered a part of the Long Depression which began with the Panic of 1873, and like that of earlier crashes, was caused by railroad overbuilding and shaky railroad financing; which set off a series of bank failures. Compounding market overbuilding and a railroad bubble was a run on the gold supply and a policy of using both gold and silver metals as a peg for the US Dollar value.
   a. 130-30 fund
   b. Panic of 1893
   c. 100-year flood
   d. 1921 recession

7. In economics, a _____ is a general slowdown in economic activity over a sustained period of time, or a business cycle contraction. During _____s, many macroeconomic indicators vary in a similar way. Production as measured by Gross Domestic Product (GDP), employment, investment spending, capacity utilization, household incomes and business profits all fall during _____s.

a. New Trade Theory
b. Fixed exchange rate
c. General equilibrium theory
d. Recession

8. Unemployment occurs when a person is available to work and seeking work but currently without work. The prevalence of unemployment is usually measured using the _____, which is defined as the percentage of those in the labor force who are unemployed. The _____ is also used in economic studies and economic indexes such as the United States' Conference Board's Index of Leading Indicators as a measure of the state of the macroeconomics.
   a. AD-IA Model
   b. ACEA agreement
   c. ACCRA Cost of Living Index
   d. Unemployment rate

9. In a company, _____ is the sum of all financial records of salaries, wages, bonuses and deductions.

A paycheck, is traditionally a paper document issued by an employer to pay an employee for services rendered. While most commonly used in the United States, recently the physical paycheck has been increasingly replaced by electronic direct deposit to bank accounts.

   a. Tax expense
   b. Payroll
   c. Total Expense Ratio
   d. 100-year flood

10. The _____, a unit of the United States Department of Labor, is the principal fact-finding agency for the U.S. government in the broad field of labor economics and statistics. The BLS is an independent national statistical agency that collects, processes, analyzes, and disseminates essential statistical data to the American public, the U.S. Congress, other Federal agencies, State and local governments, business, and labor representatives. The BLS also serves as a statistical resource to the Department of Labor.
    a. Water footprint
    b. Nonfarm payrolls
    c. Visible balance
    d. Bureau of Labor Statistics

11. In economics, a _____ is a person of legal employment age who is not actively seeking employment. This is usually due to the fact that an individual has given up looking or has had no success in finding a job, hence the term 'discouraged.' Their belief may derive from a variety of factors including: a shortage of jobs in their locality or line of work; perceived discrimination for reasons such as age, race, sex and religion; a lack of necessary skills, training or experience; or, a chronic illness or disability. Some _____s, however, are voluntarily unemployed such as stay-at-home parents, pregnant mothers, and will beneficiaries.
    a. Hedonimetry
    b. Discouraged worker
    c. Ramp up
    d. Federal Reserve districts

12. In finance, the _____ of a financial asset measures the sensitivity of the asset's price to interest rate movements. There are various definitions of _____ and derived quantities, discussed below. If not otherwise specified, '_____' generally means the Macaulay _____, as defined below.
    a. Newtonian time
    b. 100-year flood
    c. Time value of money
    d. Duration

13. Economists distinguish between various types of unemployment, including cyclical unemployment, _____, structural unemployment and classical unemployment. Some additional types of unemployment that are occasionally mentioned are seasonal unemployment, hardcore unemployment, and hidden unemployment. Real-world unemployment may combine different types.

Chapter 7. The Macroeconomy: Unemployment, Inflation, and Deflation 55

a. Structural unemployment
c. Graduate unemployment
b. Types of unemployment
d. Frictional unemployment

14. Economists distinguish between various types of unemployment, including cyclical unemployment, frictional unemployment, structural unemployment and classical unemployment. Some additional types of unemployment that are occasionally mentioned are _____, hardcore unemployment, and hidden unemployment. Real-world unemployment may combine different types.
a. Frictional unemployment
c. Graduate unemployment
b. Structural unemployment
d. Seasonal unemployment

15. _____ is long-term and chronic unemployment arising from imbalances between the skills and other characteristics of workers in the market and the needs of employers. It involves a mismatch between workers looking for jobs and the vacancies available often despite the number of vacancies being similar to the number of unemployed people. In this case, the unemployed workers lack the specific skills required for the jobs, or are located in a different geographical region to the vacant jobs.
a. Graduate unemployment
c. Frictional unemployment
b. Types of unemployment
d. Structural unemployment

16. The _____ is a group of three respected economists who advise the President of the United States on economic policy. It is a part of the Executive Office of the President of the United States, and provides much of the economic policy of the White House. The council prepares the annual Economic Report of the President.
a. Commodity fetishism
c. Labor union
b. Clap note
d. Council of Economic Advisers

17. The _____ is the central banking system of the United States. Created in 1913 by the enactment of the Federal Reserve Act (signed by Woodrow Wilson), it is a quasi-public and quasi-private (government entity with private components) banking system that comprises (1) the presidentially appointed Board of Governors of the _____ in Washington, D.C.; (2) the Federal Open Market Committee; (3) twelve regional Federal Reserve Banks located in major cities throughout the nation acting as fiscal agents for the U.S. Treasury, each with its own nine-member board of directors; (4) numerous other private U.S. member banks, which subscribe to required amounts of non-transferable stock in their regional Federal Reserve Banks; and (5) various advisory councils. Since February 2006, Ben Bernanke has served as the Chairman of the Board of Governors of the _____.
a. Federal Reserve System
c. Federal Reserve Banks
b. Federal Reserve Transparency Act
d. Federal funds rate

18. In macroeconomics, _____ is a condition of the national economy, where all or nearly all persons willing and able to work at the prevailing wages and working conditions are able to do so. It is defined either as 0% unemployment, literally, no unemployment (the rate of unemployment is the fraction of the work force unable to find work), as by James Tobin, or as the level of employment rates when there is no cyclical unemployment. It is defined by the majority of mainstream economists as being an acceptable level of natural unemployment above 0%, the discrepancy from 0% being due to non-cyclical types of unemployment.
a. SIMIC
c. War economy
b. Full employment
d. Marginal propensity to import

19. The _____ is a concept of economic activity developed in particular by Milton Friedman and Edmund Phelps in the 1960s, both recipients of the Nobel prize in economics. In both cases, the development of the concept is cited as a main motivation behind the prize. It represents the hypothetical unemployment rate consistent with aggregate production being at the 'long-run' level.
   a. Technology shock
   b. Structural change
   c. Dishoarding
   d. Natural rate of unemployment

20. In economics, _____ is a sustained decrease in the general price level of goods and services. _____ occurs when the annual inflation rate falls below zero percent, resulting in an increase in the real value of money -- a negative inflation rate. This should not be confused with disinflation, a slow-down in the inflation rate (i.e. when the inflation decreases, but still remains positive.)
   a. Deflation
   b. Labour economics
   c. Law of supply
   d. Financial crises

21. The _____ or gross domestic income (GDI), a basic measure of an economy's economic performance, is the market value of all final goods and services produced within the borders of a nation in a year. _____ can be defined in three ways, all of which are conceptually identical. First, it is equal to the total expenditures for all final goods and services produced within the country in a stipulated period of time (usually a 365-day year.)
   a. Co-operative economics
   b. Market failure
   c. Public economics
   d. Gross domestic product

22. An _____ is an economic data figure reflecting price or quantity compared with a standard or base value. The base usually equals 100 and the _____ is usually expressed as 100 times the ratio to the base value. For example, if a commodity costs twice as much in 1970 as it did in 1960, its _____ would be 200 relative to 1960.
   a. Economic depreciation
   b. International economics
   c. ACCRA Cost of Living Index
   d. Index number

23. The term _____ or commodity bundle refers to a fixed list of items used specifically to track the progress of inflation in an economy or specific market.

The most common type of _____ is the basket of consumer goods, used to define the Consumer Price Index (CPI.) Other types of baskets are used to define

- Producer Price Index (PPI), previously known as Wholesale Price Index (WPI)
- various commodity price indices

The term _____ analysis in the retail business refers to research that provides the retailer with information to understand the purchase behaviour of a buyer. This information will enable the retailer to understand the buyer's needs and rewrite the store's layout accordingly, develop cross-promotional programs, or even capture new buyers (much like the cross-selling concept.)

   a. Substitution bias
   b. Cost-weighted activity index
   c. GDP deflator
   d. Market basket

Chapter 7. The Macroeconomy: Unemployment, Inflation, and Deflation

24. In economics, _____ refers to any price or value expressed in money of the day, as opposed to real value, which adjusts for the effect of inflation. Examples include a bundle of commodities, such as gross domestic product, and income. For a series of _____s in successive years, different values could be because of differences in the price level, an index of prices.
   a. Perfect competition
   b. Law of comparative advantage
   c. Human capital
   d. Nominal value

25. _____ in economics and business is the result of an exchange and from that trade we assign a numerical monetary value to a good, service or asset. If Alice trades Bob 4 apples for an orange, the _____ of an orange is 4 apples. Inversely, the _____ of an apple is 1/4 oranges.
   a. Price
   b. Price ceiling
   c. Price dispersion
   d. Lerner Index

26. A _____ is a normalized average (typically a weighted average) of prices for a given class of goods or services in a given region, during a given interval of time. It is a statistic designed to help to compare how these prices, taken as a whole, differ between time periods or geographical locations.

Price indices have several potential uses.

   a. Price index
   b. Flat rate
   c. Pecuniary externality
   d. Point of total assumption

27. The _____ is the part of economic and administrative life that deals with the delivery of goods and services by and for the government, whether national, regional or local/municipal.

Examples of _____ activity range from delivering social security, administering urban planning and organising national defenses.

The organization of the _____ can take several forms, including:

- Direct administration funded through taxation; the delivering organization generally has no specific requirement to meet commercial success criteria, and production decisions are determined by government.
- Publicly owned corporations (in some contexts, especially manufacturing, 'state-owned enterprises'); which differ from direct administration in that they have greater commercial freedoms and are expected to operate according to commercial criteria, and production decisions are not generally taken by government (although goals may be set for them by government.)
- Partial outsourcing (of the scale many businesses do, e.g. for IT services), is considered a _____ model.

A borderline form is

- Complete outsourcing or contracting out, with a privately owned corporation delivering the entire service on behalf of government. This may be considered a mixture of private sector operations with public ownership of assets, although in some forms the private sector's control and/or risk is so great that the service may no longer be considered part of the _____.

a. Public sector
b. 100-year flood
c. 130-30 fund
d. Policy cycle

28. In economics, _____ is a rise in the general level of prices of goods and services in an economy over a period of time. When the general price level rises, each unit of currency buys fewer goods and services; consequently, _____ is also a decline in the real value of money--a loss of purchasing power in the medium of exchange which is also the monetary unit of account in the economy. A chief measure of general price-level _____ is the general _____ rate, which is the percentage change in a general price index (normally the Consumer Price Index) over time.
   a. Energy economics
   b. Opportunity cost
   c. Inflation
   d. Economic

29. _____ refers to a business or organization attempting to acquire goods or services to accomplish the goals of the enterprise. Though there are several organizations that attempt to set standards in the _____ process, processes can vary greatly between organizations. Typically the word '_____' is not used interchangeably with the word 'procurement', since procurement typically includes Expediting, Supplier Quality, and Traffic and Logistics (T'L) in addition to _____.
   a. 100-year flood
   b. Free port
   c. 130-30 fund
   d. Purchasing

30. _____ is the number of goods/services that can be purchased with a unit of currency. For example, if you had taken one dollar to a store in the 1950s, you would have been able to buy a greater number of items than you would today, indicating that you would have had a greater _____ in the 1950s. Currency can be either a commodity money, like gold or silver, or fiat currency like US dollars.
   a. Forgotten man
   b. Purchasing power
   c. Neofeudalism
   d. Female economic activity

31. _____ is the a method of technical and economic research of the systems for purpose to optimize a parity between system's consumer functions or properties and expenses to achieve those functions or properties.

This methodology for continuous perfection of production, industrial technologies, organizational structures was developed by Juryj Sobolev in 1948 at the 'Perm telephone factory'

- 1948 Juryj Sobolev - the first success in application of a method analysis at the 'Perm telephone factory'.
- 1949 - the first application for the invention as result of use of the new method.

Today in economically developed countries practically each enterprise or the company use methodology of the kind of functional-cost analysis as a practice of the quality management, most full satisfying to principles of standards of series ISO 9000.

- Interest of consumer not in products itself, but the advantage which it will receive from its usage.
- The consumer aspires to reduce his expenses
- Functions needed by consumer can be executed in the various ways, and, hence, with various efficiency and expenses. Among possible alternatives of realization of functions exist such in which the parity of quality and the price is the optimal for the consumer.

Chapter 7. The Macroeconomy: Unemployment, Inflation, and Deflation 59

The goal of _____ is achievement of the highest consumer satisfaction of production at simultaneous decrease in all kinds of industrial expenses Classical _____ has three English synonyms - Value Engineering, Value Management, Value Analysis.

a. Residual value
b. Function cost analysis
c. Monopoly wage
d. Real net output ratio

32. _____ is a broad label that refers to any individuals or households that use goods and services generated within the economy. The concept of a _____ is used in different contexts, so that the usage and significance of the term may vary.

Typically when business people and economists talk of _____s they are talking about person as _____, an aggregated commodity item with little individuality other than that expressed in the buy/not-buy decision.

a. 130-30 fund
b. 100-year flood
c. 1921 recession
d. Consumer

33. A _____ is a measure of the average price of consumer goods and services purchased by households. A _____ measures a price change for a constant market basket of goods and services from one period to the next within the same area (city, region, or nation.) It is a price index determined by measuring the price of a standard group of goods meant to represent the typical market basket of a typical urban consumer.

a. Cost-of-living index
b. Consumer Price Index
c. Lipstick index
d. Hedonic price index

34. A _____ measures average changes in prices received by domestic producers for their output. It is one of several price indices

Its importance is being undermined by the steady decline in manufactured goods as a share of spending.

A number of countries that now report a _____ previously reported a Wholesale Price Index.

a. Gross Regional Product
b. Producer Price Index
c. Lagging indicator
d. Trade weighted index

35. A _____ is the price of a representative basket of wholesale goods. Some countries (like India and The Philippines) use _____ changes as a central measure of inflation. However, India and the United States now report a producer price index instead.

a. State Domestic Product
b. Retail sales index
c. Volume index
d. Wholesale price index

36. _____ is a fee paid on borrowed assets. It is the price paid for the use of borrowed money, or, money earned by deposited funds. Assets that are sometimes lent with _____ include money, shares, consumer goods through hire purchase, major assets such as aircraft, and even entire factories in finance lease arrangements.

a. Asset protection
b. Insolvency
c. Internal debt
d. Interest

37. The _____ is the component statistic for consumption in GDP collected by the BEA. It consists of the actual and imputed expenditures of households and includes data pertaining to durable and non-durable goods, and services. It is essentially a measure of goods and services targeted towards individuals and consumed by individuals.

a. Skyscraper Index
b. Gross world product
c. Measures of national income and output
d. Personal consumption expenditure

38. In economics, the _____ is a historical inverse relation between the rate of unemployment and the rate of inflation in an economy. Stated simply, the lower the unemployment in an economy, the higher the rate of increase in nominal wages in the economy. Rate of Change of Wages against Unemployment, United Kingdom 1913-1948 from Phillips (1958)

William Phillips, a New Zealand born economist, wrote a paper in 1958 titled The Relationship between Unemployment and the Rate of Change of Money Wages in the United Kingdom 1861-1957, which was published in the quarterly journal Economica.

a. Phillips curve
b. Wage curve
c. Demand curve
d. Kuznets curve

39. _____ is a common concept in economics, and gives rise to derived concepts such as consumer debt. Generally _____ is defined by opposition to production. But the precise definition can vary because different schools of economists define production quite differently.

a. British canal system
b. Basis of futures
c. Discrete choice
d. Consumption

40. _____ is money accepted for exchange of goods in an economy. The prevalence of one money over another arises, usually, when a government designates through decrees that the government shall accept only particular notes and coins in payment for taxes. Typically, money of _____ consists of stamped coins and minted paper bills.

a. Security thread
b. Scripophily
c. Totnes pound
d. Currency

41. A _____ is a type of banknote issued by the Federal Reserve System and is the only type of U.S. banknote that is still produced today.

_____s are fiat currency, with the words 'this note is legal tender for all debts, public and private' printed on each bill. (See generally 31 U.S.C.

a. Federal Reserve System Open Market Account
b. Federal Reserve note
c. Federal banking
d. Primary Dealer Credit Facility

42. An _____ is the price a borrower pays for the use of money they do not own, for instance a small company might borrow from a bank to kick start their business, and the return a lender receives for deferring the use of funds, by lending it to the borrower. _____s are normally expressed as a percentage rate over the period of one year.

Chapter 7. The Macroeconomy: Unemployment, Inflation, and Deflation

_____s targets are also a vital tool of monetary policy and are used to control variables like investment, inflation, and unemployment.

- a. Enterprise value
- b. Interest rate
- c. ACCRA Cost of Living Index
- d. Arrow-Debreu model

43. In economics a _____ is an entity that owes a debt to someone else. The entity may be an individual, a firm, a government, a company or other legal person. The counterparty is called a creditor.
- a. Restructuring
- b. Certified International Investment Analyst
- c. Debtor
- d. Life annuity

44. The term _____ refers to economy-wide fluctuations in production or economic activity over several months or years. These fluctuations occur around a long-term growth trend, and typically involve shifts over time between periods of relatively rapid economic growth (expansion or boom), and periods of relative stagnation or decline (contraction or recession.)

These fluctuations are often measured using the growth rate of real gross domestic product.

- a. Business cycle
- b. Consumer theory
- c. Neoclassical economics
- d. Literacy rate

45. The _____ was a worldwide economic downturn starting in most places in 1929 and ending at different times in the 1930s or early 1940s for different countries. It was the largest and most important economic depression in the 20th century, and is used in the 21st century as an example of how far the world's economy can fall. The _____ originated in the United States; historians most often use as a starting date the stock market crash on October 29, 1929, known as Black Tuesday.
- a. British Empire Economic Conference
- b. Causes of the Great Depression
- c. The Great Depression
- d. Great Depression

46. _____ was a global military conflict which involved a majority of the world's nations, including all of the great powers, organized into two opposing military alliances: the Allies and the Axis. The war involved the mobilization of over 100 million military personnel, making it the most widespread war in history. In a state of 'total war', the major participants placed their entire economic, industrial, and scientific capabilities at the service of the war effort, erasing the distinction between civilian and military resources.
- a. 1921 recession
- b. 130-30 fund
- c. World War II
- d. 100-year flood

47. An _____ is a statistic about the economy. _____s allow analysis of economic performance and predictions of future performance.

_____s include various indices, earnings reports, and economic summaries, such as unemployment, housing starts, Consumer Price Index (a measure for inflation), industrial production, bankruptcies, Gross Domestic Product, broadband internet penetration, retail sales, stock market prices, and money supply changes.

a. Economic Vulnerability Index
b. Economic Indicator
c. Internationalization Index
d. ACCRA Cost of Living Index

Chapter 8. Measuring the Economy's Performance

1. _____s is the social science that studies the production, distribution, and consumption of goods and services. The term _____s comes from the Ancient Greek oá¼°κονομῖα from oá¼¶κος (oikos, 'house') + vϏμος (nomos, 'custom' or 'law'), hence 'rules of the house(hold)'. Current _____ models developed out of the broader field of political economy in the late 19th century, owing to a desire to use an empirical approach more akin to the physical sciences.
   a. Energy economics
   b. Inflation
   c. Opportunity cost
   d. Economic

2. _____ is the increase in the amount of the goods and services produced by an economy over time. It is conventionally measured as the percent rate of increase in real gross domestic product, or real GDP. Growth is usually calculated in real terms, i.e. inflation-adjusted terms, in order to net out the effect of inflation on the price of the goods and services produced.
   a. ACEA agreement
   b. ACCRA Cost of Living Index
   c. Economic growth
   d. AD-IA Model

3. The _____ or gross domestic income (GDI), a basic measure of an economy's economic performance, is the market value of all final goods and services produced within the borders of a nation in a year. _____ can be defined in three ways, all of which are conceptually identical. First, it is equal to the total expenditures for all final goods and services produced within the country in a stipulated period of time (usually a 365-day year.)
   a. Market failure
   b. Gross domestic product
   c. Public economics
   d. Co-operative economics

4. The underground economy or black market is a market where all commerce is conducted without regard to taxation, law or regulations of trade. The term is also often known as the underdog, _____, black economy, parallel economy or phantom trades.

In modern societies the underground economy covers a vast array of activities.

   a. Shadow economy
   b. Knowledge Revolution
   c. Transition economy
   d. Network Economy

5. The _____ or black market is a market where all commerce is conducted without regard to taxation, law or regulations of trade. The term is also often known as the underdog, shadow economy, black economy, parallel economy or phantom trades.

In modern societies the _____ covers a vast array of activities.

   a. Information markets
   b. Information economy
   c. Autarky
   d. Underground economy

6. Fractional-reserve banking is the banking practice in which banks keep only a fraction of their deposits in reserve (as cash and other highly liquid assets) and lend out the remainder, while maintaining the simultaneous obligation to redeem all these deposits upon demand. _____ necessarily occurs when banks lend out any fraction of the funds received from demand deposits. This practice is universal in modern banking.
   a. Certificate of deposit
   b. Bank secrecy
   c. Repo Rate
   d. Fractional reserve banking

Chapter 8. Measuring the Economy's Performance

7. _____ in economics and business is the result of an exchange and from that trade we assign a numerical monetary value to a good, service or asset. If Alice trades Bob 4 apples for an orange, the _____ of an orange is 4 apples. Inversely, the _____ of an apple is 1/4 oranges.
   a. Price dispersion
   b. Price ceiling
   c. Price
   d. Lerner Index

8. In economics, the term _____ of income or _____ refers to a simple economic model which describes the reciprocal circulation of income between producers and consumers. In the _____ model, the inter-dependent entities of producer and consumer are referred to as 'firms' and 'households' respectively and provide each other with factors in order to facilitate the flow of income. Firms provide consumers with goods and services in exchange for consumer expenditure and 'factors of production' from households.
   a. 130-30 fund
   b. 1921 recession
   c. 100-year flood
   d. Circular flow

9. In economics, the term _____ or circular flow refers to a simple economic model which describes the reciprocal circulation of income between producers and consumers. In the circular flow model, the inter-dependent entities of producer and consumer are referred to as 'firms' and 'households' respectively and provide each other with factors in order to facilitate the flow of income. Firms provide consumers with goods and services in exchange for consumer expenditure and 'factors of production' from households.
   a. 130-30 fund
   b. Circular flow of income
   c. 100-year flood
   d. 1921 recession

10. In economics, _____ are the resources employed to produce goods and services. They facilitate production but do not become part of the product (as with raw materials) or significantly transformed by the production process (as with fuel used to power machinery.) To 19th century economists, the _____ were land (natural resources, gifts from nature), labor (the ability to work), and capital goods (human-made tools and equipment.)
    a. Production function
    b. Productive capacity
    c. Long-run
    d. Factors of production

11. The _____ equals the gross domestic product (GDP) minus depreciation on a country's capital goods.

    _____ accounts for capital that has been consumed over the year in the form of housing, vehicle, or machinery deterioration. The depreciation accounted for is often referred to as capital consumption allowance and represents the amount needed in order to replace those depreciated assets.

    a. Depository Institutions Deregulation and Monetary Control Act
    b. Net domestic product
    c. Legal monopoly
    d. Cost underestimation

12. In microeconomics, _____ is quite simply the conversion of inputs into outputs. It is an economic process that uses resources to create a good or service that is suitable for exchange. This can include manufacturing, storing, shipping, and packaging.
    a. Variability
    b. Production
    c. Characteristic
    d. Bucket shop

Chapter 8. Measuring the Economy`s Performance 65

13. In Marxian economics, _____ originally referred to the means of production. Individuals, organizations and governments use _____ in the production of other goods or commodities. _____ include factories, machinery, tools, equipment, and various buildings which are used to produce other products for consumption.
 a. Capital formation
 b. Modigliani-Miller theorem
 c. Capital goods
 d. Cost of capital

14. A _____ is an object whose consumption increases the utility of the consumer, for which the quantity demanded exceeds the quantity supplied at zero price. _____s are usually modeled as having diminishing marginal utility. The first individual purchase has high utility; the second has less.
 a. Good
 b. Luxury good
 c. Search good
 d. Positional goods

15. In economics _____s are goods that are ultimately consumed rather than used in the production of another good. For example, a car sold to a consumer is a _____; the components such as tires sold to the car manufacturer are not; they are intermediate goods used to make the _____.

When used in measures of national income and output the term _____s only includes new goods.

 a. Composite good
 b. Manufactured goods
 c. Goods and services
 d. Final good

16. _____ is a mechanism that allows people easily to buy and sell products. Services are often included in the scope of the term. _____ regulation is an economic term that describes restrictions in the market.
 a. Product market
 b. Foreign investment
 c. Discretionary spending
 d. Residual claimant

17. In economics, economic output is divided into physical goods and intangible services. Consumption of _____ is assumed to produce utility. It is often used when referring to a _____ Tax.
 a. Final good
 b. Demerit good
 c. Complementary good
 d. Goods and Services

18. A variety of measures of _____ and output are used in economics to estimate total economic activity in a country or region, including gross domestic product (GDP), gross national product (GNP), and net _____

There are three main ways of calculating these numbers; the output approach, the income approach and the expenditure approach. In theory, the three must yield the same, because total expenditures on goods and services must equal the total income paid to the producers (Gnational income), and that must also equal the total value of the output of goods and services (GNP.)

 a. Gross national product
 b. Bureau of Labor Statistics
 c. Purchasing power parity
 d. National income

19. _____ or producer goods are goods used as inputs in the production of other goods, such as partly finished goods. They are goods used in production of final goods. A firm may make then use _____, or make then sell, or buy then use them.

a. Economic forecasting
b. Income distribution
c. Inflation adjustment
d. Intermediate goods

20. _____ is the a method of technical and economic research of the systems for purpose to optimize a parity between system's consumer functions or properties and expenses to achieve those functions or properties.

This methodology for continuous perfection of production, industrial technologies, organizational structures was developed by Juryj Sobolev in 1948 at the 'Perm telephone factory'

- 1948 Juryj Sobolev - the first success in application of a method analysis at the 'Perm telephone factory'.
- 1949 - the first application for the invention as result of use of the new method.

Today in economically developed countries practically each enterprise or the company use methodology of the kind of functional-cost analysis as a practice of the quality management, most full satisfying to principles of standards of series ISO 9000.

- Interest of consumer not in products itself, but the advantage which it will receive from its usage.
- The consumer aspires to reduce his expenses
- Functions needed by consumer can be executed in the various ways, and, hence, with various efficiency and expenses. Among possible alternatives of realization of functions exist such in which the parity of quality and the price is the optimal for the consumer.

The goal of _____ is achievement of the highest consumer satisfaction of production at simultaneous decrease in all kinds of industrial expenses Classical _____ has three English synonyms - Value Engineering, Value Management, Value Analysis.

a. Residual value
b. Monopoly wage
c. Real net output ratio
d. Function cost analysis

21. _____ refers to the additional value of a commodity over the cost of commodities used to produce it from the previous stage of production. An example is the price of gasoline at the pump over the price of the oil in it. In national accounts used in macroeconomics, it refers to the contribution of the factors of production, i.e., land, labor, and capital goods, to raising the value of a product and corresponds to the incomes received by the owners of these factors.

a. Demand shock
b. Fundamental psychological law
c. Value added
d. Monetary policy reaction function

22. In finance, a _____ is a debt security, in which the authorized issuer owes the holders a debt and, depending on the terms of the _____, is obliged to pay interest (the coupon) and/or to repay the principal at a later date, termed maturity. A _____ is a formal contract to repay borrowed money with interest at fixed intervals.

Thus a _____ is like a loan: the issuer is the borrower (debtor), the holder is the lender (creditor), and the coupon is the interest.

a. Bond
b. Callable
c. Carter bonds
d. Prize Bond

23. A _____ is an event or condition under the contract between a buyer and a seller to exchange an asset for payment. In accounting, it is recognized by an entry in the books of account. It involves a change in the status of the finances of two or more businesses or individuals.
   a. Tax shield
   b. Present value of costs
   c. Refinancing risk
   d. Financial transaction

24. In economics, a _____ is a redistribution of income in the market system. These payments are considered to be nonexhaustive because they do not directly absorb resources or create output. Examples of certain _____s include welfare (financial aid), social security, and government subsidies for certain businesses (firms.)
   a. 130-30 fund
   b. 1921 recession
   c. 100-year flood
   d. Transfer payment

25. A _____ is the transfer of wealth from one party (such as a person or company) to another. A _____ is usually made in exchange for the provision of goods, services or both, or to fulfill a legal obligation.

The simplest and oldest form of _____ is barter, the exchange of one good or service for another.

   a. Hard count
   b. Payment
   c. RFM
   d. Contingent payment sales

26. The _____ is 'the basic residential unit in which economic production, consumption, inheritance, child rearing, and shelter are organized and carried out'; [the _____] 'may or may not be synonomous with family'.

The _____ is the basic unit of analysis in many social, microeconomic and government models. The term refers to all individuals who live in the same dwelling.

   a. Family economics
   b. 130-30 fund
   c. 100-year flood
   d. Household

27. _____ refers to internal and external organizing and correcting factors that provide order to market and other types of societal institutions and organizations - economic, political, social and cultural - so that they may function efficiently and effectively as well as repair their failures.

The expression _____ is increasingly found in the title, abstract and text of articles, chapters and papers in the business, management, organization, strategy, social-issues, political-science and sociology literatures. The ABI/Inform Global source located 1748 such uses of both expressions in October 2008, compared with 31 in 1991 and 247 in 2002.

   a. Blanket order
   b. Nonmarket
   c. Small numbers game
   d. Net Capital Outflow

28. _____ is a set of properties and characteristics of the environment, either generalized or local, as they impinge on human beings and other organisms.

68 *Chapter 8. Measuring the Economy's Performance*

_____ is a general term which can refer to varied characteristics that relate to the natural environment as well as the built environment, such as air and water purity or pollution, noise and the potential effects which such characteristics may have on physical and mental health caused by human activities.

In the USA the term is applied with a body of federal and state standards and regulations that are monitored by regulatory agencies.

a. ACEA agreement
c. ACCRA Cost of Living Index
b. AD-IA Model
d. Environmental quality

29. The _____ is a concept in green economics and welfare economics that has been suggested to replace gross domestic product (GDP) as a metric of economic growth.

_____ is an attempt to measure whether a country's growth, increased production of goods, and expanding services have actually resulted in the improvement of the welfare (or well-being) of the people in the country. _____ advocates claim that it can more reliably measure economic progress, as it distinguishes between worthwhile growth and uneconomic growth.

a. Physical quality-of-life index
c. Human Poverty Index
b. Forgotten man
d. Genuine Progress Indicator

30. The _____ is one of three major groups of methodologies, called valuation approaches, used by appraisers. It is particularly common in commercial real estate appraisal and in business appraisal. The fundamental math is similar to the methods used for financial valuation, securities analysis, or bond pricing.

a. ACCRA Cost of Living Index
c. Urban growth boundary
b. ACEA agreement
d. Income approach

31. _____ is a common concept in economics, and gives rise to derived concepts such as consumer debt. Generally _____ is defined by opposition to production. But the precise definition can vary because different schools of economists define production quite differently.

a. Discrete choice
c. Basis of futures
b. Consumption
d. British canal system

32. _____ is a broad label that refers to any individuals or households that use goods and services generated within the economy. The concept of a _____ is used in different contexts, so that the usage and significance of the term may vary.

Typically when business people and economists talk of _____s they are talking about person as _____, an aggregated commodity item with little individuality other than that expressed in the buy/not-buy decision.

a. 100-year flood
c. 1921 recession
b. 130-30 fund
d. Consumer

Chapter 8. Measuring the Economy`s Performance

33. _____ are final goods specifically intended for the mass market. For instance, _____ do not include investment assets, like precious antiques, even though these antiques are final goods.

Manufactured goods are goods that have been processed by way of machinery.

- a. Labour battalions
- b. Government backed loan
- c. Human rights
- d. Consumer goods

34. _____ in economics refers to investment in fixed capital, i.e. tangible capital goods (real means of production or residential buildings), or to the replacement of depreciated capital goods.

Thus, _____ is investment in physical assets such as machinery, land, buildings, installations, vehicles, or technology. Normally, a company balance sheet will state both the amount of expenditure on fixed assets during the quarter or year, and the total value of the stock of fixed assets owned.

- a. Deferred financing costs
- b. Depreciation
- c. Fixed investment
- d. Salvage value

35. _____ relates to the composition of GDP. What is produced in a certain country is naturally also sold, but some of the goods produced in a given year may not be sold the same year, but in later years. Conversely, some of the goods sold in a given year might have been produced in an earlier year.

- a. Investment decisions
- b. Obelisk International
- c. Investment theory
- d. Inventory investment

36. _____ is the income of individuals or nations after adjusting for inflation. It is calculated by subtracting inflation from the nominal income. Real variables, such as _____, real GDP, and real interest rate are variables that are measured in physical units, while nominal variables such as nominal income, nominal GDP, and nominal interest rate are measured in monetary units.

- a. Pay grade
- b. Windfall gain
- c. Lerman ratio
- d. Real Income

37. In economics, an _____ is any good or commodity, transported from one country to another country in a legitimate fashion, typically for use in trade. _____ goods or services are provided to foreign consumers by domestic producers. _____ is an important part of international trade.

- a. ACCRA Cost of Living Index
- b. AD-IA Model
- c. ACEA agreement
- d. Export

38. In economics, an _____ is any good (e.g. a commodity) or service brought into one country from another country in a legitimate fashion, typically for use in trade.It is a good that is brought in from another country for sale. _____ goods or services are provided to domestic consumers by foreign producers. An _____ in the receiving country is an export to the sending country.

- a. Economic integration
- b. Incoterms
- c. Import quota
- d. Import

39. The _____ was an evolution of developed countries from an industrial/manufacturing-based wealth producing economy into a service sector asset based economy, brought about by globalization and currency manipulation by governments and their central banks. Some analysts claimed that this change in the economic structure of the United States had created a state of permanent steady growth, low unemployment, and immunity to boom and bust macroeconomic cycles. They believed that the change rendered obsolete many business practices.
   a. 130-30 fund
   b. 100-year flood
   c. 1921 recession
   d. New economy

40. _____ is a term used in accounting, economics and finance to spread the cost of an asset over the span of several years.

In simple words we can say that _____ is the reduction in the value of an asset due to usage, passage of time, wear and tear, technological outdating or obsolescence, depletion, inadequacy, rot, rust, decay or other such factors.

In accounting, _____ is a term used to describe any method of attributing the historical or purchase cost of an asset across its useful life, roughly corresponding to normal wear and tear.

   a. Net income per employee
   b. Fixed investment
   c. Salvage value
   d. Depreciation

41. The _____ is the percentage of the Gross Domestic Product (GDP) which is due to depreciation. The _____ measures the amount of expenditure that a country needs to undertake in order to maintain, as opposed to grow, its productivity. The _____ can be thought of as representing the wear-and-tear on the country's physical capital, together with the investment needed to maintain the level of human capital (eg to educate the workers needed to replace retirees.)
   a. Skyscraper Index
   b. Non-Manufacturing Business Activity Index
   c. Nonfarm payrolls
   d. Capital consumption allowance

42. The _____ was a worldwide economic downturn starting in most places in 1929 and ending at different times in the 1930s or early 1940s for different countries. It was the largest and most important economic depression in the 20th century, and is used in the 21st century as an example of how far the world's economy can fall. The _____ originated in the United States; historians most often use as a starting date the stock market crash on October 29, 1929, known as Black Tuesday.
   a. The Great Depression
   b. Great Depression
   c. Causes of the Great Depression
   d. British Empire Economic Conference

43. In economics, _____ refers to an activity of spending which increases the availability of fixed capital goods or means of production. It is the total spending on new fixed investment minus replacement investment, which simply replaces depreciated capital goods.
   a. Market sentiment
   b. Matched betting
   c. Net investment
   d. Price return

44. _____ is a fee paid on borrowed assets. It is the price paid for the use of borrowed money , or, money earned by deposited funds . Assets that are sometimes lent with _____ include money, shares, consumer goods through hire purchase, major assets such as aircraft, and even entire factories in finance lease arrangements.

a. Insolvency	b. Internal debt
c. Asset protection	d. Interest

45. A _____, or simply proprietorship is a type of business entity which legally has no separate existence from its owner. Hence, the limitations of liability enjoyed by a corporation and limited liability partnerships do not apply to sole proprietors. All debts of the business are debts of the owner.

a. Golden hello	b. Delivery schedule adherence
c. Customer centricity	d. Sole proprietorship

46. Economic _____ is defined as an excess distribution to any factor in a production process above that which is required to induce the factor into the process or any excess above that which is necessary to keep the factor in its current use..

Classical Factor _____ is primarily concerned with the fee paid for the use of fixed (e.g. natural) resources. The classical definition is expressed as any excess payment above that required to induce or provide for production.

a. 130-30 fund	b. 1921 recession
c. Rent	d. 100-year flood

47. To _____ is to impose a financial charge or other levy upon a taxpayer by a state or the functional equivalent of a state.

_____es are also imposed by many subnational entities. _____es consist of direct _____ or indirect _____, and may be paid in money or as its labour equivalent (often but not always unpaid.)

a. Tax	b. 100-year flood
c. 1921 recession	d. 130-30 fund

48. The term _____ has more than one meaning.

In the colloquial sense, an _____, or goods and services tax (GST)) is a tax collected by an intermediary (such as a retail store) from the person who bears the ultimate economic burden of the tax (such as the customer.) The intermediary later files a tax return and forwards the tax proceeds to government with the return.

a. Optimal tax	b. Olivera-Tanzi effect
c. User charge	d. Indirect Tax

49. To tax is to impose a financial charge or other levy upon a taxpayer by a state or the functional equivalent of a state.

_____ are also imposed by many subnational entities. _____ consist of direct tax or indirect tax, and may be paid in money or as its labour equivalent (often but not always unpaid.)

a. 1921 recession
b. 100-year flood
c. Taxes
d. 130-30 fund

50. Total _____ is defined by the United States' Bureau of Economic Analysis as

income received by persons from all sources. It includes income received from participation in production as well as from government and business transfer payments. It is the sum of compensation of employees (received), supplements to wages and salaries, proprietors' income with inventory valuation adjustment (IVA) and capital consumption adjustment (CCAdj), rental income of persons with CCAdj, _____ receipts on assets, and personal current transfer receipts, less contributions for government social insurance.

a. Direct Market Access
b. Malinvestment
c. Broad money
d. Personal income

51. A _____ product is a product designed for cheapness and short-term convenience rather than medium to long-term durability, with most products only intended for single use. The term is also sometimes used for products that may last several months (ex. _____ air filters) to distinguish from similar products that last indefinitely (ex.
a. Disposable
b. 1921 recession
c. 100-year flood
d. 130-30 fund

52. _____ is gross income minus income tax on that income.

Discretionary income is income after subtracting taxes and normal expenses (such as rent or mortgage, utilities, insurance, medical, transportation, property maintenance, child support, inflation, food and sundries, 'c.) to maintain a certain standard of living.

a. National War Tax Resistance Coordinating Committee
b. Privatized tax collection
c. Withholding tax
d. Disposable Income

53. The term _____ refers to a metric for valuing the price of something over time, without that metric changing due to inflation or deflation. The term specifically refers to dollars whose present value is linked to a given year.

As an example, this is a graph of 2005 _____:

_____ are used to compare the 'real value' of an income or price to put the 'nominal value' in perspective.

a. Pareto index
b. Life Quality Index
c. NCDEX Commodity Index
d. Constant dollars

54. _____ is money accepted for exchange of goods in an economy. The prevalence of one money over another arises, usually, when a government designates through decrees that the government shall accept only particular notes and coins in payment for taxes. Typically, money of _____ consists of stamped coins and minted paper bills.
a. Scripophily
b. Totnes pound
c. Security thread
d. Currency

Chapter 8. Measuring the Economy's Performance

55. In economics, _____ refers to any price or value expressed in money of the day, as opposed to real value, which adjusts for the effect of inflation. Examples include a bundle of commodities, such as gross domestic product, and income. For a series of _____s in successive years, different values could be because of differences in the price level, an index of prices.
   a. Human capital
   c. Law of comparative advantage
   b. Perfect competition
   d. Nominal value

56. A _____ is a normalized average (typically a weighted average) of prices for a given class of goods or services in a given region, during a given interval of time. It is a statistic designed to help to compare how these prices, taken as a whole, differ between time periods or geographical locations.

Price indices have several potential uses.

   a. Pecuniary externality
   c. Point of total assumption
   b. Flat rate
   d. Price index

57. An _____, in economics, is the amount by which the real Gross domestic product exceeds potential GDP. The real GDP is also known as GDP 'adjusted for inflation', 'constant prices' GDP or 'constant dollar' GDP, because it measures the aggregate output in a country's income accounts in a given year, expressed in base-year prices. On the other hand, the potential GDP is the quantity of real GDP when a country's economy is at full-employment.
   a. Inflationary gap
   c. AD-IA Model
   b. ACEA agreement
   d. ACCRA Cost of Living Index

58. _____ is a term used in accounting relating to the increase in value of an asset. In this sense it is the reverse of depreciation, which measures the fall in value of assets over their normal life-time.

_____ is a rise of a currency in a floating exchange rate.

   a. AD-IA Model
   c. ACEA agreement
   b. ACCRA Cost of Living Index
   d. Appreciation

59. A _____ is a measure of the average price of consumer goods and services purchased by households. A _____ measures a price change for a constant market basket of goods and services from one period to the next within the same area (city, region, or nation.) It is a price index determined by measuring the price of a standard group of goods meant to represent the typical market basket of a typical urban consumer.
   a. Cost-of-living index
   c. Hedonic price index
   b. Lipstick index
   d. Consumer Price Index

60. A _____ measures average changes in prices received by domestic producers for their output. It is one of several price indices

Its importance is being undermined by the steady decline in manufactured goods as a share of spending.

A number of countries that now report a _____ previously reported a Wholesale Price Index.

a. Lagging indicator
b. Trade weighted index
c. Gross Regional Product
d. Producer Price Index

61. _____ is a misspelled phrase from Latin 'pro capite' phrase meaning per head with pro meaning 'per' or 'for each' and capite meaning 'head.' Both words together equate to the phrase 'for each head.'

It is usually used in the field of statistics to indicate the average per person for any given concern, such as income, crime rate, etc.

It is also used in wills to indicate that each of the named beneficiaries should receive, by devise or bequest, equal shares of the estate. This is in contrast to a per stirpes division, in which each branch of the inheriting family inherits an equal share of the estate.

a. Per capita
b. Semiparametric regression
c. Dynamic Bayesian network
d. Posterior probability

62. _____ means how much each individual receives, in monetary terms, of the yearly income generated in the country. This is what each citizen is to receive if the yearly national income is divided equally among everyone. _____ is usually reported in units of currency per year.

a. Family income
b. Windfall gain
c. Haig-Simons income
d. Per capita Income

63. The _____ is an international organization that oversees the global financial system by following the macroeconomic policies of its member countries, in particular those with an impact on exchange rates and the balance of payments. It is an organization formed to stabilize international exchange rates and facilitate development. It also offers financial and technical assistance to its members, making it an international lender of last resort.

a. International Monetary Fund
b. ACEA agreement
c. Office of Thrift Supervision
d. ACCRA Cost of Living Index

64. The _____ is the part of economic and administrative life that deals with the delivery of goods and services by and for the government, whether national, regional or local/municipal.

Examples of _____ activity range from delivering social security, administering urban planning and organising national defenses.

Chapter 8. Measuring the Economy's Performance

The organization of the _____ can take several forms, including:

- Direct administration funded through taxation; the delivering organization generally has no specific requirement to meet commercial success criteria, and production decisions are determined by government.
- Publicly owned corporations (in some contexts, especially manufacturing, 'state-owned enterprises'); which differ from direct administration in that they have greater commercial freedoms and are expected to operate according to commercial criteria, and production decisions are not generally taken by government (although goals may be set for them by government.)
- Partial outsourcing (of the scale many businesses do, e.g. for IT services), is considered a _____ model.

A borderline form is

- Complete outsourcing or contracting out, with a privately owned corporation delivering the entire service on behalf of government. This may be considered a mixture of private sector operations with public ownership of assets, although in some forms the private sector's control and/or risk is so great that the service may no longer be considered part of the _____.

a. 130-30 fund
c. Policy cycle
b. 100-year flood
d. Public sector

65. _____ refers to a business or organization attempting to acquire goods or services to accomplish the goals of the enterprise. Though there are several organizations that attempt to set standards in the _____ process, processes can vary greatly between organizations. Typically the word '_____' is not used interchangeably with the word 'procurement', since procurement typically includes Expediting, Supplier Quality, and Traffic and Logistics (T'L) in addition to _____.
a. 100-year flood
c. 130-30 fund
b. Purchasing
d. Free port

66. _____ is the number of goods/services that can be purchased with a unit of currency. For example, if you had taken one dollar to a store in the 1950s, you would have been able to buy a greater number of items than you would today, indicating that you would have had a greater _____ in the 1950s. Currency can be either a commodity money, like gold or silver, or fiat currency like US dollars.
a. Purchasing power
c. Forgotten man
b. Female economic activity
d. Neofeudalism

67. The _____ theory uses the long-term equilibrium exchange rate of two currencies to equalize their purchasing power. Developed by Gustav Cassel in 1920, it is based on the law of one price: the theory states that, in ideally efficient markets, identical goods should have only one price.

This purchasing power SEM rate equalizes the purchasing power of different currencies in their home countries for a given basket of goods.

a. Skyscraper Index
b. Producer Price Index
c. Volume index
d. Purchasing power parity

68. The _____ is an international financial institution that provides financial and technical assistance to developing countries for development programs (e.g. bridges, roads, schools, etc.) with the stated goal of reducing poverty.

The _____ differs from the _____ Group, in that the _____ comprises only two institutions:

- International Bank for Reconstruction and Development (IBRD)
- International Development Association (IDA)

Whereas the latter incorporates these two in addition to three more:

- International Finance Corporation (IFC)
- Multilateral Investment Guarantee Agency (MIGA)
- International Centre for Settlement of Investment Disputes (ICSID)

John Maynard Keynes (right) represented the UK at the conference, and Harry Dexter White represented the US.

The _____ is one of two major financial institutions created as a result of the Bretton Woods Conference in 1944. The International Monetary Fund, a related but separate institution, is the second.

a. Black-Scholes
b. Demographic marketers
c. Dow Jones Industrial Average
d. World Bank

69. In finance, the _____s between two currencies specifies how much one currency is worth in terms of the other. It is the value of a foreign natione;s currency in terms of the home natione;s currency. For example an _____ of 102 Japanese yen to the United States dollar means that JPY 102 is worth the same as USD 1.

a. ACEA agreement
b. Exchange rate
c. Interbank market
d. ACCRA Cost of Living Index

Chapter 9. Global Economic Growth and Development

1. _____s is the social science that studies the production, distribution, and consumption of goods and services. The term _____s comes from the Ancient Greek οἰκονομία from οἶκος (oikos, 'house') + νόμος (nomos, 'custom' or 'law'), hence 'rules of the house(hold)'. Current _____ models developed out of the broader field of political economy in the late 19th century, owing to a desire to use an empirical approach more akin to the physical sciences.
   a. Inflation
   b. Opportunity cost
   c. Economic
   d. Energy economics

2. _____ is the development of economic wealth of countries or regions for the well-being of their inhabitants. It is the process by which a nation improves the economic, political, and social well being of its people. From a policy perspective, _____ can be defined as efforts that seek to improve the economic well-being and quality of life for a community by creating and/or retaining jobs and supporting or growing incomes and the tax base.
   a. Experimental economics
   b. Economic development
   c. Economic methodology
   d. Inflation

3. The _____ is an international organization that oversees the global financial system by following the macroeconomic policies of its member countries, in particular those with an impact on exchange rates and the balance of payments. It is an organization formed to stabilize international exchange rates and facilitate development. It also offers financial and technical assistance to its members, making it an international lender of last resort.
   a. ACEA agreement
   b. International Monetary Fund
   c. ACCRA Cost of Living Index
   d. Office of Thrift Supervision

4. _____ is the increase in the amount of the goods and services produced by an economy over time. It is conventionally measured as the percent rate of increase in real gross domestic product, or real GDP. Growth is usually calculated in real terms, i.e. inflation-adjusted terms, in order to net out the effect of inflation on the price of the goods and services produced.
   a. AD-IA Model
   b. ACEA agreement
   c. ACCRA Cost of Living Index
   d. Economic growth

5. In Marxian economics, _____ originally referred to the means of production. Individuals, organizations and governments use _____ in the production of other goods or commodities. _____ include factories, machinery, tools, equipment, and various buildings which are used to produce other products for consumption.
   a. Capital formation
   b. Modigliani-Miller theorem
   c. Capital goods
   d. Cost of capital

6. A _____ is an object whose consumption increases the utility of the consumer, for which the quantity demanded exceeds the quantity supplied at zero price. _____s are usually modeled as having diminishing marginal utility. The first individual purchase has high utility; the second has less.
   a. Search good
   b. Positional goods
   c. Luxury good
   d. Good

7. _____ is a type of private equity investment, most often a minority investment, in relatively mature companies that are looking for capital to expand or restructure operations, enter new markets or finance a significant acquisition without a change of control of the business.

Companies that seek _____, will often do so in order to finance a transformational event in their lifecycle. These companies are likely to be more mature than venture capital funded companies, able to generate revenue and operating profits but unable to generate sufficient cash to fund major expansions, acquisitions or other investments.

a. Seed money
b. Mezzanine capital
c. Venture capital fund
d. Growth capital

8. The _____ or gross domestic income (GDI), a basic measure of an economy's economic performance, is the market value of all final goods and services produced within the borders of a nation in a year. _____ can be defined in three ways, all of which are conceptually identical. First, it is equal to the total expenditures for all final goods and services produced within the country in a stipulated period of time (usually a 365-day year.)

a. Co-operative economics
b. Public economics
c. Market failure
d. Gross domestic product

9. _____ is the concept of adding accumulated interest back to the principal, so that interest is earned on interest from that moment on. The act of declaring interest to be principal is called compounding (i.e., interest is compounded.) A loan, for example, may have its interest compounded every month: in this case, a loan with $100 principal and 1% interest per month would have a balance of $101 at the end of the first month.

a. Domestic policy of the Reagan administration
b. Freeway Revolts
c. Lawcards
d. Compound interest

10. _____ is a fee paid on borrowed assets. It is the price paid for the use of borrowed money, or, money earned by deposited funds. Assets that are sometimes lent with _____ include money, shares, consumer goods through hire purchase, major assets such as aircraft, and even entire factories in finance lease arrangements.

a. Asset protection
b. Insolvency
c. Internal debt
d. Interest

11. _____ in economics refers to metrics and measures of output from production processes, per unit of input. Labor _____, for example, is typically measured as a ratio of output per labor-hour, an input. _____ may be conceived of as a metrics of the technical or engineering efficiency of production.

a. Productivity
b. Production-possibility frontier
c. Fordism
d. Piece work

12. In algebra, a _____ is a function depending on n that associates a scalar, det(A), to an n×n square matrix A. The fundamental geometric meaning of a _____ is a scale factor for measure when A is regarded as a linear transformation. _____s are important both in calculus, where they enter the substitution rule for several variables, and in multilinear algebra.

For a fixed nonnegative integer n, there is a unique _____ function for the n×n matrices over any commutative ring R. In particular, this function exists when R is the field of real or complex numbers.

a. 100-year flood
b. Determinant
c. 1921 recession
d. 130-30 fund

13. In finance, the _____s between two currencies specifies how much one currency is worth in terms of the other. It is the value of a foreign natione;s currency in terms of the home natione;s currency. For example an _____ of 102 Japanese yen to the United States dollar means that JPY 102 is worth the same as USD 1.
   a. ACCRA Cost of Living Index
   b. ACEA agreement
   c. Exchange rate
   d. Interbank market

14. In economics, endogenous growth theory or _____ was developed in the 1980s as a response to criticism of the neo-classical growth model.

In neo-classical growth models, the long-run rate of growth is exogenously determined by either assuming a savings rate (the Harrod-Domar model) or a rate of technical progress (Solow model.) However, the savings rate and rate of technological progress remain unexplained.

   a. Power theory of economics
   b. Dominant Design
   c. Bequest motive
   d. New growth theory

15. An _____, in economics, is the amount by which the real Gross domestic product exceeds potential GDP. The real GDP is also known as GDP 'adjusted for inflation', 'constant prices' GDP or 'constant dollar' GDP, because it measures the aggregate output in a country's income accounts in a given year, expressed in base-year prices. On the other hand, the potential GDP is the quantity of real GDP when a country's economy is at full-employment.
   a. ACEA agreement
   b. Inflationary gap
   c. AD-IA Model
   d. ACCRA Cost of Living Index

16. _____ is that which is owed; usually referencing assets owed, but the term can also cover moral obligations and other interactions not requiring money. In the case of assets, _____ is a means of using future purchasing power in the present before a summation has been earned. Some companies and corporations use _____ as a part of their overall corporate finance strategy.
   a. Non-performing loan
   b. Subordinated debt
   c. Participation loan
   d. Debt

17. In economics, _____ are the resources employed to produce goods and services. They facilitate production but do not become part of the product (as with raw materials) or significantly transformed by the production process (as with fuel used to power machinery.) To 19th century economists, the _____ were land (natural resources, gifts from nature), labor (the ability to work), and capital goods (human-made tools and equipment.)
   a. Long-run
   b. Factors of production
   c. Productive capacity
   d. Production function

18. A _____ is a set of exclusive rights granted by a state to an inventor or his assignee for a limited period of time in exchange for a disclosure of an invention.

The procedure for granting _____s, the requirements placed on the _____ee and the extent of the exclusive rights vary widely between countries according to national laws and international agreements. Typically, however, a _____ application must include one or more claims defining the invention which must be new, inventive, and useful or industrially applicable.

a. Celler-Kefauver Act
b. Patent
c. Generalized System of Preferences
d. Judgment summons

19. In microeconomics, _____ is quite simply the conversion of inputs into outputs. It is an economic process that uses resources to create a good or service that is suitable for exchange. This can include manufacturing, storing, shipping, and packaging.

a. Variability
b. Characteristic
c. Bucket shop
d. Production

20. The phrase _____, according to the Organization for Economic Co-operation and Development, refers to 'creative work undertaken on a systematic basis in order to increase the stock of knowledge, including knowledge of man, culture and society, and the use of this stock of knowledge to devise new applications [sic]'

New product design and development is more than often a crucial factor in the survival of a company. In an industry that is fast changing, firms must continually revise their design and range of products. This is necessary due to continuous technology change and development as well as other competitors and the changing preference of customers.

a. 1921 recession
b. 130-30 fund
c. 100-year flood
d. Research and development

21. In economics and especially in the theory of competition, _____ are obstacles in the path of a firm that make it difficult to enter a given market.

_____ are the source of a firm's pricing power - the ability of a firm to raise prices without losing all its customers.

The term refers to hindrances that an individual may face while trying to gain entrance into a profession or trade.

a. Net Book Agreement
b. Group boycott
c. Predatory pricing
d. Barriers to entry

Chapter 9. Global Economic Growth and Development

22. Examples of _____ include:

   - A beekeeper keeps the bees for their honey. A side effect or externality associated with his activity is the pollination of surrounding crops by the bees. The value generated by the pollination may be more important than the value of the harvested honey.

   - An individual planting an attractive garden in front of his house may provide benefits to others living in the area, and even financial benefits in the form of increased property values for all property owners.

   - An individual buying a product that is interconnected in a network (e.g., a video cellphone) will increase the usefulness of such phones to other people who have a video cellphone. When each new user of a product increases the value of the same product owned by others, the phenomenon is called a network externality or a network effect. Network externalities often have 'tipping points' where, suddenly, the product reaches general acceptance and near-universal usage, a phenomenon which can be seen in the near universal take-up of cellphones in some Scandinavian countries.

   - Knowledge spillover of inventions and information - once an invention (or most other forms of practical information) is discovered or made more easily accessible, others benefit by exploiting the invention or information. Copyright and intellectual property law are mechanisms to allow the inventor or creator to benefit from a temporary, state-protected monopoly in return for 'sharing' the information through publication or other means.

   a. Weighted average cost of carbon
   b. Negative externalities
   c. Travel cost analysis
   d. Positive externalities

23. _____ is a common concept in economics, and gives rise to derived concepts such as consumer debt. Generally _____ is defined by opposition to production. But the precise definition can vary because different schools of economists define production quite differently.
   a. Basis of futures
   b. Discrete choice
   c. British canal system
   d. Consumption

24. An _____ is an economy in which people, including businesses, can trade in goods and services with other people and businesses in the international community at large. This contrasts with a closed economy in which international trade cannot take place.

   The act of selling goods or services to a foreign country is called exporting.

   a. Attention work
   b. Indicative planning
   c. Information economy
   d. Open economy

25. The _____ is the central United States governmental body, established by the United States Constitution. The federal government has three branches: the legislative, executive, and judicial. Through a system of separation of powers and the system of 'checks and balances,' each of these branches has some authority to act on its own, some authority to regulate the other two branches, and has some of its own authority, in turn, regulated by the other branches.
   a. 100-year flood
   b. 130-30 fund
   c. 1921 recession
   d. Federal government of the United States

26. In economics, _____ is the total demand for final goods and services in the economy (Y) at a given time and price level. It is the amount of goods and services in the economy that will be purchased at all possible price levels. This is the demand for the gross domestic product of a country when inventory levels are static.
   a. Aggregate expenditure
   b. Aggregation problem
   c. Aggregate supply
   d. Aggregate demand

27. Economics:

   - _____, the desire to own something and the ability to pay for it
   - _____ curve, a graphic representation of a _____ schedule
   - _____ deposit, the money in checking accounts
   - _____ pull theory, the theory that inflation occurs when _____ for goods and services exceeds existing supplies
   - _____ schedule, a table that lists the quantity of a good a person will buy it each different price
   - _____ side economics, the school of economics at believes government spending and tax cuts open economy by raising _____

   a. Bon
   b. G20
   c. Demand
   d. Procter ' Gamble

28. A _____ is a tool used in industrial business-to-business procurement. It is a type of auction in which the role of the buyer and seller are reversed, with the primary objective to drive purchase prices downward. In an ordinary auction, buyers compete to obtain a good or service.
   a. Demand-side
   b. Vendor Managed Inventory
   c. Reverse Auction
   d. Demand side

29. The _____ consists of a number of economic theories which describe the nature of the firm, company including its existence, its behaviour, and its relationship with the market.

In simplified terms, the _____ aims to answer these questions:

1. Existence - why do firms emerge, why are not all transactions in the economy mediated over the market?
2. Boundaries - why the boundary between firms and the market is located exactly there? Which transactions are performed internally and which are negotiated on the market?
3. Organization - why are firms structured in such specific way? What is the interplay of formal and informal relationships?

Despite looking simple, these questions are not answered by the established economic theory, which usually views firms as given, and treats them as black boxes without any internal structure.

The First World War period saw a change of emphasis in economic theory away from industry-level analysis which mainly included analysing markets to analysis at the level of the firm, as it became increasingly clear that perfect competition was no longer an adequate model of how firms behaved. Economic theory till then had focussed on trying to understand markets alone and there had been little study on understanding why firms or organisations exist.

a. Neo-Ricardian school
b. Theory of the firm
c. Marginal revenue product
d. Technology gap

30. _____ refers to the stock of skills and knowledge embodied in the ability to perform labor so as to produce economic value. It is the skills and knowledge gained by a worker through education and experience. Many early economic theories refer to it simply as labor, one of three factors of production, and consider it to be a fungible resource -- homogeneous and easily interchangeable. Other conceptions of labor dispense with these assumptions.
a. Monetary inflation
b. Labour economics
c. Monopolistic competition
d. Human capital

31. _____ is a term used to describe any great reduction in a human population. It can be used to refer to longterm demographic trends, as in urban decay or rural _____, but it is also commonly employed to describe large reductions in population due to violence, disease, or other catastrophes.

History is replete with examples of large scale _____s.

a. Net reproduction rate
b. Malthusian equilibrium
c. Population momentum
d. Depopulation

32. _____ to the arrival of new individuals into a habitat or population. It is a biological concept and is important in population ecology, differentiated from emigration and migration.

_____ is a modern phenomenon.

a. Immigration
b. AD-IA Model
c. ACCRA Cost of Living Index
d. ACEA agreement

33. _____ is the change in population over time, and can be quantified as the change in the number of individuals in a population using 'per unit time' for measurement. The term _____ can technically refer to any species, but almost always refers to humans, and it is often used informally for the more specific demographic term _____ rate , and is often used to refer specifically to the growth of the population of the world.

Simple models of _____ include the Malthusian Growth Model and the logistic model.

a. Population dynamics
b. 130-30 fund
c. 100-year flood
d. Population growth

34. _____ is a branch of economics which deals with economic aspects of the development process in low-income countries. Its focus is not only on methods of promoting economic growth and structural change but also on improving the potential for the mass of the population, for example, through health and education and workplace conditions, whether through public or private channels. Thus, _____ involves the creation of theories and methods that aid in the determination of types of policies and practices and can be implemented at either the domestic or international level.
a. Singer-Prebisch thesis
b. Development economics
c. 100-year flood
d. 130-30 fund

Chapter 9. Global Economic Growth and Development

35. _____ according to Onuoha (2007) is the practice of starting new organizations or revitalizing mature organizations, particularly new businesses generally in response to identified opportunities. _____ is often a difficult undertaking, as a vast majority of new businesses fail. Entrepreneurial activities are substantially different depending on the type of organization that is being started.

a. ACCRA Cost of Living Index
b. Intrapreneurship
c. ACEA agreement
d. Entrepreneurship

36. A _____ is the exclusive authority to determine how a resource is used, whether that resource is owned by government or by individuals. All economic goods have a _____s attribute. This attribute has three broad components

1. The right to use the good
2. The right to earn income from the good
3. The right to transfer the good to others

The concept of _____s as used by economists and legal scholars are related but distinct. The distinction is largely seen in the economists' focus on the ability of an individual or collective to control the use of the good.

a. Greenfield agreement
b. Judgment summons
c. Nature of the Firm
d. Property right

37. The _____ is an international financial institution that provides financial and technical assistance to developing countries for development programs (e.g. bridges, roads, schools, etc.) with the stated goal of reducing poverty.

The _____ differs from the _____ Group, in that the _____ comprises only two institutions:

- International Bank for Reconstruction and Development (IBRD)
- International Development Association (IDA)

Whereas the latter incorporates these two in addition to three more:

- International Finance Corporation (IFC)
- Multilateral Investment Guarantee Agency (MIGA)
- International Centre for Settlement of Investment Disputes (ICSID)

John Maynard Keynes (right) represented the UK at the conference, and Harry Dexter White represented the US.

The _____ is one of two major financial institutions created as a result of the Bretton Woods Conference in 1944. The International Monetary Fund, a related but separate institution, is the second.

a. Demographic marketers
b. Dow Jones Industrial Average
c. Black-Scholes
d. World Bank

38. _____ is a set of properties and characteristics of the environment, either generalized or local, as they impinge on human beings and other organisms.

Chapter 9. Global Economic Growth and Development

_____ is a general term which can refer to varied characteristics that relate to the natural environment as well as the built environment, such as air and water purity or pollution, noise and the potential effects which such characteristics may have on physical and mental health caused by human activities.

In the USA the term is applied with a body of federal and state standards and regulations that are monitored by regulatory agencies.

- a. AD-IA Model
- b. ACCRA Cost of Living Index
- c. ACEA agreement
- d. Environmental quality

39. _____ is the shortage of common things such as food, clothing, shelter and safe drinking water, all of which determine the quality of life. It may also include the lack of access to opportunities such as education and employment which aid the escape from _____ and/or allow one to enjoy the respect of fellow citizens. According to Mollie Orshansky who developed the _____ measurements used by the U.S. government, 'to be poor is to be deprived of those goods and services and pleasures which others around us take for granted.' Ongoing debates over causes, effects and best ways to measure _____, directly influence the design and implementation of _____-reduction programs and are therefore relevant to the fields of public administration and international development.

- a. Liberal welfare reforms
- b. Secondary poverty
- c. Growth Elasticity of Poverty
- d. Poverty

40. _____ refers to confiscation of private property with the stated purpose of establishing social equality.

Unlike eminent domain, _____ takes place beyond the common law legal systems and refers to socially-motivated confiscations of any property rather than to taking away the real estate. Just compensation to owners is given.

- a. ACEA agreement
- b. ACCRA Cost of Living Index
- c. AD-IA Model
- d. Expropriation

41. _____s (economically referred to as land or raw materials) occur naturally within environments that exist relatively undisturbed by mankind, in a natural form. A _____'s is often characterized by amounts of biodiversity existent in various ecosystems.

Mining, petroleum extraction, fishing, hunting, and forestry are generally considered natural-resource industries.

- a. 130-30 fund
- b. Natural resource
- c. 1921 recession
- d. 100-year flood

42. In economics, the _____ of an industry is used as an indicator of the relative size of firms in relation to the industry as a whole. It is calculated as the sum of the percent market share of the top n industries. This may also assist in determining the market structure of the industry.

- a. De facto monopoly
- b. Price takers
- c. Rate-of-return regulation
- d. Concentration ratio

43. _____ is money accepted for exchange of goods in an economy. The prevalence of one money over another arises, usually, when a government designates through decrees that the government shall accept only particular notes and coins in payment for taxes. Typically, money of _____ consists of stamped coins and minted paper bills.
- a. Security thread
- b. Scripophily
- c. Totnes pound
- d. Currency

44. _____ is the act of taking an industry or assets into the public ownership of a national government or state. _____ usually refers to private assets, but may also mean assets owned by lower levels of government, such as municipalities, being state operated or owned by the state. The opposite of _____ is usually privatization or de-nationalisation, but may also be municipalization.
- a. Quasi-market
- b. Municipalization
- c. Ricardian equivalence
- d. Nationalization

45. A _____ is an expression that compares quantities relative to each other. The most common examples involve two quantities, but any number of quantities can be compared. _____s are represented mathematically by separating each quantity with a colon, for example the _____ 2:3, which is read as the _____ 'two to three'.
- a. 100-year flood
- b. 130-30 fund
- c. Ratio
- d. Y-intercept

46. The _____ is an international agreement administered by the World Trade Organization (WTO) that sets down minimum standards for many forms of intellectual property (IP) regulation. It was negotiated at the end of the Uruguay Round of the General Agreement on Tariffs and Trade (GATT) in 1994.

Specifically, TRIPS contains requirements that nations' laws must meet for: copyright rights, including the rights of performers, producers of sound recordings and broadcasting organizations; geographical indications, including appellations of origin; industrial designs; integrated circuit layout-designs; patents; monopolies for the developers of new plant varieties; trademarks; trade dress; and undisclosed or confidential information.

- a. ACEA agreement
- b. Agreement on Trade Related Aspects of Intellectual Property Rights
- c. ACCRA Cost of Living Index
- d. AD-IA Model

47. The notion of _____ is found in the writings of Mikhail Bakunin, Friedrich Nietzsche, and in Werner Sombart's Krieg und Kapitalismus (War and Capitalism) (1913, p. 207), where he wrote: 'again out of destruction a new spirit of creativity arises'. In Capitalism, Socialism and Democracy, the Austrian economist Joseph Schumpeter popularized and used the term to describe the process of transformation that accompanies radical innovation.
- a. 130-30 fund
- b. 100-year flood
- c. 1921 recession
- d. Creative destruction

48. _____ are legal property rights over creations of the mind, both artistic and commercial, and the corresponding fields of law. Under _____ law, owners are granted certain exclusive rights to a variety of intangible assets, such as musical, literary, and artistic works; ideas, discoveries and inventions; and words, phrases, symbols, and designs. Common types of _____ include copyrights, trademarks, patents, industrial design rights and trade secrets.
- a. Independent contractor
- b. Intellectual Property
- c. Expedited Funds Availability Act
- d. Ease of Doing Business Index

Chapter 9. Global Economic Growth and Development

49. _____ is the economic policy of restraining trade between states, through methods such as tariffs on imported goods, restrictive quotas, and a variety of other restrictive government regulations designed to discourage imports, and prevent foreign take-over of local markets and companies. This policy is closely aligned with anti-globalization, and contrasts with free trade, where government barriers to trade are kept to a minimum. The term is mostly used in the context of economics, where _____ refers to policies or doctrines which 'protect' businesses and workers within a country by restricting or regulating trade with foreign nations.
- a. Planned economy
- b. Digital economy
- c. Planned liberalism
- d. Protectionism

50. _____ is exchange of capital, goods, and services across international borders or territories. In most countries, it represents a significant share of gross domestic product (GDP.) While _____ has been present throughout much of history, its economic, social, and political importance has been on the rise in recent centuries.
- a. International trade
- b. Intra-industry trade
- c. Import license
- d. Incoterms

51. A variety of measures of _____ and output are used in economics to estimate total economic activity in a country or region, including gross domestic product (GDP), gross national product (GNP), and net _____

There are three main ways of calculating these numbers; the output approach, the income approach and the expenditure approach. In theory, the three must yield the same, because total expenditures on goods and services must equal the total income paid to the producers (Gnational income), and that must also equal the total value of the output of goods and services (GNP.)
- a. Bureau of Labor Statistics
- b. Purchasing power parity
- c. Gross national product
- d. National Income

52. _____ is a misspelled phrase from Latin 'pro capite' phrase meaning per head with pro meaning 'per' or 'for each' and capite meaning 'head.' Both words together equate to the phrase 'for each head.'

It is usually used in the field of statistics to indicate the average per person for any given concern, such as income, crime rate, etc.

It is also used in wills to indicate that each of the named beneficiaries should receive, by devise or bequest, equal shares of the estate. This is in contrast to a per stirpes division, in which each branch of the inheriting family inherits an equal share of the estate.
- a. Semiparametric regression
- b. Dynamic Bayesian network
- c. Posterior probability
- d. Per capita

53. _____ means how much each individual receives, in monetary terms, of the yearly income generated in the country. This is what each citizen is to receive if the yearly national income is divided equally among everyone. _____ is usually reported in units of currency per year.
- a. Windfall gain
- b. Per capita income
- c. Family Income
- d. Haig-Simons income

54. _____ is the income of individuals or nations after adjusting for inflation. It is calculated by subtracting inflation from the nominal income. Real variables, such as _____, real GDP, and real interest rate are variables that are measured in physical units, while nominal variables such as nominal income, nominal GDP, and nominal interest rate are measured in monetary units.
- a. Lerman ratio
- b. Pay grade
- c. Windfall gain
- d. Real income

Chapter 10. Real GDP and the Price Level in the Long Run

1. In economics, _____ is the total supply of goods and services produced by a national economy during a specific time period. It is the total amount of goods and services in the economy available at all possible price levels.
   - a. Aggregate demand
   - b. Aggregate expenditure
   - c. Aggregation problem
   - d. Aggregate supply

2. In economics, _____ is a sustained decrease in the general price level of goods and services. _____ occurs when the annual inflation rate falls below zero percent, resulting in an increase in the real value of money -- a negative inflation rate. This should not be confused with disinflation, a slow-down in the inflation rate (i.e. when the inflation decreases, but still remains positive.)
   - a. Labour economics
   - b. Law of supply
   - c. Deflation
   - d. Financial crises

3. In microeconomics, _____ is quite simply the conversion of inputs into outputs. It is an economic process that uses resources to create a good or service that is suitable for exchange. This can include manufacturing, storing, shipping, and packaging.
   - a. Characteristic
   - b. Bucket shop
   - c. Production
   - d. Variability

4. In economic models, the _____ time frame assumes no fixed factors of production. Firms can enter or leave the marketplace, and the cost (and availability) of land, labor, raw materials, and capital goods can be assumed to vary. In contrast, in the short-run time frame, certain factors are assumed to be fixed, because there is not sufficient time for them to change.
   - a. Product Pipeline
   - b. Diseconomies of scale
   - c. Short-run
   - d. Long-run

5. _____s is the social science that studies the production, distribution, and consumption of goods and services. The term _____s comes from the Ancient Greek οἰκονομῐ́α from οἶκος (oikos, 'house') + νόμος (nomos, 'custom' or 'law'), hence 'rules of the house(hold)'. Current _____ models developed out of the broader field of political economy in the late 19th century, owing to a desire to use an empirical approach more akin to the physical sciences.
   - a. Inflation
   - b. Energy economics
   - c. Economic
   - d. Opportunity cost

6. _____ is the increase in the amount of the goods and services produced by an economy over time. It is conventionally measured as the percent rate of increase in real gross domestic product, or real GDP. Growth is usually calculated in real terms, i.e. inflation-adjusted terms, in order to net out the effect of inflation on the price of the goods and services produced.
   - a. ACCRA Cost of Living Index
   - b. AD-IA Model
   - c. ACEA agreement
   - d. Economic growth

7. In Marxian economics, _____ originally referred to the means of production. Individuals, organizations and governments use _____ in the production of other goods or commodities. _____ include factories, machinery, tools, equipment, and various buildings which are used to produce other products for consumption.
   - a. Modigliani-Miller theorem
   - b. Capital goods
   - c. Capital formation
   - d. Cost of capital

8. A _____ is an object whose consumption increases the utility of the consumer, for which the quantity demanded exceeds the quantity supplied at zero price. _____s are usually modeled as having diminishing marginal utility. The first individual purchase has high utility; the second has less.
   a. Luxury good
   b. Good
   c. Search good
   d. Positional goods

9. _____ is a type of private equity investment, most often a minority investment, in relatively mature companies that are looking for capital to expand or restructure operations, enter new markets or finance a significant acquisition without a change of control of the business.

Companies that seek _____, will often do so in order to finance a transformational event in their lifecycle. These companies are likely to be more mature than venture capital funded companies, able to generate revenue and operating profits but unable to generate sufficient cash to fund major expansions, acquisitions or other investments.

   a. Growth capital
   b. Seed money
   c. Mezzanine capital
   d. Venture capital fund

10. _____ is a policy or ideology of violence intended to intimidate or cause terror for the purpose of 'exerting pressure on decision making by state bodies.' The term 'terror' is largely used to indicate clandestine, low-intensity violence that targets civilians and generates public fear. Thus 'terror' is distinct from asymmetric warfare, and violates the concept of a common law of war in which civilian life is regarded. The term '-ism' is used to indicate an ideology --typically one that claims its attacks are in the domain of a 'just war' concept, though most condemn such as crimes against humanity.
   a. 1921 recession
   b. 130-30 fund
   c. 100-year flood
   d. Terrorism

11. The _____ or gross domestic income (GDI), a basic measure of an economy's economic performance, is the market value of all final goods and services produced within the borders of a nation in a year. _____ can be defined in three ways, all of which are conceptually identical. First, it is equal to the total expenditures for all final goods and services produced within the country in a stipulated period of time (usually a 365-day year.)
   a. Gross domestic product
   b. Co-operative economics
   c. Public economics
   d. Market failure

12. _____ or government expenditure is classified by economists into three main types. Government purchases of goods and services for current use are classed as government consumption. Government purchases of goods and services intended to create future benefits, such as infrastructure investment or research spending, are classed as government investment.
   a. 130-30 fund
   b. 1921 recession
   c. 100-year flood
   d. Government spending

13. An _____, in economics, is the amount by which the real Gross domestic product exceeds potential GDP. The real GDP is also known as GDP 'adjusted for inflation', 'constant prices' GDP or 'constant dollar' GDP, because it measures the aggregate output in a country's income accounts in a given year, expressed in base-year prices. On the other hand, the potential GDP is the quantity of real GDP when a country's economy is at full-employment.

Chapter 10. Real GDP and the Price Level in the Long Run

a. ACEA agreement
b. AD-IA Model
c. Inflationary gap
d. ACCRA Cost of Living Index

14. _____ is a common concept in economics, and gives rise to derived concepts such as consumer debt. Generally _____ is defined by opposition to production. But the precise definition can vary because different schools of economists define production quite differently.
   a. Discrete choice
   b. Basis of futures
   c. British canal system
   d. Consumption

15. In economics, _____ is the total demand for final goods and services in the economy (Y) at a given time and price level. It is the amount of goods and services in the economy that will be purchased at all possible price levels. This is the demand for the gross domestic product of a country when inventory levels are static.
   a. Aggregation problem
   b. Aggregate supply
   c. Aggregate expenditure
   d. Aggregate demand

16. Economics:

   - _____, the desire to own something and the ability to pay for it
   - _____ curve, a graphic representation of a _____ schedule
   - _____ deposit, the money in checking accounts
   - _____ pull theory, the theory that inflation occurs when _____ for goods and services exceeds existing supplies
   - _____ schedule, a table that lists the quantity of a good a person will buy it each different price
   - _____ side economics, the school of economics at believes government spending and tax cuts open economy by raising _____

   a. G20
   b. Bon
   c. Procter ' Gamble
   d. Demand

17. In economics, the _____ can be defined as the graph depicting the relationship between the price of a certain commodity, and the amount of it that consumers are willing and able to purchase at that given price. It is a graphic representation of a demand schedule. The _____ for all consumers together follows from the _____ of every individual consumer: the individual demands at each price are added together.
   a. Wage curve
   b. Lorenz curve
   c. Kuznets curve
   d. Demand curve

18. _____ is a fee paid on borrowed assets. It is the price paid for the use of borrowed money, or, money earned by deposited funds. Assets that are sometimes lent with _____ include money, shares, consumer goods through hire purchase, major assets such as aircraft, and even entire factories in finance lease arrangements.
   a. Interest
   b. Asset protection
   c. Insolvency
   d. Internal debt

19. An _____ is an economy in which people, including businesses, can trade in goods and services with other people and businesses in the international community at large. This contrasts with a closed economy in which international trade cannot take place.

Chapter 10. Real GDP and the Price Level in the Long Run

The act of selling goods or services to a foreign country is called exporting.

a. Information economy
c. Indicative planning
b. Attention work
d. Open economy

20. _____ in economics and business is the result of an exchange and from that trade we assign a numerical monetary value to a good, service or asset. If Alice trades Bob 4 apples for an orange, the _____ of an orange is 4 apples. Inversely, the _____ of an apple is 1/4 oranges.

a. Price ceiling
c. Price
b. Price dispersion
d. Lerner Index

21. A _____ is a hypothetical measure of overall prices for some set of goods and services, in a given region during a given interval, normalized relative to some base set. Typically, a _____ is approximated with a price index.

The classical dichotomy is the assumption that there is a relatively clean distinction between overall increases or decreases in prices and underlying, e;reale; economic variables.

a. Relative income hypothesis
c. Federal Reserve districts
b. Price level
d. Foreign portfolio investment

22. The _____ is the Cabinet department of the United States government concerned with promoting economic growth. It was originally created as the _____ and Labor on February 14, 1903. It was subsequently renamed to the Department of Commerce on March 4, 1913, and its bureaus and agencies specializing in labor were transferred to the new Department of Labor.

a. ACEA agreement
c. ACCRA Cost of Living Index
b. United States Department of Commerce
d. AD-IA Model

23. The _____ is an economic term, referring to an increase in spending that accompanies an increase or perceived increase in wealth.

The effect would cause changes in the amounts and composition of consumer consumption caused by changes in consumer wealth. People should spend more when one of two things is true: when people actually are richer (by objective measurement, for example, a bonus or a pay raise at work, which would be an income effect), or when people perceive themselves to be 'richer' (for example, the assessed value of their home increases, or a stock they own has gone up in price recently.)

a. Wealth effect
c. Wealth condensation
b. 130-30 fund
d. 100-year flood

24. In economics, the _____ or spending multiplier is the idea that an initial amount of spending (usually by the government) leads to increased consumption spending and so results in an increase in national income greater than the initial amount of spending. In other words, an initial change in aggregate demand causes a change in aggregate output for the economy that is a multiple of the initial change.

The existence of a _____ was initially proposed by Ralph George Hawtrey in 1931.

Chapter 10. Real GDP and the Price Level in the Long Run

a. Transactions demand
b. Keynesian cross
c. Multiplier effect
d. Magical triangle

25. In economics, the term _____ of income or _____ refers to a simple economic model which describes the reciprocal circulation of income between producers and consumers. In the _____ model, the inter-dependent entities of producer and consumer are referred to as 'firms' and 'households' respectively and provide each other with factors in order to facilitate the flow of income. Firms provide consumers with goods and services in exchange for consumer expenditure and 'factors of production' from households.
   a. Circular flow
   b. 1921 recession
   c. 130-30 fund
   d. 100-year flood

26. In economics, the term _____ or circular flow refers to a simple economic model which describes the reciprocal circulation of income between producers and consumers. In the circular flow model, the inter-dependent entities of producer and consumer are referred to as 'firms' and 'households' respectively and provide each other with factors in order to facilitate the flow of income. Firms provide consumers with goods and services in exchange for consumer expenditure and 'factors of production' from households.
   a. 130-30 fund
   b. 1921 recession
   c. 100-year flood
   d. Circular flow of income

27. In economics, an _____ is any good or commodity, transported from one country to another country in a legitimate fashion, typically for use in trade. _____ goods or services are provided to foreign consumers by domestic producers. _____ is an important part of international trade.
   a. ACCRA Cost of Living Index
   b. AD-IA Model
   c. ACEA agreement
   d. Export

28. _____ and Keynesian Theory) is a macroeconomic theory based on the ideas of 20th-century British economist John Maynard Keynes. _____ argues that private sector decisions sometimes lead to inefficient macroeconomic outcomes and therefore advocates active policy responses by the public sector, including monetary policy actions by the central bank and fiscal policy actions by the government to stabilize output over the business cycle.

The theories forming the basis of _____ were first presented in The General Theory of Employment, Interest and Money, published in 1936.

   a. Rational choice theory
   b. Recession
   c. Keynesian economics
   d. Gross domestic product

29. In algebra, a _____ is a function depending on n that associates a scalar, det(A), to an n×n square matrix A. The fundamental geometric meaning of a _____ is a scale factor for measure when A is regarded as a linear transformation. _____s are important both in calculus, where they enter the substitution rule for several variables, and in multilinear algebra.

For a fixed nonnegative integer n, there is a unique _____ function for the n×n matrices over any commutative ring R. In particular, this function exists when R is the field of real or complex numbers.

a. 100-year flood
c. 1921 recession
b. 130-30 fund
d. Determinant

30. _____, Jr. (January 29, 1843 - September 14, 1901) was the 25th President of the United States, and the last veteran of the American Civil War to be elected.

By the 1880s, McKinley was a national Republican leader; his signature issue was high tariffs on imports as a formula for prosperity, as typified by his McKinley Tariff of 1890.

a. Adolf Hitler
c. Adolph Fischer
b. William McKinley
d. Adam Smith

31. In economics, _____ is a rise in the general level of prices of goods and services in an economy over a period of time. When the general price level rises, each unit of currency buys fewer goods and services; consequently, _____ is also a decline in the real value of money--a loss of purchasing power in the medium of exchange which is also the monetary unit of account in the economy. A chief measure of general price-level _____ is the general _____ rate, which is the percentage change in a general price index (normally the Consumer Price Index) over time.

a. Energy economics
c. Economic
b. Opportunity cost
d. Inflation

32. _____ , as defined by the _____ Association of America (Information technologyAA), is 'the study, design, development, implementation, support or management of computer-based information systems, particularly software applications and computer hardware.' _____ deals with the use of electronic computers and computer software to convert, store, protect, process, transmit, and securely retrieve information.

Today, the term _____ has ballooned to encompass many aspects of computing and technology, and the term has become very recognizable. The _____ umbrella can be quite large, covering many fields.

a. AD-IA Model
c. ACEA agreement
b. Information technology
d. ACCRA Cost of Living Index

33. In economics, the _____ is a historical inverse relation between the rate of unemployment and the rate of inflation in an economy. Stated simply, the lower the unemployment in an economy, the higher the rate of increase in nominal wages in the economy. Rate of Change of Wages against Unemployment, United Kingdom 1913-1948 from Phillips (1958)

William Phillips, a New Zealand born economist, wrote a paper in 1958 titled The Relationship between Unemployment and the Rate of Change of Money Wages in the United Kingdom 1861-1957, which was published in the quarterly journal Economica.

a. Wage curve
c. Demand curve
b. Kuznets curve
d. Phillips curve

34. Necessary _____s:

If x is a necessary _____ of y, then the presence of y necessarily implies the presence of x. The presence of x, however, does not imply that y will occur.

Sufficient _____s:

If x is a sufficient _____ of y, then the presence of x necessarily implies the presence of y.

a. Deductive logic
b. Global justice
c. Materialism
d. Cause

35. _____ is a school of macroeconomic thought that argues that economic growth can be most effectively created using incentives for people to produce (supply) goods and services, such as adjusting income tax and capital gains tax rates, and by allowing greater flexibility by reducing regulation. Consumers will then benefit from a greater supply of goods and services at lower prices.

The term _____ was coined by journalist Jude Wanniski in 1975, and popularized the ideas of economists Robert Mundell and Arthur Laffer.

a. Flow to Equity-Approach
b. Kibbutz volunteers
c. Categorical grants
d. Supply-side economics

36. In economics, the concept of the _____ refers to the decision-making time frame of a firm in which at least one factor of production is fixed. Costs which are fixed in the _____ have no impact on a firms decisions. For example a firm can raise output by increasing the amount of labour through overtime.

a. Marginal product
b. Hicks-neutral technical change
c. Productivity world
d. Short-run

37. The Demand side is a term used in economics to refer to a number of things:

- The demand element of a supply and demand partial equilibrium diagram, in microeconomics
- The aggregate demand in an economy, in macroeconomics
- Economic policy actions which are designed to affect aggregate demand.
- _____ learning referring to the incentive to learn how to use and modify free software as opposed to buying conventional software.

The term is also used broadly to distinguish supply-side economics from other schools, for instance Keynesian economics.

a. Demand-side
b. CPFR
c. Reverse auction
d. Delayed differentiation

38. In economics, the _____ is a measure of inflation, the rate of increase of a price index (for example, a consumer price index.)It is the percentage rate of change in price level over time. The rate of decrease in the purchasing power of money is approximately equal.

It's used to calculate the real interest rate, as well as real increases in wages, and official measurements of this rate act as input variables to COLA adjustments and Inflation derivatives prices.

a. Interest rate option
b. Edgeworth paradox
c. Equity value
d. Inflation rate

39. The _____ is a concept in green economics and welfare economics that has been suggested to replace gross domestic product (GDP) as a metric of economic growth.

_____ is an attempt to measure whether a country's growth, increased production of goods, and expanding services have actually resulted in the improvement of the welfare (or well-being) of the people in the country. _____ advocates claim that it can more reliably measure economic progress, as it distinguishes between worthwhile growth and uneconomic growth.

a. Physical quality-of-life index
b. Forgotten man
c. Human Poverty Index
d. Genuine Progress Indicator

Chapter 11. Classical and Keynesian Macro Analyses

1. _____ was a survey conducted by the U.S. Department of Justice to gauge the prevalence of alcohol and illegal drug use among prior arrestees. It was a reformulation of the prior Drug Use Forecasting (DUF) program, focused on five drugs in particular: cocaine, marijuana, methamphetamine, opiates, and PCP.

Participants were randomly selected from arrest records in major metropolitan areas; because no personally identifying information is taken from each record chosen, the resulting data can be correlated to arrest rates, but not to the total population of persons charged.

   a. Arrestee Drug Abuse Monitoring
   b. ACEA agreement
   c. AD-IA Model
   d. ACCRA Cost of Living Index

2. The _____ or gross domestic income (GDI), a basic measure of an economy's economic performance, is the market value of all final goods and services produced within the borders of a nation in a year. _____ can be defined in three ways, all of which are conceptually identical. First, it is equal to the total expenditures for all final goods and services produced within the country in a stipulated period of time (usually a 365-day year.)

   a. Co-operative economics
   b. Market failure
   c. Gross domestic product
   d. Public economics

3. _____, 1st Baron Keynes was a renowned economist from Britain whose many ideas on economic and political theories as well as on many governments' monetary policies influenced America. He advocated a government that played an active role in the lives of people regarding business, economy, etc. In this role, the government would use fiscal measures to reduce the consequences of recessions, economic depressions and booms.

   a. Adolf Hitler
   b. Adam Smith
   c. John Maynard Keynes
   d. Adolph Fischer

4. An _____, in economics, is the amount by which the real Gross domestic product exceeds potential GDP. The real GDP is also known as GDP 'adjusted for inflation', 'constant prices' GDP or 'constant dollar' GDP, because it measures the aggregate output in a country's income accounts in a given year, expressed in base-year prices. On the other hand, the potential GDP is the quantity of real GDP when a country's economy is at full-employment.

   a. ACEA agreement
   b. AD-IA Model
   c. Inflationary gap
   d. ACCRA Cost of Living Index

5. _____ was a Scottish moral philosopher and a pioneer of political economy. One of the key figures of the Scottish Enlightenment, Smith is the author of The Theory of Moral Sentiments and An Inquiry into the Nature and Causes of the Wealth of Nations. The latter, usually abbreviated as The Wealth of Nations, is considered his magnum opus and the first modern work of economics.

   a. Alan Greenspan
   b. Adolph Fischer
   c. Adolf Hitler
   d. Adam Smith

6. _____ is that which is owed; usually referencing assets owed, but the term can also cover moral obligations and other interactions not requiring money. In the case of assets, _____ is a means of using future purchasing power in the present before a summation has been earned. Some companies and corporations use _____ as a part of their overall corporate finance strategy.

   a. Participation loan
   b. Debt
   c. Non-performing loan
   d. Subordinated debt

Chapter 11. Classical and Keynesian Macro Analyses

7. _____s is the social science that studies the production, distribution, and consumption of goods and services. The term _____s comes from the Ancient Greek οἰκονομία from οἶκος (oikos, 'house') + νόμος (nomos, 'custom' or 'law'), hence 'rules of the house(hold)'. Current _____ models developed out of the broader field of political economy in the late 19th century, owing to a desire to use an empirical approach more akin to the physical sciences.

a. Inflation
b. Economic
c. Energy economics
d. Opportunity cost

8. A _____ refers to any type debt instrument, such as a loan, bond, mortgage that does not have a fixed rate of interest over the life of the instrument. Such debt typically uses an index or other base rate for establishing the interest rate for each relevant period. One of the most common rates to use as the basis for applying interest rates is the London Inter-bank Offered Rate, or LIBOR

a. Bankruptcy remote
b. Floating interest rate
c. Standard of deferred payment
d. Style investing

9. _____ is a fee paid on borrowed assets. It is the price paid for the use of borrowed money, or, money earned by deposited funds. Assets that are sometimes lent with _____ include money, shares, consumer goods through hire purchase, major assets such as aircraft, and even entire factories in finance lease arrangements.

a. Asset protection
b. Internal debt
c. Interest
d. Insolvency

10. In economics, _____ refers to the tendency of people to think of currency in nominal, rather than real, terms. In other words, the numerical/face value (nominal value) of money is mistaken for its purchasing power (real value.) This is a fallacy as modern fiat currencies have no inherent value and their real value is derived from their ability to be exchanged for goods and used for payment of taxes.

a. Swedish rounding
b. Nominal money
c. Fungibility
d. Money illusion

11. In economics, economic equilibrium is simply a state of the world where economic forces are balanced and in the absence of external influences the (equilibrium) values of economic variables will not change. It is the point at which quantity demanded and quantity supplied are equal. _____, for example, refers to a condition where a market price is established through competition such that the amount of goods or services sought by buyers is equal to the amount of goods or services produced by sellers.

a. Two-sided markets
b. Product-Market Growth Matrix
c. Contestable market
d. Market Equilibrium

12. _____ in economics and business is the result of an exchange and from that trade we assign a numerical monetary value to a good, service or asset. If Alice trades Bob 4 apples for an orange, the _____ of an orange is 4 apples. Inversely, the _____ of an apple is 1/4 oranges.

a. Lerner Index
b. Price ceiling
c. Price
d. Price dispersion

13. _____ and Keynesian Theory) is a macroeconomic theory based on the ideas of 20th-century British economist John Maynard Keynes. _____ argues that private sector decisions sometimes lead to inefficient macroeconomic outcomes and therefore advocates active policy responses by the public sector, including monetary policy actions by the central bank and fiscal policy actions by the government to stabilize output over the business cycle.

Chapter 11. Classical and Keynesian Macro Analyses 99

The theories forming the basis of _____ were first presented in The General Theory of Employment, Interest and Money, published in 1936.

a. Gross domestic product
b. Recession
c. Rational choice theory
d. Keynesian economics

14. _____ is a term that encompasses the notion of individuals and firms striving for a greater share of a market to sell or buy goods and services. Merriam-Webster defines competition in business as 'the effort of two or more parties acting independently to secure the business of a third party by offering the most favorable terms.' It was described by Adam Smith in The Wealth of Nations (1776) and later economists as allocating productive resources to their most highly-valued uses. and encouraging efficiency.

a. Cut-throat competition
b. Path dependence
c. Moral victory
d. Competition in economics

15. In a company, _____ is the sum of all financial records of salaries, wages, bonuses and deductions.

A paycheck, is traditionally a paper document issued by an employer to pay an employee for services rendered. While most commonly used in the United States, recently the physical paycheck has been increasingly replaced by electronic direct deposit to bank accounts.

a. Total Expense Ratio
b. Tax expense
c. 100-year flood
d. Payroll

16. In economics, _____ is the total supply of goods and services produced by a national economy during a specific time period. It is the total amount of goods and services in the economy available at all possible price levels.

a. Aggregate supply
b. Aggregation problem
c. Aggregate expenditure
d. Aggregate demand

17. A _____ is a hypothetical measure of overall prices for some set of goods and services, in a given region during a given interval, normalized relative to some base set. Typically, a _____ is approximated with a price index.

The classical dichotomy is the assumption that there is a relatively clean distinction between overall increases or decreases in prices and underlying, e;reale; economic variables.

a. Price level
b. Relative income hypothesis
c. Federal Reserve districts
d. Foreign portfolio investment

18. In economics, the _____ or spending multiplier is the idea that an initial amount of spending (usually by the government) leads to increased consumption spending and so results in an increase in national income greater than the initial amount of spending. In other words, an initial change in aggregate demand causes a change in aggregate output for the economy that is a multiple of the initial change.

The existence of a _____ was initially proposed by Ralph George Hawtrey in 1931.

a. Magical triangle
b. Keynesian cross
c. Transactions demand
d. Multiplier effect

19. In economics, _____ is the total demand for final goods and services in the economy (Y) at a given time and price level. It is the amount of goods and services in the economy that will be purchased at all possible price levels. This is the demand for the gross domestic product of a country when inventory levels are static.
   a. Aggregate expenditure
   b. Aggregate supply
   c. Aggregation problem
   d. Aggregate demand

20. Economics:

   - _____,the desire to own something and the ability to pay for it
   - _____ curve,a graphic representation of a _____ schedule
   - _____ deposit, the money in checking accounts
   - _____ pull theory,the theory that inflation occurs when _____ for goods and services exceeds existing supplies
   - _____ schedule,a table that lists the quantity of a good a person will buy it each different price
   - _____ side economics,the school of economics at believes government spending and tax cuts open economy by raising _____

   a. G20
   b. Bon
   c. Procter ' Gamble
   d. Demand

21. In economics, the concept of the _____ refers to the decision-making time frame of a firm in which at least one factor of production is fixed. Costs which are fixed in the _____ have no impact on a firms decisions. For example a firm can raise output by increasing the amount of labour through overtime.
   a. Hicks-neutral technical change
   b. Marginal product
   c. Productivity world
   d. Short-run

22. The _____ was a worldwide economic downturn starting in most places in 1929 and ending at different times in the 1930s or early 1940s for different countries. It was the largest and most important economic depression in the 20th century, and is used in the 21st century as an example of how far the world's economy can fall. The _____ originated in the United States; historians most often use as a starting date the stock market crash on October 29, 1929, known as Black Tuesday.
   a. The Great Depression
   b. Causes of the Great Depression
   c. British Empire Economic Conference
   d. Great Depression

23. _____ was a global military conflict which involved a majority of the world's nations, including all of the great powers, organized into two opposing military alliances: the Allies and the Axis. The war involved the mobilization of over 100 million military personnel, making it the most widespread war in history. In a state of 'total war', the major participants placed their entire economic, industrial, and scientific capabilities at the service of the war effort, erasing the distinction between civilian and military resources.
   a. World War II
   b. 100-year flood
   c. 130-30 fund
   d. 1921 recession

Chapter 11. Classical and Keynesian Macro Analyses

24. In economic models, the _____ time frame assumes no fixed factors of production. Firms can enter or leave the marketplace, and the cost (and availability) of land, labor, raw materials, and capital goods can be assumed to vary. In contrast, in the short-run time frame, certain factors are assumed to be fixed, because there is not sufficient time for them to change.
    a. Short-run
    b. Diseconomies of scale
    c. Product Pipeline
    d. Long-run

25. _____, or a _____ is the concept of a resulting effect (cf. cause and effect, arising from another action. In general terms, it is used to indicate that all human actions, particularly crime and sin, have profound effects.
    a. Variability
    b. Consequence
    c. Production
    d. Russian financial crisis

26. In economics, a _____ is a sudden event that increases or decreases demand for goods or services temporarily. A positive _____ increases demand and a negative _____ decreases demand. Prices of goods and services are affected in both cases.
    a. Secular basis
    b. War economy
    c. Demand Shock
    d. Dishoarding

27. In algebra, a _____ is a function depending on n that associates a scalar, det(A), to an n×n square matrix A. The fundamental geometric meaning of a _____ is a scale factor for measure when A is regarded as a linear transformation. _____s are important both in calculus, where they enter the substitution rule for several variables, and in multilinear algebra.

    For a fixed nonnegative integer n, there is a unique _____ function for the n×n matrices over any commutative ring R. In particular, this function exists when R is the field of real or complex numbers.

    a. Determinant
    b. 100-year flood
    c. 1921 recession
    d. 130-30 fund

28. A _____ is an event that suddenly changes the price of a commodity or service. It may be caused by a sudden increase or decrease in the supply of a particular good. This sudden change affects the equilibrium price.
    a. Marginal propensity to consume
    b. Robertson lag
    c. Potential output
    d. Supply Shock

29. In economics, a _____ is a general slowdown in economic activity over a sustained period of time, or a business cycle contraction. During _____s, many macroeconomic indicators vary in a similar way. Production as measured by Gross Domestic Product (GDP), employment, investment spending, capacity utilization, household incomes and business profits all fall during _____s.
    a. Fixed exchange rate
    b. New Trade Theory
    c. Recession
    d. General equilibrium theory

30. The GDP gap or the output gap is the difference between potential GDP and actual GDP or actual output. The calculation for the output gap is Y-Y* where Y* is potential output and Y is actual output. If this calculation yields a positive number it is called an expansionary gap and indicates an economy in expansion; if the calculation yields a negative number it is called a _____ and indicates an economy in recession.

a. 100-year flood
b. 130-30 fund
c. 1921 recession
d. Recessionary gap

31. _____ is a policy or ideology of violence intended to intimidate or cause terror for the purpose of 'exerting pressure on decision making by state bodies.' The term 'terror' is largely used to indicate clandestine, low-intensity violence that targets civilians and generates public fear. Thus 'terror' is distinct from asymmetric warfare, and violates the concept of a common law of war in which civilian life is regarded. The term '-ism' is used to indicate an ideology --typically one that claims its attacks are in the domain of a 'just war' concept, though most condemn such as crimes against humanity.
   a. 1921 recession
   b. 130-30 fund
   c. 100-year flood
   d. Terrorism

32. _____ or government expenditure is classified by economists into three main types. Government purchases of goods and services for current use are classed as government consumption. Government purchases of goods and services intended to create future benefits, such as infrastructure investment or research spending, are classed as government investment.
   a. Government spending
   b. 130-30 fund
   c. 1921 recession
   d. 100-year flood

33. _____ is a common concept in economics, and gives rise to derived concepts such as consumer debt. Generally _____ is defined by opposition to production. But the precise definition can vary because different schools of economists define production quite differently.
   a. British canal system
   b. Consumption
   c. Discrete choice
   d. Basis of futures

34. _____ is a type of inflation caused by substantial increases in the cost of important goods or services where no suitable alternative is available. A situation that has been often cited of this was the oil crisis of the 1970s, which some economists see as a major cause of the inflation experienced in the Western world in that decade. It is argued that this inflation resulted from increases in the cost of petroleum imposed by the member states of OPEC.
   a. Headline inflation
   b. Symmetrical inflation target
   c. Cost-push inflation
   d. Stealth inflation

35. _____ arises when aggregate demand in an economy outpaces aggregate supply. It involves inflation rising as real gross domestic product rises and unemployment falls, as the economy moves along the Phillips curve. This is commonly described as 'too much money chasing too few goods'.
   a. Hicksian demand function
   b. Precautionary demand
   c. Kinked demand
   d. Demand-pull inflation

36. In economics, the _____ is a historical inverse relation between the rate of unemployment and the rate of inflation in an economy. Stated simply, the lower the unemployment in an economy, the higher the rate of increase in nominal wages in the economy. Rate of Change of Wages against Unemployment, United Kingdom 1913-1948 from Phillips (1958)

William Phillips, a New Zealand born economist, wrote a paper in 1958 titled The Relationship between Unemployment and the Rate of Change of Money Wages in the United Kingdom 1861-1957, which was published in the quarterly journal Economica.

a. Demand curve
c. Wage curve
b. Kuznets curve
d. Phillips curve

37. In economics, _____ is a rise in the general level of prices of goods and services in an economy over a period of time. When the general price level rises, each unit of currency buys fewer goods and services; consequently, _____ is also a decline in the real value of money--a loss of purchasing power in the medium of exchange which is also the monetary unit of account in the economy. A chief measure of general price-level _____ is the general _____ rate, which is the percentage change in a general price index (normally the Consumer Price Index) over time.
   a. Energy economics
   c. Economic
   b. Opportunity cost
   d. Inflation

38. The Organization of the Petroleum Exporting Countries is a cartel of twelve countries made up of Algeria, Angola, Ecuador, Iran, Iraq, Kuwait, Libya, Nigeria, Qatar, Saudi Arabia, the United Arab Emirates, and Venezuela. The cartel has maintained its headquarters in Vienna since 1965, and hosts regular meetings among the oil ministers of its Member Countries. Indonesia withdrew its membership in _____ in 2008 after it became a net importer of oil, but stated it would likely return if it became a net exporter in the world.
   a. ACEA agreement
   c. ACCRA Cost of Living Index
   b. AD-IA Model
   d. OPEC

39. In international commerce and politics, an _____ is the prohibition of commerce (division of trade) and trade with a certain country, in order to isolate it and to put its government into a difficult internal situation, given that the effects of the _____ are often able to make its economy suffer from the initiative.

The _____ is usually used as a political punishment for some previous disagreed policies or acts, but its economic nature frequently raises doubts about the real interests that the prohibition serves.

One of the most comprehensive attempts at an _____ happened during the Napoleonic Wars.

   a. Overshooting model
   c. Optimum currency area
   b. International finance
   d. Embargo

40. An _____ is an economy in which people, including businesses, can trade in goods and services with other people and businesses in the international community at large. This contrasts with a closed economy in which international trade cannot take place.

The act of selling goods or services to a foreign country is called exporting.

   a. Open economy
   c. Indicative planning
   b. Information economy
   d. Attention work

Chapter 12. Consumption, Income, and the Multiplier

1. _____ is a concept found in moral, political, and bioethical philosophy. Within these contexts, it refers to the capacity of a rational individual to make an informed, un-coerced decision. In moral and political philosophy, _____ is often used as the basis for determining moral responsibility for one's actions.
   - a. AD-IA Model
   - b. ACEA agreement
   - c. ACCRA Cost of Living Index
   - d. Autonomy

2. _____ is a term used to describe consumption expenditure that occurs when income levels are zero. Such consumption is considered autonomous of income only when expenditure on these consumables does not vary with changes in income. If income levels are actually zero, this consumption counts as dissaving, because it is financed by borrowing or using up savings.
   - a. Autonomous consumption
   - b. Indexed unit of account
   - c. Economic interdependence
   - d. Austerity

3. _____ is a common concept in economics, and gives rise to derived concepts such as consumer debt. Generally _____ is defined by opposition to production. But the precise definition can vary because different schools of economists define production quite differently.
   - a. British canal system
   - b. Discrete choice
   - c. Basis of futures
   - d. Consumption

4. In economics, the _____ is a single mathematical function used to express consumer spending. It was developed by John Maynard Keynes and detailed most famously in his book The General Theory of Employment, Interest, and Money. The function is used to calculate the amount of total consumption in an economy.
   - a. Procyclical
   - b. Real exchange rate puzzles
   - c. Consumption function
   - d. Demand-Led Growth

5. A _____ is an object whose consumption increases the utility of the consumer, for which the quantity demanded exceeds the quantity supplied at zero price. _____s are usually modeled as having diminishing marginal utility. The first individual purchase has high utility; the second has less.
   - a. Positional goods
   - b. Search good
   - c. Luxury good
   - d. Good

6. _____, 1st Baron Keynes was a renowned economist from Britain whose many ideas on economic and political theories as well as on many governments' monetary policies influenced America. He advocated a government that played an active role in the lives of people regarding business, economy, etc. In this role, the government would use fiscal measures to reduce the consequences of recessions, economic depressions and booms.
   - a. John Maynard Keynes
   - b. Adam Smith
   - c. Adolph Fischer
   - d. Adolf Hitler

7. _____ and Keynesian Theory) is a macroeconomic theory based on the ideas of 20th-century British economist John Maynard Keynes. _____ argues that private sector decisions sometimes lead to inefficient macroeconomic outcomes and therefore advocates active policy responses by the public sector, including monetary policy actions by the central bank and fiscal policy actions by the government to stabilize output over the business cycle.

The theories forming the basis of _____ were first presented in The General Theory of Employment, Interest and Money, published in 1936.

Chapter 12. Consumption, Income, and the Multiplier

a. Recession
b. Keynesian economics
c. Rational choice theory
d. Gross domestic product

8. In economics, _____ is the total supply of goods and services produced by a national economy during a specific time period. It is the total amount of goods and services in the economy available at all possible price levels.
   a. Aggregate demand
   b. Aggregate supply
   c. Aggregate expenditure
   d. Aggregation problem

9. In economics, the concept of the _____ refers to the decision-making time frame of a firm in which at least one factor of production is fixed. Costs which are fixed in the _____ have no impact on a firms decisions. For example a firm can raise output by increasing the amount of labour through overtime.
   a. Short-run
   b. Productivity world
   c. Marginal product
   d. Hicks-neutral technical change

10. In Marxian economics, _____ originally referred to the means of production. Individuals, organizations and governments use _____ in the production of other goods or commodities. _____ include factories, machinery, tools, equipment, and various buildings which are used to produce other products for consumption.
    a. Capital formation
    b. Capital goods
    c. Modigliani-Miller theorem
    d. Cost of capital

11. _____ in economics refers to investment in fixed capital, i.e. tangible capital goods (real means of production or residential buildings), or to the replacement of depreciated capital goods.

Thus, _____ is investment in physical assets such as machinery, land, buildings, installations, vehicles, or technology. Normally, a company balance sheet will state both the amount of expenditure on fixed assets during the quarter or year, and the total value of the stock of fixed assets owned.

   a. Deferred financing costs
   b. Depreciation
   c. Salvage value
   d. Fixed investment

12. _____ relates to the composition of GDP. What is produced in a certain country is naturally also sold, but some of the goods produced in a given year may not be sold the same year, but in later years. Conversely, some of the goods sold in a given year might have been produced in an earlier year.
    a. Obelisk International
    b. Investment decisions
    c. Investment theory
    d. Inventory investment

13. In algebra, a _____ is a function depending on n that associates a scalar, det(A), to an n×n square matrix A. The fundamental geometric meaning of a _____ is a scale factor for measure when A is regarded as a linear transformation. _____s are important both in calculus, where they enter the substitution rule for several variables, and in multilinear algebra.

For a fixed nonnegative integer n, there is a unique _____ function for the n×n matrices over any commutative ring R. In particular, this function exists when R is the field of real or complex numbers.

a. 130-30 fund
b. 1921 recession
c. 100-year flood
d. Determinant

14. Competition law, known in the United States as _____ law, has three main elements:

- prohibiting agreements or practices that restrict free trading and competition between business entities. This includes in particular the repression of cartels.
- banning abusive behaviour by a firm dominating a market, or anti-competitive practices that tend to lead to such a dominant position. Practices controlled in this way may include predatory pricing, tying, price gouging, refusal to deal, and many others.
- supervising the mergers and acquisitions of large corporations, including some joint ventures. Transactions that are considered to threaten the competitive process can be prohibited altogether, or approved subject to 'remedies' such as an obligation to divest part of the merged business or to offer licences or access to facilities to enable other businesses to continue competing.

The substance and practice of competition law varies from jurisdiction to jurisdiction. Protecting the interests of consumers (consumer welfare) and ensuring that entrepreneurs have an opportunity to compete in the market economy are often treated as important objectives. Competition law is closely connected with law on deregulation of access to markets, state aids and subsidies, the privatisation of state owned assets and the establishment of independent sector regulators. In recent decades, competition law has been viewed as a way to provide better public services.

a. Anti-Inflation Act
b. Intellectual property law
c. Antitrust
d. United Kingdom competition law

15. _____, known in the United States as antitrust law, has three main elements:

- prohibiting agreements or practices that restrict free trading and competition between business entities. This includes in particular the repression of cartels.
- banning abusive behaviour by a firm dominating a market, or anti-competitive practices that tend to lead to such a dominant position. Practices controlled in this way may include predatory pricing, tying, price gouging, refusal to deal, and many others.
- supervising the mergers and acquisitions of large corporations, including some joint ventures. Transactions that are considered to threaten the competitive process can be prohibited altogether, or approved subject to 'remedies' such as an obligation to divest part of the merged business or to offer licences or access to facilities to enable other businesses to continue competing.

The substance and practice of _____ varies from jurisdiction to jurisdiction. Protecting the interests of consumers (consumer welfare) and ensuring that entrepreneurs have an opportunity to compete in the market economy are often treated as important objectives. _____ is closely connected with law on deregulation of access to markets, state aids and subsidies, the privatisation of state owned assets and the establishment of independent sector regulators. In recent decades, _____ has been viewed as a way to provide better public services.

a. Personal Responsibility and Work Opportunity Reconciliation Act of 1996

b. Federal Reserve Police

c. Patent

d. Competition law

16. _____ is the percentage of income spent. To find the percentage of income spent, one needs to divide consumption by income, or $APC = \dfrac{C}{Y}$. In an economy in which each individual consumer saves lots of money, there is a tendency of people losing their jobs because demand for goods and services will be low.

   a. Operating leverage
   b. Equity ratio
   c. Inventory turnover
   d. Average propensity to consume

17. The _____ is an economics term that refers to the proportion of income which is saved, usually expressed for household savings as a percentage of total household disposable income. The ratio differs considerably over time and between countries. The savings ratio can be affected by: the proportion of older people, as they have less motivation and capability to save; the rate of inflation, as expectations of rising prices encourage can encourage people to spend now rather than later

   a. Unearned income
   b. Independent income
   c. Average propensity to save
   d. Aggregate income

18. In economics and business, specifically cost accounting, the _____ point (BEP) is the point at which cost or expenses and revenue are equal: there is no net loss or gain, and one has 'broken even'. A profit or a loss has not been made, although opportunity costs have been paid, and capital has received the risk-adjusted, expected return.

For example, if the business sells less than 200 tables each month, it will make a loss, if it sells more, it will be a profit.

   a. Trailing twelve months
   b. Break-even
   c. Stylized fact
   d. Decoupling plus

19. In economics, the _____ is an empirical metric that quantifies induced consumption, the concept that the increase in personal consumer spending (consumption) that occurs with an increase in disposable income (income after taxes and transfers.) For example, if a household earns one extra dollar of disposable income, and the _____ is 0.65, then of that dollar, the household will spend 65 cents and save 35 cents.

Mathematically, the _____ (MPC) function is expressed as the derivative of the consumption (C) function with respect to disposable income (Y.)

   a. Permanent war economy
   b. Fiscal adjustment
   c. Marginal propensity to consume
   d. Macroeconomic models

20. The _____ refers to the increase in saving (non-purchase of current goods and services) that results from an increase in income. For example, if a household earns one extra dollar, and the _____ is 0.35, then of that dollar, the household will spend 65 cents and save 35 cents. It can also go the other way, referring to the decrease in saving that results from a decrease in income.

a. Permanent war economy
c. Lucas-Islands model
b. Balanced-growth equilibrium
d. Marginal propensity to save

21. _____ is a broad label that refers to any individuals or households that use goods and services generated within the economy. The concept of a _____ is used in different contexts, so that the usage and significance of the term may vary.

Typically when business people and economists talk of _____s they are talking about person as _____, an aggregated commodity item with little individuality other than that expressed in the buy/not-buy decision.

a. 1921 recession
c. 130-30 fund
b. Consumer
d. 100-year flood

22. A _____ is a measure of the average price of consumer goods and services purchased by households. A _____ measures a price change for a constant market basket of goods and services from one period to the next within the same area (city, region, or nation.) It is a price index determined by measuring the price of a standard group of goods meant to represent the typical market basket of a typical urban consumer.

a. Cost-of-living index
c. Lipstick index
b. Consumer Price Index
d. Hedonic price index

23. _____ in economics and business is the result of an exchange and from that trade we assign a numerical monetary value to a good, service or asset. If Alice trades Bob 4 apples for an orange, the _____ of an orange is 4 apples. Inversely, the _____ of an apple is 1/4 oranges.

a. Price ceiling
c. Lerner Index
b. Price
d. Price dispersion

24. A _____ is a normalized average (typically a weighted average) of prices for a given class of goods or services in a given region, during a given interval of time. It is a statistic designed to help to compare how these prices, taken as a whole, differ between time periods or geographical locations.

Price indices have several potential uses.

a. Flat rate
c. Pecuniary externality
b. Point of total assumption
d. Price Index

25. Necessary _____s:

If x is a necessary _____ of y, then the presence of y necessarily implies the presence of x. The presence of x, however, does not imply that y will occur.

Sufficient _____s:

If x is a sufficient _____ of y, then the presence of x necessarily implies the presence of y.

Chapter 12. Consumption, Income, and the Multiplier 109

    a. Deductive logic
    b. Materialism
    c. Global justice
    d. Cause

26. _____ is a specific term used in companies' financial reporting from the company-whole point of view. Because that use excludes the effects of changing ownership interest, an economic measure of _____ is necessary for financial analysis from the shareholders' point of view

_____ is defined by the Financial Accounting Standards Board, or FASB, as e;the change in equity [net assets] of a business enterprise during a period from transactions and other events and circumstances from nonowner sources. It includes all changes in equity during a period except those resulting from investments by owners and distributions to owners.e;

_____ is the sum of net income and other items that must bypass the income statement because they have not been realized, including items like an unrealized holding gain or loss from available for sale securities and foreign currency translation gains or losses.

    a. Real income
    b. Windfall gain
    c. Per capita income
    d. Comprehensive income

27. _____ , as defined by the _____ Association of America (Information technologyAA), is 'the study, design, development, implementation, support or management of computer-based information systems, particularly software applications and computer hardware.' _____ deals with the use of electronic computers and computer software to convert, store, protect, process, transmit, and securely retrieve information.

Today, the term _____ has ballooned to encompass many aspects of computing and technology, and the term has become very recognizable. The _____ umbrella can be quite large, covering many fields.

    a. Information technology
    b. ACCRA Cost of Living Index
    c. AD-IA Model
    d. ACEA agreement

28. _____ is a fee paid on borrowed assets. It is the price paid for the use of borrowed money , or, money earned by deposited funds . Assets that are sometimes lent with _____ include money, shares, consumer goods through hire purchase, major assets such as aircraft, and even entire factories in finance lease arrangements.
    a. Insolvency
    b. Interest
    c. Asset protection
    d. Internal debt

29. _____ in economics refers to metrics and measures of output from production processes, per unit of input. Labor _____, for example, is typically measured as a ratio of output per labor-hour, an input. _____ may be conceived of as a metrics of the technical or engineering efficiency of production.
    a. Fordism
    b. Production-possibility frontier
    c. Piece work
    d. Productivity

30. A variety of measures of _____ and output are used in economics to estimate total economic activity in a country or region, including gross domestic product (GDP), gross national product (GNP), and net _____

There are three main ways of calculating these numbers; the output approach, the income approach and the expenditure approach. In theory, the three must yield the same, because total expenditures on goods and services must equal the total income paid to the producers (Gnational income), and that must also equal the total value of the output of goods and services (GNP.)

a. Purchasing power parity
b. Gross national product
c. National income
d. Bureau of Labor Statistics

31. A _____ is a tax that is a fixed amount no matter what the change in circumstance of the taxed entity. (A lump-sum subsidy or lump-sum redistribution is defined similarly.) It is a regressive tax, such that the lower income is, the higher percentage of income applicable to the tax.

a. Sovereign credit
b. Government budget
c. Value capture
d. Lump-sum tax

32. To _____ is to impose a financial charge or other levy upon a taxpayer by a state or the functional equivalent of a state.

_____es are also imposed by many subnational entities. _____es consist of direct _____ or indirect _____, and may be paid in money or as its labour equivalent (often but not always unpaid.)

a. 130-30 fund
b. 1921 recession
c. Tax
d. 100-year flood

33. The balance of trade (or net exports, sometimes symbolized as NX) is the difference between the monetary value of exports and imports in an economy over a certain period of time. It is the relationship between a nation's imports and exports. A favorable balance of trade is known as a trade surplus and consists of exporting more than is imported; an unfavorable balance of trade is known as a _____ or, informally, a trade gap.

a. Backus-Kehoe-Kydland consumption correlation puzzle
b. Cash taxes
c. Trade deficit
d. Customer lifetime value

34. In economics, an _____ is any good or commodity, transported from one country to another country in a legitimate fashion, typically for use in trade. _____ goods or services are provided to foreign consumers by domestic producers. _____ is an important part of international trade.

a. ACEA agreement
b. AD-IA Model
c. ACCRA Cost of Living Index
d. Export

35. In the _____ diagram, a desired total spending (or aggregate expenditure which increases with total national output. This increase is due to the positive relationship between consumption and consumers' disposable income in the consumption function. Aggregate demand may also rise due to increases in investment (due to the accelerator effect), while this rise is reduced if imports and tax revenues rise with income.

a. Speculative demand
b. Neo-Keynesian economics
c. Keynesian cross
d. Multiplier effect

Chapter 12. Consumption, Income, and the Multiplier

36. A _____, reserve bank, or monetary authority is the entity responsible for the monetary policy of a country or of a group of member states. It is a bank that can lend money to other banks in times of need. Its primary responsibility is to maintain the stability of the national currency and money supply, but more active duties include controlling subsidized-loan interest rates, and acting as a lender of last resort to the banking sector during times of financial crisis (private banks often being integral to the national financial system.)

    a. 130-30 fund
    b. 100-year flood
    c. 1921 recession
    d. Central bank

37. In economics, the _____ or spending multiplier is the idea that an initial amount of spending (usually by the government) leads to increased consumption spending and so results in an increase in national income greater than the initial amount of spending. In other words, an initial change in aggregate demand causes a change in aggregate output for the economy that is a multiple of the initial change.

The existence of a _____ was initially proposed by Ralph George Hawtrey in 1931.

    a. Transactions demand
    b. Keynesian cross
    c. Magical triangle
    d. Multiplier effect

38. A _____ is a hypothetical measure of overall prices for some set of goods and services, in a given region during a given interval, normalized relative to some base set. Typically, a _____ is approximated with a price index.

The classical dichotomy is the assumption that there is a relatively clean distinction between overall increases or decreases in prices and underlying, e;reale; economic variables.

    a. Foreign portfolio investment
    b. Federal Reserve districts
    c. Relative income hypothesis
    d. Price level

39. In economics, _____ is the total demand for final goods and services in the economy (Y) at a given time and price level. It is the amount of goods and services in the economy that will be purchased at all possible price levels. This is the demand for the gross domestic product of a country when inventory levels are static.

    a. Aggregation problem
    b. Aggregate supply
    c. Aggregate expenditure
    d. Aggregate demand

40. Economics:

- _____, the desire to own something and the ability to pay for it
- _____ curve, a graphic representation of a _____ schedule
- _____ deposit, the money in checking accounts
- _____ pull theory, the theory that inflation occurs when _____ for goods and services exceeds existing supplies
- _____ schedule, a table that lists the quantity of a good a person will buy it each different price
- _____ side economics, the school of economics at believes government spending and tax cuts open economy by raising _____

a. Demand b. Bon
c. Procter ' Gamble d. G20

41. The _____ is the central banking system of the United States. Created in 1913 by the enactment of the Federal Reserve Act (signed by Woodrow Wilson), it is a quasi-public and quasi-private (government entity with private components) banking system that comprises (1) the presidentially appointed Board of Governors of the _____ in Washington, D.C.; (2) the Federal Open Market Committee; (3) twelve regional Federal Reserve Banks located in major cities throughout the nation acting as fiscal agents for the U.S. Treasury, each with its own nine-member board of directors; (4) numerous other private U.S. member banks, which subscribe to required amounts of non-transferable stock in their regional Federal Reserve Banks; and (5) various advisory councils. Since February 2006, Ben Bernanke has served as the Chairman of the Board of Governors of the _____.

a. Federal Reserve Banks b. Federal Reserve Transparency Act
c. Federal funds rate d. Federal Reserve System

42. A _____ is a public market for the trading of company stock and derivatives at an agreed price; these are securities listed on a stock exchange as well as those only traded privately.

The size of the world _____ was estimated at about $36.6 trillion US at the beginning of October 2008 . The total world derivatives market has been estimated at about $791 trillion face or nominal value, 11 times the size of the entire world economy.

a. 130-30 fund b. 100-year flood
c. 1921 recession d. Stock market

43. The _____ is 'the basic residential unit in which economic production, consumption, inheritance, child rearing, and shelter are organized and carried out'; [the _____] 'may or may not be synonymous with family'.

The _____ is the basic unit of analysis in many social, microeconomic and government models. The term refers to all individuals who live in the same dwelling.

a. 100-year flood b. 130-30 fund
c. Household d. Family economics

Chapter 13. Fiscal Policy

1. A _____ occurs when an entity spends more money than it takes in. The opposite of a _____ is a budget surplus. Debt is essentially an accumulated flow of deficits.
   a. Sovereign credit
   b. Budget deficit
   c. Grant-in-aid
   d. Public Financial Management

2. A _____ is a situation in which the government takes in more than it spends.
   a. 130-30 fund
   b. 100-year flood
   c. Budget set
   d. Budget surplus

3. The term _____ refers to government debt, expenditures and revenues, or to finance (particularly financial revenue) in general.

   - _____ deficit is the budget deficit of federal or local government
   - _____ policy is the discretionary spending of governments. Contrasts with monetary policy.
   - _____ year and _____ quarter are reporting periods for firms and other agencies.

   a. Russian financial crisis
   b. Consequence
   c. Freedom Park
   d. Fiscal

4. In economics, _____ is the use of government spending and revenue collection to influence the economy.

   _____ can be contrasted with the other main type of economic policy, monetary policy, which attempts to stabilize the economy by controlling interest rates and the supply of money. The two main instruments of _____ are government spending and taxation.
   a. 100-year flood
   b. Fiscalism
   c. Fiscal policy
   d. Sustainable investment rule

5. _____ in economics and business is the result of an exchange and from that trade we assign a numerical monetary value to a good, service or asset. If Alice trades Bob 4 apples for an orange, the _____ of an orange is 4 apples. Inversely, the _____ of an apple is 1/4 oranges.
   a. Price dispersion
   b. Lerner Index
   c. Price
   d. Price ceiling

6. _____ or government expenditure is classified by economists into three main types. Government purchases of goods and services for current use are classed as government consumption. Government purchases of goods and services intended to create future benefits, such as infrastructure investment or research spending, are classed as government investment.
   a. 130-30 fund
   b. Government spending
   c. 100-year flood
   d. 1921 recession

7. An _____ is a tax levied on the financial income of people, corporations, or other legal entities. Various _____ systems exist, with varying degrees of tax incidence. Income taxation can be progressive, proportional, or regressive.

a. ACCRA Cost of Living Index
b. ACEA agreement
c. AD-IA Model
d. Income tax

8. _____, 1st Baron Keynes was a renowned economist from Britain whose many ideas on economic and political theories as well as on many governments' monetary policies influenced America. He advocated a government that played an active role in the lives of people regarding business, economy, etc. In this role, the government would use fiscal measures to reduce the consequences of recessions, economic depressions and booms.
 a. John Maynard Keynes
 b. Adolph Fischer
 c. Adam Smith
 d. Adolf Hitler

9. _____ and Keynesian Theory) is a macroeconomic theory based on the ideas of 20th-century British economist John Maynard Keynes. _____ argues that private sector decisions sometimes lead to inefficient macroeconomic outcomes and therefore advocates active policy responses by the public sector, including monetary policy actions by the central bank and fiscal policy actions by the government to stabilize output over the business cycle.

The theories forming the basis of _____ were first presented in The General Theory of Employment, Interest and Money, published in 1936.

 a. Recession
 b. Keynesian economics
 c. Gross domestic product
 d. Rational choice theory

10. The GDP gap or the output gap is the difference between potential GDP and actual GDP or actual output. The calculation for the output gap is Y-Y* where Y* is potential output and Y is actual output. If this calculation yields a positive number it is called an expansionary gap and indicates an economy in expansion; if the calculation yields a negative number it is called a _____ and indicates an economy in recession.
 a. 100-year flood
 b. Recessionary gap
 c. 1921 recession
 d. 130-30 fund

11. _____ is a common concept in economics, and gives rise to derived concepts such as consumer debt. Generally _____ is defined by opposition to production. But the precise definition can vary because different schools of economists define production quite differently.
 a. British canal system
 b. Consumption
 c. Basis of futures
 d. Discrete choice

12. To _____ is to impose a financial charge or other levy upon a taxpayer by a state or the functional equivalent of a state.

_____es are also imposed by many subnational entities. _____es consist of direct _____ or indirect _____, and may be paid in money or as its labour equivalent (often but not always unpaid.)

 a. 100-year flood
 b. 130-30 fund
 c. 1921 recession
 d. Tax

Chapter 13. Fiscal Policy

13. An _____, in economics, is the amount by which the real Gross domestic product exceeds potential GDP. The real GDP is also known as GDP 'adjusted for inflation', 'constant prices' GDP or 'constant dollar' GDP, because it measures the aggregate output in a country's income accounts in a given year, expressed in base-year prices. On the other hand, the potential GDP is the quantity of real GDP when a country's economy is at full-employment.
- a. AD-IA Model
- b. ACCRA Cost of Living Index
- c. ACEA agreement
- d. Inflationary gap

14. A _____, reserve bank, or monetary authority is the entity responsible for the monetary policy of a country or of a group of member states. It is a bank that can lend money to other banks in times of need. Its primary responsibility is to maintain the stability of the national currency and money supply, but more active duties include controlling subsidized-loan interest rates, and acting as a lender of last resort to the banking sector during times of financial crisis (private banks often being integral to the national financial system.)
- a. 100-year flood
- b. Central bank
- c. 130-30 fund
- d. 1921 recession

15. To tax is to impose a financial charge or other levy upon a taxpayer by a state or the functional equivalent of a state.

_____ are also imposed by many subnational entities. _____ consist of direct tax or indirect tax, and may be paid in money or as its labour equivalent (often but not always unpaid.)
- a. Taxes
- b. 130-30 fund
- c. 1921 recession
- d. 100-year flood

16. In economics, _____ is the total supply of goods and services produced by a national economy during a specific time period. It is the total amount of goods and services in the economy available at all possible price levels.
- a. Aggregate expenditure
- b. Aggregate demand
- c. Aggregation problem
- d. Aggregate supply

17. In economic models, the _____ time frame assumes no fixed factors of production. Firms can enter or leave the marketplace, and the cost (and availability) of land, labor, raw materials, and capital goods can be assumed to vary. In contrast, in the short-run time frame, certain factors are assumed to be fixed, because there is not sufficient time for them to change.
- a. Long-run
- b. Short-run
- c. Product Pipeline
- d. Diseconomies of scale

18. _____ is a fee paid on borrowed assets. It is the price paid for the use of borrowed money , or, money earned by deposited funds . Assets that are sometimes lent with _____ include money, shares, consumer goods through hire purchase, major assets such as aircraft, and even entire factories in finance lease arrangements.
- a. Interest
- b. Asset protection
- c. Insolvency
- d. Internal debt

19. _____, is an economic theory that suggests consumers internalise the government's budget constraint and thus the timing of any tax change does not affect their change in spending. Consequently, _____ suggests that it does not matter whether a government finances its spending with debt or a tax increase, the effect on total level of demand in an economy will be the same. It was proposed, and then rejected, by the 19th-century economist David Ricardo.

a. Social discount rate
c. Compound empowerment
b. Ricardian equivalence
d. Municipalization

20. _____ is exchange of capital, goods, and services across international borders or territories. In most countries, it represents a significant share of gross domestic product (GDP.) While _____ has been present throughout much of history, its economic, social, and political importance has been on the rise in recent centuries.
    a. Import license
    b. Intra-industry trade
    c. International trade
    d. Incoterms

21. A trade union or _____ is an organization of workers who have banded together to achieve common goals in key areas and working conditions. The trade union, through its leadership, bargains with the employer on behalf of union members (rank and file members) and negotiates labor contracts (Collective bargaining) with employers. This may include the negotiation of wages, work rules, complaint procedures, rules governing hiring, firing and promotion of workers, benefits, workplace safety and policies.
    a. Controlled Foreign Corporations
    b. Labor union
    c. Differences in Differences
    d. Credible threat

22. In economics, the _____ is used to illustrate the idea that increases in the rate of taxation do not necessarily increase tax revenue. (For instance, whereas a 0% income tax rate will generate no revenue, neither will a 100% rate, as citizens will have no incentive to make money.) Increasing taxes beyond the peak of the curve point will decrease tax revenue.
    a. 100-year flood
    b. Laffer Curve
    c. 1921 recession
    d. 130-30 fund

23. _____ is a school of macroeconomic thought that argues that economic growth can be most effectively created using incentives for people to produce (supply) goods and services, such as adjusting income tax and capital gains tax rates, and by allowing greater flexibility by reducing regulation. Consumers will then benefit from a greater supply of goods and services at lower prices.

The term _____ was coined by journalist Jude Wanniski in 1975, and popularized the ideas of economists Robert Mundell and Arthur Laffer.

    a. Flow to Equity-Approach
    b. Categorical grants
    c. Kibbutz volunteers
    d. Supply-side economics

24. _____s is the social science that studies the production, distribution, and consumption of goods and services. The term _____s comes from the Ancient Greek οἰκονομῐ́α from οἶκος (oikos, 'house') + νόμος (nomos, 'custom' or 'law'), hence 'rules of the house(hold)'. Current _____ models developed out of the broader field of political economy in the late 19th century, owing to a desire to use an empirical approach more akin to the physical sciences.
    a. Inflation
    b. Opportunity cost
    c. Energy economics
    d. Economic

25. A _____ or labor union is an organization of workers who have banded together to achieve common goals in key areas and working conditions. The _____, through its leadership, bargains with the employer on behalf of union members (rank and file members) and negotiates labor contracts (Collective bargaining) with employers. This may include the negotiation of wages, work rules, complaint procedures, rules governing hiring, firing and promotion of workers, benefits, workplace safety and policies.

Chapter 13. Fiscal Policy

a. Trade union
b. Graph cuts
c. Labour vouchers
d. Dividend unit

26. The _____ is an economic and political union of 27 member states, located primarily in Europe. It was established by the Treaty of Maastricht on 1 November 1993, upon the foundations of the pre-existing European Economic Community. With a population of almost 500 million, the _____ generates an estimated 30% share (US$18.4 trillion in 2008) of the nominal gross world product.
   a. ACCRA Cost of Living Index
   b. European Union
   c. European Court of Justice
   d. ACEA agreement

27. Economics:

   - _____, the desire to own something and the ability to pay for it
   - _____ curve, a graphic representation of a _____ schedule
   - _____ deposit, the money in checking accounts
   - _____ pull theory, the theory that inflation occurs when _____ for goods and services exceeds existing supplies
   - _____ schedule, a table that lists the quantity of a good a person will buy it each different price
   - _____ side economics, the school of economics at believes government spending and tax cuts open economy by raising _____

   a. G20
   b. Procter ' Gamble
   c. Bon
   d. Demand

28. In economics, _____ is the ratio of the percent change in one variable to the percent change in another variable. It is a tool for measuring the responsiveness of a function to changes in parameters in a relative way. Commonly analyzed are _____ of substitution, price and wealth.
   a. Elasticity
   b. ACEA agreement
   c. Elasticity of demand
   d. ACCRA Cost of Living Index

29. Price _____ is defined as the measure of responsiveness in the quantity demanded for a commodity as a result of change in price of the same commodity. It is a measure of how consumers react to a change in price. In other words, it is percentage change in quantity demanded by the percentage change in price of the same commodity.
   a. ACCRA Cost of Living Index
   b. ACEA agreement
   c. Elasticity of demand
   d. Elasticity

30. Fractional-reserve banking is the banking practice in which banks keep only a fraction of their deposits in reserve (as cash and other highly liquid assets) and lend out the remainder, while maintaining the simultaneous obligation to redeem all these deposits upon demand. _____ necessarily occurs when banks lend out any fraction of the funds received from demand deposits. This practice is universal in modern banking.
   a. Repo Rate
   b. Certificate of deposit
   c. Bank secrecy
   d. Fractional reserve banking

31. _____ is defined as the measure of responsiveness in the quantity demanded for a commodity as a result of change in price of the same commodity. It is a measure of how consumers react to a change in price. In other words, it is percentage change in quantity demanded as per the percentage change in price of the same commodity.
   a. 1921 recession
   b. 100-year flood
   c. 130-30 fund
   d. Price elasticity of demand

32. The _____ is a US private, nonprofit research organization dedicated to studying the science and empirics of economics, especially the American economy. It is 'committed to undertaking and disseminating unbiased economic research among public policymakers, business professionals, and the academic community.' It publishes NBER Working Papers and books. The NBER is located in Cambridge, Massachusetts with branch offices in Palo Alto, California, and New York City.
   a. Paris Club
   b. Citizens for an Alternative Tax System
   c. National Bureau of Economic Research
   d. Luxembourg Income Study

33. A _____ is the transfer of wealth from one party (such as a person or company) to another. A _____ is usually made in exchange for the provision of goods, services or both, or to fulfill a legal obligation.

The simplest and oldest form of _____ is barter, the exchange of one good or service for another.

   a. Payment
   b. RFM
   c. Contingent payment sales
   d. Hard count

34. _____ is a broad label that refers to any individuals or households that use goods and services generated within the economy. The concept of a _____ is used in different contexts, so that the usage and significance of the term may vary.

Typically when business people and economists talk of _____s they are talking about person as _____, an aggregated commodity item with little individuality other than that expressed in the buy/not-buy decision.

   a. 1921 recession
   b. Consumer
   c. 130-30 fund
   d. 100-year flood

35. A _____ is a measure of the average price of consumer goods and services purchased by households. A _____ measures a price change for a constant market basket of goods and services from one period to the next within the same area (city, region, or nation.) It is a price index determined by measuring the price of a standard group of goods meant to represent the typical market basket of a typical urban consumer.
   a. Hedonic price index
   b. Cost-of-living index
   c. Lipstick index
   d. Consumer Price Index

36. The _____ was a worldwide economic downturn starting in most places in 1929 and ending at different times in the 1930s or early 1940s for different countries. It was the largest and most important economic depression in the 20th century, and is used in the 21st century as an example of how far the world's economy can fall. The _____ originated in the United States; historians most often use as a starting date the stock market crash on October 29, 1929, known as Black Tuesday.

a. The Great Depression
b. Causes of the Great Depression
c. British Empire Economic Conference
d. Great Depression

37. A _____ is a normalized average (typically a weighted average) of prices for a given class of goods or services in a given region, during a given interval of time. It is a statistic designed to help to compare how these prices, taken as a whole, differ between time periods or geographical locations.

Price indices have several potential uses.

a. Flat rate
b. Point of total assumption
c. Pecuniary externality
d. Price Index

38. _____ is that which is owed; usually referencing assets owed, but the term can also cover moral obligations and other interactions not requiring money. In the case of assets, _____ is a means of using future purchasing power in the present before a summation has been earned. Some companies and corporations use _____ as a part of their overall corporate finance strategy.
a. Subordinated debt
b. Debt
c. Non-performing loan
d. Participation loan

39. The _____ or gross domestic income (GDI), a basic measure of an economy's economic performance, is the market value of all final goods and services produced within the borders of a nation in a year. _____ can be defined in three ways, all of which are conceptually identical. First, it is equal to the total expenditures for all final goods and services produced within the country in a stipulated period of time (usually a 365-day year.)
a. Gross domestic product
b. Co-operative economics
c. Public economics
d. Market failure

40. The _____ is one of three major groups of methodologies, called valuation approaches, used by appraisers. It is particularly common in commercial real estate appraisal and in business appraisal. The fundamental math is similar to the methods used for financial valuation, securities analysis, or bond pricing.
a. Income approach
b. Urban growth boundary
c. ACEA agreement
d. ACCRA Cost of Living Index

41. In economics, _____ is the total demand for final goods and services in the economy (Y) at a given time and price level. It is the amount of goods and services in the economy that will be purchased at all possible price levels. This is the demand for the gross domestic product of a country when inventory levels are static.
a. Aggregate supply
b. Aggregate expenditure
c. Aggregate demand
d. Aggregation problem

42. A _____ is a hypothetical measure of overall prices for some set of goods and services, in a given region during a given interval, normalized relative to some base set. Typically, a _____ is approximated with a price index.

The classical dichotomy is the assumption that there is a relatively clean distinction between overall increases or decreases in prices and underlying, e;reale; economic variables.

a. Price level
b. Federal Reserve districts
c. Relative income hypothesis
d. Foreign portfolio investment

43. _____ is a phrase used in Indian English to mean that no bargaining is allowed over the price of a good or, less commonly, a service. As bargaining is very common in many parts of the world outside of Europe and North America, this term expresses an exception from the norm.

In the United Kingdom _____ has a similar meaning, and commonly indicates that an external party has set a price level, which may not be varied by individual sellers of a good or service.

a. Coincidence of wants
b. Contingent payment sales
c. Fixed Price
d. Trade credit

44. In economics, the _____ or spending multiplier is the idea that an initial amount of spending (usually by the government) leads to increased consumption spending and so results in an increase in national income greater than the initial amount of spending. In other words, an initial change in aggregate demand causes a change in aggregate output for the economy that is a multiple of the initial change.

The existence of a _____ was initially proposed by Ralph George Hawtrey in 1931.

a. Magical triangle
b. Transactions demand
c. Keynesian cross
d. Multiplier effect

Chapter 14. Money, Banking, and Central Banking 121

1. A _____ is a type of banknote issued by the Federal Reserve System and is the only type of U.S. banknote that is still produced today.

_____s are fiat currency, with the words 'this note is legal tender for all debts, public and private' printed on each bill. (See generally 31 U.S.C.

- a. Federal Reserve note
- b. Federal banking
- c. Federal Reserve System Open Market Account
- d. Primary Dealer Credit Facility

2. _____ is money accepted for exchange of goods in an economy. The prevalence of one money over another arises, usually, when a government designates through decrees that the government shall accept only particular notes and coins in payment for taxes. Typically, money of _____ consists of stamped coins and minted paper bills.
- a. Security thread
- b. Totnes pound
- c. Scripophily
- d. Currency

3. _____ is a reduction in the value of a currency with respect to other monetary units. In common modern usage, it specifically implies an official lowering of the value of a country's currency within a fixed exchange rate system, by which the monetary authority formally sets a new fixed rate with respect to a foreign reference currency. In contrast, (currency) depreciation is used for the unofficial decrease in the exchange rate in a floating exchange rate system.
- a. Reserve currency
- b. Petrodollar
- c. Dollarization
- d. Devaluation

4. A _____ is a currency issued by a private institution. It is often contrasted with fiat currency issued by governments.

In many countries the issue of private paper currencies is severely restricted by law.

- a. Private currency
- b. 1921 recession
- c. 100-year flood
- d. 130-30 fund

5. The _____ is the central banking system of the United States. Created in 1913 by the enactment of the Federal Reserve Act (signed by Woodrow Wilson), it is a quasi-public and quasi-private (government entity with private components) banking system that comprises (1) the presidentially appointed Board of Governors of the _____ in Washington, D.C.; (2) the Federal Open Market Committee; (3) twelve regional Federal Reserve Banks located in major cities throughout the nation acting as fiscal agents for the U.S. Treasury, each with its own nine-member board of directors; (4) numerous other private U.S. member banks, which subscribe to required amounts of non-transferable stock in their regional Federal Reserve Banks; and (5) various advisory councils. Since February 2006, Ben Bernanke has served as the Chairman of the Board of Governors of the _____.

- a. Federal funds rate
- b. Federal Reserve Transparency Act
- c. Federal Reserve Banks
- d. Federal Reserve System

6. A _____ is an intermediary used in trade to avoid the inconveniences of a pure barter system.

By contrast, as William Stanley Jevons argued, in a barter system there must be a coincidence of wants before two people can trade - one must want exactly what the other has to offer, when and where it is offered, so that the exchange can occur. A _____ permits the value of goods to be assessed and rendered in terms of the intermediary, most often, a form of money widely accepted to buy any other good.

a. Price theory
b. Labour economics
c. Medium of exchange
d. Treasury View

7. A _____ is the accepted way, in a given market, to settle a debt. For example, while the gold standard reigned, gold or any currency convertible to gold at a fixed rate constituted such a standard. As of 2003, the US dollar and the euro are the most generally accepted standards for international settlements.

a. Duration gap
b. Life annuity
c. Commuted cash value
d. Standard of deferred payment

8. To act as a _____, a commodity, a form of money stored, and retrieved - and be predictably useful when it is so retrieved.

This is distinct from the standard of deferred payment function which requires acceptability to parties one owes a debt to and a minimum of opportunity to cheat others.

a. Reserve currency
b. Store of value
c. Petrodollar recycling
d. Petrodollar

9. _____ is the a method of technical and economic research of the systems for purpose to optimize a parity between system's consumer functions or properties and expenses to achieve those functions or properties.

This methodology for continuous perfection of production, industrial technologies, organizational structures was developed by Juryj Sobolev in 1948 at the 'Perm telephone factory'

- 1948 Juryj Sobolev - the first success in application of a method analysis at the 'Perm telephone factory' .
- 1949 - the first application for the invention as result of use of the new method.

Today in economically developed countries practically each enterprise or the company use methodology of the kind of functional-cost analysis as a practice of the quality management, most full satisfying to principles of standards of series ISO 9000.

- Interest of consumer not in products itself, but the advantage which it will receive from its usage.
- The consumer aspires to reduce his expenses
- Functions needed by consumer can be executed in the various ways, and, hence, with various efficiency and expenses. Among possible alternatives of realization of functions exist such in which the parity of quality and the price is the optimal for the consumer.

The goal of _____ is achievement of the highest consumer satisfaction of production at simultaneous decrease in all kinds of industrial expenses Classical _____ has three English synonyms - Value Engineering, Value Management, Value Analysis.

a. Residual value
b. Monopoly wage
c. Function cost analysis
d. Real net output ratio

Chapter 14. Money, Banking, and Central Banking 123

10. A variety of measures of _____ and output are used in economics to estimate total economic activity in a country or region, including gross domestic product (GDP), gross national product (GNP), and net _____

There are three main ways of calculating these numbers; the output approach, the income approach and the expenditure approach. In theory, the three must yield the same, because total expenditures on goods and services must equal the total income paid to the producers (Gnational income), and that must also equal the total value of the output of goods and services (GNP.)

   a. Bureau of Labor Statistics
   b. Gross national product
   c. Purchasing power parity
   d. National income

11. A _____ is the transfer of wealth from one party (such as a person or company) to another. A _____ is usually made in exchange for the provision of goods, services or both, or to fulfill a legal obligation.

The simplest and oldest form of _____ is barter, the exchange of one good or service for another.

   a. RFM
   b. Payment
   c. Hard count
   d. Contingent payment sales

12. Bartering is a medium in which goods or services are directly exchanged for other goods and/or services, without the use of money. It can be bilateral or multilateral, and usually exists parallel to monetary systems in most developed countries, though to a very limited extent. _____ usually replaces money as the method of exchange in times of monetary crisis, when the currency is unstable and devalued by hyperinflation.
   a. Bartercard
   b. Post-capitalism
   c. New Economics Foundation
   d. Barter

13. _____ is a specific term used in companies' financial reporting from the company-whole point of view. Because that use excludes the effects of changing ownership interest, an economic measure of _____ is necessary for financial analysis from the shareholders' point of view

_____ is defined by the Financial Accounting Standards Board, or FASB, as e;the change in equity [net assets] of a business enterprise during a period from transactions and other events and circumstances from nonowner sources. It includes all changes in equity during a period except those resulting from investments by owners and distributions to owners.e;

_____ is the sum of net income and other items that must bypass the income statement because they have not been realized, including items like an unrealized holding gain or loss from available for sale securities and foreign currency translation gains or losses.

   a. Windfall gain
   b. Per capita income
   c. Real income
   d. Comprehensive income

14. The _____ problem (often 'double _____') is an important category of transaction costs that impose severe limitations on economies lacking money and thus dominated by barter or other in-kind transactions. The problem is caused by the improbability of the wants, needs or events that cause or motivate a transaction occurring at the same time and the same place.

In-kind transactions have several problems, most notably timing constraints.

    a. Payment
    b. Customer not present
    c. Hard count
    d. Coincidence of Wants

15. Market _____ is a business, economics or investment term that refers to an asset's ability to be easily converted through an act of buying or selling without causing a significant movement in the price and with minimum loss of value. Money, or cash on hand, is the most liquid asset. An act of exchange of a less liquid asset with a more liquid asset is called liquidation.
    a. 100-year flood
    b. 130-30 fund
    c. 1921 recession
    d. Liquidity

16. _____ is an equity (stock) exchange located at 11 Wall Street in lower Manhattan, New York, USA. It is the largest stock exchange in the world by dollar value of its listed companies' securities. As of October 2008, the combined capitalization of all domestic _____ listed companies was US$10.1 trillion.
    a. 100-year flood
    b. 130-30 fund
    c. New York Stock Exchange
    d. 1921 recession

17. A _____ is a corporation or mutual organization which provides trading facilities for stock brokers and traders, to trade stocks and other securities. It may be a physical trading room where the traders gather, or a formalised communications network. Creation of a _____ is a strategy of economic development.
    a. Primary shares
    b. SEAQ
    c. Stock Exchange
    d. 100-year flood

18. The _____ is the Cabinet department of the United States government concerned with promoting economic growth. It was originally created as the _____ and Labor on February 14, 1903. It was subsequently renamed to the Department of Commerce on March 4, 1913, and its bureaus and agencies specializing in labor were transferred to the new Department of Labor.
    a. AD-IA Model
    b. ACCRA Cost of Living Index
    c. ACEA agreement
    d. United States Department of Commerce

19. _____ is the value on a given date of a future payment or series of future payments, discounted to reflect the time value of money and other factors such as investment risk. _____ calculations are widely used in business and economics to provide a means to compare cash flows at different times on a meaningful 'like to like' basis.

Money value fluctuates over time: $100 today are not worth $100 in five years.

    a. Present Value
    b. Financial transaction
    c. Maturity
    d. Future value

20. _____ is a broad label that refers to any individuals or households that use goods and services generated within the economy. The concept of a _____ is used in different contexts, so that the usage and significance of the term may vary.

Chapter 14. Money, Banking, and Central Banking

Typically when business people and economists talk of _____s they are talking about person as _____, an aggregated commodity item with little individuality other than that expressed in the buy/not-buy decision.

a. Consumer
c. 100-year flood
b. 1921 recession
d. 130-30 fund

21. A _____ is a measure of the average price of consumer goods and services purchased by households. A _____ measures a price change for a constant market basket of goods and services from one period to the next within the same area (city, region, or nation.) It is a price index determined by measuring the price of a standard group of goods meant to represent the typical market basket of a typical urban consumer.

a. Cost-of-living index
c. Lipstick index
b. Hedonic price index
d. Consumer Price Index

22. _____ in economics and business is the result of an exchange and from that trade we assign a numerical monetary value to a good, service or asset. If Alice trades Bob 4 apples for an orange, the _____ of an orange is 4 apples. Inversely, the _____ of an apple is 1/4 oranges.

a. Price ceiling
c. Price dispersion
b. Lerner Index
d. Price

23. A _____ is a normalized average (typically a weighted average) of prices for a given class of goods or services in a given region, during a given interval of time. It is a statistic designed to help to compare how these prices, taken as a whole, differ between time periods or geographical locations.

Price indices have several potential uses.

a. Flat rate
c. Point of total assumption
b. Pecuniary externality
d. Price Index

24. A _____ secures the proper functioning of money by regulating economic agents, transaction types, and money supply.

_____s are traditionally formed by the policy decisions of individual governments and administrated as a domestic economic issue.

The current trend, however, is to use international trade and investment to alter the policy and legislation of individual governments.

a. Debt restructuring
c. Monetary system
b. T-Model
d. Concentrated stock

25. _____ and Keynesian Theory) is a macroeconomic theory based on the ideas of 20th-century British economist John Maynard Keynes. _____ argues that private sector decisions sometimes lead to inefficient macroeconomic outcomes and therefore advocates active policy responses by the public sector, including monetary policy actions by the central bank and fiscal policy actions by the government to stabilize output over the business cycle.

Chapter 14. Money, Banking, and Central Banking

The theories forming the basis of _____ were first presented in The General Theory of Employment, Interest and Money, published in 1936.

a. Recession
b. Rational choice theory
c. Gross domestic product
d. Keynesian economics

26. In economics, _____ is the total amount of money available in an economy at a particular point in time. There are several ways to define 'money', but standard measures usually include currency in circulation and demand deposits.

_____ data are recorded and published, usually by the government or the central bank of the country.

a. Fiscal theory of the price level
b. Monetary reform
c. Money supply
d. Monetary economy

27. A _____ association is a financial institution that specializes in accepting savings deposits and making mortgage and other loans. The S'L or thrift term is mainly used in the United States; similar institutions in the United Kingdom, Ireland and some Commonwealth countries include building societies and trustee savings banks.

They are often mutually held, meaning that the depositors and borrowers are members with voting rights, and have the ability to direct the financial and managerial goals of the organization, similar to the policyholders of a mutual insurance company.

a. Fund Platform
b. Passive management
c. Pension simplification
d. Savings and Loan

28. A _____, reserve bank, or monetary authority is the entity responsible for the monetary policy of a country or of a group of member states. It is a bank that can lend money to other banks in times of need. Its primary responsibility is to maintain the stability of the national currency and money supply, but more active duties include controlling subsidized-loan interest rates, and acting as a lender of last resort to the banking sector during times of financial crisis (private banks often being integral to the national financial system.)

a. 130-30 fund
b. Central Bank
c. 1921 recession
d. 100-year flood

29. The _____ is one of the world's most important central banks, responsible for monetary policy covering the 16 member States of the Eurozone. It was established by the European Union (EU) in 1998 with its headquarters in Frankfurt, Germany.

The predecessor to the _____ was the European Monetary Institute .

a. ACCRA Cost of Living Index
b. AD-IA Model
c. ACEA agreement
d. European Central Bank

30. _____ , as defined by the _____ Association of America (Information technologyAA), is 'the study, design, development, implementation, support or management of computer-based information systems, particularly software applications and computer hardware.' _____ deals with the use of electronic computers and computer software to convert, store, protect, process, transmit, and securely retrieve information.

Today, the term _____ has ballooned to encompass many aspects of computing and technology, and the term has become very recognizable. The _____ umbrella can be quite large, covering many fields.

a. ACEA agreement
b. ACCRA Cost of Living Index
c. Information technology
d. AD-IA Model

31. In finance, the _____ is the global financial market for short-term borrowing and lending. It provides short-term liquidity funding for the global financial system. The _____ is where short-term obligations such as Treasury bills, commercial paper and bankers' acceptances are bought and sold.

a. Bankruptcy remote
b. Money market
c. Financial rand
d. Post earnings announcement drift

32. A _____ is a money deposit at a banking institution that cannot be withdrawn for a certain 'term' or period of time. When the term is over it can be withdrawn or it can be held for another term. Generally speaking, the longer the term the better the yield on the money.

a. Diamond-Dybvig model
b. Soft probe
c. Banking agent
d. Time deposit

33. A _____ is a current account at a banking institution that allows money to be deposited and withdrawn by the account holder, with the transactions and resulting balance being recorded on the bank's books. Some banks charge a fee for this service, while others may pay the customer interest on the funds deposited.

Although restrictions placed on access depend upon the terms and conditions of the account and the provider, the account holder retains rights to have their funds repaid on demand.

a. Deposit account
b. Bank statement
c. Structuring
d. Sort code

34. The cost advantages of using _____ include:

- Reconciling conflicting preferences of lenders and borrowers

- Risk aversion- intermediaries help spread out and decrease the risks

- Economies of scale- using _____ reduces the costs of lending and borrowing

- Economies of scope- intermediaries concentrate on the demands of the lenders and borrowers and are able to enhance their products and services (use same inputs to produce different outputs)

_____ include:

- Banks
- Building societies
- Credit unions
- Financial advisers or brokers
- Insurance companies
- Collective investment schemes
- Pension funds

Financial institutions (intermediaries) perform the vital role of bringing together those economic agents with surplus funds who want to lend, with those with a shortage of funds who want to borrow.

In doing this they offer the major benefits of maturity and risk transformation. It is possible for this to be done by direct contact between the ultimate borrowers, but there are major cost disadvantages of direct finance.

Indeed, one explanation of the existence of specialist _____ is that they have a related (cost) advantage in offering financial services, which not only enables them to make profit, but also raises the overall efficiency of the economy.

a. Pensions crisis
b. Personal pension scheme
c. SICAV
d. Financial intermediaries

35. A _____ is a customs union with common policies on product regulation, and freedom of movement of the factors of production (capital and labour) and of enterprise. The goal is that the movement of capital, labour, goods, and services between the members is as easy as within them. This is the fourth stage of economic integration.

a. Quota share
b. Most favoured nation
c. Common market
d. Merchant bank

36. _____ involves the 'matching' of lenders with savings to borrowers who need money by an agent or third party, such as a bank.

If this matching is successful, the lender obtains a positive rate of return, the borrower receives a return for risk taking and entrepeneurship and the banker receives a marginal return for making the successful match. If the borrower's speculative play with the depositor's funds does not pay off, the depositor can lose the savings borrowed by the borrower and the bank can face significant losses on its loan portfolio.

a. Arranger
b. Annual percentage rate
c. Origination fee
d. Intermediation

37. A _____ is a professionally managed type of collective investment scheme that pools money from many investors and invests it in stocks, bonds, short-term money market instruments, and/or other securities. The _____ will have a fund manager that trades the pooled money on a regular basis. As of early 2008, the worldwide value of all _____s totals more than $26 trillion.

a. Mutual fund
c. Stakeholder pension scheme
b. Dark pools of liquidity
d. Net asset value

38. _____ is the revenue to a brokerage firm when commissioned securities and insurance salespeople sell a product, whether it is an investment like stocks, bonds or insurance like life insurance or long term care insurance. The commission that the agent receives is usually a percentage of this figure, although some firms like Merrill Lynch use figures called Production Credits, usually smaller than _____, to determine payouts and retain more revenue.

For example, a mutual fund with a 5.75% sales charge is sold to someone who invests $10,000.

a. Gross Dealer Concession
c. Ballpark model
b. Greater fool theory
d. Double bottom line

39. _____ is the prospect that a party insulated from risk may behave differently from the way it would behave if it were fully exposed to the risk. In insurance, _____ that occurs without conscious or malicious action is called morale hazard.

_____ is related to information asymmetry, a situation in which one party in a transaction has more information than another.

a. 1921 recession
c. Moral hazard
b. 100-year flood
d. 130-30 fund

40. _____, anti-selection insurance, statistics, and risk management. It refers to a market process in which 'bad' results occur when buyers and sellers have asymmetric information (i.e. access to different information): the 'bad' products or customers are more likely to be selected. A bank that sets one price for all its checking account customers runs the risk of being adversely selected against by its low-balance, high-activity (and hence least profitable) customers.
a. Adverse selection
c. ACCRA Cost of Living Index
b. AD-IA Model
d. ACEA agreement

41. In business and accounting, _____ are everything of value that is owned by a person or company. It is a claim on the property your income of a borrower. The balance sheet of a firm records the monetary value of the _____ owned by the firm.
a. ACCRA Cost of Living Index
c. Amortization schedule
b. Assets
d. ACEA agreement

42. The _____ consists of a number of economic theories which describe the nature of the firm, company including its existence, its behaviour, and its relationship with the market.

In simplified terms, the _____ aims to answer these questions:

1. Existence - why do firms emerge, why are not all transactions in the economy mediated over the market?
2. Boundaries - why the boundary between firms and the market is located exactly there? Which transactions are performed internally and which are negotiated on the market?
3. Organization - why are firms structured in such specific way? What is the interplay of formal and informal relationships?

Despite looking simple, these questions are not answered by the established economic theory, which usually views firms as given, and treats them as black boxes without any internal structure.

The First World War period saw a change of emphasis in economic theory away from industry-level analysis which mainly included analysing markets to analysis at the level of the firm, as it became increasingly clear that perfect competition was no longer an adequate model of how firms behaved. Economic theory till then had focussed on trying to understand markets alone and there had been little study on understanding why firms or organisations exist.

- a. Technology gap
- b. Neo-Ricardian school
- c. Theory of the firm
- d. Marginal revenue product

43. In general, a _____ is an arrangement to provide people with an income when they are no longer earning a regular income from employment.

The terms retirement plan or superannuation refer to a _____ granted upon retirement . Retirement plans may be set up by employers, insurance companies, the government or other institutions such as employer associations or trade unions.

- a. Pension insurance contract
- b. Profit-sharing agreement
- c. Merit pay
- d. Pension

44. The accounting equation relates assets, _____, and owner's equity:

Assets = _____ + Owner's Equity

The accounting equation is the mathematical structure of the balance sheet.

The Australian Accounting Research Foundation defines _____ as: 'future sacrifice of economic benefits that the entity is presently obliged to make to other entities as a result of past transactions and other past events.'

Probably the most accepted accounting definition of liability is the one used by the International Accounting Standards Board (IASB.) The following is a quotation from IFRS Framework:

A liability is a present obligation of the enterprise arising from past events, the settlement of which is expected to result in an outflow from the enterprise of resources embodying economic benefits

-

Regulations as to the recognition of _____ are different all over the world, but are roughly similar to those of the IASB.

Chapter 14. Money, Banking, and Central Banking

a. Landsbanki Freezing Order 2008
c. Liabilities
b. Due diligence
d. Human rights in Brazil

45. In economics, _____ is the monetary policy device that a country's government (i.e., sovereign power) uses to regulate the flows into and out of a country's capital account, i.e., the flows of investment-oriented money into and out of a country or currency. _____s have become more prominent in the years since the Clinton administration blessed the efforts of the world community to create the World Trade Organization (WTO), primarily because globalization has increased the acceleration of currency domain strength, in other words, giving some currencies utility far beyond their physical geographic boundaries.

One characteristic of developed economies is liquid debt markets.

a. Capital control
c. Monetary policy of Sweden
b. Second-round effect
d. Lombard credit

46. An _____ or index tracker is a collective investment scheme (usually a mutual fund or exchange-traded fund) that aims to replicate the movements of an index of a specific financial market regardless of market conditions.

Tracking can be achieved by trying to hold all of the securities in the index, in the same proportions as the index. Other methods include statistically sampling the market and holding 'representative' securities.

a. Asset management company
c. Investment trust
b. Unit trust
d. Index fund

47. _____s are deposits denominated in US dollars at banks outside the United States, and thus are not under the jurisdiction of the Federal Reserve. Consequently, such deposits are subject to much less regulation than similar deposits within the United States, allowing for higher margins. There is nothing 'European' about _____ deposits; a US dollar-denominated deposit in Tokyo or Caracas would likewise be deemed _____ deposits.
a. ACCRA Cost of Living Index
c. ACEA agreement
b. Eurodollar
d. AD-IA Model

48. _____ is that which is owed; usually referencing assets owed, but the term can also cover moral obligations and other interactions not requiring money. In the case of assets, _____ is a means of using future purchasing power in the present before a summation has been earned. Some companies and corporations use _____ as a part of their overall corporate finance strategy.
a. Non-performing loan
c. Participation loan
b. Subordinated debt
d. Debt

49. The _____ is an international financial institution that provides financial and technical assistance to developing countries for development programs (e.g. bridges, roads, schools, etc.) with the stated goal of reducing poverty.

The _____ differs from the _____ Group, in that the _____ comprises only two institutions:

- International Bank for Reconstruction and Development (IBRD)
- International Development Association (IDA)

Whereas the latter incorporates these two in addition to three more:

- International Finance Corporation (IFC)
- Multilateral Investment Guarantee Agency (MIGA)
- International Centre for Settlement of Investment Disputes (ICSID)

John Maynard Keynes (right) represented the UK at the conference, and Harry Dexter White represented the US.

The _____ is one of two major financial institutions created as a result of the Bretton Woods Conference in 1944. The International Monetary Fund, a related but separate institution, is the second.

a. World Bank
b. Black-Scholes
c. Demographic marketers
d. Dow Jones Industrial Average

50. The _____ is an Act of the 106th United States Congress which repealed part of the Glass-Steagall Act of 1933, opening up competition among banks, securities companies and insurance companies.
a. 130-30 fund
b. 100-year flood
c. 1921 recession
d. Gramm-Leach-Bliley Act

51. _____ is the central bank of Sweden and the world's oldest central bank. It is sometimes called the Swedish National Bank or the Bank of Sweden

The Riksbank began its operations in 1668, its antecedent being Stockholms Banco (also known as the Bank of Palmstruch), which was founded by Johan Palmstruch in 1656. Although the bank was private, it was the King who chose its management: in a letter to Palmstruch he gave permission to its operations according to stated regulations.

a. 130-30 fund
b. Sveriges Riksbank
c. 100-year flood
d. 1921 recession

52. _____s is the social science that studies the production, distribution, and consumption of goods and services. The term _____s comes from the Ancient Greek οἰκονομία from οἶκος (oikos, 'house') + νόμος (nomos, 'custom' or 'law'), hence 'rules of the house(hold)'. Current _____ models developed out of the broader field of political economy in the late 19th century, owing to a desire to use an empirical approach more akin to the physical sciences.
a. Inflation
b. Opportunity cost
c. Energy economics
d. Economic

53. Fractional-reserve banking is the banking practice in which banks keep only a fraction of their deposits in reserve (as cash and other highly liquid assets) and lend out the remainder, while maintaining the simultaneous obligation to redeem all these deposits upon demand. _____ necessarily occurs when banks lend out any fraction of the funds received from demand deposits. This practice is universal in modern banking.

a. Certificate of deposit
b. Repo Rate
c. Bank secrecy
d. Fractional reserve banking

54. The _____ , a component of the Federal Reserve System, is charged under United States law with overseeing the nation's open market operations. It is the Federal Reserve Committee that makes key decisions about interest rates and the growth jam of the United States money supply. It is the principal organ of United States national monetary policy.
   a. Federal Open Market Committee
   b. Taylor rule
   c. Term auction facility
   d. Federal Reserve System

55. In economics, the _____ is the term used to refer to the environment in which bonds are bought and sold between a central bank ' its regulated banks. It is not a free market process.

- To intervene in the 'business cycle', a central bank may choose to go into the _____ and buy or sell government bonds, which is known as _____ operations to increase reserves.

   a. ACCRA Cost of Living Index
   b. Outside money
   c. Open Market
   d. Inside money

56. A _____ refers to any type debt instrument, such as a loan, bond, mortgage that does not have a fixed rate of interest over the life of the instrument. Such debt typically uses an index or other base rate for establishing the interest rate for each relevant period. One of the most common rates to use as the basis for applying interest rates is the London Inter-bank Offered Rate, or LIBOR
   a. Standard of deferred payment
   b. Bankruptcy remote
   c. Style investing
   d. Floating interest rate

57. The _____ is a United States government corporation created by the Glass-Steagall Act of 1933. It provides deposit insurance, which guarantees the safety of deposits in member banks, currently up to $250,000 per depositor per bank. Funds in non-interest bearing transaction accounts are fully insured, with no limit, under the temporary Transaction Account Guarantee Program.
   a. National Bureau of Economic Research
   b. Deutsche Bank
   c. Financial Stability Board
   d. Federal Deposit Insurance Corporation

58. _____, in law and economics, is a form of risk management primarily used to hedge against the risk of a contingent loss. _____ is defined as the equitable transfer of the risk of a loss, from one entity to another, in exchange for a premium, and can be thought of as a guaranteed small loss to prevent a large, possibly devastating loss. An insurer is a company selling the _____; an insured or policyholder is the person or entity buying the _____.
   a. ACCRA Cost of Living Index
   b. ACEA agreement
   c. Insurance
   d. AD-IA Model

59. A _____ is an institution willing to extend credit when no one else will.

Originally the term referred to a reserve financial institution that secured other banks or eligible institutions, as a last resort; most often the central bank of a country. The purpose of this loan and lender is to prevent the collapse of institutions that are experiencing financial difficulty, most often near collapse.

a. Fractional reserve banking
c. Lender of last resort
b. Private money
d. Bank failure

60. The _____, an agency of the United States Department of the Treasury, is the primary regulator of federal savings associations (sometimes referred to as federal thrifts.) Federal savings associations include both federal savings banks and federal savings and loans. The OTS is also responsible for supervising savings and loan holding companies (SLHCs) and some state-chartered institutions.
   a. ACEA agreement
   c. Interstate Commerce Commission
   b. Office of Thrift Supervision
   d. ACCRA Cost of Living Index

1. _____ is the process by which the government, central bank (ii) availability of money, and (iii) cost of money or rate of interest, in order to attain a set of objectives oriented towards the growth and stability of the economy. Monetary theory provides insight into how to craft optimal _____.

_____ is referred to as either being an expansionary policy where an expansionary policy increases the total supply of money in the economy, and a contractionary policy decreases the total money supply.

a. Monetary policy
b. 130-30 fund
c. 100-year flood
d. 1921 recession

2. Fractional-reserve banking is the banking practice in which banks keep only a fraction of their deposits in reserve (as cash and other highly liquid assets) and lend out the remainder, while maintaining the simultaneous obligation to redeem all these deposits upon demand. _____ necessarily occurs when banks lend out any fraction of the funds received from demand deposits. This practice is universal in modern banking.
a. Repo Rate
b. Bank secrecy
c. Certificate of deposit
d. Fractional reserve banking

3. In economics, _____ is the total amount of money available in an economy at a particular point in time. There are several ways to define 'money', but standard measures usually include currency in circulation and demand deposits.

_____ data are recorded and published, usually by the government or the central bank of the country.

a. Fiscal theory of the price level
b. Monetary reform
c. Money supply
d. Monetary economy

4. _____s is the social science that studies the production, distribution, and consumption of goods and services. The term _____s comes from the Ancient Greek oá¼°κονομῖα from oá¼¶κος (oikos, 'house') + vÏŒμος (nomos, 'custom' or 'law'), hence 'rules of the house(hold)'. Current _____ models developed out of the broader field of political economy in the late 19th century, owing to a desire to use an empirical approach more akin to the physical sciences.
a. Economic
b. Inflation
c. Energy economics
d. Opportunity cost

5. _____, in law and economics, is a form of risk management primarily used to hedge against the risk of a contingent loss. _____ is defined as the equitable transfer of the risk of a loss, from one entity to another, in exchange for a premium, and can be thought of as a guaranteed small loss to prevent a large, possibly devastating loss. An insurer is a company selling the _____; an insured or policyholder is the person or entity buying the _____.
a. ACEA agreement
b. AD-IA Model
c. Insurance
d. ACCRA Cost of Living Index

6. The _____ is the central banking system of the United States. Created in 1913 by the enactment of the Federal Reserve Act (signed by Woodrow Wilson), it is a quasi-public and quasi-private (government entity with private components) banking system that comprises (1) the presidentially appointed Board of Governors of the _____ in Washington, D.C.; (2) the Federal Open Market Committee; (3) twelve regional Federal Reserve Banks located in major cities throughout the nation acting as fiscal agents for the U.S. Treasury, each with its own nine-member board of directors; (4) numerous other private U.S. member banks, which subscribe to required amounts of non-transferable stock in their regional Federal Reserve Banks; and (5) various advisory councils. Since February 2006, Ben Bernanke has served as the Chairman of the Board of Governors of the _____.

| a. Federal Reserve Transparency Act | b. Federal Reserve System |
| c. Federal Reserve Banks | d. Federal funds rate |

7. In economics, _____ is a rise in the general level of prices of goods and services in an economy over a period of time. When the general price level rises, each unit of currency buys fewer goods and services; consequently, _____ is also a decline in the real value of money--a loss of purchasing power in the medium of exchange which is also the monetary unit of account in the economy. A chief measure of general price-level _____ is the general _____ rate, which is the percentage change in a general price index (normally the Consumer Price Index) over time.

| a. Economic | b. Energy economics |
| c. Inflation | d. Opportunity cost |

8. In economics, the _____ is a measure of inflation, the rate of increase of a price index (for example, a consumer price index.)It is the percentage rate of change in price level over time. The rate of decrease in the purchasing power of money is approximately equal.

It's used to calculate the real interest rate, as well as real increases in wages, and official measurements of this rate act as input variables to COLA adjustments and Inflation derivatives prices.

| a. Inflation rate | b. Edgeworth paradox |
| c. Interest rate option | d. Equity value |

9. In banking, _____ are bank reserves in excess of the reserve requirement set by a central bank (in the United States, the Federal Reserve System, called the Fed; in Canada, the Bank of Canada.) They are reserves of cash more than the required amounts. Holding _____ is generally considered costly and uneconomical as no interest is earned on the excess amount.

| a. Origination fee | b. Annual percentage rate |
| c. Universal bank | d. Excess reserves |

10. A _____ is an expression that compares quantities relative to each other. The most common examples involve two quantities, but any number of quantities can be compared. _____s are represented mathematically by separating each quantity with a colon, for example the _____ 2:3, which is read as the _____ 'two to three'.

| a. 100-year flood | b. 130-30 fund |
| c. Ratio | d. Y-intercept |

11. The reserve requirement (or required _____) is a bank regulation that sets the minimum reserves each bank must hold to customer deposits and notes. It would normally be in the form of fiat currency stored in a bank vault (vault cash), or with a central bank.

The _____ is sometimes used as a tool in the monetary policy, influencing the country's economy, borrowing, and interest rates.

| a. Reserve ratio | b. Compound Interest Treasury Notes |
| c. Commodity trading advisors | d. Hybrid renewable energy systems |

Chapter 15. Money Creation and Deposit Insurance

12. The _____ is the difference between the monetary value of exports and imports in an economy over a certain period of time. It is the relationship between a nation's imports and exports. A positive _____ is known as a trade surplus and consists of exporting more than is imported; a negative _____ is known as a trade deficit or, informally, a trade gap.
    a. Technology shock
    b. Lucas-Islands model
    c. Rational expectations
    d. Balance of trade

13. In business, _____ is the total liabilitiess minus total outside assets of an individual or a company. For a company, this is called shareholders' prefernce and may be referred to as book value. _____ is stated as at a particular year in time.
    a. Floating interest rate
    b. Longevity insurance
    c. Certified International Investment Analyst
    d. Net worth

14. The _____ , a component of the Federal Reserve System, is charged under United States law with overseeing the nation's open market operations. It is the Federal Reserve Committee that makes key decisions about interest rates and the growth jam of the United States money supply. It is the principal organ of United States national monetary policy.
    a. Federal Open Market Committee
    b. Term auction facility
    c. Federal Reserve System
    d. Taylor rule

15. A _____ is a type of banknote issued by the Federal Reserve System and is the only type of U.S. banknote that is still produced today.

    _____s are fiat currency, with the words 'this note is legal tender for all debts, public and private' printed on each bill. (See generally 31 U.S.C.

    a. Federal banking
    b. Federal Reserve note
    c. Primary Dealer Credit Facility
    d. Federal Reserve System Open Market Account

16. In economics, the _____ is the term used to refer to the environment in which bonds are bought and sold between a central bank ' its regulated banks. It is not a free market process.

    - To intervene in the 'business cycle', a central bank may choose to go into the _____ and buy or sell government bonds, which is known as _____ operations to increase reserves.

    a. Open Market
    b. ACCRA Cost of Living Index
    c. Outside money
    d. Inside money

17. _____ are the means of implementing monetary policy by which a central bank controls its national money supply by buying and selling government securities, or other financial instruments. Monetary targets, such as interest rates or exchange rates, are used to guide this implementation.

    Since most money is now in the form of electronic records, rather than paper records such as banknotes, _____ are conducted simply by electronically increasing or decreasing ('crediting' or 'debiting') the amount of money that a bank has, e.g., in its reserve account at the central bank, in exchange for a bank selling or buying a financial instrument.

a. AD-IA Model
b. ACCRA Cost of Living Index
c. ACEA agreement
d. Open market operations

18. A security is a fungible, negotiable instrument representing financial value. _____ are broadly categorized into debt _____; equity _____, e.g., common stocks; and derivative (finance) contracts such as forwards, futures, options and swaps. The company or other entity issuing the security is called the issuer.
   a. Securities
   b. Pure security
   c. Street name securities
   d. Trading account assets

19. _____ is that which is owed; usually referencing assets owed, but the term can also cover moral obligations and other interactions not requiring money. In the case of assets, _____ is a means of using future purchasing power in the present before a summation has been earned. Some companies and corporations use _____ as a part of their overall corporate finance strategy.
   a. Participation loan
   b. Subordinated debt
   c. Non-performing loan
   d. Debt

20. The most common mechanism used to measure this increase in the money supply is typically called the _____. It calculates the maximum amount of money that an initial deposit can be expanded to with a given reserve ratio - such a factor is called a multiplier.

The _____, m, is the inverse of the reserve requirement, R:

$$m = \frac{1}{R}$$

This formula stems from the fact that the sum of the 'amount loaned out' column above can be expressed mathematically as a geometric series with a common ratio of 1 − R.

   a. High yield stock
   b. 43rd Elizabeth
   c. Money multiplier
   d. Lawcards

21. _____ is money accepted for exchange of goods in an economy. The prevalence of one money over another arises, usually, when a government designates through decrees that the government shall accept only particular notes and coins in payment for taxes. Typically, money of _____ consists of stamped coins and minted paper bills.
   a. Currency
   b. Totnes pound
   c. Security thread
   d. Scripophily

22. Discounting is a financial mechanism in which a debtor obtains the right to delay payments to a creditor, for a defined period of time, in exchange for a charge or fee. Essentially, the party that owes money in the present purchases the right to delay the payment until some future date. The _____, or charge, is simply the difference between the original amount owed in the present and the amount that has to be paid in the future to settle the debt.
   a. Panjer recursion
   b. Risk measure
   c. Compound annual growth rate
   d. Discount

23. The _____ is an interest rate a central bank charges depository institutions that borrow reserves from it.

The term _____ has two meanings:

- the same as interest rate; the term 'discount' does not refer to the meaning of the word, but to the purpose of using the quantity, such as computations of present value, e.g. net present value or discounted cash flow

- the annual effective _____, which is the annual interest divided by the capital including that interest; this rate is lower than the interest rate; it corresponds to using the value after a year as the nominal value, and seeing the initial value as the nominal value minus a discount; it is used for Treasury Bills and similar financial instruments

The annual effective _____ is the annual interest divided by the capital including that interest, which is the interest rate divided by 100% plus the interest rate. It is the annual discount factor to be applied to the future cash flow, to find the discount, subtracted from a future value to find the value one year earlier.

For example, suppose there is a government bond that sells for $95 and pays $100 in a year's time.

    a. LIBOR market model
    b. Current yield
    c. Stochastic volatility
    d. Discount rate

24. In the United States, _____ are overnight borrowings by banks to maintain their bank reserves at the Federal Reserve. Banks keep reserves at Federal Reserve Banks to meet their reserve requirements and to clear financial transactions. Transactions in the _____ market enable depository institutions with reserve balances in excess of reserve requirements to lend reserves to institutions with reserve deficiencies.
    a. Monetary Policy Report to the Congress
    b. Term Securities Lending Facility
    c. Federal funds rate
    d. Federal funds

25. In the United States, the _____ is the interest rate at which private depository institutions (mostly banks) lend balances (federal funds) at the Federal Reserve to other depository institutions, usually overnight. It is the interest rate banks charge each other for loans. Changing the target rate is one way the Chairman of the Federal Reserve can influence the supply of money in the U.S. economy..
    a. Federal funds rate
    b. Federal Reserve Note
    c. Federal Reserve System
    d. Monetary Policy Report to the Congress

26. Necessary _____s:

If x is a necessary _____ of y, then the presence of y necessarily implies the presence of x. The presence of x, however, does not imply that y will occur.

Sufficient _____s:

If x is a sufficient _____ of y, then the presence of x necessarily implies the presence of y.

Chapter 15. Money Creation and Deposit Insurance

a. Deductive logic
b. Global justice
c. Materialism
d. Cause

27. A _____ is an account set up at a bank or other financial institution where the funds are automatically managed between a primary cash account and secondary investment accounts.

In banking, _____s are primarily used as a legal workaround to the prohibition on paying interest on business checking accounts. In this system, the funds are described as being 'swept overnight' into an investment vehicle of some kind.

a. Double default
b. Sweep account
c. Banking license
d. Pitch Book

28. A _____, reserve bank, or monetary authority is the entity responsible for the monetary policy of a country or of a group of member states. It is a bank that can lend money to other banks in times of need. Its primary responsibility is to maintain the stability of the national currency and money supply, but more active duties include controlling subsidized-loan interest rates, and acting as a lender of last resort to the banking sector during times of financial crisis (private banks often being integral to the national financial system.)

a. 100-year flood
b. 130-30 fund
c. 1921 recession
d. Central Bank

29. _____ is sometimes referred to as _____, actually it means Economic Monetary Union.

First ideas of an economic and monetary union in Europe were raised well before establishing the European Communities. For example, already in the League of Nations, Gustav Stresemann asked in 1929 for a European currency (Link) against the background of an increased economic division due to a number of new nation states in Europe after WWI.

a. Exchange rate mechanism
b. European Monetary Union
c. European Monetary System
d. Euro Interbank Offered Rate

30. The _____ is composed of the European Central Bank (ECB) and the national central banks (NCBs) of all 27 European Union (EU) Member States.

Since not all the EU states have joined the Euro, the ESCB could not be used as the monetary authority of the eurozone. For this reason the Eurosystem (which excludes all the NCBs which have not adopted the Euro) became the institution in charge of those tasks which in principle had to be managed by the ESCB.

a. ACCRA Cost of Living Index
b. European System of Central Banks
c. AD-IA Model
d. ACEA agreement

31. The _____ is an economic and political union of 27 member states, located primarily in Europe. It was established by the Treaty of Maastricht on 1 November 1993, upon the foundations of the pre-existing European Economic Community. With a population of almost 500 million, the _____ generates an estimated 30% share (US$18.4 trillion in 2008) of the nominal gross world product.

Chapter 15. Money Creation and Deposit Insurance

a. ACEA agreement
b. European Court of Justice
c. European Union
d. ACCRA Cost of Living Index

32. An economic and _____ is a single market with a common currency. It is to be distinguished from a mere currency union, which does not involve a single market. This is the fifth stage of economic integration.

a. Certificate of origin
b. Green market
c. Metzler paradox
d. Monetary Union

33. _____ and Keynesian Theory) is a macroeconomic theory based on the ideas of 20th-century British economist John Maynard Keynes. _____ argues that private sector decisions sometimes lead to inefficient macroeconomic outcomes and therefore advocates active policy responses by the public sector, including monetary policy actions by the central bank and fiscal policy actions by the government to stabilize output over the business cycle.

The theories forming the basis of _____ were first presented in The General Theory of Employment, Interest and Money, published in 1936.

a. Gross domestic product
b. Recession
c. Rational choice theory
d. Keynesian economics

34. The _____ consists of a number of economic theories which describe the nature of the firm, company including its existence, its behaviour, and its relationship with the market.

In simplified terms, the _____ aims to answer these questions:

1. Existence - why do firms emerge, why are not all transactions in the economy mediated over the market?
2. Boundaries - why the boundary between firms and the market is located exactly there? Which transactions are performed internally and which are negotiated on the market?
3. Organization - why are firms structured in such specific way? What is the interplay of formal and informal relationships?

Despite looking simple, these questions are not answered by the established economic theory, which usually views firms as given, and treats them as black boxes without any internal structure.

The First World War period saw a change of emphasis in economic theory away from industry-level analysis which mainly included analysing markets to analysis at the level of the firm, as it became increasingly clear that perfect competition was no longer an adequate model of how firms behaved. Economic theory till then had focussed on trying to understand markets alone and there had been little study on understanding why firms or organisations exist.

a. Neo-Ricardian school
b. Technology gap
c. Marginal revenue product
d. Theory of the firm

Chapter 15. Money Creation and Deposit Insurance

35. A _____ refers to any type debt instrument, such as a loan, bond, mortgage that does not have a fixed rate of interest over the life of the instrument. Such debt typically uses an index or other base rate for establishing the interest rate for each relevant period. One of the most common rates to use as the basis for applying interest rates is the London Inter-bank Offered Rate, or LIBOR

    a. Style investing

    b. Standard of deferred payment

    c. Bankruptcy remote

    d. Floating interest rate

36. The _____ is a United States government corporation created by the Glass-Steagall Act of 1933. It provides deposit insurance, which guarantees the safety of deposits in member banks, currently up to $250,000 per depositor per bank. Funds in non-interest bearing transaction accounts are fully insured, with no limit, under the temporary Transaction Account Guarantee Program.

    a. Financial Stability Board

    b. National Bureau of Economic Research

    c. Federal Deposit Insurance Corporation

    d. Deutsche Bank

37. The _____ was an institution that administered deposit insurance for savings and loan institutions in the United States. It was abolished in 1989 by the Financial Institutions Reform, Recovery and Enforcement Act, which passed responsibility for savings and loan deposit insurance to the Federal Deposit Insurance Corporation (FDIC.)

The FSLIC was created as part of the National Housing Act of 1934 in order to insure deposits in savings and loans, a year after the FDIC was created to insure deposits in commercial banks.

    a. Net capital rule

    b. Federal Savings and Loan Insurance Corporation

    c. Federal Financial Institutions Examination Council

    d. Covered security

38. The _____ was a worldwide economic downturn starting in most places in 1929 and ending at different times in the 1930s or early 1940s for different countries. It was the largest and most important economic depression in the 20th century, and is used in the 21st century as an example of how far the world's economy can fall. The _____ originated in the United States; historians most often use as a starting date the stock market crash on October 29, 1929, known as Black Tuesday.

    a. Causes of the Great Depression

    b. British Empire Economic Conference

    c. The Great Depression

    d. Great Depression

39. A _____ association is a financial institution that specializes in accepting savings deposits and making mortgage and other loans. The S'L or thrift term is mainly used in the United States; similar institutions in the United Kingdom, Ireland and some Commonwealth countries include building societies and trustee savings banks.

They are often mutually held, meaning that the depositors and borrowers are members with voting rights, and have the ability to direct the financial and managerial goals of the organization, similar to the policyholders of a mutual insurance company.

    a. Fund Platform

    b. Passive management

    c. Savings and Loan

    d. Pension simplification

40. A _____ occurs when a bank is unable to meet its obligations to its depositors or other creditors. More specifically, a bank fails economically when the market value of its assets declines to a value that is less than the market value of its liabilities. As such, the bank is unable to fulfill the demands of all of its depositors on time.

a. Transactional account
c. Bank secrecy
b. Funds Transfer Pricing
d. Bank failure

41. A _____ occurs when a large number of bank customers withdraw their deposits because they believe the bank is insolvent. As a _____ progresses, it generates its own momentum, in a kind of self-fulfilling prophecy: as more people withdraw their deposits, the likelihood of default increases, and this encourages further withdrawals. This can destabilize the bank to the point where it faces bankruptcy.
   a. Bank run
   c. Soft probe
   b. Tier 2 capital
   d. Fractional reserve banking

42. _____, anti-selection insurance, statistics, and risk management. It refers to a market process in which 'bad' results occur when buyers and sellers have asymmetric information (i.e. access to different information): the 'bad' products or customers are more likely to be selected. A bank that sets one price for all its checking account customers runs the risk of being adversely selected against by its low-balance, high-activity (and hence least profitable) customers.
   a. ACEA agreement
   c. AD-IA Model
   b. ACCRA Cost of Living Index
   d. Adverse selection

43. _____ involves the 'matching' of lenders with savings to borrowers who need money by an agent or third party, such as a bank.

If this matching is successful, the lender obtains a positive rate of return, the borrower receives a return for risk taking and entrepeneurship and the banker receives a marginal return for making the successful match. If the borrower's speculative play with the depositor's funds does not pay off, the depositor can lose the savings borrowed by the borrower and the bank can face significant losses on its loan portfolio.

   a. Arranger
   c. Intermediation
   b. Annual percentage rate
   d. Origination fee

44. In finance, the _____ is the global financial market for short-term borrowing and lending. It provides short-term liquidity funding for the global financial system. The _____ is where short-term obligations such as Treasury bills, commercial paper and bankers' acceptances are bought and sold.
   a. Post earnings announcement drift
   c. Bankruptcy remote
   b. Financial rand
   d. Money market

45. _____ is the prospect that a party insulated from risk may behave differently from the way it would behave if it were fully exposed to the risk. In insurance, _____ that occurs without conscious or malicious action is called morale hazard.

_____ is related to information asymmetry, a situation in which one party in a transaction has more information than another.

   a. 130-30 fund
   c. 1921 recession
   b. 100-year flood
   d. Moral hazard

46. A _____ allows a borrower to use a financial security as collateral for a cash loan at a fixed rate of interest. In a repo, the borrower agrees to sell immediately a security to a lender and also agrees to buy the same security from the lender at a fixed price at some later date. A repo is equivalent to a cash transaction combined with a forward contract.

a. Constant maturity swap b. Stock market index future
c. Portfolio insurance d. Repurchase agreement

Chapter 16. Domestic and International Dimensions of Monetary Policy   145

1. A _____, reserve bank, or monetary authority is the entity responsible for the monetary policy of a country or of a group of member states. It is a bank that can lend money to other banks in times of need. Its primary responsibility is to maintain the stability of the national currency and money supply, but more active duties include controlling subsidized-loan interest rates, and acting as a lender of last resort to the banking sector during times of financial crisis (private banks often being integral to the national financial system.)

   a. 100-year flood
   b. 1921 recession
   c. 130-30 fund
   d. Central Bank

2. The _____ is one of the world's most important central banks, responsible for monetary policy covering the 16 member States of the Eurozone. It was established by the European Union (EU) in 1998 with its headquarters in Frankfurt, Germany.

   The predecessor to the _____ was the European Monetary Institute.

   a. ACCRA Cost of Living Index
   b. ACEA agreement
   c. AD-IA Model
   d. European Central Bank

3. _____ is sometimes referred to as _____, actually it means Economic Monetary Union.

   First ideas of an economic and monetary union in Europe were raised well before establishing the European Communities. For example, already in the League of Nations, Gustav Stresemann asked in 1929 for a European currency (Link) against the background of an increased economic division due to a number of new nation states in Europe after WWI.

   a. European Monetary System
   b. European Monetary Union
   c. Euro Interbank Offered Rate
   d. Exchange rate mechanism

4. The _____ is an economic and political union of 27 member states, located primarily in Europe. It was established by the Treaty of Maastricht on 1 November 1993, upon the foundations of the pre-existing European Economic Community. With a population of almost 500 million, the _____ generates an estimated 30% share (US$18.4 trillion in 2008) of the nominal gross world product.

   a. ACEA agreement
   b. European Court of Justice
   c. European Union
   d. ACCRA Cost of Living Index

5. A _____ is a type of banknote issued by the Federal Reserve System and is the only type of U.S. banknote that is still produced today.

   _____s are fiat currency, with the words 'this note is legal tender for all debts, public and private' printed on each bill. (See generally 31 U.S.C.

   a. Federal Reserve System Open Market Account
   b. Federal banking
   c. Primary Dealer Credit Facility
   d. Federal Reserve note

6. The _____ was a worldwide economic downturn starting in most places in 1929 and ending at different times in the 1930s or early 1940s for different countries. It was the largest and most important economic depression in the 20th century, and is used in the 21st century as an example of how far the world's economy can fall. The _____ originated in the United States; historians most often use as a starting date the stock market crash on October 29, 1929, known as Black Tuesday.
   a. Great Depression
   b. Causes of the Great Depression
   c. The Great Depression
   d. British Empire Economic Conference

7. An economic and _____ is a single market with a common currency. It is to be distinguished from a mere currency union, which does not involve a single market. This is the fifth stage of economic integration.
   a. Green market
   b. Metzler paradox
   c. Certificate of origin
   d. Monetary Union

8. _____ is the process by which the government, central bank (ii) availability of money, and (iii) cost of money or rate of interest, in order to attain a set of objectives oriented towards the growth and stability of the economy. Monetary theory provides insight into how to craft optimal _____.

_____ is referred to as either being an expansionary policy where an expansionary policy increases the total supply of money in the economy, and a contractionary policy decreases the total money supply.

   a. 1921 recession
   b. Monetary policy
   c. 100-year flood
   d. 130-30 fund

9. _____ refers to a business or organization attempting to acquire goods or services to accomplish the goals of the enterprise. Though there are several organizations that attempt to set standards in the _____ process, processes can vary greatly between organizations. Typically the word '_____' is not used interchangeably with the word 'procurement', since procurement typically includes Expediting, Supplier Quality, and Traffic and Logistics (T'L) in addition to _____.
   a. Purchasing
   b. Free port
   c. 130-30 fund
   d. 100-year flood

10. _____ is the number of goods/services that can be purchased with a unit of currency. For example, if you had taken one dollar to a store in the 1950s, you would have been able to buy a greater number of items than you would today, indicating that you would have had a greater _____ in the 1950s. Currency can be either a commodity money, like gold or silver, or fiat currency like US dollars.
    a. Neofeudalism
    b. Female economic activity
    c. Forgotten man
    d. Purchasing power

11. In business and accounting, _____ are everything of value that is owned by a person or company. It is a claim on the property your income of a borrower. The balance sheet of a firm records the monetary value of the _____ owned by the firm.
    a. ACEA agreement
    b. ACCRA Cost of Living Index
    c. Amortization schedule
    d. Assets

Chapter 16. Domestic and International Dimensions of Monetary Policy

12. Economics:

    - _____ ,the desire to own something and the ability to pay for it
    - _____ curve,a graphic representation of a _____ schedule
    - _____ deposit, the money in checking accounts
    - _____ pull theory,the theory that inflation occurs when _____ for goods and services exceeds existing supplies
    - _____ schedule,a table that lists the quantity of a good a person will buy it each different price
    - _____ side economics,the school of economics at believes government spending and tax cuts open economy by raising _____

    a. Demand
    b. G20
    c. Procter ' Gamble
    d. Bon

13. _____ is the demand for financial assets, such as securities, money or foreign currency; it is money people want in case of emergency.

    In economic theory, specifically Keynesian economics, _____ is one of the determinants of demand for money (and credit), the others being transactions demand and Speculative demand.

    a. Precautionary demand
    b. Marshallian demand function
    c. Kinked demand
    d. Kinked demand curve

14. _____ is the demand for financial assets, e.g., securities, money or foreign currency. It is used for purposes of business transactions and personal consumption.

    The need to accommodate a firm's expected cash transactions.

    a. Keynesian formula
    b. Keynesian Revolution
    c. Multiplier effect
    d. Transactions demand

15. The _____ is the desired holding of money balances in the form of cash or bank deposits.

    Money is dominated as store of value by interest bearing assets. However, money is necessary to carry out transactions, or in other words, it provides liquidity.

    a. Discretionary policy
    b. Cleanup clause
    c. Liquidating dividend
    d. Demand for Money

16. _____ or economic opportunity loss is the value of the next best alternative foregone as the result of making a decision. _____ analysis is an important part of a company's decision-making processes but is not treated as an actual cost in any financial statement. The next best thing that a person can engage in is referred to as the _____ of doing the best thing and ignoring the next best thing to be done.

a. Economic
b. Industrial organization
c. Economic ideology
d. Opportunity cost

17. _____ and Keynesian Theory) is a macroeconomic theory based on the ideas of 20th-century British economist John Maynard Keynes. _____ argues that private sector decisions sometimes lead to inefficient macroeconomic outcomes and therefore advocates active policy responses by the public sector, including monetary policy actions by the central bank and fiscal policy actions by the government to stabilize output over the business cycle.

The theories forming the basis of _____ were first presented in The General Theory of Employment, Interest and Money, published in 1936.

a. Rational choice theory
b. Gross domestic product
c. Recession
d. Keynesian economics

18. In economics, the _____ is the term used to refer to the environment in which bonds are bought and sold between a central bank ' its regulated banks. It is not a free market process.

- To intervene in the 'business cycle', a central bank may choose to go into the _____ and buy or sell government bonds, which is known as _____ operations to increase reserves.

a. Outside money
b. ACCRA Cost of Living Index
c. Open market
d. Inside money

19. _____ are the means of implementing monetary policy by which a central bank controls its national money supply by buying and selling government securities, or other financial instruments. Monetary targets, such as interest rates or exchange rates, are used to guide this implementation.

Since most money is now in the form of electronic records, rather than paper records such as banknotes, _____ are conducted simply by electronically increasing or decreasing ('crediting' or 'debiting') the amount of money that a bank has, e.g., in its reserve account at the central bank, in exchange for a bank selling or buying a financial instrument.

a. Open market operations
b. ACEA agreement
c. AD-IA Model
d. ACCRA Cost of Living Index

20. A security is a fungible, negotiable instrument representing financial value. _____ are broadly categorized into debt _____; equity _____, e.g., common stocks; and derivative (finance) contracts such as forwards, futures, options and swaps. The company or other entity issuing the security is called the issuer.

a. Trading account assets
b. Pure security
c. Street name securities
d. Securities

21. Discounting is a financial mechanism in which a debtor obtains the right to delay payments to a creditor, for a defined period of time, in exchange for a charge or fee. Essentially, the party that owes money in the present purchases the right to delay the payment until some future date. The _____, or charge, is simply the difference between the original amount owed in the present and the amount that has to be paid in the future to settle the debt.

Chapter 16. Domestic and International Dimensions of Monetary Policy

a. Compound annual growth rate
b. Panjer recursion
c. Risk measure
d. Discount

22. The _____ is an interest rate a central bank charges depository institutions that borrow reserves from it.

The term _____ has two meanings:

- the same as interest rate; the term 'discount' does not refer to the meaning of the word, but to the purpose of using the quantity, such as computations of present value, e.g. net present value or discounted cash flow

- the annual effective _____, which is the annual interest divided by the capital including that interest; this rate is lower than the interest rate; it corresponds to using the value after a year as the nominal value, and seeing the initial value as the nominal value minus a discount; it is used for Treasury Bills and similar financial instruments

The annual effective _____ is the annual interest divided by the capital including that interest, which is the interest rate divided by 100% plus the interest rate. It is the annual discount factor to be applied to the future cash flow, to find the discount, subtracted from a future value to find the value one year earlier.

For example, suppose there is a government bond that sells for $95 and pays $100 in a year's time.

a. Discount rate
b. Current yield
c. Stochastic volatility
d. LIBOR market model

23. In the United States, _____ are overnight borrowings by banks to maintain their bank reserves at the Federal Reserve. Banks keep reserves at Federal Reserve Banks to meet their reserve requirements and to clear financial transactions. Transactions in the _____ market enable depository institutions with reserve balances in excess of reserve requirements to lend reserves to institutions with reserve deficiencies.

a. Federal funds rate
b. Federal funds
c. Monetary Policy Report to the Congress
d. Term Securities Lending Facility

24. In the United States, the _____ is the interest rate at which private depository institutions (mostly banks) lend balances (federal funds) at the Federal Reserve to other depository institutions, usually overnight. It is the interest rate banks charge each other for loans. Changing the target rate is one way the Chairman of the Federal Reserve can influence the supply of money in the U.S. economy..

a. Federal Reserve System
b. Monetary Policy Report to the Congress
c. Federal funds rate
d. Federal Reserve Note

25. _____ is a fee paid on borrowed assets. It is the price paid for the use of borrowed money, or, money earned by deposited funds. Assets that are sometimes lent with _____ include money, shares, consumer goods through hire purchase, major assets such as aircraft, and even entire factories in finance lease arrangements.

a. Insolvency
b. Asset protection
c. Internal debt
d. Interest

Chapter 16. Domestic and International Dimensions of Monetary Policy

26. _____ in economics and business is the result of an exchange and from that trade we assign a numerical monetary value to a good, service or asset. If Alice trades Bob 4 apples for an orange, the _____ of an orange is 4 apples. Inversely, the _____ of an apple is 1/4 oranges.

   a. Price dispersion
                                                  b. Lerner Index
   c. Price
                                                         d. Price ceiling

27. In finance, a _____ is a debt security, in which the authorized issuer owes the holders a debt and, depending on the terms of the _____, is obliged to pay interest (the coupon) and/or to repay the principal at a later date, termed maturity. A _____ is a formal contract to repay borrowed money with interest at fixed intervals.

Thus a _____ is like a loan: the issuer is the borrower (debtor), the holder is the lender (creditor), and the coupon is the interest.

   a. Prize Bond
                                                   b. Callable
   c. Carter bonds
                                              d. Bond

28. An _____ is the price a borrower pays for the use of money they do not own, for instance a small company might borrow from a bank to kick start their business, and the return a lender receives for deferring the use of funds, by lending it to the borrower. _____s are normally expressed as a percentage rate over the period of one year.

_____s targets are also a vital tool of monetary policy and are used to control variables like investment, inflation, and unemployment.

   a. Arrow-Debreu model
                             b. Interest rate
   c. Enterprise value
                              d. ACCRA Cost of Living Index

29. In economics, _____ is the total amount of money available in an economy at a particular point in time. There are several ways to define 'money', but standard measures usually include currency in circulation and demand deposits.

_____ data are recorded and published, usually by the government or the central bank of the country.

   a. Monetary reform
                             b. Fiscal theory of the price level
   c. Monetary economy
                         d. Money supply

30. A _____ is an account set up at a bank or other financial institution where the funds are automatically managed between a primary cash account and secondary investment accounts.

In banking, _____s are primarily used as a legal workaround to the prohibition on paying interest on business checking accounts. In this system, the funds are described as being 'swept overnight' into an investment vehicle of some kind.

   a. Banking license
                             b. Sweep account
   c. Pitch Book
                             d. Double default

Chapter 16. Domestic and International Dimensions of Monetary Policy

31. An _____ is an economy in which people, including businesses, can trade in goods and services with other people and businesses in the international community at large. This contrasts with a closed economy in which international trade cannot take place.

The act of selling goods or services to a foreign country is called exporting.

- a. Attention work
- b. Indicative planning
- c. Information economy
- d. Open economy

32. In economics, _____ is the total demand for final goods and services in the economy (Y) at a given time and price level. It is the amount of goods and services in the economy that will be purchased at all possible price levels. This is the demand for the gross domestic product of a country when inventory levels are static.
- a. Aggregate demand
- b. Aggregation problem
- c. Aggregate supply
- d. Aggregate expenditure

33. _____ is a term used in accounting relating to the increase in value of an asset. In this sense it is the reverse of depreciation, which measures the fall in value of assets over their normal life-time.

_____ is a rise of a currency in a floating exchange rate.

- a. Appreciation
- b. ACEA agreement
- c. ACCRA Cost of Living Index
- d. AD-IA Model

34. _____ is money accepted for exchange of goods in an economy. The prevalence of one money over another arises, usually, when a government designates through decrees that the government shall accept only particular notes and coins in payment for taxes. Typically, money of _____ consists of stamped coins and minted paper bills.
- a. Totnes pound
- b. Scripophily
- c. Security thread
- d. Currency

35. The term _____ refers to government debt, expenditures and revenues, or to finance (particularly financial revenue) in general.

- _____ deficit is the budget deficit of federal or local government
- _____ policy is the discretionary spending of governments. Contrasts with monetary policy.
- _____ year and _____ quarter are reporting periods for firms and other agencies.

- a. Consequence
- b. Freedom Park
- c. Russian financial crisis
- d. Fiscal

36. In economics, _____ is the use of government spending and revenue collection to influence the economy.

_____ can be contrasted with the other main type of economic policy, monetary policy, which attempts to stabilize the economy by controlling interest rates and the supply of money. The two main instruments of _____ are government spending and taxation.

a. Fiscalism
b. 100-year flood
c. Fiscal policy
d. Sustainable investment rule

37. In finance, the _____ is the global financial market for short-term borrowing and lending. It provides short-term liquidity funding for the global financial system. The _____ is where short-term obligations such as Treasury bills, commercial paper and bankers' acceptances are bought and sold.

a. Financial rand
b. Post earnings announcement drift
c. Money market
d. Bankruptcy remote

38. In economics, an _____ is any good or commodity, transported from one country to another country in a legitimate fashion, typically for use in trade. _____ goods or services are provided to foreign consumers by domestic producers. _____ is an important part of international trade.

a. AD-IA Model
b. ACEA agreement
c. ACCRA Cost of Living Index
d. Export

39. _____ in its literal sense is the process of transformation of local or regional phenomena into global ones. It can be described as a process by which the people of the world are unified into a single society and function together.

This process is a combination of economic, technological, sociocultural and political forces.

a. Globally Integrated Enterprise
b. Helsinki Process on Globalisation and Democracy
c. Global Cosmopolitanism
d. Globalization

40. In economics, the _____ is the relation:

$$M \cdot V = P \cdot Q$$

where, for a given period,

M is the total amount of money in circulation on average in an economy.
V is the velocity of money, that is the average frequency with which a unit of money is spent.
P is the price level.

a. Open market
b. Outside money
c. Equation of exchange
d. ACCRA Cost of Living Index

41. In economics, _____ is a rise in the general level of prices of goods and services in an economy over a period of time. When the general price level rises, each unit of currency buys fewer goods and services; consequently, _____ is also a decline in the real value of money--a loss of purchasing power in the medium of exchange which is also the monetary unit of account in the economy. A chief measure of general price-level _____ is the general _____ rate, which is the percentage change in a general price index (normally the Consumer Price Index) over time.

Chapter 16. Domestic and International Dimensions of Monetary Policy   153

a. Opportunity cost
b. Energy economics
c. Economic
d. Inflation

42. In economics, the _____ of money is a theory emphasizing the positive relationship of overall prices or the nominal value of expenditures to the quantity of money.

It is the mainstream economic theory of the price level. Alternative theories include the real bills doctrine and the more recent fiscal theory of the price level.

a. War economy
b. Microsimulation
c. Quantity theory
d. World Currency Unit

43. The _____ is the average frequency with which a unit of money is spent in a specific period of time. Velocity associates the amount of economic activity associated with a given money supply. When the period is understood, the velocity may be present as a pure number; otherwise it should be given as a pure number over time.

a. Chartalism
b. Veil of money
c. Neutrality of money
d. Velocity of Money

44. In economics, _____ is inflation that is very high or 'out of control', a condition in which prices increase rapidly as a currency loses its value. Definitions used by the media vary from a cumulative inflation rate over three years approaching 100% to 'inflation exceeding 50% a month.' In informal usage the term is often applied to much lower rates. As a rule of thumb, normal inflation is reported per year, but _____ is often reported for much shorter intervals, often per month.

a. 1921 recession
b. 100-year flood
c. 130-30 fund
d. Hyperinflation

45. A _____ is a hypothetical measure of overall prices for some set of goods and services, in a given region during a given interval, normalized relative to some base set. Typically, a _____ is approximated with a price index.

The classical dichotomy is the assumption that there is a relatively clean distinction between overall increases or decreases in prices and underlying, e;reale; economic variables.

a. Federal Reserve districts
b. Foreign portfolio investment
c. Price level
d. Relative income hypothesis

46. In economics, the _____ is a theory emphasizing the positive relationship of overall prices or the nominal value of expenditures to the quantity of money.

It is the mainstream economic theory of the price level. Alternative theories include the real bills doctrine and the more recent fiscal theory of the price level.

a. Microfoundations
b. Hodrick-Prescott filter
c. Deregulation
d. Quantity theory of Money

47. In economics, the _____ is a measure of inflation, the rate of increase of a price index (for example, a consumer price index.)It is the percentage rate of change in price level over time. The rate of decrease in the purchasing power of money is approximately equal.

It's used to calculate the real interest rate, as well as real increases in wages, and official measurements of this rate act as input variables to COLA adjustments and Inflation derivatives prices.

a. Interest rate option
b. Equity value
c. Edgeworth paradox
d. Inflation rate

48. _____ is an online peer-reviewed magazine published by the Agricultural ' Applied Economics Association (AAEA) for readers interested in the policy and management of agriculture, the food industry, natural resources, rural communities, and the environment. _____ is published quarterly and is available free online. It is currently one of three outreach products offered by AAEA, along with the more timely Policy Issues and the forthcoming Shared Materials section of the AAEA Web site.

a. 100-year flood
b. Choices
c. 130-30 fund
d. 1921 recession

Chapter 16. Domestic and International Dimensions of Monetary Policy   155

49. A _____ is:

- Rewrite _____, in generative grammar and computer science
- Standardization, a formal and widely-accepted statement, fact, definition, or qualification
- Operation, a determinate _____ for performing a mathematical operation and obtaining a certain result (Mathematics, Logic)
    - Unary operation
    - Binary operation
- _____ of inference, a function from sets of formulae to formulae (Mathematics, Logic)
- _____ of thumb, principle with broad application that is not intended to be strictly accurate or reliable for every situation. Also often simply referred to as a _____
- Moral, an atomic element of a moral code for guiding choices in human behavior
- Heuristic, a quantized '_____' which shows a tendency or probability for successful function
- A regulation, as in sports
- A Production _____, as in computer science
- Procedural law, a _____ set governing the application of laws to cases
    - A law, which may informally be called a '_____'
    - A court ruling, a decision by a court
- In the U.S. Government, a regulation mandated by Congress, but written or expanded upon by the Executive Branch.
- Norm (sociology), an informal but widely accepted _____, concept, truth, definition, or qualification (social norms, legal norms, coding norms)
- Norm (philosophy), a kind of sentence or a reason to act, feel or believe
- 'Rulership' is the concept of governance by a government:
    - Military _____, governance by a military body
    - Monastic _____, a collection of precepts that guides the life of monks or nuns in a religious order where the superior holds the place of Christ
- Slide _____

- '_____,' a song by Ayumi Hamasaki
- '_____,' a song by rapper Nas
- '_____s,' an album by the band The Whitest Boy Alive
- _____s: Pyaar Ka Superhit Formula, a 2003 Bollywood film
- ruler, an instrument for measuring lengths
- _____, a component of an astrolabe, circumferator or similar instrument
- The _____s, a bestselling self-help book
- _____ Project (Run Up-to-date Linux Everywhere), a project that aims to use up-to-date Linux software on old PCs
- _____ engine, a software system that helps managing business _____s
- Ja _____, a hip hop artist
    - R.U.L.E., a 2005 greatest hits album by rapper Ja _____
- '_____s,' a KMFDM song

a. Rule
b. Russian financial crisis
c. MET
d. Bon

50. _____ was an American economist, statistician and public intellectual, and a recipient of the Nobel Memorial Prize in Economic Sciences. He is best known among scholars for his theoretical and empirical research, especially consumption analysis, monetary history and theory, and for his demonstration of the complexity of stabilization policy. A global public followed his restatement of a political philosophy that insisted on minimizing the role of government in favor of the private sector.
   a. Milton Friedman
   b. Adolph Fischer
   c. Adam Smith
   d. Adolf Hitler

Chapter 17. Stabilization in an Integrated World Economy

1. _____s is the social science that studies the production, distribution, and consumption of goods and services. The term _____s comes from the Ancient Greek oá¼°κονομῖα from oá¼¶κος (oikos, 'house') + vĭŒμος (nomos, 'custom' or 'law'), hence 'rules of the house(hold)'. Current _____ models developed out of the broader field of political economy in the late 19th century, owing to a desire to use an empirical approach more akin to the physical sciences.
   a. Opportunity cost
   b. Inflation
   c. Energy economics
   d. Economic

2. _____ is the increase in the amount of the goods and services produced by an economy over time. It is conventionally measured as the percent rate of increase in real gross domestic product, or real GDP. Growth is usually calculated in real terms, i.e. inflation-adjusted terms, in order to net out the effect of inflation on the price of the goods and services produced.
   a. ACCRA Cost of Living Index
   b. ACEA agreement
   c. AD-IA Model
   d. Economic growth

3. Unemployment occurs when a person is available to work and seeking work but currently without work. The prevalence of unemployment is usually measured using the _____, which is defined as the percentage of those in the labor force who are unemployed. The _____ is also used in economic studies and economic indexes such as the United States' Conference Board's Index of Leading Indicators as a measure of the state of the macroeconomics.
   a. ACEA agreement
   b. ACCRA Cost of Living Index
   c. AD-IA Model
   d. Unemployment rate

4. Economists distinguish between various types of unemployment, including cyclical unemployment, _____, structural unemployment and classical unemployment. Some additional types of unemployment that are occasionally mentioned are seasonal unemployment, hardcore unemployment, and hidden unemployment. Real-world unemployment may combine different types.
   a. Structural unemployment
   b. Graduate unemployment
   c. Types of unemployment
   d. Frictional unemployment

5. The _____ is a concept of economic activity developed in particular by Milton Friedman and Edmund Phelps in the 1960s, both recipients of the Nobel prize in economics. In both cases, the development of the concept is cited as a main motivation behind the prize. It represents the hypothetical unemployment rate consistent with aggregate production being at the 'long-run' level.
   a. Structural change
   b. Dishoarding
   c. Technology shock
   d. Natural rate of unemployment

6. In economics, a _____ is a general slowdown in economic activity over a sustained period of time, or a business cycle contraction. During _____s, many macroeconomic indicators vary in a similar way. Production as measured by Gross Domestic Product (GDP), employment, investment spending, capacity utilization, household incomes and business profits all fall during _____s.
   a. Recession
   b. New Trade Theory
   c. General equilibrium theory
   d. Fixed exchange rate

7. _____ is long-term and chronic unemployment arising from imbalances between the skills and other characteristics of workers in the market and the needs of employers. It involves a mismatch between workers looking for jobs and the vacancies available often despite the number of vacancies being similar to the number of unemployed people. In this case, the unemployed workers lack the specific skills required for the jobs, or are located in a different geographical region to the vacant jobs.

a. Frictional unemployment
c. Graduate unemployment
b. Types of unemployment
d. Structural unemployment

8. A _____ is:

- Rewrite _____, in generative grammar and computer science
- Standardization, a formal and widely-accepted statement, fact, definition, or qualification
- Operation, a determinate _____ for performing a mathematical operation and obtaining a certain result (Mathematics, Logic)
    - Unary operation
    - Binary operation
- _____ of inference, a function from sets of formulae to formulae (Mathematics, Logic)
- _____ of thumb, principle with broad application that is not intended to be strictly accurate or reliable for every situation. Also often simply referred to as a _____
- Moral, an atomic element of a moral code for guiding choices in human behavior
- Heuristic, a quantized '_____' which shows a tendency or probability for successful function
- A regulation, as in sports
- A Production _____, as in computer science
- Procedural law, a _____ set governing the application of laws to cases
    - A law, which may informally be called a '_____'
    - A court ruling, a decision by a court
- In the U.S. Government, a regulation mandated by Congress, but written or expanded upon by the Executive Branch.
- Norm (sociology), an informal but widely accepted _____, concept, truth, definition, or qualification (social norms, legal norms, coding norms)
- Norm (philosophy), a kind of sentence or a reason to act, feel or believe
- 'Rulership' is the concept of governance by a government:
    - Military _____, governance by a military body
    - Monastic _____, a collection of precepts that guides the life of monks or nuns in a religious order where the superior holds the place of Christ
- Slide _____

- '_____,' a song by Ayumi Hamasaki
- '_____,' a song by rapper Nas
- '_____s,' an album by the band The Whitest Boy Alive
- _____s: Pyaar Ka Superhit Formula, a 2003 Bollywood film
- ruler, an instrument for measuring lengths
- _____, a component of an astrolabe, circumferator or similar instrument
- The _____s, a bestselling self-help book
- _____ Project (Run Up-to-date Linux Everywhere), a project that aims to use up-to-date Linux software on old PCs
- _____ engine, a software system that helps managing business _____s
- Ja _____, a hip hop artist
    - R.U.L.E., a 2005 greatest hits album by rapper Ja _____
- '_____s,' a KMFDM song

Chapter 17. Stabilization in an Integrated World Economy

    a. Bon
    c. MET
    b. Russian financial crisis
    d. Rule

9. The _____ or gross domestic income (GDI), a basic measure of an economy's economic performance, is the market value of all final goods and services produced within the borders of a nation in a year. _____ can be defined in three ways, all of which are conceptually identical. First, it is equal to the total expenditures for all final goods and services produced within the country in a stipulated period of time (usually a 365-day year.)

    a. Co-operative economics
    c. Gross domestic product
    b. Public economics
    d. Market failure

10. In economics, _____ is the total demand for final goods and services in the economy (Y) at a given time and price level. It is the amount of goods and services in the economy that will be purchased at all possible price levels. This is the demand for the gross domestic product of a country when inventory levels are static.

    a. Aggregation problem
    c. Aggregate supply
    b. Aggregate demand
    d. Aggregate expenditure

11. The term _____ refers to government debt, expenditures and revenues, or to finance (particularly financial revenue) in general.

- _____ deficit is the budget deficit of federal or local government
- _____ policy is the discretionary spending of governments. Contrasts with monetary policy.
- _____ year and _____ quarter are reporting periods for firms and other agencies.

    a. Russian financial crisis
    c. Fiscal
    b. Freedom Park
    d. Consequence

12. In economics, _____ is the use of government spending and revenue collection to influence the economy.

_____ can be contrasted with the other main type of economic policy, monetary policy, which attempts to stabilize the economy by controlling interest rates and the supply of money. The two main instruments of _____ are government spending and taxation.

    a. Fiscalism
    c. 100-year flood
    b. Sustainable investment rule
    d. Fiscal policy

13. _____ is the process by which the government, central bank (ii) availability of money, and (iii) cost of money or rate of interest, in order to attain a set of objectives oriented towards the growth and stability of the economy. Monetary theory provides insight into how to craft optimal _____.

_____ is referred to as either being an expansionary policy where an expansionary policy increases the total supply of money in the economy, and a contractionary policy decreases the total money supply.

Chapter 17. Stabilization in an Integrated World Economy

a. 130-30 fund
b. 100-year flood
c. 1921 recession
d. Monetary policy

14. _____ is that which is owed; usually referencing assets owed, but the term can also cover moral obligations and other interactions not requiring money. In the case of assets, _____ is a means of using future purchasing power in the present before a summation has been earned. Some companies and corporations use _____ as a part of their overall corporate finance strategy.
   a. Subordinated debt
   b. Debt
   c. Non-performing loan
   d. Participation loan

15. Economics:

   - _____, the desire to own something and the ability to pay for it
   - _____ curve, a graphic representation of a _____ schedule
   - _____ deposit, the money in checking accounts
   - _____ pull theory, the theory that inflation occurs when _____ for goods and services exceeds existing supplies
   - _____ schedule, a table that lists the quantity of a good a person will buy it each different price
   - _____ side economics, the school of economics at believes government spending and tax cuts open economy by raising _____

   a. G20
   b. Bon
   c. Demand
   d. Procter ' Gamble

16. In economics, the _____ is a historical inverse relation between the rate of unemployment and the rate of inflation in an economy. Stated simply, the lower the unemployment in an economy, the higher the rate of increase in nominal wages in the economy. Rate of Change of Wages against Unemployment, United Kingdom 1913-1948 from Phillips (1958)

William Phillips, a New Zealand born economist, wrote a paper in 1958 titled The Relationship between Unemployment and the Rate of Change of Money Wages in the United Kingdom 1861-1957, which was published in the quarterly journal Economica.

   a. Demand curve
   b. Wage curve
   c. Kuznets curve
   d. Phillips curve

17. In economics, _____ is a rise in the general level of prices of goods and services in an economy over a period of time. When the general price level rises, each unit of currency buys fewer goods and services; consequently, _____ is also a decline in the real value of money--a loss of purchasing power in the medium of exchange which is also the monetary unit of account in the economy. A chief measure of general price-level _____ is the general _____ rate, which is the percentage change in a general price index (normally the Consumer Price Index) over time.
   a. Opportunity cost
   b. Energy economics
   c. Economic
   d. Inflation

18. _____ and Keynesian Theory) is a macroeconomic theory based on the ideas of 20th-century British economist John Maynard Keynes. _____ argues that private sector decisions sometimes lead to inefficient macroeconomic outcomes and therefore advocates active policy responses by the public sector, including monetary policy actions by the central bank and fiscal policy actions by the government to stabilize output over the business cycle.

The theories forming the basis of _____ were first presented in The General Theory of Employment, Interest and Money, published in 1936.

  a. Rational choice theory
  b. Gross domestic product
  c. Keynesian economics
  d. Recession

19. The term _____ is an acronym for Non-Accelerating Inflation Rate of Unemployment. It is a concept in economic theory significant in the interplay of macroeconomics and microeconomics. This 'full employment' unemployment rate is sometimes termed the 'inflation-threshold unemployment rate': Actual unemployment cannot fall below the _____, and the inflation rate is likely to rise quickly (accelerate) in times of strong labor demands during periods of growth.
  a. Non-Accelerating Inflation Rate of Unemployment
  b. McCloskey critique
  c. NAIRU
  d. Bequest motive

20. In economics, the _____ is a measure of inflation, the rate of increase of a price index (for example, a consumer price index.)It is the percentage rate of change in price level over time. The rate of decrease in the purchasing power of money is approximately equal.

It's used to calculate the real interest rate, as well as real increases in wages, and official measurements of this rate act as input variables to COLA adjustments and Inflation derivatives prices.

  a. Inflation rate
  b. Equity value
  c. Edgeworth paradox
  d. Interest rate option

21. _____ was an American economist, statistician and public intellectual, and a recipient of the Nobel Memorial Prize in Economic Sciences. He is best known among scholars for his theoretical and empirical research, especially consumption analysis, monetary history and theory, and for his demonstration of the complexity of stabilization policy. A global public followed his restatement of a political philosophy that insisted on minimizing the role of government in favor of the private sector.
  a. Milton Friedman
  b. Adolph Fischer
  c. Adolf Hitler
  d. Adam Smith

22. _____ is a fee paid on borrowed assets. It is the price paid for the use of borrowed money , or, money earned by deposited funds . Assets that are sometimes lent with _____ include money, shares, consumer goods through hire purchase, major assets such as aircraft, and even entire factories in finance lease arrangements.
  a. Insolvency
  b. Internal debt
  c. Asset protection
  d. Interest

23. _____ is an assumption used in many contemporary macroeconomic models, and also in other areas of contemporary economics and game theory and in other applications of rational choice theory.

Since most macroeconomic models today study decisions over many periods, the expectations of workers, consumers, and firms about future economic conditions are an essential part of the model. How to model these expectations has long been controversial, and it is well known that the macroeconomic predictions of the model may differ depending on the assumptions made about expectations

  a. Romer Model
  b. Complex multiplier
  c. Full employment
  d. Rational expectations

24. A _____ is a type of banknote issued by the Federal Reserve System and is the only type of U.S. banknote that is still produced today.

_____s are fiat currency, with the words 'this note is legal tender for all debts, public and private' printed on each bill. (See generally 31 U.S.C.

  a. Federal Reserve note
  b. Federal banking
  c. Primary Dealer Credit Facility
  d. Federal Reserve System Open Market Account

25. The Organization of the Petroleum Exporting Countries is a cartel of twelve countries made up of Algeria, Angola, Ecuador, Iran, Iraq, Kuwait, Libya, Nigeria, Qatar, Saudi Arabia, the United Arab Emirates, and Venezuela. The cartel has maintained its headquarters in Vienna since 1965, and hosts regular meetings among the oil ministers of its Member Countries. Indonesia withdrew its membership in _____ in 2008 after it became a net importer of oil, but stated it would likely return if it became a net exporter in the world.
  a. ACEA agreement
  b. ACCRA Cost of Living Index
  c. AD-IA Model
  d. OPEC

26. _____ is an economic situation in which inflation and economic stagnation occur simultaneously and remain unchecked for a period of time. The portmanteau _____ is generally attributed to British politician Iain Macleod, who coined the term in a speech to Parliament in 1965. The concept is notable partly because, in postwar macroeconomic theory, inflation and recession were regarded as mutually exclusive, and also because _____ has generally proven to be difficult and costly to eradicate once it gets started.
  a. Symmetrical inflation target
  b. Stagflation
  c. Price/wage spiral
  d. Cost-push inflation

27. The term _____ refers to economy-wide fluctuations in production or economic activity over several months or years. These fluctuations occur around a long-term growth trend, and typically involve shifts over time between periods of relatively rapid economic growth (expansion or boom), and periods of relative stagnation or decline (contraction or recession.)

These fluctuations are often measured using the growth rate of real gross domestic product.

  a. Consumer theory
  b. Neoclassical economics
  c. Literacy rate
  d. Business cycle

28. In international commerce and politics, an _____ is the prohibition of commerce (division of trade) and trade with a certain country, in order to isolate it and to put its government into a difficult internal situation, given that the effects of the _____ are often able to make its economy suffer from the initiative.

The _____ is usually used as a political punishment for some previous disagreed policies or acts, but its economic nature frequently raises doubts about the real interests that the prohibition serves.

One of the most comprehensive attempts at an _____ happened during the Napoleonic Wars.

- a. Overshooting model
- b. International finance
- c. Optimum currency area
- d. Embargo

29. _____ in economics and business is the result of an exchange and from that trade we assign a numerical monetary value to a good, service or asset. If Alice trades Bob 4 apples for an orange, the _____ of an orange is 4 apples. Inversely, the _____ of an apple is 1/4 oranges.
- a. Price ceiling
- b. Lerner Index
- c. Price dispersion
- d. Price

30. _____ Theory (or _____ Theory) is a class of macroeconomic models in which business cycle fluctuations to a large extent can be accounted for by real (in contrast to nominal) shocks. (The four primary economic fluctuations are secular (trend), business cycle, seasonal, and random.) Unlike other leading theories of the business cycle, it sees recessions and periods of economic growth as the efficient response to exogenous changes in the real economic environment.
- a. Microsimulation
- b. Supply shock
- c. Real business cycle
- d. Washington Consensus

31. _____ is a term that encompasses the notion of individuals and firms striving for a greater share of a market to sell or buy goods and services. Merriam-Webster defines competition in business as 'the effort of two or more parties acting independently to secure the business of a third party by offering the most favorable terms.' It was described by Adam Smith in The Wealth of Nations (1776) and later economists as allocating productive resources to their most highly-valued uses. and encouraging efficiency.
- a. Cut-throat competition
- b. Path dependence
- c. Moral victory
- d. Competition in economics

32. _____ is a class of macroeconomic models in which business cycle fluctuations to a large extent can be accounted for by real (in contrast to nominal) shocks. (The four primary economic fluctuations are secular (trend), business cycle, seasonal, and random.) Unlike other leading theories of the business cycle, it sees recessions and periods of economic growth as the efficient response to exogenous changes in the real economic environment.
- a. High-powered money
- b. Technology shock
- c. Real business cycle theory
- d. Fiscal adjustment

33. The _____ was a worldwide economic downturn starting in most places in 1929 and ending at different times in the 1930s or early 1940s for different countries. It was the largest and most important economic depression in the 20th century, and is used in the 21st century as an example of how far the world's economy can fall. The _____ originated in the United States; historians most often use as a starting date the stock market crash on October 20, 1929, known as Black Tuesday.

a. Great Depression
b. British Empire Economic Conference
c. The Great Depression
d. Causes of the Great Depression

34. _____, 1st Baron Keynes was a renowned economist from Britain whose many ideas on economic and political theories as well as on many governments' monetary policies influenced America. He advocated a government that played an active role in the lives of people regarding business, economy, etc. In this role, the government would use fiscal measures to reduce the consequences of recessions, economic depressions and booms.
   a. Adam Smith
   b. John Maynard Keynes
   c. Adolf Hitler
   d. Adolph Fischer

35. In labor economics, the _____ hypothesis argues that wages, at least in some markets, are determined by more than simply supply and demand. Specifically, it points to the incentive for managers to pay their employees more than the market-clearing wage in order to increase their productivity or efficiency. This increased labor productivity pays for the relatively higher wages.
   a. Exogenous growth model
   b. Efficiency wage
   c. Earnings calls
   d. Inflatable rats

36. _____ is the temporary suspension or permanent termination of employment of an employee or (more commonly) a group of employees for business reasons, such as the decision that certain positions are no longer necessary or a business slow-down or interruption in work. Originally the term '_____' referred exclusively to a temporary interruption in work, as when factory work cyclically falls off. However, in recent times the term can also refer to the permanent elimination of a position.
   a. Termination of employment
   b. 100-year flood
   c. Retirement
   d. Layoff

Chapter 18. Policies and Prospects for Global Economic Growth

1. _____s is the social science that studies the production, distribution, and consumption of goods and services. The term _____s comes from the Ancient Greek oá¼°κονομῖα from oá¼¶κος (oikos, 'house') + vÏŒμος (nomos, 'custom' or 'law'), hence 'rules of the house(hold)'. Current _____ models developed out of the broader field of political economy in the late 19th century, owing to a desire to use an empirical approach more akin to the physical sciences.
   a. Energy economics
   b. Inflation
   c. Economic
   d. Opportunity cost

2. _____ is the increase in the amount of the goods and services produced by an economy over time. It is conventionally measured as the percent rate of increase in real gross domestic product, or real GDP. Growth is usually calculated in real terms, i.e. inflation-adjusted terms, in order to net out the effect of inflation on the price of the goods and services produced.
   a. ACCRA Cost of Living Index
   b. AD-IA Model
   c. Economic growth
   d. ACEA agreement

3. _____ according to Onuoha (2007) is the practice of starting new organizations or revitalizing mature organizations, particularly new businesses generally in response to identified opportunities. _____ is often a difficult undertaking, as a vast majority of new businesses fail. Entrepreneurial activities are substantially different depending on the type of organization that is being started.
   a. Intrapreneurship
   b. ACEA agreement
   c. ACCRA Cost of Living Index
   d. Entrepreneurship

4. The _____ is an international organization that oversees the global financial system by following the macroeconomic policies of its member countries, in particular those with an impact on exchange rates and the balance of payments. It is an organization formed to stabilize international exchange rates and facilitate development. It also offers financial and technical assistance to its members, making it an international lender of last resort.
   a. International Monetary Fund
   b. ACEA agreement
   c. ACCRA Cost of Living Index
   d. Office of Thrift Supervision

5. The _____ is an international financial institution that provides financial and technical assistance to developing countries for development programs (e.g. bridges, roads, schools, etc.) with the stated goal of reducing poverty.

The _____ differs from the _____ Group, in that the _____ comprises only two institutions:

- International Bank for Reconstruction and Development (IBRD)
- International Development Association (IDA)

Whereas the latter incorporates these two in addition to three more:

- International Finance Corporation (IFC)
- Multilateral Investment Guarantee Agency (MIGA)
- International Centre for Settlement of Investment Disputes (ICSID)

John Maynard Keynes (right) represented the UK at the conference, and Harry Dexter White represented the US.

The _____ is one of two major financial institutions created as a result of the Bretton Woods Conference in 1944. The International Monetary Fund, a related but separate institution, is the second.

a. World Bank
b. Black-Scholes
c. Demographic marketers
d. Dow Jones Industrial Average

6. In Marxian economics, _____ originally referred to the means of production. Individuals, organizations and governments use _____ in the production of other goods or commodities. _____ include factories, machinery, tools, equipment, and various buildings which are used to produce other products for consumption.
   a. Capital goods
   b. Cost of capital
   c. Capital formation
   d. Modigliani-Miller theorem

7. A _____ is an object whose consumption increases the utility of the consumer, for which the quantity demanded exceeds the quantity supplied at zero price. _____s are usually modeled as having diminishing marginal utility. The first individual purchase has high utility; the second has less.
   a. Positional goods
   b. Luxury good
   c. Search good
   d. Good

8. In finance, the term _____ describes various legal measures taken to ensure that debtors, whether individuals, businesses honor their debts and make an honest effort to repay the money that they owe. Generally regarded as a subdivision of tax law, _____ is most often enforced through a combination of audits and legal restrictions. For example, a provision of the Federal Debt Collection Procedure Act states that a person or organization indebted to the United States, against whom a judgment lien has been filed, is ineligible to receive a government grant.
   a. Debt compliance
   b. Hard money loan
   c. Capital note
   d. Prosper Marketplace

9. _____ is a type of private equity investment, most often a minority investment, in relatively mature companies that are looking for capital to expand or restructure operations, enter new markets or finance a significant acquisition without a change of control of the business.

Companies that seek _____, will often do so in order to finance a transformational event in their lifecycle. These companies are likely to be more mature than venture capital funded companies, able to generate revenue and operating profits but unable to generate sufficient cash to fund major expansions, acquisitions or other investments.

   a. Venture capital fund
   b. Growth capital
   c. Mezzanine capital
   d. Seed money

10. _____ is a term used to describe any great reduction in a human population. It can be used to refer to longterm demographic trends, as in urban decay or rural _____, but it is also commonly employed to describe large reductions in population due to violence, disease, or other catastrophes.

History is replete with examples of large scale _____s.

   a. Depopulation
   b. Malthusian equilibrium
   c. Net reproduction rate
   d. Population momentum

Chapter 18. Policies and Prospects for Global Economic Growth

11. A _____, reserve bank, or monetary authority is the entity responsible for the monetary policy of a country or of a group of member states. It is a bank that can lend money to other banks in times of need. Its primary responsibility is to maintain the stability of the national currency and money supply, but more active duties include controlling subsidized-loan interest rates, and acting as a lender of last resort to the banking sector during times of financial crisis (private banks often being integral to the national financial system.)

a. 130-30 fund
b. 100-year flood
c. Central bank
d. 1921 recession

12. _____ is the change in population over time, and can be quantified as the change in the number of individuals in a population using 'per unit time' for measurement. The term _____ can technically refer to any species, but almost always refers to humans, and it is often used informally for the more specific demographic term _____ rate , and is often used to refer specifically to the growth of the population of the world.

Simple models of _____ include the Malthusian Growth Model and the logistic model.

a. 100-year flood
b. 130-30 fund
c. Population dynamics
d. Population growth

13. The _____ or gross domestic income (GDI), a basic measure of an economy's economic performance, is the market value of all final goods and services produced within the borders of a nation in a year. _____ can be defined in three ways, all of which are conceptually identical. First, it is equal to the total expenditures for all final goods and services produced within the country in a stipulated period of time (usually a 365-day year.)

a. Public economics
b. Market failure
c. Gross domestic product
d. Co-operative economics

14. _____ is a term used in economic research and policy debates. As with freedom generally, there are various definitions, but no universally accepted concept of _____. One major approach to _____ comes from the libertarian tradition emphasizing free markets and private property, while another extends the welfare economics study of individual choice, with greater _____ coming from a 'larger' (in some technical sense) set of possible choices.

a. International sanctions
b. Investment policy
c. Economic freedom
d. Economic liberalization

15. _____ is exchange of capital, goods, and services across international borders or territories. In most countries, it represents a significant share of gross domestic product (GDP.) While _____ has been present throughout much of history , its economic, social, and political importance has been on the rise in recent centuries.

a. Intra-industry trade
b. Incoterms
c. Import license
d. International trade

16. A _____ is the exclusive authority to determine how a resource is used, whether that resource is owned by government or by individuals. All economic goods have a _____s attribute. This attribute has three broad components

1. The right to use the good
2. The right to earn income from the good
3. The right to transfer the good to others

The concept of _____s as used by economists and legal scholars are related but distinct. The distinction is largely seen in the economists' focus on the ability of an individual or collective to control the use of the good.

a. Nature of the Firm
b. Property right
c. Judgment summons
d. Greenfield agreement

17. In microeconomics, _____ is quite simply the conversion of inputs into outputs. It is an economic process that uses resources to create a good or service that is suitable for exchange. This can include manufacturing, storing, shipping, and packaging.

a. Characteristic
b. Variability
c. Production
d. Bucket shop

18. A _____ is a group of people who share or are motivated by at least one common issue or interest, or work together on a specific project(s) to achieve a common objective. _____s are also characterised by attempts to share and exercise political and social power and to make decisions on a consensus-driven and egalitarian basis. _____s differ from cooperatives in that they are not necessarily focused upon an economic benefit or saving (but can be that as well.)

a. Collective
b. 1921 recession
c. 130-30 fund
d. 100-year flood

19. _____ in its classic form is defined as a company from one country making a physical investment into building a factory in another country. It is the establishment of an enterprise by a foreigner. Its definition can be extended to include investments made to acquire lasting interest in enterprises operating outside of the economy of the investor.

a. Paris Club
b. Global citizens movement
c. Financial Stability Board
d. Foreign direct investment

20. In economics and finance, _____ represents passive holdings of securities such as foreign stocks, bonds none of which entails active management or control of the securities' issuer by the investor; where such control exists, it is known as foreign direct investment. Generally, this means the investor holds less than 10% of the total shares or less than the amount needed to hold the majority vote.

Some examples of _____ are:

- purchase of shares in a foreign company.
- purchase of bonds issued by a foreign government.
- acquisition of assets in a foreign country.

Factors affecting international _____:

- tax rates on interest or dividends (investors will normally prefer countries where the tax rates are relatively low)
- interest rates (money tends to flow to countries with high interest rates)
- exchange rates (foreign investors may be attracted if the local currency is expected to strengthen)

_____ is part of the capital account on the balance of payments statistics.

Chapter 18. Policies and Prospects for Global Economic Growth

a. Marginal product of capital
c. Tangible investments
b. Capital allocation line
d. Portfolio investment

21. _____ or financing is to provide capital (funds), which means money for a project, a person, a business or any other private or public institutions.

Those funds can be allocated for either short term or long term purposes. The health fund is a new way of _____ private healthcare centers.

a. Business operations
c. Customer retention
b. Customer satisfaction
d. Funding

22. _____ is the prospect that a party insulated from risk may behave differently from the way it would behave if it were fully exposed to the risk. In insurance, _____ that occurs without conscious or malicious action is called morale hazard.

_____ is related to information asymmetry, a situation in which one party in a transaction has more information than another.

a. 100-year flood
c. 1921 recession
b. 130-30 fund
d. Moral hazard

23. _____, anti-selection insurance, statistics, and risk management. It refers to a market process in which 'bad' results occur when buyers and sellers have asymmetric information (i.e. access to different information): the 'bad' products or customers are more likely to be selected. A bank that sets one price for all its checking account customers runs the risk of being adversely selected against by its low-balance, high-activity (and hence least profitable) customers.
a. ACEA agreement
c. ACCRA Cost of Living Index
b. Adverse selection
d. AD-IA Model

24. In economics, _____ refers to the ability of a person or a country to produce a particular good at a lower marginal cost and opportunity cost than another person or country. It is the ability to produce a product most efficiently given all the other products that could be produced. It can be contrasted with absolute advantage which refers to the ability of a person or a country to produce a particular good at a lower absolute cost than another.
a. Financial export
c. Comparative Advantage
b. Small open economy
d. Dutch disease

25. _____ is money accepted for exchange of goods in an economy. The prevalence of one money over another arises, usually, when a government designates through decrees that the government shall accept only particular notes and coins in payment for taxes. Typically, money of _____ consists of stamped coins and minted paper bills.
a. Totnes pound
c. Security thread
b. Scripophily
d. Currency

26. _____ is a reduction in the value of a currency with respect to other monetary units. In common modern usage, it specifically implies an official lowering of the value of a country's currency within a fixed exchange rate system, by which the monetary authority formally sets a new fixed rate with respect to a foreign reference currency. In contrast, (currency) depreciation is used for the unofficial decrease in the exchange rate in a floating exchange rate system.

a. Petrodollar
b. Reserve currency
c. Dollarization
d. Devaluation

27. The _____ is applied broadly to a variety of situations in which some financial institutions or assets suddenly lose a large part of their value. In the 19th and early 20th centuries, many financial crises were associated with banking panics, and many recessions coincided with these panics. Other situations that are often called financial crises include stock market crashes and the bursting of other financial bubbles, currency crises, and sovereign defaults.

a. Literacy rate
b. Mercantilism
c. Market failure
d. Financial crisis

28. The _____ of monetary management established the rules for commercial and financial relations among the world's major industrial states in the mid 20th Century. The _____ was the first example of a fully negotiated monetary order intended to govern monetary relations among independent nation-states.

Preparing to rebuild the international economic system as World War II was still raging, 730 delegates from all 44 Allied nations gathered at the Mount Washington Hotel in Bretton Woods, New Hampshire, United States, for the United Nations Monetary and Financial Conference.

a. 100-year flood
b. 130-30 fund
c. Bretton Woods system
d. 1921 recession

29. The _____ business model is a business model where a customer must pay a _____ price to have access to the product/service. The model was pioneered by magazines and newspapers, but is now used by many businesses and websites. Rather than selling products individually, a _____ sells periodic (monthly or yearly or seasonal) use or access to a product or service, or, in the case of such non-profit organizations as opera companies or symphony orchestras, it sells tickets to the entire run of five to fifteen scheduled performances for an entire season.

a. Subscription
b. Freebie marketing
c. Yield management
d. Coopetition

30. _____ is the development of economic wealth of countries or regions for the well-being of their inhabitants. It is the process by which a nation improves the economic, political, and social well being of its people. From a policy perspective, _____ can be defined as efforts that seek to improve the economic well-being and quality of life for a community by creating and/or retaining jobs and supporting or growing incomes and the tax base.

a. Experimental economics
b. Economic development
c. Economic methodology
d. Inflation

31. The _____ captures an expanded spectrum of values and criteria for measuring organizational (and societal) success: economic, ecological and social. With the ratification of the United Nations and ICLEI _____ standard for urban and community accounting in early 2007, this became the dominant approach to public sector full cost accounting. Similar UN standards apply to natural capital and human capital measurement to assist in measurements required by _____, e.g. the ecoBudget standard for reporting ecological footprint.

a. Social welfare function
b. Missing market
c. Wage share
d. Triple bottom line

Chapter 19. Consumer Choice

1. _____ is a broad label that refers to any individuals or households that use goods and services generated within the economy. The concept of a _____ is used in different contexts, so that the usage and significance of the term may vary.

Typically when business people and economists talk of _____s they are talking about person as _____, an aggregated commodity item with little individuality other than that expressed in the buy/not-buy decision.

a. 130-30 fund
b. 1921 recession
c. 100-year flood
d. Consumer

2. An _____ is a tax levied on the financial income of people, corporations, or other legal entities. Various _____ systems exist, with varying degrees of tax incidence. Income taxation can be progressive, proportional, or regressive.
a. ACEA agreement
b. AD-IA Model
c. Income tax
d. ACCRA Cost of Living Index

3. To _____ is to impose a financial charge or other levy upon a taxpayer by a state or the functional equivalent of a state.

_____es are also imposed by many subnational entities. _____es consist of direct _____ or indirect _____, and may be paid in money or as its labour equivalent (often but not always unpaid.)

a. 100-year flood
b. 130-30 fund
c. Tax
d. 1921 recession

4. In economics, _____ is a measure of the relative satisfaction from consumption of various goods and services. Given this measure, one may speak meaningfully of increasing or decreasing _____, and thereby explain economic behavior in terms of attempts to increase one's _____. For illustrative purposes, changes in _____ are sometimes expressed in units called utils.
a. Expected utility hypothesis
b. Utility function
c. Ordinal utility
d. Utility

5. In economics, the _____ of a good or of a service is the utility of the specific use to which an agent would put a given increase in that good or service, or of the specific use that would be abandoned in response to a given decrease. In other words, _____ is the utility of the marginal use -- which, on the assumption of economic rationality, would be the least urgent use of the good or service, from the best feasible combination of actions in which its use is included. Under the mainstream assumptions, the _____ of a good or service is the posited quantified change in utility obtained by increasing or by decreasing use of that good or service.
a. 130-30 fund
b. 100-year flood
c. 1921 recession
d. Marginal Utility

6. _____ in economics and business is the result of an exchange and from that trade we assign a numerical monetary value to a good, service or asset. If Alice trades Bob 4 apples for an orange, the _____ of an orange is 4 apples. Inversely, the _____ of an apple is 1/4 oranges.
a. Price
b. Lerner Index
c. Price ceiling
d. Price dispersion

7. In calculus, a function f defined on a subset of the real numbers with real values is called _____, if for all x and y such that x >≤ y one has f(x) >≤ f(y), so f preserves the order. In layman's terms, the sign of the slope is always positive (the curve tending upwards) or zero (i.e., non-decreasing, or asymptotic, or depicted as a horizontal, flat line) Likewise, a function is called monotonically decreasing (non-increasing) if, whenever x >≤ y, then f(x) >≥ f(y), so it reverses the order.
   a. 100-year flood
   b. 130-30 fund
   c. 1921 recession
   d. Monotonic

Chapter 19. Consumer Choice 173

8. A _____ is:

- Rewrite _____, in generative grammar and computer science
- Standardization, a formal and widely-accepted statement, fact, definition, or qualification
- Operation, a determinate _____ for performing a mathematical operation and obtaining a certain result (Mathematics, Logic)
  - Unary operation
  - Binary operation
- _____ of inference, a function from sets of formulae to formulae (Mathematics, Logic)
- _____ of thumb, principle with broad application that is not intended to be strictly accurate or reliable for every situation. Also often simply referred to as a _____
- Moral, an atomic element of a moral code for guiding choices in human behavior
- Heuristic, a quantized '_____' which shows a tendency or probability for successful function
- A regulation, as in sports
- A Production _____, as in computer science
- Procedural law, a _____ set governing the application of laws to cases
  - A law, which may informally be called a '_____'
  - A court ruling, a decision by a court
- In the U.S. Government, a regulation mandated by Congress, but written or expanded upon by the Executive Branch.
- Norm (sociology), an informal but widely accepted _____, concept, truth, definition, or qualification (social norms, legal norms, coding norms)
- Norm (philosophy), a kind of sentence or a reason to act, feel or believe
- 'Rulership' is the concept of governance by a government:
  - Military _____, governance by a military body
  - Monastic _____, a collection of precepts that guides the life of monks or nuns in a religious order where the superior holds the place of Christ
- Slide _____

- '_____,' a song by Ayumi Hamasaki
- '_____,' a song by rapper Nas
- '_____s,' an album by the band The Whitest Boy Alive
- _____s: Pyaar Ka Superhit Formula, a 2003 Bollywood film
- ruler, an instrument for measuring lengths
- _____, a component of an astrolabe, circumferator or similar instrument
- The _____s, a bestselling self-help book
- _____ Project (Run Up-to-date Linux Everywhere), a project that aims to use up-to-date Linux software on old PCs
- _____ engine, a software system that helps managing business _____s
- Ja _____, a hip hop artist
  - R.U.L.E., a 2005 greatest hits album by rapper Ja _____
- '_____s,' a KMFDM song

a. Bon
b. Rule
c. Russian financial crisis
d. MEI

9. _____ is a specific term used in companies' financial reporting from the company-whole point of view. Because that use excludes the effects of changing ownership interest, an economic measure of _____ is necessary for financial analysis from the shareholders' point of view

_____ is defined by the Financial Accounting Standards Board, or FASB, as e;the change in equity [net assets] of a business enterprise during a period from transactions and other events and circumstances from nonowner sources. It includes all changes in equity during a period except those resulting from investments by owners and distributions to owners.e;

_____ is the sum of net income and other items that must bypass the income statement because they have not been realized, including items like an unrealized holding gain or loss from available for sale securities and foreign currency translation gains or losses.

- a. Windfall gain
- b. Comprehensive income
- c. Real income
- d. Per capita income

10. _____ refers to a business or organization attempting to acquire goods or services to accomplish the goals of the enterprise. Though there are several organizations that attempt to set standards in the _____ process, processes can vary greatly between organizations. Typically the word '_____' is not used interchangeably with the word 'procurement', since procurement typically includes Expediting, Supplier Quality, and Traffic and Logistics (T'L) in addition to _____.

- a. Free port
- b. 100-year flood
- c. Purchasing
- d. 130-30 fund

11. Economics:

- _____,the desire to own something and the ability to pay for it
- _____ curve,a graphic representation of a _____ schedule
- _____ deposit, the money in checking accounts
- _____ pull theory,the theory that inflation occurs when _____ for goods and services exceeds existing supplies
- _____ schedule,a table that lists the quantity of a good a person will buy it each different price
- _____ side economics,the school of economics at believes government spending and tax cuts open economy by raising _____

- a. Procter ' Gamble
- b. Bon
- c. G20
- d. Demand

12. In economics, the _____ can be defined as the graph depicting the relationship between the price of a certain commodity, and the amount of it that consumers are willing and able to purchase at that given price. It is a graphic representation of a demand schedule. The _____ for all consumers together follows from the _____ of every individual consumer: the individual demands at each price are added together.

- a. Kuznets curve
- b. Demand curve
- c. Lorenz curve
- d. Wage curve

Chapter 19. Consumer Choice

13. The _____ is the part of economic and administrative life that deals with the delivery of goods and services by and for the government, whether national, regional or local/municipal.

Examples of _____ activity range from delivering social security, administering urban planning and organising national defenses.

The organization of the _____ can take several forms, including:

- Direct administration funded through taxation; the delivering organization generally has no specific requirement to meet commercial success criteria, and production decisions are determined by government.
- Publicly owned corporations (in some contexts, especially manufacturing, 'state-owned enterprises'); which differ from direct administration in that they have greater commercial freedoms and are expected to operate according to commercial criteria, and production decisions are not generally taken by government (although goals may be set for them by government.)
- Partial outsourcing (of the scale many businesses do, e.g. for IT services), is considered a _____ model.

A borderline form is

- Complete outsourcing or contracting out, with a privately owned corporation delivering the entire service on behalf of government. This may be considered a mixture of private sector operations with public ownership of assets, although in some forms the private sector's control and/or risk is so great that the service may no longer be considered part of the _____.

a. Public sector
c. Policy cycle
b. 130-30 fund
d. 100-year flood

14. _____ was a survey conducted by the U.S. Department of Justice to gauge the prevalence of alcohol and illegal drug use among prior arrestees. It was a reformulation of the prior Drug Use Forecasting (DUF) program, focused on five drugs in particular: cocaine, marijuana, methamphetamine, opiates, and PCP.

Participants were randomly selected from arrest records in major metropolitan areas; because no personally identifying information is taken from each record chosen, the resulting data can be correlated to arrest rates, but not to the total population of persons charged.

a. AD-IA Model
c. ACCRA Cost of Living Index
b. ACEA agreement
d. Arrestee Drug Abuse Monitoring

15. _____ was a Scottish moral philosopher and a pioneer of political economy. One of the key figures of the Scottish Enlightenment, Smith is the author of The Theory of Moral Sentiments and An Inquiry into the Nature and Causes of the Wealth of Nations. The latter, usually abbreviated as The Wealth of Nations, is considered his magnum opus and the first modern work of economics.

a. Adolph Fischer
c. Alan Greenspan
b. Adolf Hitler
d. Adam Smith

Chapter 19. Consumer Choice

16. A _____ is a counterfeit agreement among industries. It is an informal organization of producers that agree to coordinate prices and production. _____s usually occur in an oligopolistic industry, where there is a small number of sellers and usually involve homogeneous products.
   - a. 100-year flood
   - b. Shill
   - c. Shanzhai
   - d. Cartel

17. _____ is exchange of capital, goods, and services across international borders or territories. In most countries, it represents a significant share of gross domestic product (GDP.) While _____ has been present throughout much of history, its economic, social, and political importance has been on the rise in recent centuries.
   - a. Incoterms
   - b. Intra-industry trade
   - c. Import license
   - d. International trade

18. The _____ is the apparent contradiction that although water is on the whole more useful, in terms of survival, than diamonds, diamonds command a higher price in the market. The economist Adam Smith is often considered to be the classic presenter of this paradox. Nicolaus Copernicus, John Locke, John Law and others had previously tried to explain the disparity.
   - a. St. Petersburg paradox
   - b. 130-30 fund
   - c. Paradox of value
   - d. 100-year flood

19. In economics, _____ is the ratio of the percent change in one variable to the percent change in another variable. It is a tool for measuring the responsiveness of a function to changes in parameters in a relative way. Commonly analyzed are _____ of substitution, price and wealth.
   - a. ACEA agreement
   - b. Elasticity of demand
   - c. ACCRA Cost of Living Index
   - d. Elasticity

20. In economics, the _____ is defined as a numerical measure of the responsiveness of the quantity supplied of product (A) to a change in price of product (A) alone. It is the measure of the way quantity supplied reacts to a change in price.

   For example, if, in response to a 10% rise in the price of a good, the quantity supplied increases by 20%, the _____ would be 20%/10% = 2.

   - a. Residual claimant
   - b. Price elasticity of supply
   - c. Demand side economics
   - d. Frontier markets

21. _____ is the controlled distribution of resources and scarce goods or services. _____ controls the size of the ration, one's allotted portion of the resources being distributed on a particular day or at a particular time.

   In economics, it is often common to use the word '_____' to refer to one of the roles that prices play in markets, while _____ is called 'non-price _____.' Using prices to ration means that those with the most money (or other assets) and who want a product the most are first to receive it.

Chapter 19. Consumer Choice

a. 100-year flood
b. Rationing
c. 130-30 fund
d. 1921 recession

22. A _____ represents the combinations of goods and services that a consumer can purchase given current prices and his income. Consumer theory uses the concepts of a _____ and a preference map to analyze consumer choices. Both concepts have a ready graphical representation in the two-good case.
   a. Revealed preference
   b. Budget constraint
   c. Supply and demand
   d. Quality bias

23. In microeconomic theory, an _____ is a graph showing different bundles of goods, each measured as to quantity, between which a consumer is indifferent. That is, at each point on the curve, the consumer has no preference for one bundle over another. In other words, they are all equally preferred.
   a. Engel curve
   b. Indifference map
   c. Expenditure minimization problem
   d. Indifference curve

24. In microeconomic theory a preference map or _____ is the collection of indifference curves possessed by an individual. Similar in nature to a topographical map, the contour lines of such a map demonstrating progressively more desirable options as they move upward or to the right. Because of the nature of indifference curves they cannot intersect and are effectively infinite in number, their sum defining all possible combinations of values.
   a. Expenditure minimization problem
   b. Elasticity of substitution
   c. Indifference map
   d. Engel curve

25. In economics, the _____ is the rate at which a consumer is ready to give up one good in exchange for another good while maintaining the same level of satisfaction.

Under the standard assumption of neoclassical economics that goods and services are continuously divisible, the marginal rates of substitution will be the same regardless of the direction of exchange, and will correspond to the slope of an indifference curve (more precisely, to the slope multiplied by -1) passing through the consumption bundle in question, at that point: mathematically, it is the implicit derivative. MRS of Y for X is the amount of Y for which a consumer is willing to exchange for X locally.

   a. Demand vacuum
   b. Demand Set
   c. Rational addiction
   d. Marginal rate of substitution

26. Competition law, known in the United States as _____ law, has three main elements:

   - prohibiting agreements or practices that restrict free trading and competition between business entities. This includes in particular the repression of cartels.
   - banning abusive behaviour by a firm dominating a market, or anti-competitive practices that tend to lead to such a dominant position. Practices controlled in this way may include predatory pricing, tying, price gouging, refusal to deal, and many others.
   - supervising the mergers and acquisitions of large corporations, including some joint ventures. Transactions that are considered to threaten the competitive process can be prohibited altogether, or approved subject to 'remedies' such as an obligation to divest part of the merged business or to offer licences or access to facilities to enable other businesses to continue competing.

The substance and practice of competition law varies from jurisdiction to jurisdiction. Protecting the interests of consumers (consumer welfare) and ensuring that entrepreneurs have an opportunity to compete in the market economy are often treated as important objectives. Competition law is closely connected with law on deregulation of access to markets, state aids and subsidies, the privatisation of state owned assets and the establishment of independent sector regulators. In recent decades, competition law has been viewed as a way to provide better public services.

a. Anti-Inflation Act
b. Intellectual property law
c. United Kingdom competition law
d. Antitrust

27. _____ is a common concept in economics, and gives rise to derived concepts such as consumer debt. Generally _____ is defined by opposition to production. But the precise definition can vary because different schools of economists define production quite differently.

a. British canal system
b. Discrete choice
c. Basis of futures
d. Consumption

28. In economics and business, specifically cost accounting, the _____ point (BEP) is the point at which cost or expenses and revenue are equal: there is no net loss or gain, and one has 'broken even'. A profit or a loss has not been made, although opportunity costs have been paid, and capital has received the risk-adjusted, expected return.

For example, if the business sells less than 200 tables each month, it will make a loss, if it sells more, it will be a profit.

a. Stylized fact
b. Break-even
c. Decoupling plus
d. Trailing twelve months

Chapter 20. Demand and Supply Elasticity

1. _____ in economics and business is the result of an exchange and from that trade we assign a numerical monetary value to a good, service or asset. If Alice trades Bob 4 apples for an orange, the _____ of an orange is 4 apples. Inversely, the _____ of an apple is 1/4 oranges.
    a. Lerner Index
    b. Price ceiling
    c. Price dispersion
    d. Price

2. To _____ is to impose a financial charge or other levy upon a taxpayer by a state or the functional equivalent of a state.

    _____es are also imposed by many subnational entities. _____es consist of direct _____ or indirect _____, and may be paid in money or as its labour equivalent (often but not always unpaid.)

    a. 1921 recession
    b. 130-30 fund
    c. 100-year flood
    d. Tax

3. _____ is a common concept in economics, and gives rise to derived concepts such as consumer debt. Generally _____ is defined by opposition to production. But the precise definition can vary because different schools of economists define production quite differently.
    a. British canal system
    b. Basis of futures
    c. Discrete choice
    d. Consumption

4. To tax is to impose a financial charge or other levy upon a taxpayer by a state or the functional equivalent of a state.

    _____ are also imposed by many subnational entities. _____ consist of direct tax or indirect tax, and may be paid in money or as its labour equivalent (often but not always unpaid.)

    a. 100-year flood
    b. 130-30 fund
    c. 1921 recession
    d. Taxes

5. The _____ consists of a number of economic theories which describe the nature of the firm, company including its existence, its behaviour, and its relationship with the market.

In simplified terms, the _____ aims to answer these questions:

1. Existence - why do firms emerge, why are not all transactions in the economy mediated over the market?
2. Boundaries - why the boundary between firms and the market is located exactly there? Which transactions are performed internally and which are negotiated on the market?
3. Organization - why are firms structured in such specific way? What is the interplay of formal and informal relationships?

Despite looking simple, these questions are not answered by the established economic theory, which usually views firms as given, and treats them as black boxes without any internal structure.

Chapter 20. Demand and Supply Elasticity

The First World War period saw a change of emphasis in economic theory away from industry-level analysis which mainly included analysing markets to analysis at the level of the firm, as it became increasingly clear that perfect competition was no longer an adequate model of how firms behaved. Economic theory till then had focussed on trying to understand markets alone and there had been little study on understanding why firms or organisations exist.

   a. Neo-Ricardian school
   c. Technology gap
   b. Marginal revenue product
   d. Theory of the firm

6. _____ is defined as the measure of responsiveness in the quantity demanded for a commodity as a result of change in price of the same commodity. It is a measure of how consumers react to a change in price. In other words, it is percentage change in quantity demanded as per the percentage change in price of the same commodity.
   a. 100-year flood
   b. 130-30 fund
   c. 1921 recession
   d. Price elasticity of demand

7. Economics:

   - _____,the desire to own something and the ability to pay for it
   - _____ curve,a graphic representation of a _____ schedule
   - _____ deposit, the money in checking accounts
   - _____ pull theory,the theory that inflation occurs when _____ for goods and services exceeds existing supplies
   - _____ schedule,a table that lists the quantity of a good a person will buy it each different price
   - _____ side economics,the school of economics at believes government spending and tax cuts open economy by raising _____

   a. Procter ' Gamble
   b. Bon
   c. Demand
   d. G20

8. In economics, _____ is the ratio of the percent change in one variable to the percent change in another variable. It is a tool for measuring the responsiveness of a function to changes in parameters in a relative way. Commonly analyzed are _____ of substitution, price and wealth.
   a. ACCRA Cost of Living Index
   b. Elasticity
   c. Elasticity of demand
   d. ACEA agreement

9. Price _____ is defined as the measure of responsiveness in the quantity demanded for a commodity as a result of change in price of the same commodity. It is a measure of how consumers react to a change in price. In other words, it is percentage change in quantity demanded by the percentage change in price of the same commodity.
   a. ACCRA Cost of Living Index
   b. Elasticity
   c. ACEA agreement
   d. Elasticity of demand

10. In economics, _____ describes demand that is not very sensitive to a change in price.

Chapter 20. Demand and Supply Elasticity

a. Inflation hedge
c. Effective unemployment rate
b. Export-led growth
d. Inelastic

11. _____ is the total money received from the sale of any given quantity of output.

The _____ is calculated by taking the price of the sale times the quantity sold, i.e.

_____ = price X quantity.

a. Ceteris paribus
c. Blanket order
b. Total revenue
d. Defined benefit pension plan

12. In algebra, a _____ is a function depending on n that associates a scalar, det(A), to an n×n square matrix A. The fundamental geometric meaning of a _____ is a scale factor for measure when A is regarded as a linear transformation. _____s are important both in calculus, where they enter the substitution rule for several variables, and in multilinear algebra.

For a fixed nonnegative integer n, there is a unique _____ function for the n×n matrices over any commutative ring R. In particular, this function exists when R is the field of real or complex numbers.

a. 1921 recession
c. 100-year flood
b. 130-30 fund
d. Determinant

13. A _____ occurs when an entity spends more money than it takes in. The opposite of a _____ is a budget surplus. Debt is essentially an accumulated flow of deficits.
a. Sovereign credit
c. Grant-in-aid
b. Public Financial Management
d. Budget deficit

14. In economic models, the _____ time frame assumes no fixed factors of production. Firms can enter or leave the marketplace, and the cost (and availability) of land, labor, raw materials, and capital goods can be assumed to vary. In contrast, in the short-run time frame, certain factors are assumed to be fixed, because there is not sufficient time for them to change.
a. Long-run
c. Product Pipeline
b. Diseconomies of scale
d. Short-run

15. In economics, the concept of the _____ refers to the decision-making time frame of a firm in which at least one factor of production is fixed. Costs which are fixed in the _____ have no impact on a firms decisions. For example a firm can raise output by increasing the amount of labour through overtime.
a. Productivity world
c. Marginal product
b. Hicks-neutral technical change
d. Short-run

16. A _____ is an object whose consumption increases the utility of the consumer, for which the quantity demanded exceeds the quantity supplied at zero price. _____s are usually modeled as having diminishing marginal utility. The first individual purchase has high utility; the second has less.

a. Positional goods
c. Luxury good
b. Search good
d. Good

17. In economics, the _____ of demand measures the responsiveness of the demand of a good to the change in the income of the people demanding the good. It is calculated as the ratio of the percent change in demand to the percent change in income. For example, if, in response to a 10% increase in income, the demand of a good increased by 20%, the _____ of demand would be 20%/10% = 2.
   a. Income elasticity
   c. ACCRA Cost of Living Index
   b. AD-IA Model
   d. ACEA agreement

18. In economics, the _____ measures the responsiveness of the demand of a good to the change in the income of the people demanding the good. It is calculated as the ratio of the percent change in demand to the percent change in income. For example, if, in response to a 10% increase in income, the demand of a good increased by 20%, the _____ would be 20%/10% = 2.
   a. Elasticity of substitution
   c. Expenditure minimization problem
   b. Income elasticity of demand
   d. Indifference map

19. In economics, the _____ is defined as a numerical measure of the responsiveness of the quantity supplied of product (A) to a change in price of product (A) alone. It is the measure of the way quantity supplied reacts to a change in price.

For example, if, in response to a 10% rise in the price of a good, the quantity supplied increases by 20%, the _____ would be 20%/10% = 2.

   a. Residual claimant
   c. Frontier markets
   b. Price elasticity of supply
   d. Demand side economics

20. A _____, reserve bank, or monetary authority is the entity responsible for the monetary policy of a country or of a group of member states. It is a bank that can lend money to other banks in times of need. Its primary responsibility is to maintain the stability of the national currency and money supply, but more active duties include controlling subsidized-loan interest rates, and acting as a lender of last resort to the banking sector during times of financial crisis (private banks often being integral to the national financial system.)
   a. 1921 recession
   c. 100-year flood
   b. Central bank
   d. 130-30 fund

21. In microeconomics, _____ is quite simply the conversion of inputs into outputs. It is an economic process that uses resources to create a good or service that is suitable for exchange. This can include manufacturing, storing, shipping, and packaging.
   a. Characteristic
   c. Bucket shop
   b. Variability
   d. Production

Chapter 21. Rents, Profits, and the Financial Environment of Business

1. A _____ is a public market for the trading of company stock and derivatives at an agreed price; these are securities listed on a stock exchange as well as those only traded privately.

The size of the world _____ was estimated at about $36.6 trillion US at the beginning of October 2008 . The total world derivatives market has been estimated at about $791 trillion face or nominal value, 11 times the size of the entire world economy.

 a. 1921 recession
 c. 100-year flood
 b. 130-30 fund
 d. Stock market

2. _____ are the inflation-indexed bonds issued by the U.S. Treasury. The principal is adjusted to the Consumer Price Index, the commonly used measure of inflation. The coupon rate is constant, but generates a different amount of interest when multiplied by the inflation-adjusted principal, thus protecting the holder against inflation.

 a. Treasury Inflation-Protected Securities
 c. 100-year flood
 b. 1921 recession
 d. 130-30 fund

3. _____s is the social science that studies the production, distribution, and consumption of goods and services. The term _____s comes from the Ancient Greek οἰκονομία from οἶκος (oikos, 'house') + νόμος (nomos, 'custom' or 'law'), hence 'rules of the house(hold)'. Current _____ models developed out of the broader field of political economy in the late 19th century, owing to a desire to use an empirical approach more akin to the physical sciences.

 a. Economic
 c. Inflation
 b. Energy economics
 d. Opportunity cost

4. In economics supernormal profit _____ or pure profit or excess profits, is a profit exceeding the normal profit. Normal profit equals the opportunity cost of labour and capital, while supernormal profit is the amount exceeds the normal return from these input factors in production.

_____ is usually generated by an oligopoly or a monopoly; however, these firms often try to hide this from the market to reduce risk of competition or antitrust investigation.

 a. Accounting profit
 c. Operating profit
 b. ACCRA Cost of Living Index
 d. Abnormal profit

5. Economic _____ is defined as an excess distribution to any factor in a production process above that which is required to induce the factor into the process or any excess above that which is necessary to keep the factor in its current use..

Classical Factor _____ is primarily concerned with the fee paid for the use of fixed (e.g. natural) resources. The classical definition is expressed as any excess payment above that required to induce or provide for production.

 a. 1921 recession
 c. Rent
 b. 100-year flood
 d. 130-30 fund

6. _____ refers to laws or ordinances that set price controls on the renting of residential housing. It functions as a price ceiling.

_____ exists in approximately 40 countries around the world.

a. National Housing Conference
b. Rent control
c. 100-year flood
d. Tenant rights

7. _____ is used to assign the available resources in an economic way. It is part of resource management.

In strategic planning, is a plan for using available resources, for example human resources, especially in the near term, to achieve goals for the future.

a. 1921 recession
b. Resource allocation
c. 100-year flood
d. 130-30 fund

8. _____ according to Onuoha (2007) is the practice of starting new organizations or revitalizing mature organizations, particularly new businesses generally in response to identified opportunities. _____ is often a difficult undertaking, as a vast majority of new businesses fail. Entrepreneurial activities are substantially different depending on the type of organization that is being started.

a. Entrepreneurship
b. ACEA agreement
c. ACCRA Cost of Living Index
d. Intrapreneurship

9. A _____, or simply proprietorship is a type of business entity which legally has no separate existence from its owner. Hence, the limitations of liability enjoyed by a corporation and limited liability partnerships do not apply to sole proprietors. All debts of the business are debts of the owner.

a. Sole proprietorship
b. Delivery schedule adherence
c. Customer centricity
d. Golden hello

10. In economics, the _____ is the agent who receives the net income (income after deducting all costs.)

Residual claimancy is generally required in order for there to be Moral Hazard, which is a problem typical of information asymmetry. This is specifically the case for the Principal-agent problem.

a. Recursive economics
b. Horizontal territorial allocation
c. Residual claimant
d. Price level

11. A _____ is a type of business entity in which partners (owners) share with each other the profits or losses of the business _____s are often favored over corporations for taxation purposes, as the _____ structure does not generally incur a tax on profits before it is distributed to the partners (i.e. there is no dividend tax levied.) However, depending on the _____ structure and the jurisdiction in which it operates, owners of a _____ may be exposed to greater personal liability than they would as shareholders of a corporation.

For a country-by-country listing of types of _____s, companies, etc., see Types of business entity.

a. Nature of the Firm
b. Limited liability
c. Means test
d. Partnership

Chapter 21. Rents, Profits, and the Financial Environment of Business

12. _____ is the difference between price and the costs of bringing to market whatever it is that is accounted as an enterprise (whether by harvest, extraction, manufacture, or purchase) in terms of the component costs of delivered goods and/or services and any operating or other expenses.

A key difficulty in measuring profit is in defining costs. Pure economic monetary profits can be zero or negative even in competitive equilibrium when accounted monetized costs exceed monetized price.

- a. Accounting profit
- b. Economic profit
- c. ACCRA Cost of Living Index
- d. Operating profit

13. In finance, a _____ is a debt security, in which the authorized issuer owes the holders a debt and, depending on the terms of the _____, is obliged to pay interest (the coupon) and/or to repay the principal at a later date, termed maturity. A _____ is a formal contract to repay borrowed money with interest at fixed intervals.

Thus a _____ is like a loan: the issuer is the borrower (debtor), the holder is the lender (creditor), and the coupon is the interest.

- a. Prize Bond
- b. Carter bonds
- c. Bond
- d. Callable

14. The _____ consists of a number of economic theories which describe the nature of the firm, company including its existence, its behaviour, and its relationship with the market.

In simplified terms, the _____ aims to answer these questions:

1. Existence - why do firms emerge, why are not all transactions in the economy mediated over the market?
2. Boundaries - why the boundary between firms and the market is located exactly there? Which transactions are performed internally and which are negotiated on the market?
3. Organization - why are firms structured in such specific way? What is the interplay of formal and informal relationships?

Despite looking simple, these questions are not answered by the established economic theory, which usually views firms as given, and treats them as black boxes without any internal structure.

The First World War period saw a change of emphasis in economic theory away from industry-level analysis which mainly included analysing markets to analysis at the level of the firm, as it became increasingly clear that perfect competition was no longer an adequate model of how firms behaved. Economic theory till then had focussed on trying to understand markets alone and there had been little study on understanding why firms or organisations exist.

- a. Neo-Ricardian school
- b. Technology gap
- c. Marginal revenue product
- d. Theory of the firm

15. An _____ is an easy accounted cost, such as wage, rent and materials. It can be transacted in the form of money payment and is lost directly, as opposed to monetary implicit costs.

a. Inventory valuation
b. Explicit cost
c. Average variable cost
d. Average fixed cost

16. _____ is a concept whereby a person's financial liability is limited to a fixed sum, most commonly the value of a person's investment in a company or partnership with _____. A shareholder in a limited company is not personally liable for any of the debts of the company, other than for the value of his investment in that company. The same is true for the members of a _____ partnership and the limited partners in a limited partnership.
a. Judgment summons
b. Post-sale restraint
c. Limited liability
d. Personal Responsibility and Work Opportunity Reconciliation Act of 1996

17. A mutual _____ or stockholder is an individual or company (including a corporation) that legally owns one or more shares of stock in a joint stock company. A company's _____s collectively own that company. Thus, the typical goal of such companies is to enhance _____ value.
a. Profit warning
b. Shareholder
c. Casual trading
d. Paper valuation

18. To _____ is to impose a financial charge or other levy upon a taxpayer by a state or the functional equivalent of a state.

_____es are also imposed by many subnational entities. _____es consist of direct _____ or indirect _____, and may be paid in money or as its labour equivalent (often but not always unpaid.)

a. 1921 recession
b. 130-30 fund
c. 100-year flood
d. Tax

19. _____s are payments made by a corporation to its shareholders. It is the portion of corporate profits paid out to stockholders. When a corporation earns a profit or surplus, that money can be put to two uses: it can either be re-invested in the business (called retained earnings), or it can be paid to the shareholders as a _____.
a. Dividend payout ratio
b. Dividend cover
c. Dividend imputation
d. Dividend

20. _____ is a specific term used in companies' financial reporting from the company-whole point of view. Because that use excludes the effects of changing ownership interest, an economic measure of _____ is necessary for financial analysis from the shareholders' point of view

_____ is defined by the Financial Accounting Standards Board, or FASB, as e;the change in equity [net assets] of a business enterprise during a period from transactions and other events and circumstances from nonowner sources. It includes all changes in equity during a period except those resulting from investments by owners and distributions to owners.e;

_____ is the sum of net income and other items that must bypass the income statement because they have not been realized, including items like an unrealized holding gain or loss from available for sale securities and foreign currency translation gains or losses.

a. Windfall gain   b. Real income
c. Per capita income   d. Comprehensive income

21. In economics, an _____ occurs when one foregoes an alternative action but does not make an actual payment. (For instance, the explicit cost of a night at the movies includes the moviegoer's ticket and soda, but the _____ includes the pay he would have earned if he had chosen to work instead.) _____s are related to forgone benefits of any single transaction.
   a. Implicit cost   b. Overnight trade
   c. Ostrich strategy   d. External sector

22. _____ or economic opportunity loss is the value of the next best alternative foregone as the result of making a decision. _____ analysis is an important part of a company's decision-making processes but is not treated as an actual cost in any financial statement. The next best thing that a person can engage in is referred to as the _____ of doing the best thing and ignoring the next best thing to be done.
   a. Industrial organization   b. Opportunity cost
   c. Economic   d. Economic ideology

23. In finance, _____ rate of profit or sometimes just return, is the ratio of money gained or lost on an investment relative to the amount of money invested. The amount of money gained or lost may be referred to as interest, profit/loss, gain/loss, or net income/loss. The money invested may be referred to as the asset, capital, principal, or the cost basis of the investment.
   a. Return of capital   b. Capital recovery factor
   c. Rate of return   d. Return on capital employed

24. The _____ is an expected return that the provider of capital plans to earn on their investment.

Capital (money) used for funding a business should earn returns for the capital providers who risk their capital. For an investment to be worthwhile, the expected return on capital must be greater than the _____.

   a. Wealth inequality in the United States   b. Modigliani-Miller theorem
   c. Cost of Capital   d. Capital flight

25. In economics, _____ are business expenses that are not dependent on the activities of the business They tend to be time-related, such as salaries or rents being paid per month. This is in contrast to variable costs, which are volume-related (and are paid per quantity.)

In management accounting, _____ are defined as expenses that do not change in proportion to the activity of a business, within the relevant period or scale of production.

   a. Cost allocation   b. Marginal cost
   c. Variable cost   d. Fixed costs

26. The _____ is the expected return forgone by bypassing of other potential investment activities for a given capital. It is a rate of return that investors could earn in financial markets.

a. Opportunity cost of Capital
b. ACEA agreement
c. ACCRA Cost of Living Index
d. AD-IA Model

27. _____ is the increase in the amount of the goods and services produced by an economy over time. It is conventionally measured as the percent rate of increase in real gross domestic product, or real GDP. Growth is usually calculated in real terms, i.e. inflation-adjusted terms, in order to net out the effect of inflation on the price of the goods and services produced.
a. ACCRA Cost of Living Index
b. Economic growth
c. AD-IA Model
d. ACEA agreement

28. An _____ is a person who has possession of an enterprise and assumes significant accountability for the inherent risks and the outcome. It is an ambitious leader who combines land, labor, and capital to create and market new goods or services. The term is a loanword from French and was first defined by the Irish economist Richard Cantillon.
a. ACEA agreement
b. ACCRA Cost of Living Index
c. Expansionary policies
d. Entrepreneur

29. In Marxian economics, _____ originally referred to the means of production. Individuals, organizations and governments use _____ in the production of other goods or commodities. _____ include factories, machinery, tools, equipment, and various buildings which are used to produce other products for consumption.
a. Modigliani-Miller theorem
b. Capital formation
c. Cost of capital
d. Capital goods

30. _____ is that which is owed; usually referencing assets owed, but the term can also cover moral obligations and other interactions not requiring money. In the case of assets, _____ is a means of using future purchasing power in the present before a summation has been earned. Some companies and corporations use _____ as a part of their overall corporate finance strategy.
a. Participation loan
b. Debt
c. Non-performing loan
d. Subordinated debt

31. In economics, _____ is the difference between a company's total revenue and its opportunity costs. It is the increase in wealth that an investor has from making an investment, taking into consideration all costs associated with that investment including the opportunity cost of capital.

Profit is the factor income of the entrepreneur.

a. Accounting profit
b. ACCRA Cost of Living Index
c. Operating profit
d. Economic Profit

32. A _____ is an object whose consumption increases the utility of the consumer, for which the quantity demanded exceeds the quantity supplied at zero price. _____s are usually modeled as having diminishing marginal utility. The first individual purchase has high utility; the second has less.
a. Search good
b. Positional goods
c. Luxury good
d. Good

Chapter 21. Rents, Profits, and the Financial Environment of Business

33. _____ is a type of private equity investment, most often a minority investment, in relatively mature companies that are looking for capital to expand or restructure operations, enter new markets or finance a significant acquisition without a change of control of the business.

Companies that seek _____, will often do so in order to finance a transformational event in their lifecycle. These companies are likely to be more mature than venture capital funded companies, able to generate revenue and operating profits but unable to generate sufficient cash to fund major expansions, acquisitions or other investments.

- a. Growth capital
- c. Mezzanine capital
- b. Seed money
- d. Venture capital fund

34. An _____ is a tax levied on the financial income of people, corporations, or other legal entities. Various _____ systems exist, with varying degrees of tax incidence. Income taxation can be progressive, proportional, or regressive.
- a. ACCRA Cost of Living Index
- c. ACEA agreement
- b. AD-IA Model
- d. Income tax

35. In economics, _____ is the process by which a firm determines the price and output level that returns the greatest profit. There are several approaches to this problem. The total revenue--total cost method relies on the fact that profit equals revenue minus cost, and the marginal revenue--marginal cost method is based on the fact that total profit in a perfectly competitive market reaches its maximum point where marginal revenue equals marginal cost.
- a. 100-year flood
- c. Normal profit
- b. Profit margin
- d. Profit maximization

36. In economics, _____ are the resources employed to produce goods and services. They facilitate production but do not become part of the product (as with raw materials) or significantly transformed by the production process (as with fuel used to power machinery.) To 19th century economists, the _____ were land (natural resources, gifts from nature), labor (the ability to work), and capital goods (human-made tools and equipment.)
- a. Productive capacity
- c. Long-run
- b. Production function
- d. Factors of production

37. In microeconomics, _____ is quite simply the conversion of inputs into outputs. It is an economic process that uses resources to create a good or service that is suitable for exchange. This can include manufacturing, storing, shipping, and packaging.
- a. Variability
- c. Characteristic
- b. Bucket shop
- d. Production

38. A _____ refers to any type debt instrument, such as a loan, bond, mortgage that does not have a fixed rate of interest over the life of the instrument. Such debt typically uses an index or other base rate for establishing the interest rate for each relevant period. One of the most common rates to use as the basis for applying interest rates is the London Inter-bank Offered Rate, or LIBOR
- a. Bankruptcy remote
- c. Standard of deferred payment
- b. Style investing
- d. Floating interest rate

39. _____ is a fee paid on borrowed assets. It is the price paid for the use of borrowed money, or, money earned by deposited funds. Assets that are sometimes lent with _____ include money, shares, consumer goods through hire purchase, major assets such as aircraft, and even entire factories in finance lease arrangements.

a. Asset protection
b. Internal debt
c. Insolvency
d. Interest

40. A _____, reserve bank, or monetary authority is the entity responsible for the monetary policy of a country or of a group of member states. It is a bank that can lend money to other banks in times of need. Its primary responsibility is to maintain the stability of the national currency and money supply, but more active duties include controlling subsidized-loan interest rates, and acting as a lender of last resort to the banking sector during times of financial crisis (private banks often being integral to the national financial system.)

a. 100-year flood
b. 130-30 fund
c. 1921 recession
d. Central Bank

41. _____ is the value on a given date of a future payment or series of future payments, discounted to reflect the time value of money and other factors such as investment risk. _____ calculations are widely used in business and economics to provide a means to compare cash flows at different times on a meaningful 'like to like' basis.

Money value fluctuates over time: $100 today are not worth $100 in five years.

a. Present value
b. Financial transaction
c. Future value
d. Maturity

42. _____ is the development of economic wealth of countries or regions for the well-being of their inhabitants. It is the process by which a nation improves the economic, political, and social well being of its people. From a policy perspective, _____ can be defined as efforts that seek to improve the economic well-being and quality of life for a community by creating and/or retaining jobs and supporting or growing incomes and the tax base.

a. Inflation
b. Economic development
c. Economic methodology
d. Experimental economics

43. An _____ is the price a borrower pays for the use of money they do not own, for instance a small company might borrow from a bank to kick start their business, and the return a lender receives for deferring the use of funds, by lending it to the borrower. _____s are normally expressed as a percentage rate over the period of one year.

_____s targets are also a vital tool of monetary policy and are used to control variables like investment, inflation, and unemployment.

a. Arrow-Debreu model
b. ACCRA Cost of Living Index
c. Enterprise value
d. Interest rate

44. _____ is the a method of technical and economic research of the systems for purpose to optimize a parity between system's consumer functions or properties and expenses to achieve those functions or properties.

Chapter 21. Rents, Profits, and the Financial Environment of Business

This methodology for continuous perfection of production, industrial technologies, organizational structures was developed by Juryj Sobolev in 1948 at the 'Perm telephone factory'

- 1948 Juryj Sobolev - the first success in application of a method analysis at the 'Perm telephone factory' .
- 1949 - the first application for the invention as result of use of the new method.

Today in economically developed countries practically each enterprise or the company use methodology of the kind of functional-cost analysis as a practice of the quality management, most full satisfying to principles of standards of series ISO 9000.

- Interest of consumer not in products itself, but the advantage which it will receive from its usage.
- The consumer aspires to reduce his expenses
- Functions needed by consumer can be executed in the various ways, and, hence, with various efficiency and expenses. Among possible alternatives of realization of functions exist such in which the parity of quality and the price is the optimal for the consumer.

The goal of _____ is achievement of the highest consumer satisfaction of production at simultaneous decrease in all kinds of industrial expenses Classical _____ has three English synonyms - Value Engineering, Value Management, Value Analysis.

 a. Residual value
 c. Monopoly wage
 b. Function cost analysis
 d. Real net output ratio

45. _____ is a financial mechanism in which a debtor obtains the right to delay payments to a creditor, for a defined period of time, in exchange for a charge or fee. Essentially, the party that owes money in the present purchases the right to delay the payment until some future date. The discount, or charge, is simply the difference between the original amount owed in the present and the amount that has to be paid in the future to settle the debt.
 a. RiskMetrics
 c. Catastrophe modeling
 b. Risk measure
 d. Discounting

46. Discounting is a financial mechanism in which a debtor obtains the right to delay payments to a creditor, for a defined period of time, in exchange for a charge or fee. Essentially, the party that owes money in the present purchases the right to delay the payment until some future date. The _____, or charge, is simply the difference between the original amount owed in the present and the amount that has to be paid in the future to settle the debt.
 a. Compound annual growth rate
 c. Risk measure
 b. Panjer recursion
 d. Discount

47. _____ is money accepted for exchange of goods in an economy. The prevalence of one money over another arises, usually, when a government designates through decrees that the government shall accept only particular notes and coins in payment for taxes. Typically, money of _____ consists of stamped coins and minted paper bills.
 a. Security thread
 c. Totnes pound
 b. Scripophily
 d. Currency

Chapter 21. Rents, Profits, and the Financial Environment of Business

48. The _____ was a trading company, which was established in 1602, when the States-General of the Netherlands granted it a 21-year monopoly to carry out colonial activities in Asia. It was the first multinational corporation in the world and the first company to issue stock. It was also arguably the world's first megacorporation, possessing quasi-governmental powers, including the ability to wage war, negotiate treaties, coin money, and establish colonies.
   a. 130-30 fund
   b. 100-year flood
   c. 1921 recession
   d. Dutch East India Company

49. The _____ was an early English joint-stock company that was formed initially for pursuing trade with the East Indies, but that ended up trading with the Indian subcontinent and China. The oldest among several similarly formed European East India Companies, the Company was granted an English Royal Charter, under the name Governor and Company of Merchants of London Trading into the East Indies, by Elizabeth I on 31 December 1600. After a rival English company challenged its monopoly in the late 17th century, the two companies were merged in 1708 to form the United Company of Merchants of England Trading to the East Indies, commonly styled the Honourable _____, and abbreviated, HEast India Company; the Company was colloquially referred to as John Company, and in India as Company Bahadur .
   a. ACCRA Cost of Living Index
   b. East India Company
   c. AD-IA Model
   d. ACEA agreement

50. _____ is typically a 'higher ranking' stock than voting shares, and its terms are negotiated between the corporation and the investor.

   _____ usually carries no voting rights, but may carry priority over common stock in the payment of dividends and upon liquidation. _____ may carry a dividend that is paid out prior to any dividends being paid to common stock holders.

   a. Bookrunner
   b. Financial accelerator
   c. Capital budgeting
   d. Preferred stock

51. _____ is a term used in accounting relating to the increase in value of an asset. In this sense it is the reverse of depreciation, which measures the fall in value of assets over their normal life-time.

   _____ is a rise of a currency in a floating exchange rate.

   a. Appreciation
   b. AD-IA Model
   c. ACEA agreement
   d. ACCRA Cost of Living Index

52. _____ is an equity (stock) exchange located at 11 Wall Street in lower Manhattan, New York, USA. It is the largest stock exchange in the world by dollar value of its listed companies' securities. As of October 2008, the combined capitalization of all domestic _____ listed companies was US$10.1 trillion.
   a. 1921 recession
   b. New York Stock Exchange
   c. 130-30 fund
   d. 100-year flood

53. A security is a fungible, negotiable instrument representing financial value. _____ are broadly categorized into debt _____; equity _____, e.g., common stocks; and derivative (finance) contracts such as forwards, futures, options and swaps. The company or other entity issuing the security is called the issuer.

Chapter 21. Rents, Profits, and the Financial Environment of Business

a. Pure security
c. Street name securities
b. Trading account assets
d. Securities

54. A _____ is a corporation or mutual organization which provides trading facilities for stock brokers and traders, to trade stocks and other securities. It may be a physical trading room where the traders gather, or a formalised communications network. Creation of a _____ is a strategy of economic development.
   a. Stock Exchange
   c. Primary shares
   b. 100-year flood
   d. SEAQ

55. A United States Treasury security is a government debt issued by the United States Department of the Treasury through the Bureau of the Public Debt. Treasury securities are the debt financing instruments of the United States Federal government, and they are often referred to simply as Treasuries. There are four types of marketable treasury securities: _____, Treasury notes, Treasury bonds, and Treasury Inflation Protected Securities (TIPS.)
   a. Hicks-optimal outcome
   c. Treasury bills
   b. Cash taxes
   d. G-20 Leaders Summit on Financial Markets and the World Economy

56. A _____ is the transfer of wealth from one party (such as a person or company) to another. A _____ is usually made in exchange for the provision of goods, services or both, or to fulfill a legal obligation.

The simplest and oldest form of _____ is barter, the exchange of one good or service for another.

   a. Contingent payment sales
   c. Hard count
   b. RFM
   d. Payment

57. The _____ is an American stock exchange. It is the largest electronic screen-based equity securities trading market in the United States. With approximately 3,800 companies, it has more trading volume per hour than any other stock exchange in the world.
   a. 130-30 fund
   c. 1921 recession
   b. 100-year flood
   d. Nasdaq

58. _____ is a concept with somewhat disparate meanings in several fields. It also has a common meaning which has a loose connection with some of those more definite meanings.

Casually, it is typically used to denote a lack of order, or purpose, or cause.

   a. 100-year flood
   c. Randomness
   b. 130-30 fund
   d. 1921 recession

59. A _____, sometimes denoted _____, is a mathematical formalization of a trajectory that consists of taking successive random steps. The results of _____ analysis have been applied to computer science, physics, ecology, economics, and a number of other fields as a fundamental model for random processes in time. For example, the path traced by a molecule as it travels in a liquid or a gas, the search path of a foraging animal, the price of a fluctuating stock and the financial status of a gambler can all be modeled as _____s.

a. 100-year flood
c. 1921 recession
b. 130-30 fund
d. Random walk

60. _____ in economics and business is the result of an exchange and from that trade we assign a numerical monetary value to a good, service or asset. If Alice trades Bob 4 apples for an orange, the _____ of an orange is 4 apples. Inversely, the _____ of an apple is 1/4 oranges.
   a. Price ceiling
   b. Price
   c. Price dispersion
   d. Lerner Index

61. _____ is the controlled distribution of resources and scarce goods or services. _____ controls the size of the ration, one's allotted portion of the resources being distributed on a particular day or at a particular time.

In economics, it is often common to use the word '_____' to refer to one of the roles that prices play in markets, while _____ is called 'non-price _____.' Using prices to ration means that those with the most money (or other assets) and who want a product the most are first to receive it.

   a. 1921 recession
   b. 130-30 fund
   c. 100-year flood
   d. Rationing

62. A _____ is an expression that compares quantities relative to each other. The most common examples involve two quantities, but any number of quantities can be compared. _____s are represented mathematically by separating each quantity with a colon, for example the _____ 2:3, which is read as the _____ 'two to three'.
   a. 100-year flood
   b. Y-intercept
   c. 130-30 fund
   d. Ratio

Chapter 22. The Firm: Cost and Output Determination

1. The _____ Corporation (1857-2003), based in Bethlehem, Pennsylvania, was once the second-largest steel producer in the United States, after Pittsburgh, Pennsylvania-based U.S. Steel. After a decline in the U.S. steel industry and management problems leading to the company's 2001 bankruptcy, the company was dissolved and the remaining assets sold to International Steel Group in 2003. In 2005, ISG merged with Mittal Steel, ending U.S. ownership of the assets of _____.

   a. 130-30 fund
   b. 100-year flood
   c. 1921 recession
   d. Bethlehem Steel

2. The _____ consists of a number of economic theories which describe the nature of the firm, company including its existence, its behaviour, and its relationship with the market.

   In simplified terms, the _____ aims to answer these questions:

   1. Existence - why do firms emerge, why are not all transactions in the economy mediated over the market?
   2. Boundaries - why the boundary between firms and the market is located exactly there? Which transactions are performed internally and which are negotiated on the market?
   3. Organization - why are firms structured in such specific way? What is the interplay of formal and informal relationships?

   Despite looking simple, these questions are not answered by the established economic theory, which usually views firms as given, and treats them as black boxes without any internal structure.

   The First World War period saw a change of emphasis in economic theory away from industry-level analysis which mainly included analysing markets to analysis at the level of the firm, as it became increasingly clear that perfect competition was no longer an adequate model of how firms behaved. Economic theory till then had focussed on trying to understand markets alone and there had been little study on understanding why firms or organisations exist.

   a. Marginal revenue product
   b. Technology gap
   c. Neo-Ricardian school
   d. Theory of the firm

3. _____ is the term denoting either an entrance or changes which are inserted into a system and which activate/modify a process. It is an abstract concept, used in the modeling, system(s) design and system(s) exploitation. It is usually connected with other terms, e.g., _____ field, _____ variable, _____ parameter, _____ value, _____ signal, _____ device and _____ file.

   a. Input
   b. AD-IA Model
   c. ACCRA Cost of Living Index
   d. ACEA agreement

4. In microeconomics, _____ is quite simply the conversion of inputs into outputs. It is an economic process that uses resources to create a good or service that is suitable for exchange. This can include manufacturing, storing, shipping, and packaging.

   a. Production
   b. Characteristic
   c. Bucket shop
   d. Variability

5. In Marxian economics, _____ originally referred to the means of production. Individuals, organizations and governments use _____ in the production of other goods or commodities. _____ include factories, machinery, tools, equipment, and various buildings which are used to produce other products for consumption.

Chapter 22. The Firm: Cost and Output Determination

a. Capital formation
c. Modigliani-Miller theorem
b. Cost of capital
d. Capital goods

6. Economics:

- _____,the desire to own something and the ability to pay for it
- _____ curve,a graphic representation of a _____ schedule
- _____ deposit, the money in checking accounts
- _____ pull theory,the theory that inflation occurs when _____ for goods and services exceeds existing supplies
- _____ schedule,a table that lists the quantity of a good a person will buy it each different price
- _____ side economics,the school of economics at believes government spending and tax cuts open economy by raising _____

a. Bon
c. G20
b. Demand
d. Procter ' Gamble

7. In economics, _____ is the ratio of the percent change in one variable to the percent change in another variable. It is a tool for measuring the responsiveness of a function to changes in parameters in a relative way. Commonly analyzed are _____ of substitution, price and wealth.
   a. Elasticity of demand
   c. ACCRA Cost of Living Index
   b. ACEA agreement
   d. Elasticity

8. A _____ is an object whose consumption increases the utility of the consumer, for which the quantity demanded exceeds the quantity supplied at zero price. _____s are usually modeled as having diminishing marginal utility. The first individual purchase has high utility; the second has less.
   a. Luxury good
   c. Search good
   b. Positional goods
   d. Good

9. _____ is the temporary suspension or permanent termination of employment of an employee or (more commonly) a group of employees for business reasons, such as the decision that certain positions are no longer necessary or a business slow-down or interruption in work. Originally the term '_____' referred exclusively to a temporary interruption in work, as when factory work cyclically falls off. However, in recent times the term can also refer to the permanent elimination of a position.
   a. Retirement
   c. Termination of employment
   b. 100-year flood
   d. Layoff

10. In economics, the concept of the _____ refers to the decision-making time frame of a firm in which at least one factor of production is fixed. Costs which are fixed in the _____ have no impact on a firms decisions. For example a firm can raise output by increasing the amount of labour through overtime.
    a. Hicks-neutral technical change
    c. Short-run
    b. Productivity world
    d. Marginal product

Chapter 22. The Firm: Cost and Output Determination

11. Competition law, known in the United States as _____ law, has three main elements:

    - prohibiting agreements or practices that restrict free trading and competition between business entities. This includes in particular the repression of cartels.
    - banning abusive behaviour by a firm dominating a market, or anti-competitive practices that tend to lead to such a dominant position. Practices controlled in this way may include predatory pricing, tying, price gouging, refusal to deal, and many others.
    - supervising the mergers and acquisitions of large corporations, including some joint ventures. Transactions that are considered to threaten the competitive process can be prohibited altogether, or approved subject to 'remedies' such as an obligation to divest part of the merged business or to offer licences or access to facilities to enable other businesses to continue competing.

    The substance and practice of competition law varies from jurisdiction to jurisdiction. Protecting the interests of consumers (consumer welfare) and ensuring that entrepreneurs have an opportunity to compete in the market economy are often treated as important objectives. Competition law is closely connected with law on deregulation of access to markets, state aids and subsidies, the privatisation of state owned assets and the establishment of independent sector regulators. In recent decades, competition law has been viewed as a way to provide better public services.

    a. Anti-Inflation Act
    c. Intellectual property law
    b. Antitrust
    d. United Kingdom competition law

12. In economics, _____ refers to how the marginal contribution of a factor of production usually decreases as more of the factor is used. According to this relationship, in a production system with fixed and variable inputs, beyond some point, each additional unit of the variable input yields smaller and smaller increases in output. Conversely, producing one more unit of output costs more and more in variable inputs.

    a. Law of increasing relative cost
    c. Diminishing returns
    b. Cobden-Chevalier Treaty
    d. Harvester Judgment

13. In economics, and cost accounting, _____ describes the total economic cost of production and is made up of variable costs, which vary according to the quantity of a good produced and include inputs such as labor and raw materials, plus fixed costs, which are independent of the quantity of a good produced and include inputs (capital) that cannot be varied in the short term, such as buildings and machinery. _____ in economics includes the total opportunity cost of each factor of production in addition to fixed and variable costs.

    The rate at which _____ changes as the amount produced changes is called marginal cost.

    a. 130-30 fund
    c. 1921 recession
    b. 100-year flood
    d. Total cost

14. In economics, the marginal product or _____ is the extra output produced by one more unit of an input (for instance, the difference in output when a firm's labour is increased from five to six units.) Assuming that no other inputs to production change, the marginal product of a given input (X) can be expressed as:

    $MP = \Delta Y/\Delta X$ = (the change of Y)/(the change of X.)

In neoclassical economics, this is the mathematical derivative of the production function....

a. Hicks-neutral technical change
b. Short-run
c. Factors of production
d. Marginal physical product

15. This concept is also known as the law of diminishing marginal returns, the _____, or the law of increasing opportunity cost.

The concept of diminishing returns can be traced back to the concerns of early economists such as Johann Heinrich von Thünen, Turgot, Thomas Malthus and David Ricardo.

Suppose that one kilogram of seed applied to a plot of land of a fixed size produces one ton of crop.

a. Post-sale restraint
b. Feoffee
c. Directive 76/207/EEC
d. Law of increasing relative cost

16. In economics, _____ is the process by which a firm determines the price and output level that returns the greatest profit. There are several approaches to this problem. The total revenue--total cost method relies on the fact that profit equals revenue minus cost, and the marginal revenue--marginal cost method is based on the fact that total profit in a perfectly competitive market reaches its maximum point where marginal revenue equals marginal cost.

a. Profit margin
b. Normal profit
c. 100-year flood
d. Profit maximization

17. In economics and business, specifically cost accounting, the _____ point (BEP) is the point at which cost or expenses and revenue are equal: there is no net loss or gain, and one has 'broken even'. A profit or a loss has not been made, although opportunity costs have been paid, and capital has received the risk-adjusted, expected return.

For example, if the business sells less than 200 tables each month, it will make a loss, if it sells more, it will be a profit.

a. Trailing twelve months
b. Decoupling plus
c. Stylized fact
d. Break-even

18. _____ is the total money received from the sale of any given quantity of output.

The _____ is calculated by taking the price of the sale times the quantity sold, i.e.

_____ = price X quantity.

a. Defined benefit pension plan
b. Blanket order
c. Ceteris paribus
d. Total revenue

Chapter 22. The Firm: Cost and Output Determination

19. In economics, a _____ is a graph of the costs of production as a function of total quantity produced. In a free market economy, productively efficient firms use these curves to find the optimal point of production, where they make the most profits. There are a few different types of _____s, each relevant to a different area of economics.

a. Phillips curve
b. Lorenz curve
c. Demand curve
d. Cost curve

20. In economics, _____ are business expenses that are not dependent on the activities of the business They tend to be time-related, such as salaries or rents being paid per month. This is in contrast to variable costs, which are volume-related (and are paid per quantity.)

In management accounting, _____ are defined as expenses that do not change in proportion to the activity of a business, within the relevant period or scale of production.

a. Variable cost
b. Fixed costs
c. Marginal cost
d. Cost allocation

21. _____s are expenses that change in proportion to the activity of a business. In other words, _____ is the sum of marginal costs. It can also be considered normal costs.

a. Variable cost
b. Cost-Volume-Profit Analysis
c. Marginal cost
d. Cost overrun

22. In economics, _____ is the total supply of goods and services produced by a national economy during a specific time period. It is the total amount of goods and services in the economy available at all possible price levels.

a. Aggregate expenditure
b. Aggregation problem
c. Aggregate demand
d. Aggregate supply

23. In economics, _____ is equal to total cost divided by the number of goods produced (the output quantity, Q.) It is also equal to the sum of average variable costs (total variable costs divided by Q) plus average fixed costs (total fixed costs divided by Q.) _____s may be dependent on the time period considered (increasing production may be expensive or impossible in the short term, for example.)

a. Average Cost
b. Average variable cost
c. Explicit cost
d. Average fixed cost

24. _____ is an economics term used to describe the total fixed costs (TFC) divided by the quantity (Q) of units produced.

$$AFC = \frac{TFC}{Q}$$

_____ is a per-unit measure of fixed costs. As the total number of goods produced increases, the _____ decreases because the same amount of fixed costs are being spread over a larger number of units.

a. Average fixed cost
b. Explicit cost
c. Average variable cost
d. Inventory valuation

Chapter 22. The Firm: Cost and Output Determination

25. _____ is an economics term to describe a firms variable costs (labor, electricity, etc.) divided by the quantity (Q) of total units of output.

$$AVC = \frac{TVC}{Q}$$

Where:

- TVC = Total Variable Cost
- _____ = Average variable cost
- Q = Quantity of Units Produced

_____ plus average fixed cost equals average total cost:

_____ + AFC = ATC.

a. Average variable cost
b. Average fixed cost
c. Inventory valuation
d. Explicit cost

26. _____s is the social science that studies the production, distribution, and consumption of goods and services. The term _____s comes from the Ancient Greek oá¼°κονομῖα from oá¼¶κος (oikos, 'house') + vÏŒμος (nomos, 'custom' or 'law'), hence 'rules of the house(hold)'. Current _____ models developed out of the broader field of political economy in the late 19th century, owing to a desire to use an empirical approach more akin to the physical sciences.

a. Economic
b. Inflation
c. Energy economics
d. Opportunity cost

27. _____ is the increase in the amount of the goods and services produced by an economy over time. It is conventionally measured as the percent rate of increase in real gross domestic product, or real GDP. Growth is usually calculated in real terms, i.e. inflation-adjusted terms, in order to net out the effect of inflation on the price of the goods and services produced.

a. ACEA agreement
b. Economic growth
c. ACCRA Cost of Living Index
d. AD-IA Model

28. _____ in economics and business is the result of an exchange and from that trade we assign a numerical monetary value to a good, service or asset. If Alice trades Bob 4 apples for an orange, the _____ of an orange is 4 apples. Inversely, the _____ of an apple is 1/4 oranges.

a. Price
b. Lerner Index
c. Price dispersion
d. Price ceiling

29. In economics and finance, _____ is the change in total cost that arises when the quantity produced changes by one unit. It is the cost of producing one more unit of a good. Mathematically, the _____ function is expressed as the first derivative of the total cost (TC) function with respect to quantity (Q.)

Chapter 22. The Firm: Cost and Output Determination

a. Fixed costs
c. Quality costs
b. Marginal cost
d. Cost allocation

30. In economic models, the _____ time frame assumes no fixed factors of production. Firms can enter or leave the marketplace, and the cost (and availability) of land, labor, raw materials, and capital goods can be assumed to vary. In contrast, in the short-run time frame, certain factors are assumed to be fixed, because there is not sufficient time for them to change.
   a. Long-run
   c. Product Pipeline
   b. Short-run
   d. Diseconomies of scale

31. In production, returns to scale refers to changes in output subsequent to a proportional change in all inputs (where all inputs increase by a constant factor.) If output increases by that same proportional change then there are _____ If output increases by less than that proportional change, there are decreasing returns to scale (DRS.)
   a. Lexicographic preferences
   c. Market demand schedule
   b. Constant returns to scale
   d. Mohring effect

32. _____ are the forces that cause larger firms to produce goods and services at increased per-unit costs. They are less well known than what economists have long understood as 'economies of scale', the forces which enable larger firms to produce goods and services at reduced per-unit costs.

Some of the forces which cause a diseconomy of scale are listed below:

Ideally, all employees of a firm would have one-on-one communication with each other so they know exactly what the other workers are doing.

   a. Diseconomies of scale
   c. Price/performance ratio
   b. Post-Fordism
   d. Factor prices

33. _____, in microeconomics, are the cost advantages that a business obtains due to expansion. They are factors that cause a producere;s average cost per unit to fall as scale is increased. _____ is a long run concept and refers to reductions in unit cost as the size of a facility, or scale, increases.
   a. Economic production quantity
   c. Isoquant
   b. Underinvestment employment relationship
   d. Economies of scale

34. In economics and especially in the theory of competition, _____ are obstacles in the path of a firm that make it difficult to enter a given market.

_____ are the source of a firm's pricing power - the ability of a firm to raise prices without losing all its customers.

The term refers to hindrances that an individual may face while trying to gain entrance into a profession or trade.

   a. Predatory pricing
   c. Net Book Agreement
   b. Group boycott
   d. Barriers to entry

35. In economics, _____ and economies of scale are related terms that describe what happens as the scale of production increases. They are different terms and should not be used interchangeably.

_____ refers to a technical property of production that examines changes in output subsequent to a proportional change in all inputs (where all inputs increase by a constant factor.)

a. Marginal revenue
c. Necessity good
b. Customer equity
d. Returns to scale

36. _____ is a term used to collectively describe topics relating to the operations of firms with interests in multiple countries. Such firms are sometimes called multinational corporations . Well known MNCs include fast food companies McDonald's and Yum Brands, vehicle manufacturers such as General Motors and Toyota, consumer electronics companies like Samsung, LG and Sony, and energy companies such as ExxonMobil and BP.

a. ACEA agreement
c. AD-IA Model
b. ACCRA Cost of Living Index
d. International Business

Chapter 23. Perfect Competition

1. _____ is a fee paid on borrowed assets. It is the price paid for the use of borrowed money, or, money earned by deposited funds. Assets that are sometimes lent with _____ include money, shares, consumer goods through hire purchase, major assets such as aircraft, and even entire factories in finance lease arrangements.
   - a. Interest
   - b. Insolvency
   - c. Asset protection
   - d. Internal debt

2. In neoclassical economics and microeconomics, _____ describes the perfect being a market in which there are many small firms, all producing homogeneous goods. In the short term, such markets are productively inefficient as output will not occur where mc is equal to ac, but allocatively efficient, as output under _____ will always occur where mc is equal to mr, and therefore where mc equals ar. However, in the long term, such markets are both allocatively and productively efficient.
   - a. Perfect competition
   - b. Co-operative economics
   - c. Nominal value
   - d. Law and economics

3. In economics, a _____ 'purchase') is a market form in which only one buyer faces many sellers. It is an example of imperfect competition, similar to a monopoly, in which only one seller faces many buyers. As the only purchaser of a good or service, the 'monopsonist' may dictate terms to its suppliers in the same manner that a monopolist controls the market for its buyers.
   - a. Monopsony
   - b. 100-year flood
   - c. 1921 recession
   - d. 130-30 fund

4. _____ in economics and business is the result of an exchange and from that trade we assign a numerical monetary value to a good, service or asset. If Alice trades Bob 4 apples for an orange, the _____ of an orange is 4 apples. Inversely, the _____ of an apple is 1/4 oranges.
   - a. Price ceiling
   - b. Price
   - c. Price dispersion
   - d. Lerner Index

5. Monopoly power is an example of market failure which occurs when one or more of the participants has the ability to influence the price or other outcomes in some general or specialized market. The most commonly discussed form of market power is that of a monopoly, but other forms such as monopsony, and more moderate versions of these two extremes, exist. Market participants that have market power are sometimes referred to as 'price makers', while those without are sometimes called '_____'.
   - a. De facto monopoly
   - b. Quasi-rent
   - c. Market concentration
   - d. Price takers

204 Chapter 23. Perfect Competition

6. _____ has several particular meanings:

   - in mathematics
     - _____ function
     - Euler _____
     - _____
     - _____ subgroup
     - method of _____s (partial differential equations)
   - in physics and engineering
     - any _____ curve that shows the relationship between certain input- and output parameters, e.g.
     - an I-V or current-voltage _____ is the current in a circuit as a function of the applied voltage
     - Receiver-Operator _____
   - in fiction
     - in Dungeons ' Dragons, _____ is another name for ability score

   a. Characteristic
   b. Drawdown
   c. Fiscal
   d. Procter ' Gamble

7. Economics:

   - _____, the desire to own something and the ability to pay for it
   - _____ curve, a graphic representation of a _____ schedule
   - _____ deposit, the money in checking accounts
   - _____ pull theory, the theory that inflation occurs when _____ for goods and services exceeds existing supplies
   - _____ schedule, a table that lists the quantity of a good a person will buy it each different price
   - _____ side economics, the school of economics at believes government spending and tax cuts open economy by raising _____

   a. G20
   b. Bon
   c. Procter ' Gamble
   d. Demand

8. In economics, the _____ can be defined as the graph depicting the relationship between the price of a certain commodity, and the amount of it that consumers are willing and able to purchase at that given price. It is a graphic representation of a demand schedule. The _____ for all consumers together follows from the _____ of every individual consumer: the individual demands at each price are added together.
   a. Wage curve
   b. Lorenz curve
   c. Kuznets curve
   d. Demand curve

9. In microeconomics, _____ is quite simply the conversion of inputs into outputs. It is an economic process that uses resources to create a good or service that is suitable for exchange. This can include manufacturing, storing, shipping, and packaging.

a. Characteristic	b. Variability
c. Bucket shop	d. Production

10. In economics, _____ is the process by which a firm determines the price and output level that returns the greatest profit. There are several approaches to this problem. The total revenue--total cost method relies on the fact that profit equals revenue minus cost, and the marginal revenue--marginal cost method is based on the fact that total profit in a perfectly competitive market reaches its maximum point where marginal revenue equals marginal cost.

a. Profit maximization	b. Normal profit
c. 100-year flood	d. Profit margin

11. _____ is the total money received from the sale of any given quantity of output.

The _____ is calculated by taking the price of the sale times the quantity sold, i.e.

_____ = price X quantity.

a. Defined benefit pension plan	b. Ceteris paribus
c. Total revenue	d. Blanket order

12. In Marxian economics, _____ originally referred to the means of production. Individuals, organizations and governments use _____ in the production of other goods or commodities. _____ include factories, machinery, tools, equipment, and various buildings which are used to produce other products for consumption.

a. Modigliani-Miller theorem	b. Capital goods
c. Capital formation	d. Cost of capital

13. In economics, _____ are the resources employed to produce goods and services. They facilitate production but do not become part of the product (as with raw materials) or significantly transformed by the production process (as with fuel used to power machinery.) To 19th century economists, the _____ were land (natural resources, gifts from nature), labor (the ability to work), and capital goods (human-made tools and equipment.)

a. Factors of production	b. Long-run
c. Production function	d. Productive capacity

14. A _____ is an object whose consumption increases the utility of the consumer, for which the quantity demanded exceeds the quantity supplied at zero price. _____s are usually modeled as having diminishing marginal utility. The first individual purchase has high utility; the second has less.

a. Positional goods	b. Search good
c. Luxury good	d. Good

15. In economics, and cost accounting, _____ describes the total economic cost of production and is made up of variable costs, which vary according to the quantity of a good produced and include inputs such as labor and raw materials, plus fixed costs, which are independent of the quantity of a good produced and include inputs (capital) that cannot be varied in the short term, such as buildings and machinery. _____ in economics includes the total opportunity cost of each factor of production in addition to fixed and variable costs.

The rate at which _____ changes as the amount produced changes is called marginal cost.

a. 100-year flood
b. Total cost
c. 130-30 fund
d. 1921 recession

16. In economics, the concept of the _____ refers to the decision-making time frame of a firm in which at least one factor of production is fixed. Costs which are fixed in the _____ have no impact on a firms decisions. For example a firm can raise output by increasing the amount of labour through overtime.
   a. Hicks-neutral technical change
   b. Productivity world
   c. Short-run
   d. Marginal product

17. _____s is the social science that studies the production, distribution, and consumption of goods and services. The term _____s comes from the Ancient Greek οἰκονομία from οἶκος (oikos, 'house') + νόμος (nomos, 'custom' or 'law'), hence 'rules of the house(hold)'. Current _____ models developed out of the broader field of political economy in the late 19th century, owing to a desire to use an empirical approach more akin to the physical sciences.
   a. Opportunity cost
   b. Energy economics
   c. Inflation
   d. Economic

18. _____ is the increase in the amount of the goods and services produced by an economy over time. It is conventionally measured as the percent rate of increase in real gross domestic product, or real GDP. Growth is usually calculated in real terms, i.e. inflation-adjusted terms, in order to net out the effect of inflation on the price of the goods and services produced.
   a. ACCRA Cost of Living Index
   b. ACEA agreement
   c. AD-IA Model
   d. Economic growth

19. _____ is the controlled distribution of resources and scarce goods or services. _____ controls the size of the ration, one's allotted portion of the resources being distributed on a particular day or at a particular time.

In economics, it is often common to use the word '_____' to refer to one of the roles that prices play in markets, while _____ is called 'non-price _____.' Using prices to ration means that those with the most money (or other assets) and who want a product the most are first to receive it.

   a. 130-30 fund
   b. 1921 recession
   c. 100-year flood
   d. Rationing

20. _____ is a type of private equity investment, most often a minority investment, in relatively mature companies that are looking for capital to expand or restructure operations, enter new markets or finance a significant acquisition without a change of control of the business.

Companies that seek _____, will often do so in order to finance a transformational event in their lifecycle. These companies are likely to be more mature than venture capital funded companies, able to generate revenue and operating profits but unable to generate sufficient cash to fund major expansions, acquisitions or other investments.

   a. Mezzanine capital
   b. Seed money
   c. Venture capital fund
   d. Growth capital

Chapter 23. Perfect Competition

21. In economics and business, specifically cost accounting, the _____ point (BEP) is the point at which cost or expenses and revenue are equal: there is no net loss or gain, and one has 'broken even'. A profit or a loss has not been made, although opportunity costs have been paid, and capital has received the risk-adjusted, expected return.

For example, if the business sells less than 200 tables each month, it will make a loss, if it sells more, it will be a profit.

a. Break-even
b. Decoupling plus
c. Stylized fact
d. Trailing twelve months

22. CÄ"terÄ«s paribus is a Latin phrase, literally translated as 'with other things the same.' It is commonly rendered in English as 'all other things being equal.' A prediction, or a statement about causal or logical connections between two states of affairs, is qualified by _____ in order to acknowledge, and to rule out, the possibility of other factors which could override the relationship between the antecedent and the consequent.

A _____ assumption is often fundamental to the predictive purpose of scientific inquiry. In order to formulate scientific laws, it is usually necessary to rule out factors which interfere with examining a specific causal relationship.

a. Dead cat bounce
b. Regrettables
c. Deflator
d. Ceteris paribus

23. In economics, the _____ of an industry is used as an indicator of the relative size of firms in relation to the industry as a whole. It is calculated as the sum of the percent market share of the top n industries. This may also assist in determining the market structure of the industry.

a. Price takers
b. De facto monopoly
c. Rate-of-return regulation
d. Concentration ratio

24. A _____ is an expression that compares quantities relative to each other. The most common examples involve two quantities, but any number of quantities can be compared. _____s are represented mathematically by separating each quantity with a colon, for example the _____ 2:3, which is read as the _____ 'two to three'.

a. 130-30 fund
b. 100-year flood
c. Y-intercept
d. Ratio

25. In economics, _____ is inflation that is very high or 'out of control', a condition in which prices increase rapidly as a currency loses its value. Definitions used by the media vary from a cumulative inflation rate over three years approaching 100% to 'inflation exceeding 50% a month.' In informal usage the term is often applied to much lower rates. As a rule of thumb, normal inflation is reported per year, but _____ is often reported for much shorter intervals, often per month.

a. 100-year flood
b. 1921 recession
c. 130-30 fund
d. Hyperinflation

26. _____ is exchange of capital, goods, and services across international borders or territories. In most countries, it represents a significant share of gross domestic product (GDP.) While _____ has been present throughout much of history, its economic, social, and political importance has been on the rise in recent centuries.

a. International trade
b. Intra-industry trade
c. Import license
d. Incoterms

27. In economic models, the _____ time frame assumes no fixed factors of production. Firms can enter or leave the marketplace, and the cost (and availability) of land, labor, raw materials, and capital goods can be assumed to vary. In contrast, in the short-run time frame, certain factors are assumed to be fixed, because there is not sufficient time for them to change.
   a. Long-run
   b. Short-run
   c. Product Pipeline
   d. Diseconomies of scale

28. _____ and Keynesian Theory) is a macroeconomic theory based on the ideas of 20th-century British economist John Maynard Keynes. _____ argues that private sector decisions sometimes lead to inefficient macroeconomic outcomes and therefore advocates active policy responses by the public sector, including monetary policy actions by the central bank and fiscal policy actions by the government to stabilize output over the business cycle.

The theories forming the basis of _____ were first presented in The General Theory of Employment, Interest and Money, published in 1936.

   a. Rational choice theory
   b. Recession
   c. Gross domestic product
   d. Keynesian economics

29. In economics and finance, _____ is the change in total cost that arises when the quantity produced changes by one unit. It is the cost of producing one more unit of a good. Mathematically, the _____ function is expressed as the first derivative of the total cost (TC) function with respect to quantity (Q.)
   a. Quality costs
   b. Marginal cost
   c. Fixed costs
   d. Cost allocation

30. _____ is one of the four Ps of the marketing mix. The other three aspects are product, promotion, and place. It is also a key variable in microeconomic price allocation theory.
   a. Big ticket item
   b. Nonlinear pricing
   c. Two-part tariff
   d. Pricing

31. The _____ consists of a number of economic theories which describe the nature of the firm, company including its existence, its behaviour, and its relationship with the market.

In simplified terms, the _____ aims to answer these questions:

1. Existence - why do firms emerge, why are not all transactions in the economy mediated over the market?
2. Boundaries - why the boundary between firms and the market is located exactly there? Which transactions are performed internally and which are negotiated on the market?
3. Organization - why are firms structured in such specific way? What is the interplay of formal and informal relationships?

Despite looking simple, these questions are not answered by the established economic theory, which usually views firms as given, and treats them as black boxes without any internal structure.

Chapter 23. Perfect Competition

The First World War period saw a change of emphasis in economic theory away from industry-level analysis which mainly included analysing markets to analysis at the level of the firm, as it became increasingly clear that perfect competition was no longer an adequate model of how firms behaved. Economic theory till then had focussed on trying to understand markets alone and there had been little study on understanding why firms or organisations exist.

- a. Neo-Ricardian school
- c. Theory of the firm
- b. Technology gap
- d. Marginal revenue product

32. In economics, a _____ exists when the production or use of goods and services by the market is not efficient. That is, there exists another outcome where all involved can be made better off. _____s can be viewed as scenarios where individuals' pursuit of pure self-interest leads to results that are not efficient - that can be improved upon from the societal point-of-view.
- a. Consumer theory
- c. New Keynesian economics
- b. Perfect competition
- d. Market failure

Chapter 24. Monopoly

1. In economics, a _____ exists when a specific individual or enterprise has sufficient control over a particular product or service to determine significantly the terms on which other individuals shall have access to it. Monopolies are thus characterized by a lack of economic competition for the good or service that they provide and a lack of viable substitute goods. The verb 'monopolize' refers to the process by which a firm gains persistently greater market share than what is expected under perfect competition.
    a. Monopoly
    c. 100-year flood
    b. 1921 recession
    d. 130-30 fund

2. _____ in economics and business is the result of an exchange and from that trade we assign a numerical monetary value to a good, service or asset. If Alice trades Bob 4 apples for an orange, the _____ of an orange is 4 apples. Inversely, the _____ of an apple is 1/4 oranges.
    a. Price ceiling
    c. Price dispersion
    b. Lerner Index
    d. Price

3. In economics and especially in the theory of competition, _____ are obstacles in the path of a firm that make it difficult to enter a given market.

    _____ are the source of a firm's pricing power - the ability of a firm to raise prices without losing all its customers.

    The term refers to hindrances that an individual may face while trying to gain entrance into a profession or trade.

    a. Barriers to entry
    c. Predatory pricing
    b. Net Book Agreement
    d. Group boycott

4. _____ is a fee paid on borrowed assets. It is the price paid for the use of borrowed money , or, money earned by deposited funds . Assets that are sometimes lent with _____ include money, shares, consumer goods through hire purchase, major assets such as aircraft, and even entire factories in finance lease arrangements.
    a. Interest
    c. Insolvency
    b. Internal debt
    d. Asset protection

5. The Organization of the Petroleum Exporting Countries is a cartel of twelve countries made up of Algeria, Angola, Ecuador, Iran, Iraq, Kuwait, Libya, Nigeria, Qatar, Saudi Arabia, the United Arab Emirates, and Venezuela. The cartel has maintained its headquarters in Vienna since 1965, and hosts regular meetings among the oil ministers of its Member Countries. Indonesia withdrew its membership in _____ in 2008 after it became a net importer of oil, but stated it would likely return if it became a net exporter in the world.
    a. ACEA agreement
    c. ACCRA Cost of Living Index
    b. OPEC
    d. AD-IA Model

6. _____s is the social science that studies the production, distribution, and consumption of goods and services. The term _____s comes from the Ancient Greek οá¼°κονομῖα from οá¼¶κος (oikos, 'house') + vἴŒμος (nomos, 'custom' or 'law'), hence 'rules of the house(hold)'. Current _____ models developed out of the broader field of political economy in the late 19th century, owing to a desire to use an empirical approach more akin to the physical sciences.
    a. Opportunity cost
    c. Energy economics
    b. Economic
    d. Inflation

Chapter 24. Monopoly

7. _____ is the increase in the amount of the goods and services produced by an economy over time. It is conventionally measured as the percent rate of increase in real gross domestic product, or real GDP. Growth is usually calculated in real terms, i.e. inflation-adjusted terms, in order to net out the effect of inflation on the price of the goods and services produced.
   a. AD-IA Model
   b. ACCRA Cost of Living Index
   c. ACEA agreement
   d. Economic growth

8. _____, in microeconomics, are the cost advantages that a business obtains due to expansion. They are factors that cause a producere;s average cost per unit to fall as scale is increased. _____ is a long run concept and refers to reductions in unit cost as the size of a facility, or scale, increases.
   a. Isoquant
   b. Underinvestment employment relationship
   c. Economies of scale
   d. Economic production quantity

9. In economics, a _____ occurs when, due to the economies of scale of a particular industry, the maximum efficiency of production and distribution is realized through a single supplier.

Natural monopolies arise where the largest supplier in an industry, often the first supplier in a market, has an overwhelming cost advantage over other actual or potential competitors. This tends to be the case in industries where capital costs predominate, creating economies of scale which are large in relation to the size of the market, and hence high barriers to entry; examples include water services and electricity.

   a. Privatizing profits and socializing losses
   b. Government monopoly
   c. Government failure
   d. Natural monopoly

10. In economics, a _____ is a graph of the costs of production as a function of total quantity produced. In a free market economy, productively efficient firms use these curves to find the optimal point of production, where they make the most profits. There are a few different types of _____s, each relevant to a different area of economics.
    a. Cost curve
    b. Demand curve
    c. Lorenz curve
    d. Phillips curve

11. In economics, a _____ 'purchase') is a market form in which only one buyer faces many sellers. It is an example of imperfect competition, similar to a monopoly, in which only one seller faces many buyers. As the only purchaser of a good or service, the 'monopsonist' may dictate terms to its suppliers in the same manner that a monopolist controls the market for its buyers.
    a. 130-30 fund
    b. 100-year flood
    c. Monopsony
    d. 1921 recession

12. A _____ is a counterfeit agreement among industries. It is an informal organization of producers that agree to coordinate prices and production. _____s usually occur in an oligopolistic industry, where there is a small number of sellers and usually involve homogeneous products.
    a. 100-year flood
    b. Shill
    c. Shanzhai
    d. Cartel

13. _____ are legal property rights over creations of the mind, both artistic and commercial, and the corresponding fields of law. Under _____ law, owners are granted certain exclusive rights to a variety of intangible assets, such as musical, literary, and artistic works; ideas, discoveries and inventions; and words, phrases, symbols, and designs. Common types of _____ include copyrights, trademarks, patents, industrial design rights and trade secrets.

- a. Intellectual property
- b. Independent contractor
- c. Expedited Funds Availability Act
- d. Ease of Doing Business Index

14. A _____ is a set of exclusive rights granted by a state to an inventor or his assignee for a limited period of time in exchange for a disclosure of an invention.

The procedure for granting _____s, the requirements placed on the _____ee and the extent of the exclusive rights vary widely between countries according to national laws and international agreements. Typically, however, a _____ application must include one or more claims defining the invention which must be new, inventive, and useful or industrially applicable.

- a. Celler-Kefauver Act
- b. Judgment summons
- c. Generalized System of Preferences
- d. Patent

15. A _____ is a duty imposed on goods when they are moved across a political boundary. They are usually associated with protectionism, the economic policy of restraining trade between nations. For political reasons, _____s are usually imposed on imported goods, although they may also be imposed on exported goods.

- a. 100-year flood
- b. 1921 recession
- c. 130-30 fund
- d. Tariff

16. Competition law, known in the United States as _____ law, has three main elements:

- prohibiting agreements or practices that restrict free trading and competition between business entities. This includes in particular the repression of cartels.
- banning abusive behaviour by a firm dominating a market, or anti-competitive practices that tend to lead to such a dominant position. Practices controlled in this way may include predatory pricing, tying, price gouging, refusal to deal, and many others.
- supervising the mergers and acquisitions of large corporations, including some joint ventures. Transactions that are considered to threaten the competitive process can be prohibited altogether, or approved subject to 'remedies' such as an obligation to divest part of the merged business or to offer licences or access to facilities to enable other businesses to continue competing.

The substance and practice of competition law varies from jurisdiction to jurisdiction. Protecting the interests of consumers (consumer welfare) and ensuring that entrepreneurs have an opportunity to compete in the market economy are often treated as important objectives. Competition law is closely connected with law on deregulation of access to markets, state aids and subsidies, the privatisation of state owned assets and the establishment of independent sector regulators. In recent decades, competition law has been viewed as a way to provide better public services.

- a. Anti-Inflation Act
- b. Intellectual property law
- c. United Kingdom competition law
- d. Antitrust

Chapter 24. Monopoly

17. _____ is the removal or simplification of government rules and regulations that constrain the operation of market forces. _____ does not mean elimination of laws against fraud, but eliminating or reducing government control of how business is done, thereby moving toward a more free market.

The stated rationale for '_____' is often that fewer and simpler regulations will lead to a raised level of competitiveness, therefore higher productivity, more efficiency and lower prices overall.

    a. Lucas-Islands model   b. Monetary policy reaction function
    c. SIMIC   d. Deregulation

18. _____ is exchange of capital, goods, and services across international borders or territories. In most countries, it represents a significant share of gross domestic product (GDP.) While _____ has been present throughout much of history , its economic, social, and political importance has been on the rise in recent centuries.
    a. Incoterms   b. Intra-industry trade
    c. Import license   d. International trade

19. A _____, reserve bank, or monetary authority is the entity responsible for the monetary policy of a country or of a group of member states. It is a bank that can lend money to other banks in times of need. Its primary responsibility is to maintain the stability of the national currency and money supply, but more active duties include controlling subsidized-loan interest rates, and acting as a lender of last resort to the banking sector during times of financial crisis (private banks often being integral to the national financial system.)
    a. Central Bank   b. 1921 recession
    c. 130-30 fund   d. 100-year flood

20. Economics:

- _____,the desire to own something and the ability to pay for it
- _____ curve,a graphic representation of a _____ schedule
- _____ deposit, the money in checking accounts
- _____ pull theory,the theory that inflation occurs when _____ for goods and services exceeds existing supplies
- _____ schedule,a table that lists the quantity of a good a person will buy it each different price
- _____ side economics,the school of economics at believes government spending and tax cuts open economy by raising _____

    a. Procter ' Gamble   b. Bon
    c. G20   d. Demand

21. In economics, the _____ can be defined as the graph depicting the relationship between the price of a certain commodity, and the amount of it that consumers are willing and able to purchase at that given price. It is a graphic representation of a demand schedule. The _____ for all consumers together follows from the _____ of every individual consumer: the individual demands at each price are added together.
    a. Demand curve   b. Wage ourvc
    c. Kuznets curve   d. Lorenz curve

22. In microeconomics, _____ is quite simply the conversion of inputs into outputs. It is an economic process that uses resources to create a good or service that is suitable for exchange. This can include manufacturing, storing, shipping, and packaging.
    a. Bucket shop
    b. Characteristic
    c. Variability
    d. Production

23. In Marxian economics, _____ originally referred to the means of production. Individuals, organizations and governments use _____ in the production of other goods or commodities. _____ include factories, machinery, tools, equipment, and various buildings which are used to produce other products for consumption.
    a. Cost of capital
    b. Modigliani-Miller theorem
    c. Capital formation
    d. Capital goods

24. A _____ is an object whose consumption increases the utility of the consumer, for which the quantity demanded exceeds the quantity supplied at zero price. _____s are usually modeled as having diminishing marginal utility. The first individual purchase has high utility; the second has less.
    a. Luxury good
    b. Search good
    c. Positional goods
    d. Good

25. In calculus, a function f defined on a subset of the real numbers with real values is called _____, if for all x and y such that $x \geq y$ one has $f(x) \geq f(y)$, so f preserves the order. In layman's terms, the sign of the slope is always positive (the curve tending upwards) or zero (i.e., non-decreasing, or asymptotic, or depicted as a horizontal, flat line) Likewise, a function is called monotonically decreasing (non-increasing) if, whenever $x \geq y$, then $f(x) \geq f(y)$, so it reverses the order.
    a. 100-year flood
    b. 1921 recession
    c. 130-30 fund
    d. Monotonic

26. In economics, _____ describes the state of a market with respect to competition.

- Perfect competition, in which the market consists of a very large number of firms producing a homogeneous product.
- Monopolistic competition where there are a large number of independent firms which have a very small proportion of the market share.
- Oligopoly, in which a market is dominated by a small number of firms which own more than 40% of the market share.
- Oligopsony, a market dominated by many sellers and a few buyers.
- Monopoly, where there is only one provider of a product or service.
- Natural monopoly, a monopoly in which economies of scale cause efficiency to increase continuously with the size of the firm. A firm is a natural monopoly if it is able to serve the entire market demand at a lower cost than any combination of two or more smaller, more specialized firms.
- Monopsony, when there is only one buyer in a market.

The imperfectly competitive structure is quite identical to the realistic market conditions where some monopolistic competitors, monopolists, oligopolists, and duopolists exist and dominate the market conditions. The elements of _____ include the number and size distribution of firms, entry conditions, and the extent of differentiation.

These somewhat abstract concerns tend to determine some but not all details of a specific concrete market system where buyers and sellers actually meet and commit to trade.

Chapter 24. Monopoly

a. Monetary economics
b. Mainstream economics
c. Market structure
d. Law of demand

27. Monopoly power is an example of market failure which occurs when one or more of the participants has the ability to influence the price or other outcomes in some general or specialized market. The most commonly discussed form of market power is that of a monopoly, but other forms such as monopsony, and more moderate versions of these two extremes, exist. Market participants that have market power are sometimes referred to as 'price makers', while those without are sometimes called '_____'.

a. Market concentration
b. De facto monopoly
c. Price takers
d. Quasi-rent

28. In microeconomics, _____ is the extra revenue that an additional unit of product will bring. It is the additional income from selling one more unit of a good; sometimes equal to price. It can also be described as the change in total revenue/change in number of units sold.

a. Mohring effect
b. Social surplus
c. Marginal revenue
d. Product proliferation

29. _____ is a common market structure where many competing producers sell products that are differentiated from one another (ie. the products are substitutes, but are not exactly alike.) Many markets are monopolistically competitive, common examples include the markets for restaurants, cereal, clothing, shoes and service industries in large cities.

a. Co-operative economics
b. Perfect competition
c. Deflation
d. Monopolistic Competition

30. In economics, _____ is the ratio of the percent change in one variable to the percent change in another variable. It is a tool for measuring the responsiveness of a function to changes in parameters in a relative way. Commonly analyzed are _____ of substitution, price and wealth.

a. ACCRA Cost of Living Index
b. ACEA agreement
c. Elasticity of demand
d. Elasticity

31. In economics and finance, _____ is the change in total cost that arises when the quantity produced changes by one unit. It is the cost of producing one more unit of a good. Mathematically, the _____ function is expressed as the first derivative of the total cost (TC) function with respect to quantity (Q.)

a. Quality costs
b. Fixed costs
c. Cost allocation
d. Marginal cost

32. In economics, _____ is the process by which a firm determines the price and output level that returns the greatest profit. There are several approaches to this problem. The total revenue--total cost method relies on the fact that profit equals revenue minus cost, and the marginal revenue--marginal cost method is based on the fact that total profit in a perfectly competitive market reaches its maximum point where marginal revenue equals marginal cost.

a. 100-year flood
b. Profit margin
c. Profit maximization
d. Normal profit

33. In economics, and cost accounting, _____ describes the total economic cost of production and is made up of variable costs, which vary according to the quantity of a good produced and include inputs such as labor and raw materials, plus fixed costs, which are independent of the quantity of a good produced and include inputs (capital) that cannot be varied in the short term, such as buildings and machinery. _____ in economics includes the total opportunity cost of each factor of production in addition to fixed and variable costs.

The rate at which _____ changes as the amount produced changes is called marginal cost.

- a. 130-30 fund
- b. 100-year flood
- c. 1921 recession
- d. Total cost

34. _____ is the total money received from the sale of any given quantity of output.

The _____ is calculated by taking the price of the sale times the quantity sold, i.e.

_____ = price X quantity.

- a. Defined benefit pension plan
- b. Total revenue
- c. Blanket order
- d. Ceteris paribus

35. In economics, _____ are the resources employed to produce goods and services. They facilitate production but do not become part of the product (as with raw materials) or significantly transformed by the production process (as with fuel used to power machinery.) To 19th century economists, the _____ were land (natural resources, gifts from nature), labor (the ability to work), and capital goods (human-made tools and equipment.)

- a. Production function
- b. Long-run
- c. Productive capacity
- d. Factors of production

36. In economics, a firm is said to reap _____s when a lack of viable market competition allows it to set its prices above the equilibrium price for a good or service without losing profits to competitors. _____ is a type of economic profit, that is, it is a profit greater than the normal profit that is typical in a perfectly competitive industry. The resulting price is known as the monopoly price.

- a. January effect
- b. Legal monopoly
- c. Correlation trading
- d. Monopoly profit

37. In international commerce and politics, an _____ is the prohibition of commerce (division of trade) and trade with a certain country, in order to isolate it and to put its government into a difficult internal situation, given that the effects of the _____ are often able to make its economy suffer from the initiative.

The _____ is usually used as a political punishment for some previous disagreed policies or acts, but its economic nature frequently raises doubts about the real interests that the prohibition serves.

One of the most comprehensive attempts at an _____ happened during the Napoleonic Wars.

Chapter 24. Monopoly

a. International finance
c. Optimum currency area
b. Overshooting model
d. Embargo

38. _____ exists when sales of identical goods or services are transacted at different prices from the same provider. In a theoretical market with perfect information, no transaction costs or prohibition on secondary exchange (or re-selling) to prevent arbitrage, _____ can only be a feature of monopoly and oligopoly markets, where market power can be exercised. Otherwise, the moment the seller tries to sell the same good at different prices, the buyer at the lower price can arbitrage by selling to the consumer buying at the higher price but with a tiny discount.
   a. Competitor indexing
   c. Price discrimination
   b. Price points
   d. Break even analysis

39. In neoclassical economics and microeconomics, _____ describes the perfect being a market in which there are many small firms, all producing homogeneous goods. In the short term, such markets are productively inefficient as output will not occur where mc is equal to ac, but allocatively efficient, as output under _____ will always occur where mc is equal to mr, and therefore where mc equals ar. However, in the long term, such markets are both allocatively and productively efficient.
   a. Perfect competition
   c. Nominal value
   b. Law and economics
   d. Co-operative economics

40. In economics _____ is defined as the sum of private and external costs. Economic theorists ascribe individual decision-making to a calculation costs and benefits. Rational choice theory assumes that individuals only consider their own private costs when making decisions, not the costs that may be borne by others.
   a. Transaction cost
   c. Social cost
   b. Total absorption costing
   d. Variable cost

41. In economics, the _____ of an industry is used as an indicator of the relative size of firms in relation to the industry as a whole. It is calculated as the sum of the percent market share of the top n industries. This may also assist in determining the market structure of the industry.
   a. Rate-of-return regulation
   c. Price takers
   b. Concentration ratio
   d. De facto monopoly

42. A _____ is an expression that compares quantities relative to each other. The most common examples involve two quantities, but any number of quantities can be compared. _____s are represented mathematically by separating each quantity with a colon, for example the _____ 2:3, which is read as the _____ 'two to three'.
   a. Y-intercept
   c. 130-30 fund
   b. Ratio
   d. 100-year flood

Chapter 25. Monopolistic Competition

1. _____ is a common market structure where many competing producers sell products that are differentiated from one another (ie. the products are substitutes, but are not exactly alike.) Many markets are monopolistically competitive, common examples include the markets for restaurants, cereal, clothing, shoes and service industries in large cities.

   a. Deflation
   b. Perfect competition
   c. Co-operative economics
   d. Monopolistic competition

2. _____s is the social science that studies the production, distribution, and consumption of goods and services. The term _____s comes from the Ancient Greek oá¼°κονομῖα from oá¼¶κος (oikos, 'house') + vÏŒμος (nomos, 'custom' or 'law'), hence 'rules of the house(hold)'. Current _____ models developed out of the broader field of political economy in the late 19th century, owing to a desire to use an empirical approach more akin to the physical sciences.

   a. Opportunity cost
   b. Energy economics
   c. Inflation
   d. Economic

3. In economic theory, _____ is the competitive situation in any market where the conditions necessary for perfect competition are not satisfied. It is a market structure that does not meet the conditions of perfect competition.

   Forms of _____ include:

   - Monopoly, in which there is only one seller of a good.
   - Oligopoly, in which there is a small number of sellers.
   - Monopolistic competition, in which there are many sellers producing highly differentiated goods.
   - Monopsony, in which there is only one buyer of a good.
   - Oligopsony, in which there is a small number of buyers.

   There may also be _____ in markets due to buyers or sellers lacking information about prices and the goods being traded.

   There may also be _____ due to a time lag in a market.

   a. ACCRA Cost of Living Index
   b. Imperfect Competition
   c. AD-IA Model
   d. ACEA agreement

4. _____ is a specific term used in companies' financial reporting from the company-whole point of view. Because that use excludes the effects of changing ownership interest, an economic measure of _____ is necessary for financial analysis from the shareholders' point of view

   _____ is defined by the Financial Accounting Standards Board, or FASB, as e;the change in equity [net assets] of a business enterprise during a period from transactions and other events and circumstances from nonowner sources. It includes all changes in equity during a period except those resulting from investments by owners and distributions to owners.e;

   _____ is the sum of net income and other items that must bypass the income statement because they have not been realized, including items like an unrealized holding gain or loss from available for sale securities and foreign currency translation gains or losses.

Chapter 25. Monopolistic Competition

a. Windfall gain
c. Real income

b. Per capita income
d. Comprehensive income

5. In economics, the term _____ of income or _____ refers to a simple economic model which describes the reciprocal circulation of income between producers and consumers. In the _____ model, the inter-dependent entities of producer and consumer are referred to as 'firms' and 'households' respectively and provide each other with factors in order to facilitate the flow of income. Firms provide consumers with goods and services in exchange for consumer expenditure and 'factors of production' from households.

a. 100-year flood
c. 1921 recession

b. 130-30 fund
d. Circular flow

6. In marketing, _____ is the process of distinguishing the differences of a product or offering from others, to make it more attractive to a particular target market. This involves differentiating it from competitors' products as well as one's own product offerings.

Differentiation is a source of competitive advantage.

a. Market sector
c. Market segment

b. Customer relationship management
d. Product differentiation

7. In economics, a _____ is a graph of the costs of production as a function of total quantity produced. In a free market economy, productively efficient firms use these curves to find the optimal point of production, where they make the most profits. There are a few different types of _____s, each relevant to a different area of economics.

a. Phillips curve
c. Lorenz curve

b. Cost curve
d. Demand curve

8. Economics:

- _____,the desire to own something and the ability to pay for it
- _____ curve,a graphic representation of a _____ schedule
- _____ deposit, the money in checking accounts
- _____ pull theory,the theory that inflation occurs when _____ for goods and services exceeds existing supplies
- _____ schedule,a table that lists the quantity of a good a person will buy it each different price
- _____ side economics,the school of economics at believes government spending and tax cuts open economy by raising _____

a. G20
c. Bon

b. Procter ' Gamble
d. Demand

9. In economics, the _____ can be defined as the graph depicting the relationship between the price of a certain commodity, and the amount of it that consumers are willing and able to purchase at that given price. It is a graphic representation of a demand schedule. The _____ for all consumers together followo from the _____ of every individual consumer: the individual demands at each price are added together.

a. Wage curve
b. Demand curve
c. Lorenz curve
d. Kuznets curve

10. _____ is a fee paid on borrowed assets. It is the price paid for the use of borrowed money, or, money earned by deposited funds. Assets that are sometimes lent with _____ include money, shares, consumer goods through hire purchase, major assets such as aircraft, and even entire factories in finance lease arrangements.
   a. Insolvency
   b. Internal debt
   c. Asset protection
   d. Interest

11. _____ and Keynesian Theory) is a macroeconomic theory based on the ideas of 20th-century British economist John Maynard Keynes. _____ argues that private sector decisions sometimes lead to inefficient macroeconomic outcomes and therefore advocates active policy responses by the public sector, including monetary policy actions by the central bank and fiscal policy actions by the government to stabilize output over the business cycle.

The theories forming the basis of _____ were first presented in The General Theory of Employment, Interest and Money, published in 1936.

   a. Rational choice theory
   b. Recession
   c. Gross domestic product
   d. Keynesian economics

12. In economic models, the _____ time frame assumes no fixed factors of production. Firms can enter or leave the marketplace, and the cost (and availability) of land, labor, raw materials, and capital goods can be assumed to vary. In contrast, in the short-run time frame, certain factors are assumed to be fixed, because there is not sufficient time for them to change.
   a. Diseconomies of scale
   b. Short-run
   c. Long-run
   d. Product Pipeline

13. In economics, the concept of the _____ refers to the decision-making time frame of a firm in which at least one factor of production is fixed. Costs which are fixed in the _____ have no impact on a firms decisions. For example a firm can raise output by increasing the amount of labour through overtime.
   a. Short-run
   b. Marginal product
   c. Productivity world
   d. Hicks-neutral technical change

14. _____ in economics and business is the result of an exchange and from that trade we assign a numerical monetary value to a good, service or asset. If Alice trades Bob 4 apples for an orange, the _____ of an orange is 4 apples. Inversely, the _____ of an apple is 1/4 oranges.
   a. Lerner Index
   b. Price ceiling
   c. Price
   d. Price dispersion

15. _____ is the increase in the amount of the goods and services produced by an economy over time. It is conventionally measured as the percent rate of increase in real gross domestic product, or real GDP. Growth is usually calculated in real terms, i.e. inflation-adjusted terms, in order to net out the effect of inflation on the price of the goods and services produced.
   a. ACCRA Cost of Living Index
   b. Economic growth
   c. AD-IA Model
   d. ACEA agreement

Chapter 25. Monopolistic Competition

16. In Marxian economics, _____ originally referred to the means of production. Individuals, organizations and governments use _____ in the production of other goods or commodities. _____ include factories, machinery, tools, equipment, and various buildings which are used to produce other products for consumption.
    a. Capital formation
    b. Modigliani-Miller theorem
    c. Cost of capital
    d. Capital goods

17. In economics, _____ is the difference between a company's total revenue and its opportunity costs. It is the increase in wealth that an investor has from making an investment, taking into consideration all costs associated with that investment including the opportunity cost of capital.

    Profit is the factor income of the entrepreneur.

    a. Accounting profit
    b. Operating profit
    c. ACCRA Cost of Living Index
    d. Economic profit

18. A _____ is an object whose consumption increases the utility of the consumer, for which the quantity demanded exceeds the quantity supplied at zero price. _____s are usually modeled as having diminishing marginal utility. The first individual purchase has high utility; the second has less.
    a. Luxury good
    b. Search good
    c. Positional goods
    d. Good

19. _____ is a type of private equity investment, most often a minority investment, in relatively mature companies that are looking for capital to expand or restructure operations, enter new markets or finance a significant acquisition without a change of control of the business.

    Companies that seek _____, will often do so in order to finance a transformational event in their lifecycle. These companies are likely to be more mature than venture capital funded companies, able to generate revenue and operating profits but unable to generate sufficient cash to fund major expansions, acquisitions or other investments.

    a. Venture capital fund
    b. Seed money
    c. Mezzanine capital
    d. Growth capital

20. In neoclassical economics and microeconomics, _____ describes the perfect being a market in which there are many small firms, all producing homogeneous goods. In the short term, such markets are productively inefficient as output will not occur where mc is equal to ac, but allocatively efficient, as output under _____ will always occur where mc is equal to mr, and therefore where mc equals ar. However, in the long term, such markets are both allocatively and productively efficient.
    a. Perfect competition
    b. Nominal value
    c. Co-operative economics
    d. Law and economics

21. _____ are legal property rights over creations of the mind, both artistic and commercial, and the corresponding fields of law. Under _____ law, owners are granted certain exclusive rights to a variety of intangible assets, such as musical, literary, and artistic works; ideas, discoveries and inventions; and words, phrases, symbols, and designs. Common types of _____ include copyrights, trademarks, patents, industrial design rights and trade secrets.

a. Intellectual property
b. Expedited Funds Availability Act
c. Independent contractor
d. Ease of Doing Business Index

22. The _____ is the central United States governmental body, established by the United States Constitution. The federal government has three branches: the legislative, executive, and judicial. Through a system of separation of powers and the system of 'checks and balances,' each of these branches has some authority to act on its own, some authority to regulate the other two branches, and has some of its own authority, in turn, regulated by the other branches.

a. 130-30 fund
b. 1921 recession
c. 100-year flood
d. Federal government of the United States

23. _____ is exchange of capital, goods, and services across international borders or territories. In most countries, it represents a significant share of gross domestic product (GDP.) While _____ has been present throughout much of history, its economic, social, and political importance has been on the rise in recent centuries.

a. Intra-industry trade
b. Import license
c. Incoterms
d. International trade

24. _____ is the a method of technical and economic research of the systems for purpose to optimize a parity between system's consumer functions or properties and expenses to achieve those functions or properties.

This methodology for continuous perfection of production, industrial technologies, organizational structures was developed by Juryj Sobolev in 1948 at the 'Perm telephone factory'

- 1948 Juryj Sobolev - the first success in application of a method analysis at the 'Perm telephone factory' .
- 1949 - the first application for the invention as result of use of the new method.

Today in economically developed countries practically each enterprise or the company use methodology of the kind of functional-cost analysis as a practice of the quality management, most full satisfying to principles of standards of series ISO 9000.

- Interest of consumer not in products itself, but the advantage which it will receive from its usage.
- The consumer aspires to reduce his expenses
- Functions needed by consumer can be executed in the various ways, and, hence, with various efficiency and expenses. Among possible alternatives of realization of functions exist such in which the parity of quality and the price is the optimal for the consumer.

The goal of _____ is achievement of the highest consumer satisfaction of production at simultaneous decrease in all kinds of industrial expenses Classical _____ has three English synonyms - Value Engineering, Value Management, Value Analysis.

a. Function cost analysis
b. Monopoly wage
c. Residual value
d. Real net output ratio

25. In economics, an _____ is a product or service where product characteristics such as quality or price are difficult to observe in advance, but these characteristics can be ascertained upon consumption. The concept is originally due to Philip Nelson, who contrasted an _____ with a search good.

Chapter 25. Monopolistic Competition

_____s pose difficulties for consumers in accurately making consumption choices.

a. Experience good
b. Export-oriented
c. Independent goods
d. Information good

26. In economics, a _____ is a product or service with features and characteristics easily evaluated before purchase. In a distinction originally due to Philip Nelson, a _____ is contrasted with an experience good.

_____s are more subject to substitution and price competition, as consumers can easily verify the price of the product and alternatives at other outlets and make sure that the products are comparable.

a. Merit good
b. Composite good
c. Superior goods
d. Search good

27. The _____ consists of a number of economic theories which describe the nature of the firm, company including its existence, its behaviour, and its relationship with the market.

In simplified terms, the _____ aims to answer these questions:

1. Existence - why do firms emerge, why are not all transactions in the economy mediated over the market?
2. Boundaries - why the boundary between firms and the market is located exactly there? Which transactions are performed internally and which are negotiated on the market?
3. Organization - why are firms structured in such specific way? What is the interplay of formal and informal relationships?

Despite looking simple, these questions are not answered by the established economic theory, which usually views firms as given, and treats them as black boxes without any internal structure.

The First World War period saw a change of emphasis in economic theory away from industry-level analysis which mainly included analysing markets to analysis at the level of the firm, as it became increasingly clear that perfect competition was no longer an adequate model of how firms behaved. Economic theory till then had focussed on trying to understand markets alone and there had been little study on understanding why firms or organisations exist.

a. Marginal revenue product
b. Neo-Ricardian school
c. Technology gap
d. Theory of the firm

28. _____, in microeconomics, are the cost advantages that a business obtains due to expansion. They are factors that cause a producere;s average cost per unit to fall as scale is increased. _____ is a long run concept and refers to reductions in unit cost as the size of a facility, or scale, increases.

a. Underinvestment employment relationship
b. Economic production quantity
c. Isoquant
d. Economies of scale

29. In economics, _____ are business expenses that are not dependent on the activities of the business They tend to be time-related, such as salaries or rents being paid per month. This is in contrast to variable costs, which are volume-related (and are paid per quantity.)

In management accounting, _____ are defined as expenses that do not change in proportion to the activity of a business, within the relevant period or scale of production.

   a. Variable cost
   c. Marginal cost
   b. Cost allocation
   d. Fixed costs

30. In economics, _____ is the total supply of goods and services produced by a national economy during a specific time period. It is the total amount of goods and services in the economy available at all possible price levels.
   a. Aggregate demand
   c. Aggregation problem
   b. Aggregate expenditure
   d. Aggregate supply

31. In economics, _____ is equal to total cost divided by the number of goods produced (the output quantity, Q.) It is also equal to the sum of average variable costs (total variable costs divided by Q) plus average fixed costs (total fixed costs divided by Q.) _____s may be dependent on the time period considered (increasing production may be expensive or impossible in the short term, for example.)
   a. Average Cost
   c. Average fixed cost
   b. Explicit cost
   d. Average variable cost

32. In economics and especially in the theory of competition, _____ are obstacles in the path of a firm that make it difficult to enter a given market.

_____ are the source of a firm's pricing power - the ability of a firm to raise prices without losing all its customers.

The term refers to hindrances that an individual may face while trying to gain entrance into a profession or trade.

   a. Predatory pricing
   c. Group boycott
   b. Barriers to entry
   d. Net Book Agreement

Chapter 25. Monopolistic Competition

33. _____ has several particular meanings:

- in mathematics
  - _____ function
  - Euler _____
  - _____
  - _____ subgroup
  - method of _____ s (partial differential equations)
- in physics and engineering
  - any _____ curve that shows the relationship between certain input- and output parameters, e.g.
  - an I-V or current-voltage _____ is the current in a circuit as a function of the applied voltage
  - Receiver-Operator _____
- in fiction
  - in Dungeons ' Dragons, _____ is another name for ability score

a. Procter ' Gamble
c. Fiscal
b. Drawdown
d. Characteristic

34. An _____ is an economy in which people, including businesses, can trade in goods and services with other people and businesses in the international community at large. This contrasts with a closed economy in which international trade cannot take place.

The act of selling goods or services to a foreign country is called exporting.

a. Open Economy
c. Attention work
b. Indicative planning
d. Information economy

35. In economics and finance, _____ is the change in total cost that arises when the quantity produced changes by one unit. It is the cost of producing one more unit of a good. Mathematically, the _____ function is expressed as the first derivative of the total cost (TC) function with respect to quantity (Q.)

a. Marginal cost
c. Cost allocation
b. Fixed costs
d. Quality costs

36. _____ is one of the four Ps of the marketing mix. The other three aspects are product, promotion, and place. It is also a key variable in microeconomic price allocation theory.

a. Nonlinear pricing
c. Pricing
b. Big ticket item
d. Two-part tariff

37. In economics, and cost accounting, _____ describes the total economic cost of production and is made up of variable costs, which vary according to the quantity of a good produced and include inputs such as labor and raw materials, plus fixed costs, which are independent of the quantity of a good produced and include inputs (capital) that cannot be varied in the short term, such as buildings and machinery. _____ in economics includes the total opportunity cost of each factor of production in addition to fixed and variable costs.

The rate at which _____ changes as the amount produced changes is called marginal cost.

a. 100-year flood
c. 130-30 fund
b. 1921 recession
d. Total cost

Chapter 26. Oligopoly and Strategic Behavior

1. An _____ is a market form in which a market or industry is dominated by a small number of sellers (oligopolists.) Because there are few participants in this type of market, each oligopolist is aware of the actions of the others. The decisions of one firm influence, and are influenced by, the decisions of other firms.

    a. Oligopoly   b. Oligopsony

    c. ACEA agreement   d. ACCRA Cost of Living Index

2. The _____ consists of a number of economic theories which describe the nature of the firm, company including its existence, its behaviour, and its relationship with the market.

In simplified terms, the _____ aims to answer these questions:

1. Existence - why do firms emerge, why are not all transactions in the economy mediated over the market?
2. Boundaries - why the boundary between firms and the market is located exactly there? Which transactions are performed internally and which are negotiated on the market?
3. Organization - why are firms structured in such specific way? What is the interplay of formal and informal relationships?

Despite looking simple, these questions are not answered by the established economic theory, which usually views firms as given, and treats them as black boxes without any internal structure.

The First World War period saw a change of emphasis in economic theory away from industry-level analysis which mainly included analysing markets to analysis at the level of the firm, as it became increasingly clear that perfect competition was no longer an adequate model of how firms behaved. Economic theory till then had focussed on trying to understand markets alone and there had been little study on understanding why firms or organisations exist.

    a. Technology gap   b. Neo-Ricardian school

    c. Marginal revenue product   d. Theory of the firm

3. The _____ comprises government and commercial industry involved in research, development, production, and service of military equipment and facilities. It includes:

- Defense contractors: business organizations or individuals that provide products or services to a defense department of a government.
- The Arms industry, which produces guns, ammunition, missiles, military aircraft, and their associated consumables and systems.

It can also include:

- Private military contractors: private companies that provide logistics, manpower, and other expenditures for a military force.
- European defence procurement, which is more or less analogous to the U.S. 'military-industrial complex.'

a. 1921 recession
b. 130-30 fund
c. 100-year flood
d. Defense industry

4. _____ has several particular meanings:

- in mathematics
   - _____ function
   - Euler _____
   - _____
   - _____ subgroup
   - method of _____s (partial differential equations)
- in physics and engineering
   - any _____ curve that shows the relationship between certain input- and output parameters, e.g.
   - an I-V or current-voltage _____ is the current in a circuit as a function of the applied voltage
   - Receiver-Operator _____
- in fiction
   - in Dungeons ' Dragons, _____ is another name for ability score

a. Drawdown
b. Procter ' Gamble
c. Fiscal
d. Characteristic

5. In economics and especially in the theory of competition, _____ are obstacles in the path of a firm that make it difficult to enter a given market.

_____ are the source of a firm's pricing power - the ability of a firm to raise prices without losing all its customers.

The term refers to hindrances that an individual may face while trying to gain entrance into a profession or trade.

a. Barriers to entry
b. Net Book Agreement
c. Group boycott
d. Predatory pricing

6. _____, in microeconomics, are the cost advantages that a business obtains due to expansion. They are factors that cause a producere;s average cost per unit to fall as scale is increased. _____ is a long run concept and refers to reductions in unit cost as the size of a facility, or scale, increases.

a. Underinvestment employment relationship
b. Economic production quantity
c. Isoquant
d. Economies of scale

7. In economics, a _____ is the combination of two or more firms competing in the same market with the same good or service. See Horizontal integration.

a. Product market
b. Market dominance
c. Ramp up
d. Horizontal merger

Chapter 26. Oligopoly and Strategic Behavior

8. In economics, market concentration is a function of the number of firms and their respective shares of the total production (alternatively, total capacity or total reserves) in a market. Alternative terms are _____ and Seller concentration.

Market concentration is related to the concept of industrial concentration, which concerns the distribution of production within an industry, as opposed to a market.

    a. ACEA agreement
    b. AD-IA Model
    c. ACCRA Cost of Living Index
    d. Industry concentration

9. In economics, the _____ of an industry is used as an indicator of the relative size of firms in relation to the industry as a whole. It is calculated as the sum of the percent market share of the top n industries. This may also assist in determining the market structure of the industry.
    a. Rate-of-return regulation
    b. De facto monopoly
    c. Price takers
    d. Concentration ratio

10. A _____ is an expression that compares quantities relative to each other. The most common examples involve two quantities, but any number of quantities can be compared. _____s are represented mathematically by separating each quantity with a colon, for example the _____ 2:3, which is read as the _____ 'two to three'.
    a. 100-year flood
    b. Y-intercept
    c. 130-30 fund
    d. Ratio

11. In economics, _____ is a theory of utility under which the utility (roughly, satisfaction) gained from a particular good or service can be measured and that the magnitude of the measurement is meaningful. Under _____ theory, the util is a unit of measurement much like the metre or second. A util has a fixed size, making comparisons based on ratios of utils possible.
    a. 130-30 fund
    b. Generalized expected utility
    c. 100-year flood
    d. Cardinal utility

12. In economics, _____ is a measure of the relative satisfaction from consumption of various goods and services. Given this measure, one may speak meaningfully of increasing or decreasing _____, and thereby explain economic behavior in terms of attempts to increase one's _____. For illustrative purposes, changes in _____ are sometimes expressed in units called utils.
    a. Utility function
    b. Expected utility hypothesis
    c. Ordinal utility
    d. Utility

13. _____ is a branch of applied mathematics that is used in the social sciences (most notably economics), biology, engineering, political science, international relations, computer science, and philosophy. _____ attempts to mathematically capture behavior in strategic situations, in which an individual's success in making choices depends on the choices of others. While initially developed to analyze competitions in which one individual does better at another's expense (zero sum games), it has been expanded to treat a wide class of interactions, which are classified according to several criteria.
    a. Discriminatory price auction
    b. Dollar auction
    c. Pareto efficiency
    d. Game theory

14. In economics, _____ is the ability of a firm to alter the market price of a good or service. A firm with _____ can raise prices without losing all customers to competitors.

When a firm has _____ it faces a downward-sloping demand curve.

a. Rate-of-return regulation
b. Monopolization
c. Revenue-cap regulation
d. Market power

15. _____ is an economic concept with commonplace familiarity. It is the price that a good or service is offered at, or will fetch, in the marketplace. It is of interest mainly in the study of microeconomics.

a. Market anomaly
b. Paper trading
c. Market price
d. Noisy market hypothesis

16. _____ is used to assign the available resources in an economic way. It is part of resource management.

In strategic planning, is a plan for using available resources, for example human resources, especially in the near term, to achieve goals for the future.

a. 100-year flood
b. 130-30 fund
c. 1921 recession
d. Resource allocation

17. _____ s is the social science that studies the production, distribution, and consumption of goods and services. The term _____ s comes from the Ancient Greek οἰκονομία from οἶκος (oikos, 'house') + νόμος (nomos, 'custom' or 'law'), hence 'rules of the house(hold)'. Current _____ models developed out of the broader field of political economy in the late 19th century, owing to a desire to use an empirical approach more akin to the physical sciences.

a. Opportunity cost
b. Energy economics
c. Inflation
d. Economic

18. In economics supernormal profit _____ or pure profit or excess profits, is a profit exceeding the normal profit. Normal profit equals the opportunity cost of labour and capital, while supernormal profit is the amount exceeds the normal return from these input factors in production.

_____ is usually generated by an oligopoly or a monopoly; however, these firms often try to hide this from the market to reduce risk of competition or antitrust investigation.

a. Operating profit
b. Accounting profit
c. ACCRA Cost of Living Index
d. Abnormal profit

19. _____ in economics and business is the result of an exchange and from that trade we assign a numerical monetary value to a good, service or asset. If Alice trades Bob 4 apples for an orange, the _____ of an orange is 4 apples. Inversely, the _____ of an apple is 1/4 oranges.

a. Price ceiling
b. Lerner Index
c. Price dispersion
d. Price

Chapter 26. Oligopoly and Strategic Behavior

20. Economic _____ is defined as an excess distribution to any factor in a production process above that which is required to induce the factor into the process or any excess above that which is necessary to keep the factor in its current use..

Classical Factor _____ is primarily concerned with the fee paid for the use of fixed (e.g. natural) resources. The classical definition is expressed as any excess payment above that required to induce or provide for production.

a. Rent
c. 1921 recession

b. 100-year flood
d. 130-30 fund

21. _____ is a policy or ideology of violence intended to intimidate or cause terror for the purpose of 'exerting pressure on decision making by state bodies.' The term 'terror' is largely used to indicate clandestine, low-intensity violence that targets civilians and generates public fear. Thus 'terror' is distinct from asymmetric warfare, and violates the concept of a common law of war in which civilian life is regarded. The term '-ism' is used to indicate an ideology --typically one that claims its attacks are in the domain of a 'just war' concept, though most condemn such as crimes against humanity.

a. 100-year flood
c. 130-30 fund

b. 1921 recession
d. Terrorism

22. The concept was first developed in game theory and consequently zero-sum situations are often called _____s though this does not imply that the concept applies only to what are commonly referred to as games.

For 2-player finite _____s, the different game theoretic Solution concepts of Nash equilibrium, minimax, and maximin all give the same solution. In the solution, players play a mixed strategy.

a. Zero-sum game
c. Human Rights Act 1993

b. Black-Scholes
d. Digital credentials

23. _____, in law and economics, is a form of risk management primarily used to hedge against the risk of a contingent loss. _____ is defined as the equitable transfer of the risk of a loss, from one entity to another, in exchange for a premium, and can be thought of as a guaranteed small loss to prevent a large, possibly devastating loss. An insurer is a company selling the _____; an insured or policyholder is the person or entity buying the _____.

a. Insurance
c. AD-IA Model

b. ACCRA Cost of Living Index
d. ACEA agreement

24. _____ is the controlled distribution of resources and scarce goods or services. _____ controls the size of the ration, one's allotted portion of the resources being distributed on a particular day or at a particular time.

In economics, it is often common to use the word '_____' to refer to one of the roles that prices play in markets, while _____ is called 'non-price _____.' Using prices to ration means that those with the most money (or other assets) and who want a product the most are first to receive it.

a. 130-30 fund
c. 100-year flood

b. 1921 recession
d. Rationing

25. _____ is one of the four Ps of the marketing mix. The other three aspects are product, promotion, and place. It is also a key variable in microeconomic price allocation theory.
   a. Nonlinear pricing
   b. Big ticket item
   c. Two-part tariff
   d. Pricing

26. The _____ curve theory is an economic theory regarding oligopoly and monopolistic competition. When it was created, the idea fundamentally challenged classical economic tenets such as efficient markets and rapidly-changing prices, ideas that underly basic supply and demand models. _____ was an initial attempt to explain sticky prices.
   a. Marginal demand
   b. Hicksian demand function
   c. Kinked demand
   d. Marshallian demand function

27. The _____ theory is an economic theory regarding oligopoly and monopolistic competition. When it was created, the idea fundamentally challenged classical economic tenets such as efficient markets and rapidly-changing prices, ideas that underly basic supply and demand models. Kinked demand was an initial attempt to explain sticky prices.
   a. Marshallian demand function
   b. Kinked demand
   c. Marginal demand
   d. Kinked demand curve

28. Economics:

   - _____, the desire to own something and the ability to pay for it
   - _____ curve, a graphic representation of a _____ schedule
   - _____ deposit, the money in checking accounts
   - _____ pull theory, the theory that inflation occurs when _____ for goods and services exceeds existing supplies
   - _____ schedule, a table that lists the quantity of a good a person will buy it each different price
   - _____ side economics, the school of economics at believes government spending and tax cuts open economy by raising _____

   a. Bon
   b. G20
   c. Procter ' Gamble
   d. Demand

29. In economics, the _____ can be defined as the graph depicting the relationship between the price of a certain commodity, and the amount of it that consumers are willing and able to purchase at that given price. It is a graphic representation of a demand schedule. The _____ for all consumers together follows from the _____ of every individual consumer: the individual demands at each price are added together.
   a. Kuznets curve
   b. Lorenz curve
   c. Demand curve
   d. Wage curve

30. The Organization of the Petroleum Exporting Countries is a cartel of twelve countries made up of Algeria, Angola, Ecuador, Iran, Iraq, Kuwait, Libya, Nigeria, Qatar, Saudi Arabia, the United Arab Emirates, and Venezuela. The cartel has maintained its headquarters in Vienna since 1965, and hosts regular meetings among the oil ministers of its Member Countries. Indonesia withdrew its membership in _____ in 2008 after it became a net importer of oil, but stated it would likely return if it became a net exporter in the world.

a. OPEC
c. AD-IA Model
b. ACCRA Cost of Living Index
d. ACEA agreement

31. _____ is a term used in business to indicate a state of intense competitive rivalry accompanied by a multi-lateral series of price reduction. One competitor will lower its price, then others will lower their prices to match. If one of them reduces their price again, a new round of reductions starts.
   a. Best available rate
   c. Pecuniary externality
   b. Point of total assumption
   d. Price war

32. In international commerce and politics, an _____ is the prohibition of commerce (division of trade) and trade with a certain country, in order to isolate it and to put its government into a difficult internal situation, given that the effects of the _____ are often able to make its economy suffer from the initiative.

The _____ is usually used as a political punishment for some previous disagreed policies or acts, but its economic nature frequently raises doubts about the real interests that the prohibition serves.

One of the most comprehensive attempts at an _____ happened during the Napoleonic Wars.

   a. International finance
   c. Optimum currency area
   b. Overshooting model
   d. Embargo

33. In economics, _____ is the process by which a firm determines the price and output level that returns the greatest profit. There are several approaches to this problem. The total revenue--total cost method relies on the fact that profit equals revenue minus cost, and the marginal revenue--marginal cost method is based on the fact that total profit in a perfectly competitive market reaches its maximum point where marginal revenue equals marginal cost.
   a. Profit margin
   c. Normal profit
   b. Profit maximization
   d. 100-year flood

34. In economics, _____ are the resources employed to produce goods and services. They facilitate production but do not become part of the product (as with raw materials) or significantly transformed by the production process (as with fuel used to power machinery.) To 19th century economists, the _____ were land (natural resources, gifts from nature), labor (the ability to work), and capital goods (human-made tools and equipment.)
   a. Production function
   c. Productive capacity
   b. Long-run
   d. Factors of production

35. In microeconomics, _____ is quite simply the conversion of inputs into outputs. It is an economic process that uses resources to create a good or service that is suitable for exchange. This can include manufacturing, storing, shipping, and packaging.
   a. Production
   c. Bucket shop
   b. Characteristic
   d. Variability

36. _____ is the development of economic wealth of countries or regions for the well-being of their inhabitants. It is the process by which a nation improves the economic, political, and social well being of its people. From a policy perspective, _____ can be defined as efforts that seek to improve the economic well-being and quality of life for a community by creating and/or retaining jobs and supporting or growing incomes and the tax base.

a. Economic methodology
b. Economic development
c. Inflation
d. Experimental economics

37. _____ occurs when cartels are illegal or overt collusion is absent. Put another way, two firms agree to play a certain strategy without explicitly saying so. This is also known as price leadership, as firms may stay within the law but still tacitly collude by monitoring each other's prices and keeping them the same.
   a. Commodity broker
   b. Tacit collusion
   c. Staple port
   d. Personal offshoring

38. _____ is an agreement, usually secretive, which occurs between two or more persons to deceive, mislead or to obtain an objective forbidden by law typically involving fraud or gaining an unfair advantage. It is an agreement among firms to divide the market, set prices kickbacks, or misrepresenting the independence of the relationship between the colluding parties.' All acts effected by _____ are considered void.
   a. Collusion
   b. Group boycott
   c. Limit pricing
   d. Net Book Agreement

39. _____ is a fee paid on borrowed assets. It is the price paid for the use of borrowed money , or, money earned by deposited funds . Assets that are sometimes lent with _____ include money, shares, consumer goods through hire purchase, major assets such as aircraft, and even entire factories in finance lease arrangements.
   a. Insolvency
   b. Internal debt
   c. Asset protection
   d. Interest

40. In calculus, a function f defined on a subset of the real numbers with real values is called _____, if for all x and y such that x >≤ y one has f(x) >≤ f(y), so f preserves the order. In layman's terms, the sign of the slope is always positive (the curve tending upwards) or zero (i.e., non-decreasing, or asymptotic, or depicted as a horizontal, flat line) Likewise, a function is called monotonically decreasing (non-increasing) if, whenever x >≤ y, then f(x) >≥ f(y), so it reverses the order.
   a. Monotonic
   b. 1921 recession
   c. 100-year flood
   d. 130-30 fund

41. In economics and business, a _____ is the effect that one user of a good or service has on the value of that product to other people.

The classic example is the telephone. The more people own telephones, the more valuable the telephone is to each owner.

   a. Cluster effect
   b. Pigou effect
   c. Penn effect
   d. Network effect

42. In economics _____ is defined as the sum of private and external costs. Economic theorists ascribe individual decision-making to a calculation costs and benefits. Rational choice theory assumes that individuals only consider their own private costs when making decisions, not the costs that may be borne by others.
   a. Social Cost
   b. Transaction cost
   c. Variable cost
   d. Total absorption costing

43. _____ is a specific term used in companies' financial reporting from the company-whole point of view. Because that use excludes the effects of changing ownership interest, an economic measure of _____ is necessary for financial analysis from the shareholders' point of view

_____ is defined by the Financial Accounting Standards Board, or FASB, as e;the change in equity [net assets] of a business enterprise during a period from transactions and other events and circumstances from nonowner sources. It includes all changes in equity during a period except those resulting from investments by owners and distributions to owners.e;

_____ is the sum of net income and other items that must bypass the income statement because they have not been realized, including items like an unrealized holding gain or loss from available for sale securities and foreign currency translation gains or losses.

- a. Per capita income
- b. Windfall gain
- c. Real income
- d. Comprehensive income

44. _____ is a common market structure where many competing producers sell products that are differentiated from one another (ie. the products are substitutes, but are not exactly alike.) Many markets are monopolistically competitive, common examples include the markets for restaurants, cereal, clothing, shoes and service industries in large cities.
- a. Perfect competition
- b. Co-operative economics
- c. Deflation
- d. Monopolistic competition

45. In neoclassical economics and microeconomics, _____ describes the perfect being a market in which there are many small firms, all producing homogeneous goods. In the short term, such markets are productively inefficient as output will not occur where mc is equal to ac, but allocatively efficient, as output under _____ will always occur where mc is equal to mr, and therefore where mc equals ar. However, in the long term, such markets are both allocatively and productively efficient.
- a. Law and economics
- b. Perfect competition
- c. Nominal value
- d. Co-operative economics

46. In economics, _____ describes the state of a market with respect to competition.

- Perfect competition, in which the market consists of a very large number of firms producing a homogeneous product.
- Monopolistic competition where there are a large number of independent firms which have a very small proportion of the market share.
- Oligopoly, in which a market is dominated by a small number of firms which own more than 40% of the market share.
- Oligopsony, a market dominated by many sellers and a few buyers.
- Monopoly, where there is only one provider of a product or service.
- Natural monopoly, a monopoly in which economies of scale cause efficiency to increase continuously with the size of the firm. A firm is a natural monopoly if it is able to serve the entire market demand at a lower cost than any combination of two or more smaller, more specialized firms.
- Monopsony, when there is only one buyer in a market.

The imperfectly competitive structure is quite identical to the realistic market conditions where some monopolistic competitors, monopolists, oligopolists, and duopolists exist and dominate the market conditions. The elements of _____ include the number and size distribution of firms, entry conditions, and the extent of differentiation.

These somewhat abstract concerns tend to determine some but not all details of a specific concrete market system where buyers and sellers actually meet and commit to trade.

a. Monetary economics
b. Market structure
c. Law of demand
d. Mainstream economics

Chapter 27. Regulation and Antitrust Policy in a Globalized Economy

1. The _____ is an economic and political union of 27 member states, located primarily in Europe. It was established by the Treaty of Maastricht on 1 November 1993, upon the foundations of the pre-existing European Economic Community. With a population of almost 500 million, the _____ generates an estimated 30% share (US$18.4 trillion in 2008) of the nominal gross world product.
   - a. ACEA agreement
   - b. ACCRA Cost of Living Index
   - c. European Court of Justice
   - d. European Union

2.

The _____ is an independent agency of the United States government, created, directed, and empowered by Congressional statute , and with the majority of its commissioners appointed by the current President. The _____ works towards six strategic goals in the areas of broadband, competition, the spectrum, the media, public safety and homeland security, and modernizing the _____.

   - a. Federal Communications Commission
   - b. 100-year flood
   - c. 1921 recession
   - d. 130-30 fund

3. _____ is a fee paid on borrowed assets. It is the price paid for the use of borrowed money , or, money earned by deposited funds . Assets that are sometimes lent with _____ include money, shares, consumer goods through hire purchase, major assets such as aircraft, and even entire factories in finance lease arrangements.
   - a. Asset protection
   - b. Internal debt
   - c. Insolvency
   - d. Interest

4. In economics, a _____ occurs when, due to the economies of scale of a particular industry, the maximum efficiency of production and distribution is realized through a single supplier.

Natural monopolies arise where the largest supplier in an industry, often the first supplier in a market, has an overwhelming cost advantage over other actual or potential competitors. This tends to be the case in industries where capital costs predominate, creating economies of scale which are large in relation to the size of the market, and hence high barriers to entry; examples include water services and electricity.

   - a. Privatizing profits and socializing losses
   - b. Government failure
   - c. Government monopoly
   - d. Natural monopoly

5. _____ is a legally declared inability or impairment of ability of an individual or organization to pay its creditors. Creditors may file a _____ petition against a debtor ('involuntary _____') in an effort to recoup a portion of what they are owed or initiate a restructuring. In the majority of cases, however, _____ is initiated by the debtor (a 'voluntary _____' that is filed by the insolvent individual or organization.)
   - a. National bankruptcy
   - b. Liquidation
   - c. Debt settlement
   - d. Bankruptcy

6. In economics, a _____ is a graph of the costs of production as a function of total quantity produced. In a free market economy, productively efficient firms use these curves to find the optimal point of production, where they make the most profits. There are a few different types of _____s, each relevant to a different area of economics.
   - a. Phillips curve
   - b. Demand curve
   - c. Lorenz curve
   - d. Cost curve

7. In economics, a _____ exists when a specific individual or enterprise has sufficient control over a particular product or service to determine significantly the terms on which other individuals shall have access to it. Monopolies are thus characterized by a lack of economic competition for the good or service that they provide and a lack of viable substitute goods. The verb 'monopolize' refers to the process by which a firm gains persistently greater market share than what is expected under perfect competition.
- a. Monopoly
- b. 100-year flood
- c. 1921 recession
- d. 130-30 fund

8. In economics and finance, _____ is the change in total cost that arises when the quantity produced changes by one unit. It is the cost of producing one more unit of a good. Mathematically, the _____ function is expressed as the first derivative of the total cost (TC) function with respect to quantity (Q.)
- a. Quality costs
- b. Fixed costs
- c. Cost allocation
- d. Marginal cost

9. In economics, _____ is the process by which a firm determines the price and output level that returns the greatest profit. There are several approaches to this problem. The total revenue--total cost method relies on the fact that profit equals revenue minus cost, and the marginal revenue--marginal cost method is based on the fact that total profit in a perfectly competitive market reaches its maximum point where marginal revenue equals marginal cost.
- a. 100-year flood
- b. Normal profit
- c. Profit margin
- d. Profit maximization

10. In economics, _____ are the resources employed to produce goods and services. They facilitate production but do not become part of the product (as with raw materials) or significantly transformed by the production process (as with fuel used to power machinery.) To 19th century economists, the _____ were land (natural resources, gifts from nature), labor (the ability to work), and capital goods (human-made tools and equipment.)
- a. Long-run
- b. Factors of production
- c. Productive capacity
- d. Production function

11. In economics, a firm is said to reap _____s when a lack of viable market competition allows it to set its prices above the equilibrium price for a good or service without losing profits to competitors. _____ is a type of economic profit, that is, it is a profit greater than the normal profit that is typical in a perfectly competitive industry. The resulting price is known as the monopoly price.
- a. Correlation trading
- b. January effect
- c. Legal monopoly
- d. Monopoly profit

12. _____ is one of the four Ps of the marketing mix. The other three aspects are product, promotion, and place. It is also a key variable in microeconomic price allocation theory.
- a. Nonlinear pricing
- b. Two-part tariff
- c. Big ticket item
- d. Pricing

13. In microeconomics, _____ is quite simply the conversion of inputs into outputs. It is an economic process that uses resources to create a good or service that is suitable for exchange. This can include manufacturing, storing, shipping, and packaging.
- a. Bucket shop
- b. Characteristic
- c. Variability
- d. Production

14. _____s is the social science that studies the production, distribution, and consumption of goods and services. The term _____s comes from the Ancient Greek oá¼°κονομῖα from oá¼¶κος (oikos, 'house') + vĺŒµος (nomos, 'custom' or 'law'), hence 'rules of the house(hold)'. Current _____ models developed out of the broader field of political economy in the late 19th century, owing to a desire to use an empirical approach more akin to the physical sciences.

a. Inflation
b. Economic
c. Energy economics
d. Opportunity cost

15. In economics and business, a _____ is the effect that one user of a good or service has on the value of that product to other people.

The classic example is the telephone. The more people own telephones, the more valuable the telephone is to each owner.

a. Cluster effect
b. Penn effect
c. Pigou effect
d. Network effect

16. _____ is a system for setting the prices charged by regulated monopolies. The central idea is that monopoly firms should be required to charge the price that would prevail in a competitive market, which is equal to efficient costs of production plus a market-determined rate of return on capital.

_____ has been criticized because it encourages cost-padding, and because, if the allowable rate is set too high, it encourages the adoption of an inefficiently high capital-labor ratio.

a. Complementary monopoly
b. Rate-of-return regulation
c. Bilateral monopoly
d. Revenue-cap regulation

17. A consumer price index (_____) is a measure of the average price of consumer goods and services purchased by households. A consumer price index measures a price change for a constant market basket of goods and services from one period to the next within the same area (city, region, or nation.) It is a price index determined by measuring the price of a standard group of goods meant to represent the typical market basket of a typical urban consumer.

a. Lipstick index
b. Hedonic price index
c. Cost-of-living index
d. CPI

18. _____ is a broad label that refers to any individuals or households that use goods and services generated within the economy. The concept of a _____ is used in different contexts, so that the usage and significance of the term may vary.

Typically when business people and economists talk of _____s they are talking about person as _____, an aggregated commodity item with little individuality other than that expressed in the buy/not-buy decision.

a. Consumer
b. 130-30 fund
c. 100-year flood
d. 1921 recession

19. The U.S. _____ (EEOC) is a federal agency whose goal is ending employment discrimination. The _____ investigates discrimination complaints based on an individual's race, color, national origin, religion, sex, age, disability and retaliation for reporting and/or opposing a discriminatory practice. The Commission is also tasked with filing suits on behalf of alleged victim(s) of discrimination against employers and as an adjudicatory for claims of discrimination brought against federal agencies.
   a. ACCRA Cost of Living Index
   b. EEOC
   c. ACEA agreement
   d. AD-IA Model

20. _____ is a practice of protecting the environment, on individual, organisational or governmental level, for the benefit of the natural environment and (or) humans.

Due to the pressures of population and technology the biophysical environment is being degraded, sometimes permanently. This has been recognised and governments began placing restraints on activities that caused environmental degradation.

   a. AD-IA Model
   b. ACCRA Cost of Living Index
   c. ACEA agreement
   d. Environmental Protection

21. The U.S. _____ is a federal agency whose goal is ending employment discrimination. The _____ investigates discrimination complaints based on an individual's race, color, national origin, religion, sex, age, disability and retaliation for reporting and/or opposing a discriminatory practice. The Commission is also tasked with filing suits on behalf of alleged victim(s) of discrimination against employers and as an adjudicatory for claims of discrimination brought against federal agencies.
   a. AD-IA Model
   b. ACCRA Cost of Living Index
   c. ACEA agreement
   d. Equal Employment Opportunity Commission

22. _____ is a cross-disciplinary area concerned with protecting the safety, health and welfare of people engaged in work or employment. As a secondary effect, it may also protect co-workers, family members, employers, customers, suppliers, nearby communities, and other members of the public who are impacted by the workplace environment. It may involve interactions among many subject areas, including occupational medicine, occupational (or industrial) hygiene, public health, safety engineering, chemistry, health physics, ergonomics, toxicology, epidemiology, environmental health, industrial relations, public policy, sociology, and occupational health psychology.
   a. AD-IA Model
   b. ACEA agreement
   c. Occupational Safety and Health
   d. ACCRA Cost of Living Index

23. The United States _____ is an agency of the United States Department of Labor. It was created by Congress under the Occupational Safety and Health Act, signed by President Richard M. Nixon, on December 29, 1970. Its mission is to prevent work-related injuries, illnesses, and deaths by issuing and enforcing rules (called standards) for workplace safety and health.
   a. ACCRA Cost of Living Index
   b. AD-IA Model
   c. ACEA agreement
   d. Occupational Safety and Health Administration

24. _____ in economics and business is the result of an exchange and from that trade we assign a numerical monetary value to a good, service or asset. If Alice trades Bob 4 apples for an orange, the _____ of an orange is 4 apples. Inversely, the _____ of an apple is 1/4 oranges.

Chapter 27. Regulation and Antitrust Policy in a Globalized Economy   241

a. Price
c. Price dispersion
b. Price ceiling
d. Lerner Index

25. The _____ is an independent agency of the United States government, established in 1914 by the _____ Act. Its principal mission is the promotion of 'consumer protection' and the elimination and prevention of what regulators perceive to be harmfully 'anti-competitive' business practices, such as coercive monopoly.

The _____ Act was one of President Wilson's major acts against trusts.

a. 130-30 fund
c. 100-year flood
b. 1921 recession
d. Federal Trade Commission

26. The U.S. _____ is an independent agency of the United States government which holds primary responsibility for enforcing the federal securities laws and regulating the securities industry, the nation's stock and options exchanges, and other electronic securities markets. The SEC was created by section 4 of the Securities Exchange Act of 1934 (now codified as 15 U.S.C. § 78d and commonly referred to as the 1934 Act.)

a. 100-year flood
c. 1921 recession
b. 130-30 fund
d. Securities and Exchange Commission

27. A security is a fungible, negotiable instrument representing financial value. _____ are broadly categorized into debt _____; equity _____, e.g., common stocks; and derivative (finance) contracts such as forwards, futures, options and swaps. The company or other entity issuing the security is called the issuer.

a. Street name securities
c. Pure security
b. Trading account assets
d. Securities

28. _____ is the removal or simplification of government rules and regulations that constrain the operation of market forces. _____ does not mean elimination of laws against fraud, but eliminating or reducing government control of how business is done, thereby moving toward a more free market.

The stated rationale for '_____' is often that fewer and simpler regulations will lead to a raised level of competitiveness, therefore higher productivity, more efficiency and lower prices overall.

a. Deregulation
c. Monetary policy reaction function
b. Lucas-Islands model
d. SIMIC

29. In 1940, President Franklin Roosevelt split the authority into two agencies, the Civil Aeronautics Administration (CAA) and the _____ The CAA was responsible for air traffic control, safety programs, and airway development. The _____ was entrusted with safety rulemaking, accident investigation, and economic regulation of the airlines.

a. 100-year flood
c. 1921 recession
b. 130-30 fund
d. Civil Aeronautics Board

30. The _____ was a regulatory body in the United States created by the Interstate Commerce Act of 1887, which was signed into law by President Grover Cleveland. The agency was abolished in 1995, and the agency's remaining functions were transferred to the Surface Transportation Board.

The Commission's five members were appointed by the President with the consent of the United States Senate.

a. Office of Thrift Supervision
b. ACEA agreement
c. Interstate Commerce Commission
d. ACCRA Cost of Living Index

31. _____ is an equity (stock) exchange located at 11 Wall Street in lower Manhattan, New York, USA. It is the largest stock exchange in the world by dollar value of its listed companies' securities. As of October 2008, the combined capitalization of all domestic _____ listed companies was US$10.1 trillion.
   a. 130-30 fund
   b. 1921 recession
   c. 100-year flood
   d. New York Stock Exchange

32. A _____ is a corporation or mutual organization which provides trading facilities for stock brokers and traders, to trade stocks and other securities. It may be a physical trading room where the traders gather, or a formalised communications network. Creation of a _____ is a strategy of economic development.
   a. 100-year flood
   b. Primary shares
   c. SEAQ
   d. Stock Exchange

33. In economics, the concept of the _____ refers to the decision-making time frame of a firm in which at least one factor of production is fixed. Costs which are fixed in the _____ have no impact on a firms decisions. For example a firm can raise output by increasing the amount of labour through overtime.
   a. Productivity world
   b. Marginal product
   c. Hicks-neutral technical change
   d. Short-run

34. In economics, a _____ is a market served by only one firm, but with mandated 'competitive' pricing, so as to second the monopoly held by said firm on said market. Its fundamental feature is low barriers to entry and exit; a perfectly _____ would have no barriers to entry or exit. _____s are characteristed by 'hit and run' entry.
   a. Partial equilibrium
   b. Marketization
   c. Competitive equilibrium
   d. Contestable market

35. Competition law, known in the United States as _____ law, has three main elements:

   - prohibiting agreements or practices that restrict free trading and competition between business entities. This includes in particular the repression of cartels.
   - banning abusive behaviour by a firm dominating a market, or anti-competitive practices that tend to lead to such a dominant position. Practices controlled in this way may include predatory pricing, tying, price gouging, refusal to deal, and many others.
   - supervising the mergers and acquisitions of large corporations, including some joint ventures. Transactions that are considered to threaten the competitive process can be prohibited altogether, or approved subject to 'remedies' such as an obligation to divest part of the merged business or to offer licences or access to facilities to enable other businesses to continue competing.

The substance and practice of competition law varies from jurisdiction to jurisdiction. Protecting the interests of consumers (consumer welfare) and ensuring that entrepreneurs have an opportunity to compete in the market economy are often treated as important objectives. Competition law is closely connected with law on deregulation of access to markets, state aids and subsidies, the privatisation of state owned assets and the establishment of independent sector regulators. In recent decades, competition law has been viewed as a way to provide better public services.

Chapter 27. Regulation and Antitrust Policy in a Globalized Economy

a. Intellectual property law
b. United Kingdom competition law
c. Anti-Inflation Act
d. Antitrust

36. _____, known in the United States as antitrust law, has three main elements:

- prohibiting agreements or practices that restrict free trading and competition between business entities. This includes in particular the repression of cartels.
- banning abusive behaviour by a firm dominating a market, or anti-competitive practices that tend to lead to such a dominant position. Practices controlled in this way may include predatory pricing, tying, price gouging, refusal to deal, and many others.
- supervising the mergers and acquisitions of large corporations, including some joint ventures. Transactions that are considered to threaten the competitive process can be prohibited altogether, or approved subject to 'remedies' such as an obligation to divest part of the merged business or to offer licences or access to facilities to enable other businesses to continue competing.

The substance and practice of _____ varies from jurisdiction to jurisdiction. Protecting the interests of consumers (consumer welfare) and ensuring that entrepreneurs have an opportunity to compete in the market economy are often treated as important objectives. _____ is closely connected with law on deregulation of access to markets, state aids and subsidies, the privatisation of state owned assets and the establishment of independent sector regulators. In recent decades, _____ has been viewed as a way to provide better public services.

a. Patent
b. Federal Reserve Police
c. Personal Responsibility and Work Opportunity Reconciliation Act of 1996
d. Competition law

37. _____ is a term that refers both to:

- a formal discipline used to help appraise, or assess, the case for a project or proposal, which itself is a process known as project appraisal; and
- an informal approach to making decisions of any kind.

Under both definitions the process involves, whether explicitly or implicitly, weighing the total expected costs against the total expected benefits of one or more actions in order to choose the best or most profitable option. The formal process is often referred to as either CBA (_____) or BCost-benefit analysis

A hallmark of CBA is that all benefits and all costs are expressed in money terms, and are adjusted for the time value of money, so that all flows of benefits and flows of project costs over time (which tend to occur at different points in time) are expressed on a common basis in terms of their e;present value.e; Closely related, but slightly different, formal techniques include Cost-effectiveness analysis, Economic impact analysis, Fiscal impact analysis and Social Return on Investment(SROI) analysis. The latter builds upon the logic of _____, but differs in that it is explicitly designed to inform the practical decision-making of enterprise managers and investors focused on optimising their social and environmental impacts.

a. 100-year flood
c. 130-30 fund
b. Decision theory
d. Cost-benefit analysis

38. The term _____ refers to an offense under Section 2 of the American Sherman Antitrust Act, passed in 1890. Section 2 states that any person 'who shall monopolize .

a. Price takers
c. De facto monopoly
b. Concentration ratio
d. Monopolization

39. _____ is a common law doctrine relating to the enforceability of contractual restrictions on freedom to conduct business. In an old leading case of Mitchell v. Reynolds (1711) Lord Smith L.C. said,

'it is the privilege of a trader in a free country, in all matters not contrary to law, to regulate his own mode of carrying it on according to his own discretion and choice.

a. Restraint of trade
c. Group boycott
b. Bid rigging
d. Limit pricing

40.

The _____ was the first United States Federal statute to limit cartels and monopolies. It falls under antitrust law.

The Act provides: 'Every contract, combination in the form of trust or otherwise, or conspiracy, in restraint of trade or commerce among the several States, or with foreign nations, is declared to be illegal'. The Act also provides: 'Every person who shall monopolize, or attempt to monopolize, or combine or conspire with any other person or persons, to monopolize any part of the trade or commerce among the several States, or with foreign nations, shall be deemed guilty of a felony [. . .]' The Act put responsibility upon government attorneys and district courts to pursue and investigate trusts, companies and organizations suspected of violating the Act. The Clayton Act extended the right to sue under the antitrust laws to 'any person who shall be injured in his business or property by reason of anything forbidden in the antitrust laws.' Under the Clayton Act, private parties may sue in U.S. district court and should they prevail, they may be awarded treble damages and the cost of suit, including reasonable attorney's fees.

a. 1921 recession
c. 100-year flood
b. 130-30 fund
d. Sherman Antitrust Act

41. _____ was a predominant American integrated oil producing, transporting, refining, and marketing company. Established in 1870 as an Ohio Corporation, it was the largest oil refiner in the world and operated as a major company trust and was one of the world's first and largest multinational corporations until it was broken up by the United States Supreme Court in 1911. John D. Rockefeller was a founder, chairman and major shareholder, and the company made him a billionaire and eventually the richest man in history.

a. 1921 recession
c. 100-year flood
b. 130-30 fund
d. Standard Oil

Chapter 27. Regulation and Antitrust Policy in a Globalized Economy

42. _____ is exchange of capital, goods, and services across international borders or territories. In most countries, it represents a significant share of gross domestic product (GDP.) While _____ has been present throughout much of history, its economic, social, and political importance has been on the rise in recent centuries.

a. International Trade
b. Intra-industry trade
c. Incoterms
d. Import license

43. The _____ consists of a number of economic theories which describe the nature of the firm, company including its existence, its behaviour, and its relationship with the market.

In simplified terms, the _____ aims to answer these questions:

1. Existence - why do firms emerge, why are not all transactions in the economy mediated over the market?
2. Boundaries - why the boundary between firms and the market is located exactly there? Which transactions are performed internally and which are negotiated on the market?
3. Organization - why are firms structured in such specific way? What is the interplay of formal and informal relationships?

Despite looking simple, these questions are not answered by the established economic theory, which usually views firms as given, and treats them as black boxes without any internal structure.

The First World War period saw a change of emphasis in economic theory away from industry-level analysis which mainly included analysing markets to analysis at the level of the firm, as it became increasingly clear that perfect competition was no longer an adequate model of how firms behaved. Economic theory till then had focussed on trying to understand markets alone and there had been little study on understanding why firms or organisations exist.

a. Technology gap
b. Neo-Ricardian school
c. Marginal revenue product
d. Theory of the firm

44. The _____ of 1914 (15 U.S.C §§ 41-58, as amended) established the Federal Trade Commission (FTC), a bipartisan body of five members appointed by the President of the United States for seven year terms. This Commission was authorized to issue Cease and Desist orders to large corporations to curb unfair trade practices. This Act also gave more flexibility to the US congress for judicial matters.

a. Bennett Amendment
b. Deficiency judgment
c. Loss of use
d. Federal Trade Commission Act

45. The _____ is a conflict of laws rule applied to the proprietary aspects of security transactions, especially collateral transactions. It is an alternative approach to the historically important look-through approach, and was a in its earliest form the basis for the initial draft of the Hague Securities Convention.

Unlike the look-through approach, PRIMA does not look through the various tiers of intermediaries to the underlying securities.

a. Securities fraud
b. Securities lending
c. Book entry
d. Place of the Relevant Intermediary Approach

46. The _____ of 1936 (or Anti-Price Discrimination Act, 15 U.S.C. § 13) is a United States federal law that prohibits what were considered, at the time of passage, to be anticompetitive practices by producers, specifically price discrimination. It grew out of practices in which chain stores were allowed to purchase goods at lower prices than other retailers.

a. Legal tender
b. Robinson-Patman Act
c. Prior appropriation water rights
d. Competition law

47. The _____ of 1938 is a United States federal law that amended the Federal Trade Commission Act to add the clause 'unfair or deceptive acts or practices in commerce are hereby declared unlawful' to the Section 5 prohibition of unfair methods of competition, in order to protect consumers as well as competition.

1938 amendment to the federal trade commission act that authorized the FTC to restrict unfair or deceptive acts; also called the advertising act. Until this amendment was passed, the FTC could only restrict practices that were unfair to competitors.

a. No Child Left Behind
b. Human rights in Brazil
c. Buydown
d. Wheeler-Lea Act

48. _____, in strategic management and marketing is, according to Carlton O'Neal, the percentage or proportion of the total available market or market segment that is being serviced by a company. It can be expressed as a company's sales revenue (from that market) divided by the total sales revenue available in that market. It can also be expressed as a company's unit sales volume (in a market) divided by the total volume of units sold in that market.

a. Market share
b. Market sector
c. Technology acceptance model
d. Customer relationship management

49. In competition law the _____ defines the market in which one or more goods compete. Therefore, the _____ defines whether two or more products can be considered substitute goods and whether they constitute a particular and separate market for competition analysis.

The _____ combines the product market and the geographic market, defined as follows:

1. A relevant product market comprises all those products and/or services which are regarded as interchangeable or substitutable by the consumer by reason of the products' characteristics, their prices and their intended use;
2. A relevant geographic market comprises the area in which the firms concerned are involved in the supply of products or services and in which the conditions of competition are sufficiently homogeneous.

The notion of _____ is used in order to identify the products and undertakings which are directly competing in a business. Therefore, the _____ is the market where the competition takes place.

a. Flextime
b. Leave of absence
c. Judgment summons
d. Relevant market

Chapter 27. Regulation and Antitrust Policy in a Globalized Economy

50. _____ is a term used in economics to describe how an economic quantity is related to economic fluctuations. It is the opposite of procyclical. However, it has more than one meaning.

a. Deflation
b. Countercyclical
c. Mercantilism
d. Price theory

51. The phrase _____ and acquisitions refers to the aspect of corporate strategy, corporate finance and management dealing with the buying, selling and combining of different companies that can aid, finance, or help a growing company in a given industry grow rapidly without having to create another business entity.

An acquisition, also known as a takeover or a buyout, is the buying of one company (the 'target') by another. An acquisition may be friendly or hostile.

a. Political economy
b. Dirigisme
c. Peace dividend
d. Mergers

52. _____ AG is an international Universal bank with its headquarters in Frankfurt, Germany. The bank employs more than 81,000 people in 76 countries, and has a large presence in Europe, the Americas, Asia Pacific and the emerging markets.

_____ has offices in major financial centers, such as London, Moscow, New York, São Paulo, Singapore, Sydney, Hong Kong and Tokyo.

a. Rakon
b. Global citizens movement
c. Deutsche Bank
d. Great Leap Forward

Chapter 28. Labor Demand and Supply

1. Unemployment occurs when a person is available to work and seeking work but currently without work. The prevalence of unemployment is usually measured using the _____, which is defined as the percentage of those in the labor force who are unemployed. The _____ is also used in economic studies and economic indexes such as the United States' Conference Board's Index of Leading Indicators as a measure of the state of the macroeconomics.
   - a. ACEA agreement
   - b. AD-IA Model
   - c. ACCRA Cost of Living Index
   - d. Unemployment rate

2. In economics, the marginal product or _____ is the extra output produced by one more unit of an input (for instance, the difference in output when a firm's labour is increased from five to six units.) Assuming that no other inputs to production change, the marginal product of a given input (X) can be expressed as:

   MP = ΔY/ΔX = (the change of Y)/(the change of X.)

   In neoclassical economics, this is the mathematical derivative of the production function....

   - a. Factors of production
   - b. Short-run
   - c. Hicks-neutral technical change
   - d. Marginal physical product

3. A _____ is the lowest hourly, daily or monthly wage that employers may legally pay to employees or workers. Equivalently, it is the lowest wage at which workers may sell their labor. Although _____ laws are in effect in a great many jurisdictions, there are differences of opinion about the benefits and drawbacks of a _____.
   - a. Deregulation
   - b. Permanent income hypothesis
   - c. Permanent war economy
   - d. Minimum wage

4. _____ in economics and business is the result of an exchange and from that trade we assign a numerical monetary value to a good, service or asset. If Alice trades Bob 4 apples for an orange, the _____ of an orange is 4 apples. Inversely, the _____ of an apple is 1/4 oranges.
   - a. Price ceiling
   - b. Price
   - c. Price dispersion
   - d. Lerner Index

5. Monopoly power is an example of market failure which occurs when one or more of the participants has the ability to influence the price or other outcomes in some general or specialized market. The most commonly discussed form of market power is that of a monopoly, but other forms such as monopsony, and more moderate versions of these two extremes, exist. Market participants that have market power are sometimes referred to as 'price makers', while those without are sometimes called '_____'.
   - a. Quasi-rent
   - b. Price takers
   - c. Market concentration
   - d. De facto monopoly

6. _____ is a mechanism that allows people easily to buy and sell products. Services are often included in the scope of the term. _____ regulation is an economic term that describes restrictions in the market.
   - a. Product market
   - b. Residual claimant
   - c. Discretionary spending
   - d. Foreign investment

Chapter 28. Labor Demand and Supply

7. _____ is a term that encompasses the notion of individuals and firms striving for a greater share of a market to sell or buy goods and services. Merriam-Webster defines competition in business as 'the effort of two or more parties acting independently to secure the business of a third party by offering the most favorable terms.' It was described by Adam Smith in The Wealth of Nations (1776) and later economists as allocating productive resources to their most highly-valued uses. and encouraging efficiency.

    a. Cut-throat competition
    c. Path dependence
    b. Moral victory
    d. Competition in economics

8. In neoclassical economics and microeconomics, _____ describes the perfect being a market in which there are many small firms, all producing homogeneous goods. In the short term, such markets are productively inefficient as output will not occur where mc is equal to ac, but allocatively efficient, as output under _____ will always occur where mc is equal to mr, and therefore where mc equals ar. However, in the long term, such markets are both allocatively and productively efficient.

    a. Perfect Competition
    c. Law and economics
    b. Nominal value
    d. Co-operative economics

250 Chapter 28. Labor Demand and Supply

9. A _____ is:

- Rewrite _____, in generative grammar and computer science
- Standardization, a formal and widely-accepted statement, fact, definition, or qualification
- Operation, a determinate _____ for performing a mathematical operation and obtaining a certain result (Mathematics, Logic)
    - Unary operation
    - Binary operation
- _____ of inference, a function from sets of formulae to formulae (Mathematics, Logic)
- _____ of thumb, principle with broad application that is not intended to be strictly accurate or reliable for every situation. Also often simply referred to as a _____
- Moral, an atomic element of a moral code for guiding choices in human behavior
- Heuristic, a quantized '_____' which shows a tendency or probability for successful function
- A regulation, as in sports
- A Production _____, as in computer science
- Procedural law, a _____ set governing the application of laws to cases
    - A law, which may informally be called a '_____'
    - A court ruling, a decision by a court
- In the U.S. Government, a regulation mandated by Congress, but written or expanded upon by the Executive Branch.
- Norm (sociology), an informal but widely accepted _____, concept, truth, definition, or qualification (social norms, legal norms, coding norms)
- Norm (philosophy), a kind of sentence or a reason to act, feel or believe
- 'Rulership' is the concept of governance by a government:
    - Military _____, governance by a military body
    - Monastic _____, a collection of precepts that guides the life of monks or nuns in a religious order where the superior holds the place of Christ
- Slide _____

- '_____,' a song by Ayumi Hamasaki
- '_____,' a song by rapper Nas
- '_____s,' an album by the band The Whitest Boy Alive
- _____s: Pyaar Ka Superhit Formula, a 2003 Bollywood film
- ruler, an instrument for measuring lengths
- _____, a component of an astrolabe, circumferator or similar instrument
- The _____s, a bestselling self-help book
- _____ Project (Run Up-to-date Linux Everywhere), a project that aims to use up-to-date Linux software on old PCs
- _____ engine, a software system that helps managing business _____s
- Ja _____, a hip hop artist
    - R.U.L.E., a 2005 greatest hits album by rapper Ja _____
- '_____s,' a KMFDM song

a. Bon
c. MET
b. Russian financial crisis
d. Rule

Chapter 28. Labor Demand and Supply

10. In microeconomics, _____ is the extra revenue that an additional unit of product will bring. It is the additional income from selling one more unit of a good; sometimes equal to price. It can also be described as the change in total revenue/change in number of units sold.

   a. Marginal revenue
   b. Mohring effect
   c. Social surplus
   d. Product proliferation

11. The marginal revenue productivity theory of wages, also referred to as the _____ of labor, is the change in total revenue earned by a firm that results from employing one more unit of labor. It is a neoclassical model that determines, under some conditions, the optimal number of workers to employ at an exogenously determined market wage rate.

   The _____ of a worker is equal to the product of the marginal product of labor (MP) and the marginal revenue (MR), given by MR×MP = _____.

   a. Developmentalism
   b. Marginal revenue product
   c. Peak gas
   d. Historical school of economics

12. _____ or national income by type of income is a measure of national income or output based on the cost of factors of production, instead of market prices. This allows the effect of any subsidy or indirect tax to be removed from the final measure.

   a. Linkage principle
   b. Capital guarantee
   c. Black-Litterman model
   d. Factor cost

13. Economics:

   - _____,the desire to own something and the ability to pay for it
   - _____ curve,a graphic representation of a _____ schedule
   - _____ deposit, the money in checking accounts
   - _____ pull theory,the theory that inflation occurs when _____ for goods and services exceeds existing supplies
   - _____ schedule,a table that lists the quantity of a good a person will buy it each different price
   - _____ side economics,the school of economics at believes government spending and tax cuts open economy by raising _____

   a. G20
   b. Bon
   c. Procter ' Gamble
   d. Demand

14. _____ is a term in economics, where demand for one good or service occurs as a result of demand for another. This may occur as the former is a part of production of the second. For example, demand for coal leads to _____ for mining, as coal must be mined for coal to be consumed.

   a. Situation analysis
   b. Monopoly wage
   c. Lateral expansion
   d. Derived demand

Chapter 28. Labor Demand and Supply

15. _____ is the term denoting either an entrance or changes which are inserted into a system and which activate/modify a process. It is an abstract concept, used in the modeling, system(s) design and system(s) exploitation. It is usually connected with other terms, e.g., _____ field, _____ variable, _____ parameter, _____ value, _____ signal, _____ device and _____ file.
   a. ACEA agreement
   b. Input
   c. AD-IA Model
   d. ACCRA Cost of Living Index

16. _____ is defined as the measure of responsiveness in the quantity demanded for a commodity as a result of change in price of the same commodity. It is a measure of how consumers react to a change in price. In other words, it is percentage change in quantity demanded as per the percentage change in price of the same commodity.
   a. Price elasticity of demand
   b. 130-30 fund
   c. 100-year flood
   d. 1921 recession

17. In economics, _____ is the ratio of the percent change in one variable to the percent change in another variable. It is a tool for measuring the responsiveness of a function to changes in parameters in a relative way. Commonly analyzed are _____ of substitution, price and wealth.
   a. ACCRA Cost of Living Index
   b. ACEA agreement
   c. Elasticity
   d. Elasticity of demand

18. Price _____ is defined as the measure of responsiveness in the quantity demanded for a commodity as a result of change in price of the same commodity. It is a measure of how consumers react to a change in price. In other words, it is percentage change in quantity demanded by the percentage change in price of the same commodity.
   a. Elasticity of demand
   b. ACEA agreement
   c. ACCRA Cost of Living Index
   d. Elasticity

19. In economics, the _____ is the wage rate that produces neither an access supply of workers nor an excess demand for workers and labor market. See economic equilibrium.
   a. Effective unemployment rate
   b. International free trade agreement
   c. Economic stability
   d. Equilibrium wage

20. In labor economics, the _____ hypothesis argues that wages, at least in some markets, are determined by more than simply supply and demand. Specifically, it points to the incentive for managers to pay their employees more than the market-clearing wage in order to increase their productivity or efficiency. This increased labor productivity pays for the relatively higher wages.
   a. Inflatable rats
   b. Earnings calls
   c. Exogenous growth model
   d. Efficiency wage

21. _____ is that which is owed; usually referencing assets owed, but the term can also cover moral obligations and other interactions not requiring money. In the case of assets, _____ is a means of using future purchasing power in the present before a summation has been earned. Some companies and corporations use _____ as a part of their overall corporate finance strategy.
   a. Non-performing loan
   b. Debt
   c. Participation loan
   d. Subordinated debt

Chapter 28. Labor Demand and Supply

22. In economics, the _____ can be defined as the graph depicting the relationship between the price of a certain commodity, and the amount of it that consumers are willing and able to purchase at that given price. It is a graphic representation of a demand schedule. The _____ for all consumers together follows from the _____ of every individual consumer: the individual demands at each price are added together.
    a. Lorenz curve
    b. Demand curve
    c. Wage curve
    d. Kuznets curve

23. _____ in economics refers to metrics and measures of output from production processes, per unit of input. Labor _____, for example, is typically measured as a ratio of output per labor-hour, an input. _____ may be conceived of as a metrics of the technical or engineering efficiency of production.
    a. Production-possibility frontier
    b. Fordism
    c. Piece work
    d. Productivity

24. In economics, _____ are the resources employed to produce goods and services. They facilitate production but do not become part of the product (as with raw materials) or significantly transformed by the production process (as with fuel used to power machinery.) To 19th century economists, the _____ were land (natural resources, gifts from nature), labor (the ability to work), and capital goods (human-made tools and equipment.)
    a. Factors of production
    b. Long-run
    c. Productive capacity
    d. Production function

25. _____ is the controlled distribution of resources and scarce goods or services. _____ controls the size of the ration, one's allotted portion of the resources being distributed on a particular day or at a particular time.

    In economics, it is often common to use the word '_____' to refer to one of the roles that prices play in markets, while _____ is called 'non-price _____.' Using prices to ration means that those with the most money (or other assets) and who want a product the most are first to receive it.

    a. 130-30 fund
    b. Rationing
    c. 1921 recession
    d. 100-year flood

26. In algebra, a _____ is a function depending on n that associates a scalar, det(A), to an n×n square matrix A. The fundamental geometric meaning of a _____ is a scale factor for measure when A is regarded as a linear transformation. _____ s are important both in calculus, where they enter the substitution rule for several variables, and in multilinear algebra.

    For a fixed nonnegative integer n, there is a unique _____ function for the n×n matrices over any commutative ring R. In particular, this function exists when R is the field of real or complex numbers.

    a. Determinant
    b. 1921 recession
    c. 100-year flood
    d. 130-30 fund

27. In a company, _____ is the sum of all financial records of salaries, wages, bonuses and deductions.

A paycheck, is traditionally a paper document issued by an employer to pay an employee for services rendered. While most commonly used in the United States, recently the physical paycheck has been increasingly replaced by electronic direct deposit to bank accounts.

Chapter 28. Labor Demand and Supply

    a. Payroll
    b. Total Expense Ratio
    c. Tax expense
    d. 100-year flood

28. In microeconomics, _____ is quite simply the conversion of inputs into outputs. It is an economic process that uses resources to create a good or service that is suitable for exchange. This can include manufacturing, storing, shipping, and packaging.
    a. Variability
    b. Production
    c. Characteristic
    d. Bucket shop

29. An _____ is a tax levied on the financial income of people, corporations, or other legal entities. Various _____ systems exist, with varying degrees of tax incidence. Income taxation can be progressive, proportional, or regressive.
    a. AD-IA Model
    b. ACCRA Cost of Living Index
    c. Income tax
    d. ACEA agreement

30. In economics, a _____ is any economic system that effects its distribution of goods and services with prices and employing any form of money or debt tokens. Except for possible remote and primitive communities, all modern societies use _____s to allocate resources. However, _____s are not used for all resource allocation decisions today.
    a. Heavy-Chemical Industry Drive
    b. History of capitalism
    c. Price system
    d. Tenant-in-chief

31. To _____ is to impose a financial charge or other levy upon a taxpayer by a state or the functional equivalent of a state.

_____es are also imposed by many subnational entities. _____es consist of direct _____ or indirect _____, and may be paid in money or as its labour equivalent (often but not always unpaid.)

    a. 100-year flood
    b. 1921 recession
    c. 130-30 fund
    d. Tax

32. The supply of labor is the number of total hours that workers wish to work at a given real wage rate.

_____ curves are derived from the 'labor-leisure' trade-off. More hours worked earn higher incomes but necessitate a cut in the amount of leisure that workers enjoy.

    a. Neo-Capitalism
    b. Narco-capitalism
    c. Wage labour
    d. Labor supply

33. To tax is to impose a financial charge or other levy upon a taxpayer by a state or the functional equivalent of a state.

_____ are also imposed by many subnational entities. _____ consist of direct tax or indirect tax, and may be paid in money or as its labour equivalent (often but not always unpaid.)

    a. 1921 recession
    b. 130-30 fund
    c. 100-year flood
    d. Taxes

Chapter 28. Labor Demand and Supply

34. In economics, a _____ exists when a specific individual or enterprise has sufficient control over a particular product or service to determine significantly the terms on which other individuals shall have access to it. Monopolies are thus characterized by a lack of economic competition for the good or service that they provide and a lack of viable substitute goods. The verb 'monopolize' refers to the process by which a firm gains persistently greater market share than what is expected under perfect competition.
   a. 130-30 fund
   b. 1921 recession
   c. 100-year flood
   d. Monopoly

35. In economics and especially in the theory of competition, _____ are obstacles in the path of a firm that make it difficult to enter a given market.

   _____ are the source of a firm's pricing power - the ability of a firm to raise prices without losing all its customers.

   The term refers to hindrances that an individual may face while trying to gain entrance into a profession or trade.

   a. Predatory pricing
   b. Net Book Agreement
   c. Group boycott
   d. Barriers to entry

36. In economics, _____ is the process by which a firm determines the price and output level that returns the greatest profit. There are several approaches to this problem. The total revenue--total cost method relies on the fact that profit equals revenue minus cost, and the marginal revenue--marginal cost method is based on the fact that total profit in a perfectly competitive market reaches its maximum point where marginal revenue equals marginal cost.
   a. Normal profit
   b. 100-year flood
   c. Profit maximization
   d. Profit margin

37. _____s is the social science that studies the production, distribution, and consumption of goods and services. The term _____s comes from the Ancient Greek oá¼°κονομῖα from oá¼¶κος (oikos, 'house') + vϓμος (nomos, 'custom' or 'law'), hence 'rules of the house(hold)'. Current _____ models developed out of the broader field of political economy in the late 19th century, owing to a desire to use an empirical approach more akin to the physical sciences.
   a. Economic
   b. Energy economics
   c. Opportunity cost
   d. Inflation

38. _____ is the increase in the amount of the goods and services produced by an economy over time. It is conventionally measured as the percent rate of increase in real gross domestic product, or real GDP. Growth is usually calculated in real terms, i.e. inflation-adjusted terms, in order to net out the effect of inflation on the price of the goods and services produced.
   a. ACCRA Cost of Living Index
   b. AD-IA Model
   c. ACEA agreement
   d. Economic growth

Chapter 29. Unions and Labor Market Monopoly Power

1. The International Union, United Automobile, Aerospace and Agricultural Implement Workers of America, better known as the _____ , is a labor union which represents workers in the United States and Puerto Rico. Founded in order to represent workers in the automobile manufacturing industry, _____ members in the 21st century work in industries as diverse as health care, casino gaming and higher education. Headquartered in Detroit, Michigan, the union has approximately 800 local unions, which negotiated 3,100 contracts with some 2,000 employers.
    a. United Auto Workers
    b. ACEA agreement
    c. AD-IA Model
    d. ACCRA Cost of Living Index

2. The _____ was one of the first federations of labor unions in the United States. It was founded in Columbus, Ohio in 1886 by Samuel Gompers as a reorganization of its predecessor, the Federation of Organized Trades and Labor Unions. Gompers became president of the AFL in 1886 and was reelected every year except one until his death on December 13, 1924.
    a. AD-IA Model
    b. ACEA agreement
    c. ACCRA Cost of Living Index
    d. American Federation of Labor

3. A _____ is a group of people who share or are motivated by at least one common issue or interest, or work together on a specific project(s) to achieve a common objective. _____s are also characterised by attempts to share and exercise political and social power and to make decisions on a consensus-driven and egalitarian basis. _____s differ from cooperatives in that they are not necessarily focused upon an economic benefit or saving (but can be that as well.)
    a. 1921 recession
    b. 100-year flood
    c. 130-30 fund
    d. Collective

4. In organized labor, _____ is the method whereby workers organize together (usually in unions) to meet, converse, and negotiate upon the work conditions with their employers normally resulting in a written contract setting forth the wages, hours, and other conditions to be observed for a stipulated period. It is the practice in which union and company representatives meet to negotiate a new labor contract. In various national labor and employment law contexts, _____ takes on a more specific legal meaning and so, in a broad sense, however, it is the coming together of workers to negotiate their employment.

    A collective agreement is a labor contract between an employer and one or more unions.

    a. Designated Suppliers Program
    b. Swedish labour movement
    c. Division of labour
    d. Collective bargaining

5. _____ refers to organizing a union in a manner that seeks to unify workers in a particular industry along the lines of the particular craft or trade that they work in by class or skill level. It contrasts with industrial unionism, in which all workers in the same industry are organized into the same union, regardless of differences in skill.

    _____ is perhaps best exemplified by many of the construction unions that formed the backbone of the old American Federation of Labor (which later merged with the industrial unions of the Congress of Industrial Organizations to form the AFL-CIO.)

    a. 1921 recession
    b. 100-year flood
    c. 130-30 fund
    d. Craft unionism

Chapter 29. Unions and Labor Market Monopoly Power

6. _____s are deposits denominated in US dollars at banks outside the United States, and thus are not under the jurisdiction of the Federal Reserve. Consequently, such deposits are subject to much less regulation than similar deposits within the United States, allowing for higher margins. There is nothing 'European' about _____ deposits; a US dollar-denominated deposit in Tokyo or Caracas would likewise be deemed _____ deposits.
   - a. ACEA agreement
   - b. AD-IA Model
   - c. ACCRA Cost of Living Index
   - d. Eurodollar

7. _____s function as professionals who deal with trade, dealing in commodities that they do not produce themselves, in order to produce profit.

   _____s can be of two types:

   1. A wholesale _____ operates in the chain between producer and retail _____. Some wholesale _____s only organize the movement of goods rather than move the goods themselves.
   2. A retail _____ or retailer, sells commodities to consumers (including businesses.) A shop owner is a retail _____.

   A _____ class characterizes many pre-modern societies. Its status can range from high (even achieving titles like that of _____ prince or nabob) to low, such as in Chinese culture, due to the soiling capabilities of profiting from 'mere' trade, rather than from the labor of others reflected in agricultural produce, craftsmanship, and tribute.

   In the United States, '_____' is defined (under the Uniform Commercial Code) as any person while engaged in a business or profession or a seller who deals regularly in the type of goods sold.
   - a. Merchant
   - b. Social gravity
   - c. Perfect tender rule
   - d. Buy-sell agreement

8. _____, often referred to by his initials _____, was the 32nd President of the United States. He was a central figure of the 20th century during a time of worldwide economic crisis and world war. Elected to four terms in office, he served from 1933 to 1945 and is the only U.S. president to have served more than two terms.
   - a. Adolph Fischer
   - b. Adolf Hitler
   - c. Adam Smith
   - d. Franklin Delano Roosevelt

9. A _____ or labor union is an organization of workers who have banded together to achieve common goals in key areas and working conditions. The _____, through its leadership, bargains with the employer on behalf of union members (rank and file members) and negotiates labor contracts (Collective bargaining) with employers. This may include the negotiation of wages, work rules, complaint procedures, rules governing hiring, firing and promotion of workers, benefits, workplace safety and policies.
   - a. Dividend unit
   - b. Graph cuts
   - c. Labour vouchers
   - d. Trade union

10. The _____ proposed by John L. Lewis in 1932, was a federation of unions that organized workers in industrial unions in the United States and Canada from 1935 to 1955. The Taft-Hartley Act of 1947 required union leaders to swear that they were not Communists. Many CIO leaders refused to obey that requirement, later found unconstitutional.

a. Citizens for an Alternative Tax System
b. Freddie Mac
c. Great Leap Forward
d. Congress of Industrial Organizations

11. _____ is a field of economics that studies the strategic behavior of firms, the structure of markets and their interactions. The study of _____ adds to the perfectly competitive model real-world frictions such as limited information, transaction cost, cost of adjusting prices, government actions, and barriers to entry by new firms into a market. It then considers how firms are organized and how they compete.
a. Inflation
b. Economic ideology
c. Industrial Organization
d. Economic

12. _____ are statutes enforced in twenty-two U.S. states, mostly in the southern or western U.S., allowed under provisions of the Taft-Hartley Act, which prohibit agreements between trade unions and employers making membership or payment of union dues or 'fees' a condition of employment, either before or after hiring.

Prior to the passage of the Taft-Hartley Act by Congress over President Harry S. Truman's veto in 1947, unions and employers covered by the National Labor Relations Act could lawfully agree to a 'closed shop,' in which employees at unionized workplaces are required to be members of the union as a condition of employment. Under the law in effect before the Taft-Hartley amendments, an employee who ceased being a member of the union for whatever reason, from failure to pay dues to expulsion from the union as an internal disciplinary punishment, could also be fired even if the employee did not violate any of the employer's rules.

a. Cobden-Chevalier Treaty
b. Deficiency judgment
c. Generalized System of Preferences
d. Right-to-work laws

13. A _____ is an attempt by labor to convince others to stop doing business with a particular firm because that firm does business with another firm that is the subject of a strike and/or a primary boycott.

This type of action is illegal in many countries. In the U.S. it is banned by the interpretation of the Sherman Antitrust Act, by the Taft-Hartley Act, which amends the National Labor Relations Act of 1935, also known as the Wagner Act.

a. 100-year flood
b. 130-30 fund
c. 1921 recession
d. Secondary boycott

14. The _____ is a labor union in the United States and Canada. Formed in 1903 by the merger of several local and regional locals of teamsters, the union now represents a diverse membership of blue-collar and professional workers in both the public and private sectors. The union had approximately 1.4 million members in 2007.
a. ACCRA Cost of Living Index
b. International Brotherhood of Teamsters
c. AD-IA Model
d. ACEA agreement

Chapter 29. Unions and Labor Market Monopoly Power

15. Competition law, known in the United States as _____ law, has three main elements:

- prohibiting agreements or practices that restrict free trading and competition between business entities. This includes in particular the repression of cartels.
- banning abusive behaviour by a firm dominating a market, or anti-competitive practices that tend to lead to such a dominant position. Practices controlled in this way may include predatory pricing, tying, price gouging, refusal to deal, and many others.
- supervising the mergers and acquisitions of large corporations, including some joint ventures. Transactions that are considered to threaten the competitive process can be prohibited altogether, or approved subject to 'remedies' such as an obligation to divest part of the merged business or to offer licences or access to facilities to enable other businesses to continue competing.

The substance and practice of competition law varies from jurisdiction to jurisdiction. Protecting the interests of consumers (consumer welfare) and ensuring that entrepreneurs have an opportunity to compete in the market economy are often treated as important objectives. Competition law is closely connected with law on deregulation of access to markets, state aids and subsidies, the privatisation of state owned assets and the establishment of independent sector regulators. In recent decades, competition law has been viewed as a way to provide better public services.

a. Anti-Inflation Act
b. Intellectual property law
c. Antitrust
d. United Kingdom competition law

16. In finance, a _____ is a debt security, in which the authorized issuer owes the holders a debt and, depending on the terms of the _____, is obliged to pay interest (the coupon) and/or to repay the principal at a later date, termed maturity. A _____ is a formal contract to repay borrowed money with interest at fixed intervals.

Thus a _____ is like a loan: the issuer is the borrower (debtor), the holder is the lender (creditor), and the coupon is the interest.

a. Carter bonds
b. Callable
c. Prize Bond
d. Bond

17. The _____ is a United States labor law which protects employees, their families, and communities by requiring most employers with 100 or more employees to provide sixty- (60) calendar-day advance notification of plant closings and mass layoffs of employees. It was enacted in 1989.

Employees entitled to notice under the WARN Act include managers and supervisors, hourly wage, and salaried workers.

a. Worker Adjustment and Retraining Notification Act
b. Celler-Kefauver Act
c. Lang Law
d. Letter of credit

18. A _____ is a person who works despite an ongoing strike. _____s are usually individuals who are not employed by the company prior to the trade union dispute, but rather hired prior to or during the strike to keep production or services going. '_____s' may also refer to be workers who cross picket lines to work.

Chapter 29. Unions and Labor Market Monopoly Power

a. Work-life balance
c. Departmentalization
b. Collective bargaining
d. Strikebreaker

19. _____ is the controlled distribution of resources and scarce goods or services. _____ controls the size of the ration, one's allotted portion of the resources being distributed on a particular day or at a particular time.

In economics, it is often common to use the word '_____' to refer to one of the roles that prices play in markets, while _____ is called 'non-price _____.' Using prices to ration means that those with the most money (or other assets) and who want a product the most are first to receive it.

a. 1921 recession
c. 100-year flood
b. Rationing
d. 130-30 fund

20. In macroeconomics, _____ is a condition of the national economy, where all or nearly all persons willing and able to work at the prevailing wages and working conditions are able to do so. It is defined either as 0% unemployment, literally, no unemployment (the rate of unemployment is the fraction of the work force unable to find work), as by James Tobin, or as the level of employment rates when there is no cyclical unemployment. It is defined by the majority of mainstream economists as being an acceptable level of natural unemployment above 0%, the discrepancy from 0% being due to non-cyclical types of unemployment.

a. Full employment
c. SIMIC
b. War economy
d. Marginal propensity to import

21. In a company, _____ is the sum of all financial records of salaries, wages, bonuses and deductions.

A paycheck, is traditionally a paper document issued by an employer to pay an employee for services rendered. While most commonly used in the United States, recently the physical paycheck has been increasingly replaced by electronic direct deposit to bank accounts.

a. Total Expense Ratio
c. 100-year flood
b. Tax expense
d. Payroll

22. Economics:

- _____,the desire to own something and the ability to pay for it
- _____ curve,a graphic representation of a _____ schedule
- _____ deposit, the money in checking accounts
- _____ pull theory,the theory that inflation occurs when _____ for goods and services exceeds existing supplies
- _____ schedule,a table that lists the quantity of a good a person will buy it each different price
- _____ side economics,the school of economics at believes government spending and tax cuts open economy by raising _____

a. Bon
c. Procter ' Gamble
b. G20
d. Demand

Chapter 29. Unions and Labor Market Monopoly Power

23. _____ in economics refers to metrics and measures of output from production processes, per unit of input. Labor _____, for example, is typically measured as a ratio of output per labor-hour, an input. _____ may be conceived of as a metrics of the technical or engineering efficiency of production.

   a. Fordism
   b. Production-possibility frontier
   c. Piece work
   d. Productivity

24. In algebra, a _____ is a function depending on n that associates a scalar, det(A), to an n×n square matrix A. The fundamental geometric meaning of a _____ is a scale factor for measure when A is regarded as a linear transformation. _____s are important both in calculus, where they enter the substitution rule for several variables, and in multilinear algebra.

   For a fixed nonnegative integer n, there is a unique _____ function for the n×n matrices over any commutative ring R. In particular, this function exists when R is the field of real or complex numbers.

   a. 100-year flood
   b. 1921 recession
   c. 130-30 fund
   d. Determinant

25. In finance, the _____s between two currencies specifies how much one currency is worth in terms of the other. It is the value of a foreign natione;s currency in terms of the home natione;s currency. For example an _____ of 102 Japanese yen to the United States dollar means that JPY 102 is worth the same as USD 1.

   a. Exchange rate
   b. ACEA agreement
   c. Interbank market
   d. ACCRA Cost of Living Index

26. In calculus, a function f defined on a subset of the real numbers with real values is called _____, if for all x and y such that x >≤ y one has f(x) >≤ f(y), so f preserves the order. In layman's terms, the sign of the slope is always positive (the curve tending upwards) or zero (i.e., non-decreasing, or asymptotic, or depicted as a horizontal, flat line) Likewise, a function is called monotonically decreasing (non-increasing) if, whenever x >≤ y, then f(x) >≥ f(y), so it reverses the order.

   a. 100-year flood
   b. 130-30 fund
   c. 1921 recession
   d. Monotonic

27. _____ is a pejorative term for the practice of hiring more workers than are needed to perform a given job complex and time-consuming merely to employ additional workers. The term 'make-work' is sometimes used as a synonym for _____.

   The term '_____' is usually used by management to describe behaviors and rules sought by workers.

   a. Featherbedding
   b. Customer centricity
   c. Small business
   d. Business process automation

28. A _____ is an object whose consumption increases the utility of the consumer, for which the quantity demanded exceeds the quantity supplied at zero price. _____s are usually modeled as having diminishing marginal utility. The first individual purchase has high utility; the second has less.

   a. Luxury good
   b. Search good
   c. Positional goods
   d. Good

Chapter 29. Unions and Labor Market Monopoly Power

29. _____, when used as a special term, refers to various incentive plans introduced by businesses that provide direct or indirect payments to employees that depend on company's profitability in addition to employees' regular salary and bonuses. In publicly traded companies these plans typically amount to allocation of shares to employees.

The _____ plans are based on predetermined economic sharing rules that define the split of gains between the company as a principal and the employee as an agent.

a. Living wage
b. Merit pay
c. Pension insurance contract
d. Profit sharing

30. In economics, a _____ is a graph of the costs of production as a function of total quantity produced. In a free market economy, productively efficient firms use these curves to find the optimal point of production, where they make the most profits. There are a few different types of _____s, each relevant to a different area of economics.

a. Lorenz curve
b. Demand curve
c. Phillips curve
d. Cost curve

31. In economics, a monopsony 'purchase') is a market form in which only one buyer faces many sellers. It is an example of imperfect competition, similar to a monopoly, in which only one seller faces many buyers. As the only purchaser of a good or service, the '_____' may dictate terms to its suppliers in the same manner that a monopolist controls the market for its buyers.

a. Monopsonist
b. 100-year flood
c. 1921 recession
d. 130-30 fund

32. In economics, a _____ 'purchase') is a market form in which only one buyer faces many sellers. It is an example of imperfect competition, similar to a monopoly, in which only one seller faces many buyers. As the only purchaser of a good or service, the 'monopsonist' may dictate terms to its suppliers in the same manner that a monopolist controls the market for its buyers.

a. 130-30 fund
b. Monopsony
c. 1921 recession
d. 100-year flood

33. _____ or national income by type of income is a measure of national income or output based on the cost of factors of production, instead of market prices. This allows the effect of any subsidy or indirect tax to be removed from the final measure.

a. Factor cost
b. Black-Litterman model
c. Linkage principle
d. Capital guarantee

34. In economic models, the _____ time frame assumes no fixed factors of production. Firms can enter or leave the marketplace, and the cost (and availability) of land, labor, raw materials, and capital goods can be assumed to vary. In contrast, in the short-run time frame, certain factors are assumed to be fixed, because there is not sufficient time for them to change.

a. Short-run
b. Diseconomies of scale
c. Product Pipeline
d. Long-run

35. _____ is a fee paid on borrowed assets. It is the price paid for the use of borrowed money , or, money earned by deposited funds . Assets that are sometimes lent with _____ include money, shares, consumer goods through hire purchase, major assets such as aircraft, and even entire factories in finance lease arrangements.

Chapter 29. Unions and Labor Market Monopoly Power

a. Internal debt
c. Insolvency
b. Asset protection
d. Interest

36. _____ is the term denoting either an entrance or changes which are inserted into a system and which activate/modify a process. It is an abstract concept, used in the modeling, system(s) design and system(s) exploitation. It is usually connected with other terms, e.g., _____ field, _____ variable, _____ parameter, _____ value, _____ signal, _____ device and _____ file.

a. ACEA agreement
c. AD-IA Model
b. ACCRA Cost of Living Index
d. Input

37. A _____ is the lowest hourly, daily or monthly wage that employers may legally pay to employees or workers. Equivalently, it is the lowest wage at which workers may sell their labor. Although _____ laws are in effect in a great many jurisdictions, there are differences of opinion about the benefits and drawbacks of a _____.

a. Deregulation
c. Minimum Wage
b. Permanent income hypothesis
d. Permanent war economy

38. _____ in economics and business is the result of an exchange and from that trade we assign a numerical monetary value to a good, service or asset. If Alice trades Bob 4 apples for an orange, the _____ of an orange is 4 apples. Inversely, the _____ of an apple is 1/4 oranges.

a. Price dispersion
c. Price ceiling
b. Lerner Index
d. Price

39. In a _____ there is both a monopoly (a single seller) and monopsony (a single buyer) in the same market.

In such market price and output will be determined by the non economic forces like bargaining power of both buyer and seller. A _____ model is often used in situations where the switching costs of both sides are prohibitively high.

a. Market concentration
c. De facto monopoly
b. Price makers
d. Bilateral monopoly

40. In economics and especially in the theory of competition, _____ are obstacles in the path of a firm that make it difficult to enter a given market.

_____ are the source of a firm's pricing power - the ability of a firm to raise prices without losing all its customers.

The term refers to hindrances that an individual may face while trying to gain entrance into a profession or trade.

a. Barriers to entry
c. Net Book Agreement
b. Group boycott
d. Predatory pricing

41. _____ is a term that encompasses the notion of individuals and firms striving for a greater share of a market to sell or buy goods and services. Merriam-Webster defines competition in business as 'the effort of two or more parties acting independently to secure the business of a third party by offering the most favorable terms.' It was described by Adam Smith in The Wealth of Nations (1776) and later economists as allocating productive resources to their most highly-valued uses. and encouraging efficiency.
- a. Moral victory
- b. Competition in economics
- c. Path dependence
- d. Cut-throat competition

42. In economics, a _____ exists when a specific individual or enterprise has sufficient control over a particular product or service to determine significantly the terms on which other individuals shall have access to it. Monopolies are thus characterized by a lack of economic competition for the good or service that they provide and a lack of viable substitute goods. The verb 'monopolize' refers to the process by which a firm gains persistently greater market share than what is expected under perfect competition.
- a. 100-year flood
- b. 130-30 fund
- c. 1921 recession
- d. Monopoly

Chapter 30. Income, Poverty, and Health Care

1. _____ is a common concept in economics, and gives rise to derived concepts such as consumer debt. Generally _____ is defined by opposition to production. But the precise definition can vary because different schools of economists define production quite differently.
   a. Discrete choice
   b. British canal system
   c. Basis of futures
   d. Consumption

2. In economics, _____ is how a natione;s total economy is distributed among its population. ._____ has always been a central concern of economic theory and economic policy. Classical economists such as Adam Smith, Thomas Malthus and David Ricardo were mainly concerned with factor _____, that is, the distribution of income between the main factors of production, land, labour and capital.
   a. Eco commerce
   b. Income distribution
   c. Equipment trust certificate
   d. Authorised capital

3. In economics, the _____ is a graphical representation of the cumulative distribution function of a probability distribution; it is a graph showing the proportion of the distribution assumed by the bottom y% of the values. It is a curve that illustrates income distribution. It is often used to represent income distribution, where it shows for the bottom x% of households, what percentage y% of the total income they have.
   a. Cost curve
   b. Wage curve
   c. Kuznets curve
   d. Lorenz curve

4. The _____ is the central banking system of the United States. Created in 1913 by the enactment of the Federal Reserve Act (signed by Woodrow Wilson), it is a quasi-public and quasi-private (government entity with private components) banking system that comprises (1) the presidentially appointed Board of Governors of the _____ in Washington, D.C.; (2) the Federal Open Market Committee; (3) twelve regional Federal Reserve Banks located in major cities throughout the nation acting as fiscal agents for the U.S. Treasury, each with its own nine-member board of directors; (4) numerous other private U.S. member banks, which subscribe to required amounts of non-transferable stock in their regional Federal Reserve Banks; and (5) various advisory councils. Since February 2006, Ben Bernanke has served as the Chairman of the Board of Governors of the _____.
   a. Federal Reserve Transparency Act
   b. Federal Reserve Banks
   c. Federal Reserve System
   d. Federal funds rate

5. The _____ is the broad group of people in contemporary society who fall socioeconomically between the working class and upper class. This socioeconomic class encompasses the sub-classes of lower middle, middle middle, and upper middle, and includes professionals, highly skilled workers, and management. As in all socioeconomic classes, the _____ is associated with a shared and complex set of cultural values.
   a. 130-30 fund
   b. Middle class
   c. Dominant minority
   d. 100-year flood

6. In algebra, a _____ is a function depending on n that associates a scalar, det(A), to an n×n square matrix A. The fundamental geometric meaning of a _____ is a scale factor for measure when A is regarded as a linear transformation. _____s are important both in calculus, where they enter the substitution rule for several variables, and in multilinear algebra.

For a fixed nonnegative integer n, there is a unique _____ function for the n×n matrices over any commutative ring R. In particular, this function exists when R is the field of real or complex numbers.

a. Determinant
b. 1921 recession
c. 100-year flood
d. 130-30 fund

7. In economics, the _____ or marginal physical product is the extra output produced by one more unit of an input (for instance, the difference in output when a firm's labour is increased from five to six units.) Assuming that no other inputs to production change, the _____ of a given input (X) can be expressed as:

_____ = ΔY/ΔX = (the change of Y)/(the change of X.)

-
  -
    - Pending approval by Thomas Sowell***

In neoclassical economics, this is the mathematical derivative of the production function.... Note that the 'product' (Y) is typically defined ignoring external costs and benefits.

a. Marginal product
b. Productivity world
c. Diseconomies of scale
d. Labor problem

8. _____ in economics refers to metrics and measures of output from production processes, per unit of input. Labor _____, for example, is typically measured as a ratio of output per labor-hour, an input. _____ may be conceived of as a metrics of the technical or engineering efficiency of production.

a. Piece work
b. Fordism
c. Productivity
d. Production-possibility frontier

9. In finance, the _____s between two currencies specifies how much one currency is worth in terms of the other. It is the value of a foreign natione;s currency in terms of the home natione;s currency. For example an _____ of 102 Japanese yen to the United States dollar means that JPY 102 is worth the same as USD 1.

a. ACEA agreement
b. Exchange rate
c. Interbank market
d. ACCRA Cost of Living Index

10. _____ refers to the stock of skills and knowledge embodied in the ability to perform labor so as to produce economic value. It is the skills and knowledge gained by a worker through education and experience.Many early economic theories refer to it simply as labor, one of three factors of production, and consider it to be a fungible resource -- homogeneous and easily interchangeable. Other conceptions of labor dispense with these assumptions.

a. Monetary inflation
b. Labour economics
c. Monopolistic competition
d. Human capital

11. _____ is a fee paid on borrowed assets. It is the price paid for the use of borrowed money , or, money earned by deposited funds . Assets that are sometimes lent with _____ include money, shares, consumer goods through hire purchase, major assets such as aircraft, and even entire factories in finance lease arrangements.

a. Interest
b. Internal debt
c. Asset protection
d. Insolvency

12.

_____ was a German philosopher, political economist, historian, political theorist, sociologist, communist and revolutionary credited as the founder of communism.

Marx summarized his approach to history and politics in the opening line of the first chapter of The Communist Manifesto : e;The history of all hitherto existing society is the history of class struggles.e; Marx argued that capitalism, like previous socioeconomic systems, will produce internal tensions which will lead to its destruction. Just as capitalism replaced feudalism, socialism will in its turn replace capitalism and lead to a stateless, classless society which will emerge after a transitional period, the 'dictatorship of the proletariat'.

a. Marxism
b. Adam Smith
c. Neo-Gramscianism
d. Karl Heinrich Marx

13. _____ is the shortage of common things such as food, clothing, shelter and safe drinking water, all of which determine the quality of life. It may also include the lack of access to opportunities such as education and employment which aid the escape from _____ and/or allow one to enjoy the respect of fellow citizens. According to Mollie Orshansky who developed the _____ measurements used by the U.S. government, 'to be poor is to be deprived of those goods and services and pleasures which others around us take for granted.' Ongoing debates over causes, effects and best ways to measure _____, directly influence the design and implementation of _____-reduction programs and are therefore relevant to the fields of public administration and international development.

a. Poverty
b. Secondary poverty
c. Growth Elasticity of Poverty
d. Liberal welfare reforms

14. _____ is a broad label that refers to any individuals or households that use goods and services generated within the economy. The concept of a _____ is used in different contexts, so that the usage and significance of the term may vary.

Typically when business people and economists talk of _____s they are talking about person as _____, an aggregated commodity item with little individuality other than that expressed in the buy/not-buy decision.

a. Consumer
b. 130-30 fund
c. 100-year flood
d. 1921 recession

15. A _____ is a measure of the average price of consumer goods and services purchased by households. A _____ measures a price change for a constant market basket of goods and services from one period to the next within the same area (city, region, or nation.) It is a price index determined by measuring the price of a standard group of goods meant to represent the typical market basket of a typical urban consumer.

a. Hedonic price index
b. Consumer Price Index
c. Lipstick index
d. Cost-of-living index

16. _____ in economics and business is the result of an exchange and from that trade we assign a numerical monetary value to a good, service or asset. If Alice trades Bob 4 apples for an orange, the _____ of an orange is 4 apples. Inversely, the _____ of an apple is 1/4 oranges.

a. Price ceiling
b. Lerner Index
c. Price dispersion
d. Price

17. A _____ is a normalized average (typically a weighted average) of prices for a given class of goods or services in a given region, during a given interval of time. It is a statistic designed to help to compare how these prices, taken as a whole, differ between time periods or geographical locations.

Price indices have several potential uses.

a. Flat rate
b. Point of total assumption
c. Pecuniary externality
d. Price Index

18. A _____, reserve bank, or monetary authority is the entity responsible for the monetary policy of a country or of a group of member states. It is a bank that can lend money to other banks in times of need. Its primary responsibility is to maintain the stability of the national currency and money supply, but more active duties include controlling subsidized-loan interest rates, and acting as a lender of last resort to the banking sector during times of financial crisis (private banks often being integral to the national financial system.)

a. 100-year flood
b. 1921 recession
c. Central bank
d. 130-30 fund

19. In economics, a _____ is a redistribution of income in the market system. These payments are considered to be nonexhaustive because they do not directly absorb resources or create output. Examples of certain _____s include welfare (financial aid), social security, and government subsidies for certain businesses (firms.)

a. 1921 recession
b. Transfer payment
c. 100-year flood
d. 130-30 fund

20. _____, often called disability income insurance, is a form of insurance that insures the beneficiary's earned income against the risk that disability will make working (and therefore earning) impossible. It includes paid sick leave, short-term disability benefits, and long-term disability benefits.

In most developed countries, the single most important form of _____ is that provided by the national government for all citizens.

a. 1921 recession
b. 100-year flood
c. 130-30 fund
d. Disability insurance

21. _____, in law and economics, is a form of risk management primarily used to hedge against the risk of a contingent loss. _____ is defined as the equitable transfer of the risk of a loss, from one entity to another, in exchange for a premium, and can be thought of as a guaranteed small loss to prevent a large, possibly devastating loss. An insurer is a company selling the _____; an insured or policyholder is the person or entity buying the _____.

a. ACEA agreement
b. AD-IA Model
c. ACCRA Cost of Living Index
d. Insurance

22. A _____ is the transfer of wealth from one party (such as a person or company) to another. A _____ is usually made in exchange for the provision of goods, services or both, or to fulfill a legal obligation.

The simplest and oldest form of _____ is barter, the exchange of one good or service for another.

a. RFM
c. Contingent payment sales
b. Hard count
d. Payment

23. To _____ is to impose a financial charge or other levy upon a taxpayer by a state or the functional equivalent of a state.

_____es are also imposed by many subnational entities. _____es consist of direct _____ or indirect _____, and may be paid in money or as its labour equivalent (often but not always unpaid.)

a. 100-year flood
c. 130-30 fund
b. 1921 recession
d. Tax

24. To tax is to impose a financial charge or other levy upon a taxpayer by a state or the functional equivalent of a state.

_____ are also imposed by many subnational entities. _____ consist of direct tax or indirect tax, and may be paid in money or as its labour equivalent (often but not always unpaid.)

a. 130-30 fund
c. 1921 recession
b. 100-year flood
d. Taxes

25. _____ is the United States of America's federal assistance program, formerly known as 'welfare'. It began on July 1, 1997, and succeeded the Aid to Families with Dependent Children program, providing cash assistance to indigent American families with dependent children through the United States Department of Health and Human Services. Prior to 1997, the federal government designed the overall program requirements and guidelines, while states administered the program and determined eligibility for benefits.

a. 1921 recession
c. 130-30 fund
b. 100-year flood
d. Temporary Assistance for Needy Families

26. _____ is a voluntary transfer of resources from one country to another, given at least partly with the objective of benefiting the recipient country. It may have other functions as well: it may be given as a signal of diplomatic approval, or to strengthen a military ally, to reward a government for behaviour desired by the donor, to extend the donor's cultural influence, to provide infrastructure needed by the donor for resource extraction from the recipient country, or to gain other kinds of commercial access. Humanitarianism and altruism are, nevertheless, significant motivations for the giving of _____.

a. ACCRA Cost of Living Index
c. AD-IA Model
b. Aid
d. ACEA agreement

27. _____ was a federal assistance program in effect from 1935 to 1997, which was administered by the United States Department of Health and Human Services. This program provided financial assistance to children whose families had low or no income.

The program was created under the name Aid to Dependent Children (ADC) by the Social Security Act of 1935 as part of the New Deal; the words 'families with' were added to the name in 1960, partly due to concern that the program's rules discouraged marriage.

a. Aid to Families with Dependent Children
b. ACCRA Cost of Living Index
c. ACEA agreement
d. AD-IA Model

28. A _____ refers to any type debt instrument, such as a loan, bond, mortgage that does not have a fixed rate of interest over the life of the instrument. Such debt typically uses an index or other base rate for establishing the interest rate for each relevant period. One of the most common rates to use as the basis for applying interest rates is the London Inter-bank Offered Rate, or LIBOR
   a. Standard of deferred payment
   b. Style investing
   c. Bankruptcy remote
   d. Floating interest rate

29. The United States federal _____ is a refundable tax credit. For tax year 2008, a claimant with one qualifying child can receive a maximum credit of $2,917. For two or more qualifying children, the maximum credit is $4,824.
   a. ACEA agreement
   b. AD-IA Model
   c. Earned Income Tax Credit
   d. ACCRA Cost of Living Index

30. An _____ is a tax levied on the financial income of people, corporations, or other legal entities. Various _____ systems exist, with varying degrees of tax incidence. Income taxation can be progressive, proportional, or regressive.
   a. ACEA agreement
   b. ACCRA Cost of Living Index
   c. Income Tax
   d. AD-IA Model

31. The term _____ describes two different concepts:

   - The first is a recognition of partial payment already made towards taxes due.
   - The second is a state benefit paid to workers through the tax system, which has the effect of increasing (rather than reducing) net income.

Within the Australian, Canadian, United Kingdom, and United States tax systems, a _____ is a recognition of partial payment already made towards taxes due. A similar concept exists (fr:Avoir fiscal) in the French tax system. This situation arises, for example, when standard rate tax has been deducted at source , but the tax-payer is subject to further taxation at a higher rate. It also applies in dividend imputation systems.

   a. 100-year flood
   b. 1921 recession
   c. Tax Credit
   d. 130-30 fund

32. _____ is that which is owed; usually referencing assets owed, but the term can also cover moral obligations and other interactions not requiring money. In the case of assets, _____ is a means of using future purchasing power in the present before a summation has been earned. Some companies and corporations use _____ as a part of their overall corporate finance strategy.
   a. Participation loan
   b. Debt
   c. Non-performing loan
   d. Subordinated debt

Chapter 30. Income, Poverty, and Health Care

33. The term _____ refers to government debt, expenditures and revenues, or to finance (particularly financial revenue) in general.

- _____ deficit is the budget deficit of federal or local government
- _____ policy is the discretionary spending of governments. Contrasts with monetary policy.
- _____ year and _____ quarter are reporting periods for firms and other agencies.

a. Consequence
c. Freedom Park
b. Fiscal
d. Russian financial crisis

34. In economics, _____ is the use of government spending and revenue collection to influence the economy.

_____ can be contrasted with the other main type of economic policy, monetary policy, which attempts to stabilize the economy by controlling interest rates and the supply of money. The two main instruments of _____ are government spending and taxation.

a. Sustainable investment rule
c. 100-year flood
b. Fiscal policy
d. Fiscalism

35. _____ is a misspelled phrase from Latin 'pro capite' phrase meaning per head with pro meaning 'per' or 'for each' and capite meaning 'head.' Both words together equate to the phrase 'for each head.'

It is usually used in the field of statistics to indicate the average per person for any given concern, such as income, crime rate, etc.

It is also used in wills to indicate that each of the named beneficiaries should receive, by devise or bequest, equal shares of the estate. This is in contrast to a per stirpes division, in which each branch of the inheriting family inherits an equal share of the estate.

a. Posterior probability
c. Semiparametric regression
b. Dynamic Bayesian network
d. Per capita

36. In an insurance policy, the _____ or excess (UK term) is the portion of any claim that is not covered by the insurance provider. It is the amount of expenses that must be paid out of pocket before an insurer will cover any expenses. It is normally quoted as a fixed quantity and is a part of most policies covering losses to the policy holder.

a. Dual trigger insurance
c. Loss reserving
b. Probable maximum loss
d. Deductible

272   Chapter 30. Income, Poverty, and Health Care

37. Economics:

- _____, the desire to own something and the ability to pay for it
- _____ curve, a graphic representation of a _____ schedule
- _____ deposit, the money in checking accounts
- _____ pull theory, the theory that inflation occurs when _____ for goods and services exceeds existing supplies
- _____ schedule, a table that lists the quantity of a good a person will buy it each different price
- _____ side economics, the school of economics at believes government spending and tax cuts open economy by raising _____

a. Bon
b. Demand
c. Procter ' Gamble
d. G20

38. _____ is the prospect that a party insulated from risk may behave differently from the way it would behave if it were fully exposed to the risk. In insurance, _____ that occurs without conscious or malicious action is called morale hazard.

_____ is related to information asymmetry, a situation in which one party in a transaction has more information than another.

a. 100-year flood
b. 1921 recession
c. Moral hazard
d. 130-30 fund

39. _____ and Keynesian Theory) is a macroeconomic theory based on the ideas of 20th-century British economist John Maynard Keynes. _____ argues that private sector decisions sometimes lead to inefficient macroeconomic outcomes and therefore advocates active policy responses by the public sector, including monetary policy actions by the central bank and fiscal policy actions by the government to stabilize output over the business cycle.

The theories forming the basis of _____ were first presented in The General Theory of Employment, Interest and Money, published in 1936.

a. Recession
b. Keynesian economics
c. Gross domestic product
d. Rational choice theory

40. In financial accounting, the _____ is one of the accounts in shareholders' equity. Sole proprietorships have a single _____ in the owner's equity. Partnerships maintain a _____ for each of the partners.

a. Current account
b. Compensation of employees
c. Gross private domestic investment
d. Capital Account

41. _____s are accounts maintained by retail financial institutions that pay interest but can not be used directly as money (for example, by writing a cheque.) These accounts let customers set aside a portion of their liquid assets while earning a monetary return.

_____s are offered by commercial banks, savings and loan associations, credit unions, building societies and mutual savings banks.

a. Savings account
c. Bank run
b. Capital requirement
d. Narrow banking

Chapter 31. Environmental Economics

1. _____ is the logging and/or burning of trees in a forested area. There are several reasons for doing so: trees or derived charcoal can be sold as a commodity and used by humans, while cleared land is used as pasture, plantations of commodities and human settlement. The removal of trees without sufficient reforestation has resulted in damage to habitat, biodiversity loss and aridity.
   a. Carbon offset
   b. Carbon emissions trading
   c. Post-Kyoto negotiations
   d. Deforestation

2. _____s is the social science that studies the production, distribution, and consumption of goods and services. The term _____s comes from the Ancient Greek οἰκονομῖα from οἶκος (oikos, 'house') + νόμος (nomos, 'custom' or 'law'), hence 'rules of the house(hold)'. Current _____ models developed out of the broader field of political economy in the late 19th century, owing to a desire to use an empirical approach more akin to the physical sciences.
   a. Energy economics
   b. Economic
   c. Inflation
   d. Opportunity cost

3. Many _____ are related to the environmental consequences of production and use

   - Systemic risk describes the risks to the overall economy arising from the risks which the banking system takes. That the private costs of banking failure may be smaller than the social costs justifies banking regulations, although regulations could create a moral hazard.

   - Anthropogenic climate change is attributed to greenhouse gas emissions from burning oil, gas, and coal. Global warming has been ranked as the #1 externality of all economic activity, in the magnitude of potential harms and yet remains unmitigated.

   a. Contingent valuation
   b. Positive externalities
   c. Total Economic Value
   d. Negative externalities

4. In economics _____ is defined as the sum of private and external costs. Economic theorists ascribe individual decision-making to a calculation costs and benefits. Rational choice theory assumes that individuals only consider their own private costs when making decisions, not the costs that may be borne by others.
   a. Total absorption costing
   b. Variable cost
   c. Transaction cost
   d. Social cost

5. In economics, an _____ or spillover of an economic transaction is an impact on a party that is not directly involved in the transaction. In such a case, prices do not reflect the full costs or benefits in production or consumption of a product or service. A positive impact is called an external benefit, while a negative impact is called an external cost.
   a. Externality
   b. Environmental impact assessment
   c. Environmental tariff
   d. Existence value

6. In economics, a common-pool resource, alternatively termed a _____ resource, is a particular type of good consisting of a natural or human-made resource system, the size or characteristics of which makes it costly, but not impossible, to exclude potential beneficiaries from obtaining benefits from its use. Unlike pure public goods, common pool resources face problems of congestion or overuse, because they are subtractable. A common-pool resource typically consists of a core resource, which defines the stock variable, while providing a limited quantity of extractable fringe units, which defines the flow variable.

a. Price-cap regulation
b. Tragedy of the anticommons
c. Government failure
d. Common property

7. _____ or economic opportunity loss is the value of the next best alternative foregone as the result of making a decision. _____ analysis is an important part of a company's decision-making processes but is not treated as an actual cost in any financial statement. The next best thing that a person can engage in is referred to as the _____ of doing the best thing and ignoring the next best thing to be done.
   a. Economic ideology
   b. Economic
   c. Opportunity Cost
   d. Industrial organization

8. The _____ of a decision depends on both the cost of the alternative chosen and the benefit that the best alternative would have provided if chosen. _____ differs from accounting cost because it includes opportunity cost.
   a. Isocost
   b. Inventory analysis
   c. Epstein-Zin preferences
   d. Economic cost

9. _____ is an online peer-reviewed magazine published by the Agricultural ' Applied Economics Association (AAEA) for readers interested in the policy and management of agriculture, the food industry, natural resources, rural communities, and the environment. _____ is published quarterly and is available free online. It is currently one of three outreach products offered by AAEA, along with the more timely Policy Issues and the forthcoming Shared Materials section of the AAEA Web site.
   a. 130-30 fund
   b. 100-year flood
   c. 1921 recession
   d. Choices

10. To _____ is to impose a financial charge or other levy upon a taxpayer by a state or the functional equivalent of a state.

_____es are also imposed by many subnational entities. _____es consist of direct _____ or indirect _____, and may be paid in money or as its labour equivalent (often but not always unpaid.)

   a. 130-30 fund
   b. 100-year flood
   c. 1921 recession
   d. Tax

11. In economics and finance, _____ is the change in total cost that arises when the quantity produced changes by one unit. It is the cost of producing one more unit of a good. Mathematically, the _____ function is expressed as the first derivative of the total cost (TC) function with respect to quantity (Q.)
   a. Quality costs
   b. Cost allocation
   c. Fixed costs
   d. Marginal cost

12. _____ is a practice of protecting the environment, on individual, organisational or governmental level, for the benefit of the natural environment and (or) humans.

Due to the pressures of population and technology the biophysical environment is being degraded, sometimes permanently. This has been recognised and governments began placing restraints on activities that caused environmental degradation.

a. ACCRA Cost of Living Index
b. ACEA agreement
c. AD-IA Model
d. Environmental Protection

13. A _____ is the exclusive authority to determine how a resource is used, whether that resource is owned by government or by individuals. All economic goods have a _____s attribute. This attribute has three broad components

1. The right to use the good
2. The right to earn income from the good
3. The right to transfer the good to others

The concept of _____s as used by economists and legal scholars are related but distinct. The distinction is largely seen in the economists' focus on the ability of an individual or collective to control the use of the good.

a. Greenfield agreement
b. Nature of the Firm
c. Judgment summons
d. Property right

14. The _____ is the apparent contradiction that although water is on the whole more useful, in terms of survival, than diamonds, diamonds command a higher price in the market. The economist Adam Smith is often considered to be the classic presenter of this paradox. Nicolaus Copernicus, John Locke, John Law and others had previously tried to explain the disparity.

a. Paradox of value
b. 100-year flood
c. 130-30 fund
d. St. Petersburg paradox

15. _____ is a type of trade policy that allows traders to act and transact without interference from government. Thus, the policy permits trading partners mutual gains from trade, with goods and services produced according to the theory of comparative advantage.

Under a _____ policy, prices are a reflection of true supply and demand, and are the sole determinant of resource allocation.

a. 130-30 fund
b. Free Trade
c. 1921 recession
d. 100-year flood

16. The _____ is a trilateral trade bloc in North America created by the governments of the United States, Canada, and Mexico. The agreement creating the trade bloc came into force on January 1, 1994. It superseded the Canada-United States Free Trade Agreement between the U.S. and Canada.

a. North American Free Trade Agreement
b. Guaranteed investment contracts
c. Dividend unit
d. Hybrid renewable energy systems

17. In economics and related disciplines, a _____ is a cost incurred in making an economic exchange. For example, most people, when buying or selling a stock, must pay a commission to their broker; that commission is a _____ of doing the stock deal. Or consider buying a banana from a store; to purchase the banana, your costs will be not only the price of the banana itself, but also the energy and effort it requires to find out which of the various banana products you prefer, where to get them and at what price, the cost of traveling from your house to the store and back, the time waiting in line, and the effort of the paying itself; the costs above and beyond the cost of the banana are the _____s.

a. Cost allocation
b. Psychic cost
c. Total absorption costing
d. Transaction cost

18. _____ is money accepted for exchange of goods in an economy. The prevalence of one money over another arises, usually, when a government designates through decrees that the government shall accept only particular notes and coins in payment for taxes. Typically, money of _____ consists of stamped coins and minted paper bills.
a. Security thread
b. Currency
c. Totnes pound
d. Scripophily

19. _____ is a reduction in the value of a currency with respect to other monetary units. In common modern usage, it specifically implies an official lowering of the value of a country's currency within a fixed exchange rate system, by which the monetary authority formally sets a new fixed rate with respect to a foreign reference currency. In contrast, (currency) depreciation is used for the unofficial decrease in the exchange rate in a floating exchange rate system.
a. Reserve currency
b. Dollarization
c. Devaluation
d. Petrodollar

20. _____ is the act of taking an industry or assets into the public ownership of a national government or state. _____ usually refers to private assets, but may also mean assets owned by lower levels of government, such as municipalities, being state operated or owned by the state. The opposite of _____ is usually privatization or de-nationalisation, but may also be municipalization.
a. Quasi-market
b. Ricardian equivalence
c. Municipalization
d. Nationalization

21. _____ is a misspelled phrase from Latin 'pro capite' phrase meaning per head with pro meaning 'per' or 'for each' and capite meaning 'head.' Both words together equate to the phrase 'for each head.'

It is usually used in the field of statistics to indicate the average per person for any given concern, such as income, crime rate, etc.

It is also used in wills to indicate that each of the named beneficiaries should receive, by devise or bequest, equal shares of the estate. This is in contrast to a per stirpes division, in which each branch of the inheriting family inherits an equal share of the estate.

a. Posterior probability
b. Dynamic Bayesian network
c. Per capita
d. Semiparametric regression

22. _____ is a common concept in economics, and gives rise to derived concepts such as consumer debt. Generally _____ is defined by opposition to production. But the precise definition can vary because different schools of economists define production quite differently.
a. Basis of futures
b. Consumption
c. British canal system
d. Discrete choice

23. In economics, and cost accounting, _____ describes the total economic cost of production and is made up of variable costs, which vary according to the quantity of a good produced and include inputs such as labor and raw materials, plus fixed costs, which are independent of the quantity of a good produced and include inputs (capital) that cannot be varied in the short term, such as buildings and machinery. _____ in economics includes the total opportunity cost of each factor of production in addition to fixed and variable costs.

The rate at which _____ changes as the amount produced changes is called marginal cost.

   a. 1921 recession
   c. 100-year flood
   b. 130-30 fund
   d. Total Cost

24. _____ is the increase in the amount of the goods and services produced by an economy over time. It is conventionally measured as the percent rate of increase in real gross domestic product, or real GDP. Growth is usually calculated in real terms, i.e. inflation-adjusted terms, in order to net out the effect of inflation on the price of the goods and services produced.

   a. ACCRA Cost of Living Index
   c. Economic growth
   b. AD-IA Model
   d. ACEA agreement

25. The term _____ is applied broadly to a variety of situations in which some financial institutions or assets suddenly lose a large part of their value. In the 19th and early 20th centuries, many financial crises were associated with banking panics, and many recessions coincided with these panics. Other situations that are often called financial crises include stock market crashes and the bursting of other financial bubbles, currency crises, and sovereign defaults.

   a. Mercantilism
   c. Market failure
   b. Literacy rate
   d. Financial crisis

26. A _____ is a situation that involves losing one quality or aspect of something in return for gaining another quality or aspect. It implies a decision to be made with full comprehension of both the upside and downside of a particular choice.

In economics the term is expressed as opportunity cost, referring the most preferred alternative given up.

   a. Capital outflow
   c. Market microstructure
   b. Trade-off
   d. Stylized fact

27. _____s (economically referred to as land or raw materials) occur naturally within environments that exist relatively undisturbed by mankind, in a natural form. A _____'s is often characterized by amounts of biodiversity existent in various ecosystems.

Mining, petroleum extraction, fishing, hunting, and forestry are generally considered natural-resource industries.

   a. 130-30 fund
   c. 100-year flood
   b. Natural resource
   d. 1921 recession

28. _____ involves processing used materials into new products in order to prevent waste of potentially useful materials, reduce the consumption of fresh raw materials, reduce energy usage, reduce air pollution (from incineration) and water pollution (from landfilling) by reducing the need for 'conventional' waste disposal, and lower greenhouse gas emissions as compared to virgin production. _____ is a key component of modern waste management and is the third component of the 'Reduce, Reuse, Recycle' waste hierarchy.

Recyclable materials include many kinds of glass, paper, metal, plastic, textiles, and electronics.

a. Blotto game
c. Human rights
b. Demographics of India
d. Recycling

29. _____ is a fee paid on borrowed assets. It is the price paid for the use of borrowed money , or, money earned by deposited funds . Assets that are sometimes lent with _____ include money, shares, consumer goods through hire purchase, major assets such as aircraft, and even entire factories in finance lease arrangements.

a. Internal debt
c. Asset protection
b. Insolvency
d. Interest

30. _____ in economics and business is the result of an exchange and from that trade we assign a numerical monetary value to a good, service or asset. If Alice trades Bob 4 apples for an orange, the _____ of an orange is 4 apples. Inversely, the _____ of an apple is 1/4 oranges.

a. Price dispersion
c. Price ceiling
b. Lerner Index
d. Price

Chapter 32. Comparative Advantage and the Open Economy

1. _____s is the social science that studies the production, distribution, and consumption of goods and services. The term _____s comes from the Ancient Greek οá¼°κονομῖα from οá¼¶κος (oikos, 'house') + vϊŒμος (nomos, 'custom' or 'law'), hence 'rules of the house(hold)'. Current _____ models developed out of the broader field of political economy in the late 19th century, owing to a desire to use an empirical approach more akin to the physical sciences.
   a. Inflation
   b. Economic
   c. Energy economics
   d. Opportunity cost

2. The _____ is an economic and political union of 27 member states, located primarily in Europe. It was established by the Treaty of Maastricht on 1 November 1993, upon the foundations of the pre-existing European Economic Community. With a population of almost 500 million, the _____ generates an estimated 30% share (US$18.4 trillion in 2008) of the nominal gross world product.
   a. ACEA agreement
   b. European Court of Justice
   c. European Union
   d. ACCRA Cost of Living Index

3. _____ is a type of trade policy that allows traders to act and transact without interference from government. Thus, the policy permits trading partners mutual gains from trade, with goods and services produced according to the theory of comparative advantage.

   Under a _____ policy, prices are a reflection of true supply and demand, and are the sole determinant of resource allocation.
   a. 100-year flood
   b. 130-30 fund
   c. 1921 recession
   d. Free Trade

4. The _____ is a trilateral trade bloc in North America created by the governments of the United States, Canada, and Mexico. The agreement creating the trade bloc came into force on January 1, 1994. It superseded the Canada-United States Free Trade Agreement between the U.S. and Canada.
   a. Dividend unit
   b. Hybrid renewable energy systems
   c. Guaranteed investment contracts
   d. North American Free Trade Agreement

5. In economics, _____ refers to the ability of a person or a country to produce a particular good at a lower marginal cost and opportunity cost than another person or country. It is the ability to produce a product most efficiently given all the other products that could be produced. It can be contrasted with absolute advantage which refers to the ability of a person or a country to produce a particular good at a lower absolute cost than another.
   a. Small open economy
   b. Financial export
   c. Dutch disease
   d. Comparative advantage

6. In economics, an _____ is any good (e.g. a commodity) or service brought into one country from another country in a legitimate fashion, typically for use in trade.It is a good that is brought in from another country for sale. _____ goods or services are provided to domestic consumers by foreign producers. An _____ in the receiving country is an export to the sending country.
   a. Import quota
   b. Incoterms
   c. Economic integration
   d. Import

7. _____ is exchange of capital, goods, and services across international borders or territories. In most countries, it represents a significant share of gross domestic product (GDP.) While _____ has been present throughout much of history , its economic, social, and political importance has been on the rise in recent centuries.

a. International trade
b. Incoterms
c. Intra-industry trade
d. Import license

8. The _____ is the largest national economy in the world. Its gross domestic product (GDP) was estimated as $14.2 trillion in 2008. The U.S. economy maintains a high level of output per person (GDP per capita, $46,800 in 2008, ranked at around number ten in the world.)
   a. AD-IA Model
   b. ACCRA Cost of Living Index
   c. ACEA agreement
   d. Economy of the United States

9. In economics, an _____ is any good or commodity, transported from one country to another country in a legitimate fashion, typically for use in trade. _____ goods or services are provided to foreign consumers by domestic producers. _____ is an important part of international trade.
   a. AD-IA Model
   b. ACEA agreement
   c. Export
   d. ACCRA Cost of Living Index

10. In economics, _____ refers to the ability of a party to produce a good or service using fewer real resources than another entity producing the same good or service..A party has an _____ when using the same input as another party, it can produce a greater output. Since _____ is determined by a simple comparison of labor productivities, it is possible for a a party to have no _____ in anything. It can be contrasted with the concept of comparative advantage which refers to the ability to produce a particular good at a lower opportunity cost.
   a. Index number
   b. International economics
   c. Absolute advantage
   d. ACCRA Cost of Living Index

11. _____ or economic opportunity loss is the value of the next best alternative foregone as the result of making a decision. _____ analysis is an important part of a company's decision-making processes but is not treated as an actual cost in any financial statement. The next best thing that a person can engage in is referred to as the _____ of doing the best thing and ignoring the next best thing to be done.
   a. Economic
   b. Industrial organization
   c. Economic ideology
   d. Opportunity cost

12. _____ are legal property rights over creations of the mind, both artistic and commercial, and the corresponding fields of law. Under _____ law, owners are granted certain exclusive rights to a variety of intangible assets, such as musical, literary, and artistic works; ideas, discoveries and inventions; and words, phrases, symbols, and designs. Common types of _____ include copyrights, trademarks, patents, industrial design rights and trade secrets.
   a. Ease of Doing Business Index
   b. Expedited Funds Availability Act
   c. Independent contractor
   d. Intellectual property

13. _____ is that which is owed; usually referencing assets owed, but the term can also cover moral obligations and other interactions not requiring money. In the case of assets, _____ is a means of using future purchasing power in the present before a summation has been earned. Some companies and corporations use _____ as a part of their overall corporate finance strategy.
   a. Non-performing loan
   b. Subordinated debt
   c. Debt
   d. Participation loan

14. _____ according to Onuoha (2007) is the practice of starting new organizations or revitalizing mature organizations, particularly new businesses generally in response to identified opportunities. _____ is often a difficult undertaking, as a vast majority of new businesses fail. Entrepreneurial activities are substantially different depending on the type of organization that is being started.
   a. Entrepreneurship
   b. ACEA agreement
   c. Intrapreneurship
   d. ACCRA Cost of Living Index

15. The _____ is a region that spans southwestern Asia and northeastern Africa. It has no clear boundaries, often used as a synonym to Near East, in opposition to Far East. The term '_____' was popularized around 1900 in the United Kingdom.
   a. 130-30 fund
   b. Middle East
   c. 100-year flood
   d. 1921 recession

16. _____ is a comparative concept of the ability and performance of a firm, sub-sector or country to sell and supply goods and/or services in a given market. Although widely used in economics and business management, the usefulness of the concept, particularly in the context of national _____, is vigorously disputed by economists, such as Paul Krugman.

The term may also be applied to markets, where it is used to refer to the extent to which the market structure may be regarded as perfectly competitive.

   a. Market access
   b. Kennedy Round
   c. Competitiveness
   d. Mutual recognition agreement

17. _____ occurs when the economy is operating at its production possibility frontier (PPF.) This takes place when production of one good is achieved at the lowest cost possible, given the production of the other good(s.) Equivalently, it is when the highest possible output of one good is produced, given the production level of the other good(s.)
   a. Lean consumption
   b. Fixed exchange rate system
   c. Recursive economics
   d. Productive efficiency

18. The _____ is an economic reason for protectionism. The crux of the argument is that nascent industries often do not have the economies of scale that their older competitors from other countries may have, and thus need to be protected until they can attain similar economies of scale. It was first used by Alexander Hamilton in 1790 and later by Friedrich List, in 1841, to support protection for German manufacturing against British industry.
   a. ACCRA Cost of Living Index
   b. AD-IA Model
   c. Infant industry argument
   d. ACEA agreement

19. In economics, the _____ of an industry is used as an indicator of the relative size of firms in relation to the industry as a whole. It is calculated as the sum of the percent market share of the top n industries. This may also assist in determining the market structure of the industry.
   a. De facto monopoly
   b. Concentration ratio
   c. Price takers
   d. Rate-of-return regulation

20. A _____ is an expression that compares quantities relative to each other. The most common examples involve two quantities, but any number of quantities can be compared. _____s are represented mathematically by separating each quantity with a colon, for example the _____ 2:3, which is read as the _____ 'two to three'.

Chapter 32. Comparative Advantage and the Open Economy

a. Y-intercept
c. 130-30 fund
b. 100-year flood
d. Ratio

21. _____ is the branch of economics that incorporates value judgments (that is, normative judgements) about what the economy ought to be like or what particular policy actions ought to be recommended to achieve a desirable goal. _____ looks at the desirability of certain aspects of the economy. It underlies expressions of support for particular economic policies.
   a. Broad money
   c. Normative economics
   b. Bord halfpenny
   d. Buy-side analyst

22. _____ is the development of economic wealth of countries or regions for the well-being of their inhabitants. It is the process by which a nation improves the economic, political, and social well being of its people. From a policy perspective, _____ can be defined as efforts that seek to improve the economic well-being and quality of life for a community by creating and/or retaining jobs and supporting or growing incomes and the tax base.
   a. Experimental economics
   c. Inflation
   b. Economic methodology
   d. Economic development

23. _____ is a branch of economics with three main subdisciplines international trade, monetary economics and international finance.

   - International trade studies goods-and-services flows across international boundaries from supply-and-demand factors, economic integration, and policy variables such as tariff rates and trade quotas.
   - International finance studies the flow of capital across international financial markets, and the effects of these movements on exchange rates.
   - International monetary economics and macroeconomics studies money and macro flows across countries.
   - Stanley W. Black (2008.) 'international monetary institutions,' The New Palgrave Dictionary of Economics. 2nd Edition.

   a. Index number
   c. Economic depreciation
   b. ACCRA Cost of Living Index
   d. International Economics

24. A _____ is a duty imposed on goods when they are moved across a political boundary. They are usually associated with protectionism, the economic policy of restraining trade between nations. For political reasons, _____s are usually imposed on imported goods, although they may also be imposed on exported goods.
   a. Tariff
   c. 130-30 fund
   b. 1921 recession
   d. 100-year flood

25. The _____ is a term used for industries primarily concerned with the design or manufacture of clothing as well as the distribution and use of textiles.

Prior to the manufacturing processes were mechanized, textiles were produced in the home, and excess sold for extra money. Most cloth was made from either wool, cotton, or flax, depending on the era and location.

   a. 100-year flood
   c. Textile manufacture during the Industrial Revolution
   b. Textile industry
   d. 130-30 fund

Chapter 32. Comparative Advantage and the Open Economy

26. A _____, reserve bank, or monetary authority is the entity responsible for the monetary policy of a country or of a group of member states. It is a bank that can lend money to other banks in times of need. Its primary responsibility is to maintain the stability of the national currency and money supply, but more active duties include controlling subsidized-loan interest rates, and acting as a lender of last resort to the banking sector during times of financial crisis (private banks often being integral to the national financial system.)
   a. 130-30 fund
   b. 1921 recession
   c. 100-year flood
   d. Central bank

27. The General Agreement on Tariffs and Trade was the outcome of the failure of negotiating governments to create the International Trade Organization (ITO.) _____ was formed in 1947 and lasted until 1994, when it was replaced by the World Trade Organization. The Bretton Woods Conference had introduced the idea for an organization to regulate trade as part of a larger plan for economic recovery after World War II.
   a. Dutch-Scandinavian Economic Pact
   b. General Agreement on Tariffs and Trade
   c. General Agreement on Trade in Services
   d. GATT

28. The _____ of 1974 (actually enacted January 3, 1975 as Pub.L. 93-618, 88 Stat. 1978, 19 U.S.C. ch.12) was passed to help industry in the United States become more competitive or phase workers into other industries or occupations. It created fast track authority for the President to negotiate trade agreements that Congress can approve or disapprove but cannot amend or filibuster. The fast track authority created under the Act extended to 1994 and was restored in 2002 by the _____ of 2002.
   a. 1921 recession
   b. Trade Act
   c. 130-30 fund
   d. 100-year flood

29. The _____ was the outcome of the failure of negotiating governments to create the International Trade Organization (ITO.) GATT was formed in 1947 and lasted until 1994, when it was replaced by the World Trade Organization. The Bretton Woods Conference had introduced the idea for an organization to regulate trade as part of a larger plan for economic recovery after World War II.
   a. GATT
   b. General Agreement on Tariffs and Trade
   c. Dutch-Scandinavian Economic Pact
   d. General Agreement on Trade in Services

30. The _____ was an act signed into law on June 17, 1930, that raised U.S. tariffs on over 20,000 imported goods to record levels. In the United States 1,028 economists signed a petition against this legislation, and after it was passed, many countries retaliated with their own increased tariffs on U.S. goods, and American exports and imports were reduced by more than half.

Although rated capacity had increased tremendously, actual output, income, and expenditure had not.

   a. Napoleonic code
   b. Due diligence
   c. Smoot-Hawley Tariff Act
   d. Competition law

31. The _____ commenced in September 1986 and continued until April 1994. The round, based on the General Agreement on Tariffs and Trade (GATT) ministerial meeting in Geneva (1982), was launched in Punta del Este in Uruguay (hence the name), followed by negotiations in Montreal, Geneva, Brussels, Washington, D.C., and Tokyo, with the 20 agreements finally being signed in Marrakech - the Marrakesh Agreement. The Round transformed the GATT into the World Trade Organization.

a. ACCRA Cost of Living Index
b. Uruguay Round
c. AD-IA Model
d. ACEA agreement

32. The _____ is an important selective, mainly private, international organization designed by its founders to supervise and liberalize international trade. The organization officially commenced on 1 January 1995, under the Marrakesh Agreement, succeeding the 1947 General Agreement on Tariffs and Trade (GATT.)

The _____ deals with regulation of trade between participating countries; it provides a framework for negotiating and formalising trade agreements, and a dispute resolution process aimed at enforcing participants' adherence to _____ agreements which are signed by representatives of member governments and ratified by their parliaments.

a. Differences in Differences
b. Blotto game
c. Differential games
d. World Trade Organization

33. _____ is a Regional Trade Agreement among Argentina, Brazil, Paraguay and Uruguay founded in 1991 by the Treaty of Asunci>ón, which was later amended and updated by the 1994 Treaty of Ouro Preto. Its purpose is to promote free trade and the fluid movement of goods, people, and currency.

_____ origins trace back to 1985 when Presidents Ra>úl Alfons>ín of Argentina and Jos>é Sarney of Brazil signed the Argentina-Brazil Integration and Economics Cooperation Program or PICE .

a. 100-year flood
b. 130-30 fund
c. Free trade area
d. Mercosur

34. In economics, _____ is a measure of the relative satisfaction from consumption of various goods and services. Given this measure, one may speak meaningfully of increasing or decreasing _____, and thereby explain economic behavior in terms of attempts to increase one's _____. For illustrative purposes, changes in _____ are sometimes expressed in units called utils.

a. Expected utility hypothesis
b. Utility function
c. Ordinal utility
d. Utility

Chapter 33. Exchange Rates and the Balance of Payments

1. A _____, reserve bank, or monetary authority is the entity responsible for the monetary policy of a country or of a group of member states. It is a bank that can lend money to other banks in times of need. Its primary responsibility is to maintain the stability of the national currency and money supply, but more active duties include controlling subsidized-loan interest rates, and acting as a lender of last resort to the banking sector during times of financial crisis (private banks often being integral to the national financial system.)
   - a. 1921 recession
   - b. 130-30 fund
   - c. 100-year flood
   - d. Central Bank

2. The _____ is one of the world's most important central banks, responsible for monetary policy covering the 16 member States of the Eurozone. It was established by the European Union (EU) in 1998 with its headquarters in Frankfurt, Germany.

   The predecessor to the _____ was the European Monetary Institute.

   - a. ACCRA Cost of Living Index
   - b. ACEA agreement
   - c. AD-IA Model
   - d. European Central Bank

3. _____ is sometimes referred to as _____, actually it means Economic Monetary Union.

   First ideas of an economic and monetary union in Europe were raised well before establishing the European Communities. For example, already in the League of Nations, Gustav Stresemann asked in 1929 for a European currency (Link) against the background of an increased economic division due to a number of new nation states in Europe after WWI.

   - a. European Monetary System
   - b. Exchange rate mechanism
   - c. European Monetary Union
   - d. Euro Interbank Offered Rate

4. The _____ is an economic and political union of 27 member states, located primarily in Europe. It was established by the Treaty of Maastricht on 1 November 1993, upon the foundations of the pre-existing European Economic Community. With a population of almost 500 million, the _____ generates an estimated 30% share (US$18.4 trillion in 2008) of the nominal gross world product.
   - a. European Union
   - b. European Court of Justice
   - c. ACEA agreement
   - d. ACCRA Cost of Living Index

5. An economic and _____ is a single market with a common currency. It is to be distinguished from a mere currency union, which does not involve a single market. This is the fifth stage of economic integration.
   - a. Green market
   - b. Certificate of origin
   - c. Metzler paradox
   - d. Monetary Union

6. The _____ is the official currency of 16 of the 27 member states of the European Union (EU.) The states, known collectively as the Eurozone, are Austria, Belgium, Cyprus, Finland, France, Germany, Greece, Ireland, Italy, Luxembourg, Malta, the Netherlands, Portugal, Slovakia, Slovenia, and Spain. The currency is also used in a further five European countries, with and without formal agreements and is consequently used daily by some 327 million Europeans.
   - a. IRS Code 3401
   - b. Equity capital market
   - c. Import and Export Price Indices
   - d. Euro

Chapter 33. Exchange Rates and the Balance of Payments

7. _____ in economics and business is the result of an exchange and from that trade we assign a numerical monetary value to a good, service or asset. If Alice trades Bob 4 apples for an orange, the _____ of an orange is 4 apples. Inversely, the _____ of an apple is 1/4 oranges.
   a. Price
   b. Price dispersion
   c. Price ceiling
   d. Lerner Index

8. In economics, the _____ measures the payments that flow between any individual country and all other countries. It is used to summarize all international economic transactions for that country during a specific time period, usually a year. The _____ is determined by the country's exports and imports of goods, services, and financial capital, as well as financial transfers.
   a. Skyscraper Index
   b. Purchasing power parity
   c. Balance of payments
   d. Real gross domestic product

9. The _____ is the difference between the monetary value of exports and imports in an economy over a certain period of time. It is the relationship between a nation's imports and exports. A positive _____ is known as a trade surplus and consists of exporting more than is imported; a negative _____ is known as a trade deficit or, informally, a trade gap.
   a. Technology shock
   b. Rational expectations
   c. Lucas-Islands model
   d. Balance of trade

10. _____ is money accepted for exchange of goods in an economy. The prevalence of one money over another arises, usually, when a government designates through decrees that the government shall accept only particular notes and coins in payment for taxes. Typically, money of _____ consists of stamped coins and minted paper bills.
    a. Totnes pound
    b. Scripophily
    c. Security thread
    d. Currency

11. _____ is a reduction in the value of a currency with respect to other monetary units. In common modern usage, it specifically implies an official lowering of the value of a country's currency within a fixed exchange rate system, by which the monetary authority formally sets a new fixed rate with respect to a foreign reference currency. In contrast, (currency) depreciation is used for the unofficial decrease in the exchange rate in a floating exchange rate system.
    a. Dollarization
    b. Devaluation
    c. Petrodollar
    d. Reserve currency

12. _____ refers to the stock of skills and knowledge embodied in the ability to perform labor so as to produce economic value. It is the skills and knowledge gained by a worker through education and experience. Many early economic theories refer to it simply as labor, one of three factors of production, and consider it to be a fungible resource -- homogeneous and easily interchangeable. Other conceptions of labor dispense with these assumptions.
    a. Labour economics
    b. Monetary inflation
    c. Monopolistic competition
    d. Human Capital

13. A _____ is the transfer of wealth from one party (such as a person or company) to another. A _____ is usually made in exchange for the provision of goods, services or both, or to fulfill a legal obligation.

The simplest and oldest form of _____ is barter, the exchange of one good or service for another.

a. Contingent payment sales
b. RFM
c. Payment
d. Hard count

14. In economics, the _____ is one of the two primary components of the balance of payments, the other being the capital account. It is the sum of the balance of trade (exports minus imports of goods and services), net factor income (such as interest and dividends) and net transfer payments (such as foreign aid.)

$$\text{Current account} = \text{Balance of trade}$$
$$+ \text{Net factor income from abroad}$$
$$+ \text{Net unilateral transfers from abroad}$$

The _____ balance is one of two major metrics of the nature of a country's foreign trade (the other being the net capital outflow.)

a. Gross private domestic investment
b. National Income and Product Accounts
c. Net national product
d. Current account

15. In economics, an _____ is any good or commodity, transported from one country to another country in a legitimate fashion, typically for use in trade. _____ goods or services are provided to foreign consumers by domestic producers. _____ is an important part of international trade.

a. Export
b. ACEA agreement
c. ACCRA Cost of Living Index
d. AD-IA Model

16. In economics, an _____ is any good (e.g. a commodity) or service brought into one country from another country in a legitimate fashion, typically for use in trade. It is a good that is brought in from another country for sale. _____ goods or services are provided to domestic consumers by foreign producers. An _____ in the receiving country is an export to the sending country.

a. Import quota
b. Import
c. Incoterms
d. Economic integration

17. A _____ is the procedure of systematically acquiring and recording information about the members of a given population. It is a regularly occurring and official count of a particular population. The term is used mostly in connection with national 'population and door to door _____es' (to be taken every 10 years according to United Nations recommendations), agriculture, and business _____es.

a. 100-year flood
b. 130-30 fund
c. Census
d. 1921 recession

18. The balance of trade (or net exports, sometimes symbolized as NX) is the difference between the monetary value of exports and imports in an economy over a certain period of time. It is the relationship between a nation's imports and exports. A favorable balance of trade is known as a trade surplus and consists of exporting more than is imported; an unfavorable balance of trade is known as a _____ or, informally, a trade gap.

a. Customer lifetime value
b. Backus-Kehoe-Kydland consumption correlation puzzle
c. Cash taxes
d. Trade deficit

19. The _____ of monetary management established the rules for commercial and financial relations among the world's major industrial states in the mid 20th Century. The _____ was the first example of a fully negotiated monetary order intended to govern monetary relations among independent nation-states.

Chapter 33. Exchange Rates and the Balance of Payments

Preparing to rebuild the international economic system as World War II was still raging, 730 delegates from all 44 Allied nations gathered at the Mount Washington Hotel in Bretton Woods, New Hampshire, United States, for the United Nations Monetary and Financial Conference.

a. 1921 recession
b. 130-30 fund
c. 100-year flood
d. Bretton Woods system

20. In financial accounting, the _____ is one of the accounts in shareholders' equity. Sole proprietorships have a single _____ in the owner's equity. Partnerships maintain a _____ for each of the partners.
    a. Current account
    b. Capital account
    c. Gross private domestic investment
    d. Compensation of employees

21. _____ are potential claims on the freely usable currencies of International Monetary Fund members. _____s have the ISO 4217 currency code XDR.

_____s are defined in terms of a basket of major currencies used in international trade and finance.

a. Common market
b. Global financial system
c. Kennedy Round
d. Special drawing rights

22. The _____, a unit of the United States Department of Labor, is the principal fact-finding agency for the U.S. government in the broad field of labor economics and statistics. The BLS is an independent national statistical agency that collects, processes, analyzes, and disseminates essential statistical data to the American public, the U.S. Congress, other Federal agencies, State and local governments, business, and labor representatives. The BLS also serves as a statistical resource to the Department of Labor.
    a. Bureau of Labor Statistics
    b. Water footprint
    c. Nonfarm payrolls
    d. Visible balance

23. _____, in economics, occurs when assets and/or money rapidly flow out of a country, due to an economic event that disturbs investors and causes them to lower their valuation of the assets in that country, or otherwise to lose confidence in its economic strength. This leads to a disappearance of wealth and is usually accompanied by a sharp drop in the exchange rate of the affected country (depreciation in a variable exchange rate regime, or a forced devaluation in a fixed exchange rate regime.)

This fall is particularly damaging when the capital belongs to the people of the affected country, because not only are the citizens now burdened by the loss of faith in the economy and devaluation of their currency, but probably also their assets have lost much of their nominal value.

a. Capital goods
b. Consumption of fixed capital
c. Capital flight
d. Capital intensity

24. The _____ is where currency trading takes place. It is where banks and other official institutions facilitate the buying and selling of foreign currencies. FX transactions typically involve one party purchasing a quantity of one currency in exchange for paying a quantity of another.

a. Continuous linked settlement
b. Foreign exchange trading
c. Foreign exchange option
d. Foreign exchange market

25. In finance, the _____s between two currencies specifies how much one currency is worth in terms of the other. It is the value of a foreign natione;s currency in terms of the home natione;s currency. For example an _____ of 102 Japanese yen to the United States dollar means that JPY 102 is worth the same as USD 1.
    a. Interbank market
    b. ACCRA Cost of Living Index
    c. ACEA agreement
    d. Exchange rate

26. Economics:

    - _____,the desire to own something and the ability to pay for it
    - _____ curve,a graphic representation of a _____ schedule
    - _____ deposit, the money in checking accounts
    - _____ pull theory,the theory that inflation occurs when _____ for goods and services exceeds existing supplies
    - _____ schedule,a table that lists the quantity of a good a person will buy it each different price
    - _____ side economics,the school of economics at believes government spending and tax cuts open economy by raising _____

    a. Bon
    b. G20
    c. Procter ' Gamble
    d. Demand

27. A _____ is an object whose consumption increases the utility of the consumer, for which the quantity demanded exceeds the quantity supplied at zero price. _____s are usually modeled as having diminishing marginal utility. The first individual purchase has high utility; the second has less.
    a. Positional goods
    b. Search good
    c. Luxury good
    d. Good

28. _____ is a term used in accounting relating to the increase in value of an asset. In this sense it is the reverse of depreciation, which measures the fall in value of assets over their normal life-time.

    _____ is a rise of a currency in a floating exchange rate.

    a. Appreciation
    b. ACCRA Cost of Living Index
    c. AD-IA Model
    d. ACEA agreement

29. _____ is a term used in accounting, economics and finance to spread the cost of an asset over the span of several years.

In simple words we can say that _____ is the reduction in the value of an asset due to usage, passage of time, wear and tear, technological outdating or obsolescence, depletion, inadequacy, rot, rust, decay or other such factors.

Chapter 33. Exchange Rates and the Balance of Payments 291

In accounting, _____ is a term used to describe any method of attributing the historical or purchase cost of an asset across its useful life, roughly corresponding to normal wear and tear.

a. Net income per employee
c. Salvage value
b. Fixed investment
d. Depreciation

30. _____ is a term in economics, where demand for one good or service occurs as a result of demand for another. This may occur as the former is a part of production of the second. For example, demand for coal leads to _____ for mining, as coal must be mined for coal to be consumed.

a. Lateral expansion
c. Situation analysis
b. Monopoly wage
d. Derived demand

31. A _____ is a tax system with a constant tax rate. Usually the term _____ would refer to household income (and sometimes corporate profits) being taxed at one marginal rate, in contrast with progressive taxes that may vary according to such parameters as income or usage levels. _____es generally offer simplicity in the tax code, which has been reported to increase compliance and decrease administration costs.

a. 1921 recession
c. 100-year flood
b. 130-30 fund
d. Flat tax

32. The _____ or gross domestic income (GDI), a basic measure of an economy's economic performance, is the market value of all final goods and services produced within the borders of a nation in a year. _____ can be defined in three ways, all of which are conceptually identical. First, it is equal to the total expenditures for all final goods and services produced within the country in a stipulated period of time (usually a 365-day year.)

a. Gross domestic product
c. Market failure
b. Co-operative economics
d. Public economics

33. To _____ is to impose a financial charge or other levy upon a taxpayer by a state or the functional equivalent of a state.

_____es are also imposed by many subnational entities. _____es consist of direct _____ or indirect _____, and may be paid in money or as its labour equivalent (often but not always unpaid.)

a. 1921 recession
c. Tax
b. 130-30 fund
d. 100-year flood

34. In economics, a _____ is a table that lists the quantity of a good a person will buy it each different price See Demand curve.

a. Rational irrationality
c. Discouraged worker
b. Dynamic efficiency
d. Demand schedule

35. In algebra, a _____ is a function depending on n that associates a scalar, det(A), to an n×n square matrix A. The fundamental geometric meaning of a _____ is a scale factor for measure when A is regarded as a linear transformation. _____s are important both in calculus, where they enter the substitution rule for several variables, and in multilinear algebra.

For a fixed nonnegative integer n, there is a unique _____ function for the n×n matrices over any commutative ring R. In particular, this function exists when R is the field of real or complex numbers.

- a. Determinant
- b. 1921 recession
- c. 100-year flood
- d. 130-30 fund

36. _____ is a broad label that refers to any individuals or households that use goods and services generated within the economy. The concept of a _____ is used in different contexts, so that the usage and significance of the term may vary.

Typically when business people and economists talk of _____s they are talking about person as _____, an aggregated commodity item with little individuality other than that expressed in the buy/not-buy decision.

- a. 1921 recession
- b. Consumer
- c. 130-30 fund
- d. 100-year flood

37. _____s is the social science that studies the production, distribution, and consumption of goods and services. The term _____s comes from the Ancient Greek oá¼°κονομῖα from oá¼¶κος (oikos, 'house') + vΐŒμος (nomos, 'custom' or 'law'), hence 'rules of the house(hold)'. Current _____ models developed out of the broader field of political economy in the late 19th century, owing to a desire to use an empirical approach more akin to the physical sciences.

- a. Economic
- b. Energy economics
- c. Inflation
- d. Opportunity cost

38. _____ refers to an absence of excessive fluctuations in the macroeconomy. An economy with fairly constant output growth and low and stable inflation would be considered economically stable. An economy with frequent large recessions, a pronounced business cycle, very high or variable inflation, or frequent financial crises would be considered economically unstable.

- a. Income effect
- b. Export subsidy
- c. Export-led growth
- d. Economic stability

39. The _____ is a monetary system in which a region's common medium of exchange are paper notes that are normally freely convertible into pre-set, fixed quantities of gold. The _____ is not currently used by any government, having been replaced completely by fiat currency. Gold certificates were used as paper currency in the United States from 1882 to 1933, these certificates were freely convertable into gold coins.

In the 1790s Britain suffered a massive shortage of silver coinage and ceased to mint larger silver coins.

- a. 1921 recession
- b. 100-year flood
- c. 130-30 fund
- d. Gold standard

40. _____ is a fee paid on borrowed assets. It is the price paid for the use of borrowed money , or, money earned by deposited funds . Assets that are sometimes lent with _____ include money, shares, consumer goods through hire purchase, major assets such as aircraft, and even entire factories in finance lease arrangements.

Chapter 33. Exchange Rates and the Balance of Payments

a. Internal debt
c. Insolvency
b. Asset protection
d. Interest

41. An _____ is the price a borrower pays for the use of money they do not own, for instance a small company might borrow from a bank to kick start their business, and the return a lender receives for deferring the use of funds, by lending it to the borrower. _____s are normally expressed as a percentage rate over the period of one year.

_____s targets are also a vital tool of monetary policy and are used to control variables like investment, inflation, and unemployment.

a. Enterprise value
c. ACCRA Cost of Living Index
b. Arrow-Debreu model
d. Interest rate

42. _____ in economics refers to metrics and measures of output from production processes, per unit of input. Labor _____, for example, is typically measured as a ratio of output per labor-hour, an input. _____ may be conceived of as a metrics of the technical or engineering efficiency of production.
a. Piece work
c. Production-possibility frontier
b. Fordism
d. Productivity

43. _____ is an online peer-reviewed magazine published by the Agricultural ' Applied Economics Association (AAEA) for readers interested in the policy and management of agriculture, the food industry, natural resources, rural communities, and the environment. _____ is published quarterly and is available free online. It is currently one of three outreach products offered by AAEA, along with the more timely Policy Issues and the forthcoming Shared Materials section of the AAEA Web site.
a. Choices
c. 100-year flood
b. 1921 recession
d. 130-30 fund

44. Preparing to rebuild the international economic system as World War II was still raging, 730 delegates from all 44 Allied nations gathered at the Mount Washington Hotel in Bretton Woods, New Hampshire, United States, for the United Nations Monetary and Financial Conference. The delegates deliberated upon and signed the _____ during the first three weeks of July 1944.

Setting up a system of rules, institutions, and procedures to regulate the international monetary system, the planners at Bretton Woods established the International Monetary Fund (IMF) and the International Bank for Reconstruction and Development (IBRD), which today is part of the World Bank Group.

a. Dromography
c. Bretton Woods Agreements
b. Commercial Revolution
d. Celtic Tiger

45. _____ is the a method of technical and economic research of the systems for purpose to optimize a parity between system's consumer functions or properties and expenses to achieve those functions or properties.

Chapter 33. Exchange Rates and the Balance of Payments

This methodology for continuous perfection of production, industrial technologies, organizational structures was developed by Juryj Sobolev in 1948 at the 'Perm telephone factory'

- 1948 Juryj Sobolev - the first success in application of a method analysis at the 'Perm telephone factory'.
- 1949 - the first application for the invention as result of use of the new method.

Today in economically developed countries practically each enterprise or the company use methodology of the kind of functional-cost analysis as a practice of the quality management, most full satisfying to principles of standards of series ISO 9000.

- Interest of consumer not in products itself, but the advantage which it will receive from its usage.
- The consumer aspires to reduce his expenses
- Functions needed by consumer can be executed in the various ways, and, hence, with various efficiency and expenses. Among possible alternatives of realization of functions exist such in which the parity of quality and the price is the optimal for the consumer.

The goal of _____ is achievement of the highest consumer satisfaction of production at simultaneous decrease in all kinds of industrial expenses Classical _____ has three English synonyms - Value Engineering, Value Management, Value Analysis.

a. Residual value
b. Real net output ratio
c. Monopoly wage
d. Function cost analysis

46. A _____, sometimes called a pegged exchange rate, is a type of exchange rate regime wherein a currency's value is matched to the value of another single currency or to a basket of other currencies such as gold.

A _____ is usually used to stabilize the value of a currency, vis-a-vis the currency it is pegged to. This facilitates trade and investments between the two countries, and is especially useful for small economies where external trade forms a large part of their GDP.

a. Human capital
b. Price theory
c. Leading indicators
d. Fixed exchange rate

47. A _____ or a flexible exchange rate is a type of exchange rate regime wherein a currency's value is allowed to fluctuate according to the foreign exchange market. A currency that uses a _____ is known as a floating currency. The opposite of a _____ is a fixed exchange rate.

a. Percentage in point
b. Floating exchange rate
c. Covered interest arbitrage
d. Foreign exchange trading

48. In economics, _____ refers to any price or value expressed in money of the day, as opposed to real value, which adjusts for the effect of inflation. Examples include a bundle of commodities, such as gross domestic product, and income. For a series of _____s in successive years, different values could be because of differences in the price level, an index of prices.

Chapter 33. Exchange Rates and the Balance of Payments

a. Law of comparative advantage
c. Perfect competition
b. Human capital
d. Nominal Value

49. _____ in a strict sense are only the foreign currency deposits and bonds held by central banks and monetary authorities. However, the term in popular usage commonly includes foreign exchange and gold, SDRs and IMF reserve positions. This broader figure is more readily available, but it is more accurately termed official international reserves or international reserves.

a. Percentage in point
c. Spot market
b. Currency swap
d. Foreign exchange reserves

50. A _____ is a foreign exchange agreement between two parties to exchange principal and fixed rate interest payments on a loan in one currency for principal and fixed rate interest payments on an equal (regarding net present value) loan in another currency. _____s are motivated by comparative advantage. _____s were introduced by the World Bank in 1981 to obtain Swiss franks and German marks by exchanging cash flows with IBM.

a. Strong dollar policy
c. Foreign exchange spot trading
b. Currency swap
d. Foreign exchange option

51. _____ is a form of risk that arises from the change in price of one currency against another. Whenever investors or companies have assets or business operations across national borders, they face _____ if their positions are not hedged.

- Transaction risk is the risk that exchange rates will change unfavourably over time. It can be hedged against using forward currency contracts;
- Translation risk is an accounting risk, proportional to the amount of assets held in foreign currencies. Changes in the exchange rate over time will render a report inaccurate, and so assets are usually balanced by borrowings in that currency.

The exchange risk associated with a foreign denominated instrument is a key element in foreign investment. This risk flows from differential monetary policy and growth in real productivity, which results in differential inflation rates.

a. Risk neutral
c. Transaction risk
b. Currency risk
d. Taleb distribution

52. The _____ is an international organization that oversees the global financial system by following the macroeconomic policies of its member countries, in particular those with an impact on exchange rates and the balance of payments. It is an organization formed to stabilize international exchange rates and facilitate development. It also offers financial and technical assistance to its members, making it an international lender of last resort.

a. International Monetary Fund
c. ACEA agreement
b. ACCRA Cost of Living Index
d. Office of Thrift Supervision

53. The _____ is the central banking system of the United States. Created in 1913 by the enactment of the Federal Reserve Act (signed by Woodrow Wilson), it is a quasi-public and quasi-private (government entity with private components) banking system that comprises (1) the presidentially appointed Board of Governors of the _____ in Washington, D.C.; (2) the Federal Open Market Committee; (3) twelve regional Federal Reserve Banks located in major cities throughout the nation acting as fiscal agents for the U.S. Treasury, each with its own nine-member board of directors; (4) numerous other private U.S. member banks, which subscribe to required amounts of non-transferable stock in their regional Federal Reserve Banks; and (5) various advisory councils. Since February 2006, Ben Bernanke has served as the Chairman of the Board of Governors of the _____.

   a. Federal Reserve Transparency Act   b. Federal Reserve System
   c. Federal Reserve Banks   d. Federal funds rate

54. _____ is that which is owed; usually referencing assets owed, but the term can also cover moral obligations and other interactions not requiring money. In the case of assets, _____ is a means of using future purchasing power in the present before a summation has been earned. Some companies and corporations use _____ as a part of their overall corporate finance strategy.

   a. Non-performing loan   b. Subordinated debt
   c. Participation loan   d. Debt

55. A _____ is a monetary authority which is required to maintain a fixed exchange rate with a foreign currency. This policy objective requires the conventional objectives of a central bank to be subordinated to the exchange rate target.

The main qualities of an orthodox _____ are:

- A _____'s foreign currency reserves must be sufficient to ensure that all holders of its notes and coins (and all banks creditor of a Reserve Account at the _____) can convert them into the reserve currency (usually 110-115% of the monetary base M0.)
- A _____ maintains absolute, unlimited convertibility between its notes and coins and the currency against which they are pegged (the anchor currency), at a fixed rate of exchange, with no restrictions on current-account or capital-account transactions.
- A _____ only earns profit from interests on foreign reserves (less the expense of note-issuing), and does not engage in forward-exchange transactions. These foreign reserves exist (1) because local notes have been issued in exchange, or (2) because commercial banks must by regulation deposit a minimum reserve at the _____. (1) generates a seignorage revenue. (2) is the revenue on minimum reserves (revenue of investment activities less cost of minimum reserves remuneration)
- A _____ has no discretionary powers to effect monetary policy and does not lend to the government. Governments cannot print money, and can only tax or borrow to meet their spending commitments.
- A _____ does not act as a lender of last resort to commercial banks, and does not regulate reserve requirements.
- A _____ does not attempt to manipulate interest rates by establishing a discount rate like a central bank. The peg with the foreign currency tends to keep interest rates and inflation very closely aligned to those in the country against whose currency the peg is fixed.

The _____ in question will no longer issue fiat money but instead will only issue one unit of local currency for each unit (or decided amount) of foreign currency it has in its vault (often a hard currency such as the U.S. dollar or the euro.) The surplus on the balance of payments of that country is reflected by higher deposits local banks hold at the central bank as well as (initially) higher deposits of the (net) exporting firms at their local banks.

a. Hard currency
b. Devaluation
c. World currency
d. Currency board

56. _____ occurs when the inhabitants of a country use foreign currency in parallel to or instead of the domestic currency.

_____ can occur

- unofficially, when private agents prefer the foreign currency over the domestic currency. They hold for example deposits in the foreign currency because of a bad track record of the local currency.
- semiofficially (or officially bimonetary systems), where foreign currency is legal tender, but plays a secondary role to domestic currency
- officially, when a country ceases to issue the domestic currency and uses only foreign currency. It adopts the foreign currency as legal tender.

The term _____ is not only applied to usage of the United States dollar, but also generally to the use of any foreign currency as the national currency.

a. Currency competition
b. Dollarization
c. Hard currency
d. Fiat money

Chapter 1
1. d	2. a	3. c	4. b	5. a	6. d	7. a	8. c	9. d	10. c
11. b	12. d	13. d	14. d	15. d	16. d	17. d	18. d	19. d	20. d
21. c	22. c	23. a	24. d	25. d	26. d	27. d	28. b	29. a	30. a

Chapter 2
1. b	2. d	3. b	4. d	5. d	6. c	7. c	8. b	9. d	10. d
11. b	12. b	13. b	14. d	15. d	16. d	17. d	18. d	19. b	20. d
21. b	22. a	23. a	24. d	25. c	26. d	27. c	28. a	29. d	30. b
31. c	32. b	33. b	34. d	35. c	36. c	37. b	38. d	39. b	40. c
41. d	42. d	43. d	44. d	45. d	46. b	47. d	48. d	49. b	

Chapter 3
1. b	2. c	3. d	4. b	5. d	6. a	7. b	8. c	9. a	10. d
11. c	12. d	13. d	14. a	15. c	16. d	17. d	18. a	19. d	20. d
21. d	22. b	23. d	24. d	25. d	26. d	27. b	28. d	29. c	30. d
31. d	32. d	33. b	34. a	35. c	36. b	37. c	38. d	39. c	40. b
41. b	42. a								

Chapter 4
1. d	2. b	3. c	4. b	5. d	6. d	7. a	8. c	9. d	10. b
11. d	12. a	13. a	14. c	15. d	16. d	17. d	18. d	19. d	20. b
21. c	22. c	23. d	24. b	25. d	26. c	27. d	28. b	29. b	30. d

Chapter 5
1. a	2. b	3. a	4. c	5. d	6. d	7. d	8. a	9. d	10. d
11. d	12. d	13. d	14. b	15. a	16. a	17. d	18. d	19. d	20. b
21. d	22. d	23. c	24. d	25. a	26. a	27. d	28. a	29. d	30. a
31. b	32. d	33. d	34. a	35. a	36. b	37. d	38. d	39. d	40. a
41. d	42. d	43. c	44. d	45. c	46. d	47. b	48. b	49. d	50. a
51. d	52. a	53. d	54. d	55. d	56. b	57. d	58. b	59. a	60. c
61. b	62. d	63. d	64. b						

Chapter 6
1. d	2. b	3. d	4. b	5. c	6. d	7. d	8. b	9. d	10. c
11. d	12. d	13. d	14. b	15. c	16. d	17. b	18. b	19. b	20. c
21. d	22. c	23. a	24. b	25. d	26. d	27. c	28. d	29. d	

Chapter 7
1. d	2. d	3. b	4. c	5. d	6. b	7. d	8. d	9. b	10. d
11. b	12. d	13. d	14. d	15. d	16. d	17. a	18. b	19. d	20. a
21. d	22. d	23. d	24. d	25. a	26. a	27. a	28. c	29. d	30. b
31. b	32. d	33. b	34. b	35. d	36. d	37. d	38. a	39. d	40. d
41. b	42. b	43. c	44. a	45. d	46. c	47. b			

ANSWER KEY

Chapter 8

1. d	2. c	3. b	4. a	5. d	6. d	7. c	8. d	9. b	10. d
11. b	12. b	13. c	14. a	15. d	16. a	17. d	18. d	19. d	20. d
21. c	22. a	23. d	24. d	25. b	26. d	27. b	28. d	29. d	30. d
31. b	32. d	33. d	34. c	35. d	36. d	37. d	38. d	39. d	40. d
41. d	42. b	43. c	44. d	45. d	46. c	47. a	48. d	49. c	50. d
51. a	52. d	53. d	54. d	55. d	56. d	57. a	58. d	59. d	60. d
61. a	62. d	63. a	64. d	65. b	66. a	67. d	68. d	69. b	

Chapter 9

1. c	2. b	3. b	4. d	5. c	6. d	7. d	8. d	9. d	10. d
11. a	12. b	13. c	14. d	15. b	16. d	17. b	18. b	19. d	20. d
21. d	22. d	23. d	24. d	25. d	26. d	27. c	28. c	29. b	30. d
31. d	32. a	33. d	34. b	35. d	36. d	37. d	38. d	39. d	40. d
41. b	42. d	43. d	44. d	45. c	46. b	47. d	48. b	49. d	50. a
51. d	52. d	53. b	54. d						

Chapter 10

1. d	2. c	3. c	4. d	5. c	6. d	7. b	8. b	9. a	10. d
11. a	12. d	13. c	14. d	15. d	16. d	17. d	18. a	19. d	20. c
21. b	22. b	23. a	24. c	25. a	26. d	27. d	28. c	29. d	30. b
31. d	32. b	33. d	34. d	35. d	36. d	37. a	38. d	39. d	

Chapter 11

1. a	2. c	3. c	4. c	5. d	6. b	7. b	8. b	9. c	10. d
11. d	12. c	13. d	14. d	15. d	16. a	17. a	18. d	19. d	20. d
21. d	22. d	23. a	24. d	25. b	26. c	27. a	28. d	29. c	30. d
31. d	32. a	33. b	34. c	35. d	36. d	37. d	38. d	39. d	40. a

Chapter 12

1. d	2. a	3. d	4. c	5. d	6. a	7. b	8. b	9. a	10. b
11. d	12. d	13. d	14. c	15. d	16. d	17. c	18. b	19. c	20. d
21. b	22. b	23. b	24. d	25. d	26. d	27. a	28. b	29. d	30. c
31. d	32. c	33. c	34. d	35. c	36. d	37. d	38. d	39. d	40. a
41. d	42. d	43. c							

Chapter 13

1. b	2. d	3. d	4. c	5. c	6. b	7. d	8. a	9. b	10. b
11. b	12. d	13. d	14. b	15. a	16. d	17. a	18. a	19. b	20. c
21. b	22. b	23. d	24. d	25. a	26. b	27. d	28. a	29. c	30. d
31. d	32. c	33. a	34. b	35. d	36. d	37. d	38. b	39. a	40. a
41. c	42. a	43. c	44. d						

Chapter 14

1. a	2. d	3. d	4. a	5. d	6. c	7. d	8. b	9. c	10. d
11. b	12. d	13. d	14. d	15. d	16. c	17. c	18. d	19. a	20. a
21. d	22. d	23. d	24. c	25. d	26. c	27. d	28. b	29. d	30. c
31. b	32. d	33. a	34. d	35. c	36. d	37. a	38. a	39. c	40. a
41. b	42. c	43. d	44. c	45. a	46. d	47. b	48. d	49. a	50. d
51. b	52. d	53. d	54. a	55. c	56. d	57. d	58. c	59. c	60. b

Chapter 15

1. a	2. d	3. c	4. a	5. c	6. b	7. c	8. a	9. d	10. c
11. a	12. d	13. d	14. a	15. b	16. a	17. d	18. a	19. d	20. c
21. a	22. d	23. d	24. d	25. a	26. d	27. b	28. d	29. b	30. b
31. c	32. d	33. d	34. d	35. d	36. c	37. b	38. d	39. c	40. d
41. a	42. d	43. c	44. d	45. d	46. d				

Chapter 16

1. d	2. d	3. b	4. c	5. d	6. a	7. d	8. b	9. a	10. d
11. d	12. a	13. a	14. d	15. d	16. d	17. d	18. c	19. a	20. d
21. d	22. a	23. b	24. c	25. d	26. c	27. d	28. b	29. d	30. b
31. d	32. a	33. a	34. d	35. d	36. c	37. c	38. d	39. d	40. c
41. d	42. c	43. d	44. d	45. c	46. d	47. d	48. b	49. a	50. a

Chapter 17

1. d	2. d	3. d	4. d	5. d	6. a	7. d	8. d	9. c	10. b
11. c	12. d	13. d	14. b	15. c	16. d	17. d	18. c	19. c	20. a
21. a	22. d	23. d	24. a	25. d	26. b	27. d	28. d	29. d	30. c
31. d	32. c	33. a	34. b	35. b	36. d				

Chapter 18

1. c	2. c	3. d	4. a	5. a	6. a	7. d	8. a	9. b	10. a
11. c	12. d	13. c	14. c	15. d	16. b	17. c	18. a	19. d	20. d
21. d	22. d	23. b	24. c	25. d	26. d	27. d	28. c	29. a	30. b
31. d									

Chapter 19

1. d	2. c	3. c	4. d	5. d	6. a	7. d	8. b	9. b	10. c
11. d	12. b	13. a	14. d	15. d	16. d	17. d	18. c	19. d	20. b
21. b	22. b	23. d	24. c	25. d	26. d	27. d	28. b		

Chapter 20

1. d	2. d	3. d	4. d	5. d	6. d	7. c	8. b	9. d	10. d
11. b	12. d	13. d	14. a	15. d	16. d	17. a	18. b	19. b	20. b
21. d									

ANSWER KEY

Chapter 21

1. d	2. a	3. a	4. d	5. c	6. b	7. b	8. a	9. a	10. c
11. d	12. a	13. c	14. d	15. b	16. c	17. b	18. d	19. d	20. d
21. a	22. b	23. c	24. c	25. d	26. a	27. b	28. d	29. d	30. b
31. d	32. d	33. a	34. d	35. d	36. d	37. d	38. d	39. d	40. d
41. a	42. b	43. d	44. b	45. d	46. d	47. d	48. d	49. b	50. d
51. a	52. b	53. d	54. a	55. c	56. d	57. d	58. c	59. d	60. b
61. d	62. d								

Chapter 22

1. d	2. d	3. a	4. a	5. d	6. b	7. d	8. d	9. d	10. c
11. b	12. c	13. d	14. d	15. d	16. d	17. d	18. d	19. d	20. b
21. a	22. d	23. a	24. a	25. a	26. a	27. b	28. a	29. b	30. a
31. b	32. a	33. d	34. d	35. d	36. d				

Chapter 23

1. a	2. a	3. a	4. b	5. d	6. a	7. d	8. d	9. d	10. a
11. c	12. b	13. a	14. d	15. b	16. c	17. d	18. d	19. d	20. d
21. a	22. d	23. d	24. d	25. d	26. a	27. a	28. d	29. b	30. d
31. c	32. d								

Chapter 24

1. a	2. d	3. a	4. a	5. b	6. b	7. d	8. c	9. d	10. a
11. c	12. d	13. a	14. d	15. d	16. d	17. d	18. d	19. a	20. d
21. a	22. d	23. d	24. d	25. d	26. c	27. c	28. c	29. d	30. d
31. d	32. c	33. d	34. b	35. d	36. d	37. d	38. c	39. a	40. c
41. b	42. b								

Chapter 25

1. d	2. d	3. b	4. d	5. d	6. d	7. b	8. d	9. b	10. d
11. d	12. c	13. a	14. c	15. b	16. d	17. d	18. d	19. d	20. a
21. a	22. d	23. d	24. a	25. a	26. d	27. d	28. d	29. d	30. d
31. a	32. b	33. d	34. a	35. a	36. c	37. d			

Chapter 26

1. a	2. d	3. d	4. d	5. a	6. d	7. d	8. d	9. d	10. d
11. d	12. d	13. d	14. d	15. c	16. d	17. d	18. d	19. d	20. a
21. d	22. a	23. a	24. d	25. d	26. c	27. d	28. d	29. c	30. a
31. d	32. d	33. b	34. d	35. a	36. b	37. b	38. a	39. d	40. a
41. d	42. a	43. d	44. d	45. b	46. b				

Chapter 27

1. d	2. a	3. d	4. d	5. d	6. d	7. a	8. d	9. d	10. b
11. d	12. d	13. d	14. b	15. d	16. b	17. d	18. a	19. b	20. d
21. d	22. c	23. d	24. a	25. d	26. d	27. d	28. a	29. d	30. c
31. d	32. d	33. d	34. d	35. d	36. d	37. d	38. d	39. a	40. d
41. d	42. a	43. d	44. d	45. d	46. b	47. d	48. a	49. d	50. b
51. d	52. c								

Chapter 28

1. d	2. d	3. d	4. b	5. b	6. a	7. d	8. a	9. d	10. a
11. b	12. d	13. d	14. d	15. b	16. a	17. c	18. a	19. d	20. d
21. b	22. b	23. d	24. a	25. b	26. a	27. a	28. b	29. c	30. c
31. d	32. d	33. d	34. d	35. d	36. c	37. a	38. d		

Chapter 29

1. a	2. d	3. d	4. d	5. d	6. d	7. a	8. d	9. d	10. d
11. c	12. d	13. d	14. b	15. c	16. d	17. a	18. d	19. b	20. a
21. d	22. d	23. d	24. d	25. a	26. d	27. a	28. d	29. d	30. d
31. a	32. b	33. a	34. d	35. d	36. d	37. c	38. d	39. d	40. a
41. b	42. d								

Chapter 30

1. d	2. b	3. d	4. c	5. b	6. a	7. a	8. c	9. b	10. d
11. a	12. d	13. a	14. a	15. b	16. d	17. d	18. c	19. b	20. d
21. d	22. d	23. d	24. d	25. d	26. b	27. a	28. d	29. c	30. c
31. c	32. b	33. b	34. b	35. d	36. d	37. b	38. c	39. b	40. d
41. a									

Chapter 31

1. d	2. b	3. d	4. d	5. a	6. d	7. c	8. d	9. d	10. d
11. d	12. d	13. d	14. a	15. b	16. a	17. d	18. b	19. c	20. d
21. c	22. b	23. d	24. c	25. d	26. b	27. b	28. d	29. d	30. d

Chapter 32

1. b	2. c	3. d	4. d	5. d	6. d	7. a	8. d	9. c	10. c
11. d	12. d	13. c	14. a	15. b	16. c	17. d	18. c	19. b	20. d
21. c	22. d	23. d	24. a	25. b	26. d	27. d	28. b	29. b	30. c
31. b	32. d	33. d	34. d						

Chapter 33

1. d	2. d	3. c	4. a	5. d	6. d	7. a	8. c	9. d	10. d
11. b	12. d	13. c	14. d	15. a	16. b	17. c	18. d	19. d	20. b
21. d	22. a	23. c	24. d	25. d	26. d	27. d	28. a	29. d	30. d
31. d	32. a	33. c	34. d	35. a	36. b	37. a	38. d	39. d	40. d
41. d	42. d	43. a	44. c	45. d	46. d	47. b	48. d	49. d	50. b
51. b	52. a	53. b	54. d	55. d	56. b				

www.ingramcontent.com/pod-product-compliance
Lightning Source LLC
Chambersburg PA
CBHW080543230426
43663CB00015B/2693